C A P I T A L
PUNISHMENT

A Reference Handbook

Second Edition

Other Titles in ABC-CLIO's
**Contemporary
World Issues**
Series

Affirmative Action, Lynne Eisaguirre
American Homelessness, 3d edition, Mary Ellen Hombs
Censorship in America, Mary E. Hull
Consumer Fraud, Lee E. Norrgard and Julia M. Norrgard
Hate Crimes, Donald Altschiller
New Slavery, Kevin Bales
Police Misconduct in America, Dean J. Champion
Pornography in America, Joseph W. Slade
Prisons in America, Nicole Hahn Rafter and Debra L. Stanley
Religion and Politics, John W. Storey and Glenn H. Utter
Tax Reform, James John Jurinski
The Religious Right, 2d edition, Glenn H. Utter and John W. Storey
Urban Sprawl, Donald C. Williams
Work and Family in America, Leslie F. Stebbins
World Population, Geoffrey Gilbert

Books in the Contemporary World Issues series address vital issues in today's society such as genetic engineering, pollution, and biodiversity. Written by professional writers, scholars, and nonacademic experts, these books are authoritative, clearly written, up-to-date, and objective. They provide a good starting point for research by high school and college students, scholars, and general readers as well as by legislators, businesspeople, activists, and others.

Each book, carefully organized and easy to use, contains an overview of the subject, a detailed chronology, biographical sketches, facts and data and/or documents and other primary-source material, a directory of organizations and agencies, annotated lists of print and nonprint resources, and an index.

Readers of books in the Contemporary World Issues series will find the information they need in order to have a better understanding of the social, political, environmental, and economic issues facing the world today.

C A P I T A L
PUNISHMENT

A Reference Handbook

Second Edition

Michael Kronenwetter

**CONTEMPORARY
WORLD ISSUES**

ABC-CLIO

Santa Barbara, California   Denver, Colorado   Oxford, England

Library of Congress Cataloging-in-Publication Data
Kronenwetter, Michael.
    Capital punishment : a reference handbook / Michael Kronenwetter.—
2nd ed.
       p.   cm. — (Contemporary world issues)
    Includes bibliographical references and index.
    ISBN 1-57607-432-3 (hardcover : acid-free paper); 1-57607-433-1
(e-book)
    1. Capital punishment—United States.   2. Capital punishment.
I. Title.   II. Series.
HV8699.U5 K76 2001
364.66—dc21
                                                                    2001005512

06   05   04   03   02   01   10   9   8   7   6   5   4   3   2   1

This book is also available on the World Wide Web as an e-book. Visit abc-clio.com for details.

ABC-CLIO, Inc.
130 Cremona Drive, P.O. Box 1911
Santa Barbara, California 93116–1911

This book is printed on acid-free paper ∞.
Manufactured in the United States of America

Contents

Preface to the Second Edition, xi

1   **Capital Punishment in Context,** 1
    Why Death? 2
        Controlling the "Uncontrollable Brutes," 3
        Deterrence, 5
        A Sense of Justice, 6
        Keeping Order, 9
    The Origins of Capital Punishment, 11
        Class Distinctions, 13
        Killing Machines: Methods of Execution
          in England and Europe, 13
        The American Colonies, 15
        The Early United States, 16
        Elsewhere, 19
    Conclusion, 21

2   **Problems and Controversies,** 25
    The Question of Deterrence, 26
    Does the Death Penalty Encourage Crime? 30
    Is the Death Penalty Needed to Protect Society
        from Those Who Would Kill Again? 33
    Is Life-without-the-Possibility-of-Parole an Effective
        Alternative to the Death Penalty? 35
    Does the Death Penalty Mean Fewer Convictions? 36
    The Question of Cost, 37
    Does the Death Penalty Violate (or Uphold)
        the Sanctity of Human Life? 40
    Is Death the Ultimate Punishment? 42

Hope, 43
Private Vengeance/Public Retribution, 44
Questions of Fairness, 47
    The Indigent, 47
    Race, 48
    Underrepresented Groups, 52
    Summary, 52
Inconsistency, 52
Shame and Excitement—the Public's Response, 55
The Risk of Mistake, 58
Clemency: The Potential for Mercy, 62
"Cruel and Unusual Punishment," 64
Brutalization, 66
Executing the Incompetent, 68
    The Mentally Ill, 68
    The Young, 69
    The Retarded, 71
Judeo-Christian Beliefs, 72
The Political Question, 75
    Life Imprisonment, 75
    Rehabilitation, 76
    Improved Law Enforcement, 77
Summary, 78

3 The International Perspective, 87
    The World Divided, 87
    Religious Influence on National and International
        Attitudes toward the Death Penalty, 90
    Legitimacy of the Death Penalty in
        the Modern World, 95
    Binding Treaties, 97
    Near Unanimity on the Execution of Juveniles, 99
    International Pressures, 100

4 Chronology, 107

5 People and Events, 157
    People, 158
        Anthony Guy Amsterdam (1935–), 158
        Cesare Beccaria (1738–1794), 159
        Hugo Adam Bedau (1926–), 161
        Jeremy Bentham (1748–1832), 161

Walter Berns (1919–), 162
Marvin H. Bovee (1827–1888), 163
William Joseph Brennan, Jr. (1906–1997), 163
Rev. George Cheever (1807–1890), 165
Newton M. Curtis (1835–1910), 167
George Mifflin Dallas (1792–1864), 168
Clarence Darrow (1857–1938), 169
Joseph-Ignace Guillotin (1738–1814), 170
Rev. Joe Ingle (1948–), 171
Jack Ketch (?–1686), 172
Lewis E. Lawes (1883–1947), 173
Edward Livingston (1764–1836), 174
Thurgood Marshall (1908–1993), 174
Albert Pierrepoint (1905–1992), 176
William Hubbs Rehnquist (1924–), 177
Sir Samuel Romilly (1757–1818), 178
Dr. Benjamin Rush (1745–1813), 179
Harvey Schwartzchild (1926–), 180
Potter Stewart (1915–1985), 181
Events, 182
A Plea for the Lives of the Notorious "Thrill"
Killers Leopold and Loeb, 182
The Futile Struggle of Caryl Chessman
(1920–1960), 186
The Trial and Execution of Sacco and Vanzetti, 188
Gary Mark Gilmore Gets His Wish (1940–1977), 190

6 **Facts and Statistics,** 193
Key Death Penalty Decisions of the United States
Supreme Court, 193
Common Contemporary Methods of Execution, 199
Shooting, 199
Hanging, 200
Gas, 200
Electrocution, 200
Lethal Injection, 201
Less Commonly Used Methods of Execution, 201
Stoning, 201
Beheading or Decapitation, 202
Ancient Methods of Execution, 202
Crucifixion, 202
Burning, 203

Breaking on the Wheel, 203
Drawing and Quartering, 203
Peine forte et dure, 204
Garrotting, 204
Other Historical Methods, 205
Tables and Figures, 206

7 **Documents,** 229
A Nineteenth-Century Execution by Guillotine, 229
Excerpt from Pope John Paul II's Encyclical Letter,
On the Value and Inviolability of Human Life, 233
The U.S. Supreme Court Allows the Resumption
of Executions, 237
A Justice Dissents, 259
European Parliament Resolution on the
Death Penalty, 264
South Africa Abolishes the Death Penalty, 267
The European Union Explains Its Views to a Friend, 286

8 **Organizations,** 295
Selected Organizations Based in the United States, 295
Selected Oranizations Based Abroad, 303

9 **Print and Nonprint Resources,** 307
Books, 307
Pamphlets and Monographs, 324
Print Articles and Reports, 325
Videos, 330
Selected General Information Web Sites, 337
Abolitionist Web Sites, 338
Selected Abolitionist Web Sites (State Specific), 340
Retentionist Web Sites, 341
Selected Web Sites Devoted to Specific Cases
or to Material by Inmates, 342
Selected Web-Site Articles and Essays, 343

Glossary, 347

Index, 355
About the Author, 369

Preface to the Second Edition

D eath is widely considered the most terrible penalty that the government can inflict on an individual. This is not only because it is the most violent of all legal punishments, but because it is the most complete and final. Execution deprives its victims not only of their freedom, but of their very future—of all human potential.

As the U.S. Supreme Court Justice William Brennan wrote in his dissent to the majority's opinion in the case of *Gregg* v. *Georgia:* "Death for whatever crime and all circumstances is truly an awesome punishment. The calculated killing of a human being by the state involves, by its very nature, a denial of the executed person's humanity . . . an executed person has indeed 'lost' the right to have rights."

Attitudes toward capital punishment are in transition. Not long ago, in historical terms, the death penalty was prescribed as a punishment in the laws of virtually every country of the world; and not long before that, many governments employed it as a routine punishment for many crimes. Today, however, roughly half of the world's nations have effectively abandoned capital punishment, while many of the rest employ it only in exceptional circumstances, if at all. But this is only part of the story. Even while many countries have been moving away from the death penalty and toward what they see as the more humane punishment of life imprisonment, others have moved in the opposite direction. Far from restricting the use of the death penalty, some countries are actually increasing its use. The most notable of these is the United States, which currently executes far more people than any other western nation.

The first edition of *Capital Punishment: A Reference Handbook* focused on the use of the death penalty in the United States and on the waxing and waning of the abolition movement in this country. This second edition both complements and supplants the first. Much of the original material has been significantly revised and updated, while at the same time the focus of the book has been expanded. The current volume devotes more attention to the international ramifications of capital punishment: to the worldwide status of the death penalty, to developments concerning it in other countries, and to how that status and those developments affect the United States. To this end, an entirely new chapter has been added, and the scope of the others has been broadened to include a more comprehensive examination of the issue of capital punishment from an international perspective.

The body of this new edition is designed to make the book as useful and easy-to-use as possible both for students and for general readers, no matter which aspects of the issue they may be interested in pursuing. It is divided into nine chapters.

Chapter One provides an introduction to the issue of capital punishment. It includes a brief history of the death penalty, presents the primary reasons and justifications for the practice, and places the issue in context in the modern world.

Chapter Two examines the many controversies—penological, practical, moral, and political—that surround the use of the death penalty.

Chapter Three—which is entirely new to this edition—examines how the death penalty is viewed by other nations, and by the international community as a whole. It includes a discussion of the ways in which U.S. policies on capital punishment affect its relations with other countries.

Chapter Four provides a handy chronology, highlighting and linking key events in the history of capital punishment, and in the evolution of national and international policies relating to it.

Chapter Five provides sketches of some of those people and events that have most influenced the debate over capital punishment.

Chapter Six presents a wealth of statistical and other information relevant to the capital punishment debate, much of it in the form of easy-to-read tables, charts, and graphs.

Chapter Seven provides a selection of documents, and excerpts from documents, important to an understanding of the capital punishment debate. The selection, which is entirely different from that contained in the first edition of this book, includes documents of foreign and international origin, as well as the historic U.S. Supreme Court decision in the case of *Gregg v. Georgia,* which affirmed the use of the death penalty in the United States, and a key dissent from that decision.

Chapter Eight provides readers with a selective list of organizations and websites that provide information and/or advocacy on capital punishment.

Chapter Nine directs readers to an annotated selection of the many other sources of information available on the death penalty. These include books, journals, and articles, as well as videotapes and other non-print resources. The book concludes with a glossary of key terms and a detailed index.

This revised edition of *Capital Punishment* would have been impossible without the invaluable assistance of my daughter, Catherine Kronenwetter, who not only aided in the research and in the preparation of the manuscript, but was my patient and indefatigable guide to the mysteries of the computer.

1

Capital Punishment in Context

All punishment is based on the same simple proposition: There must be a penalty for wrongdoing. Most systems of religion or ethics teach that bad actions lead to bad consequences. Although these consequences may not be immediately apparent, they are both natural and inevitable. They will be felt, if not in this world, in some future one—and if not by the perpetrator of the bad actions, then by others, or by society as a whole. Most human societies, however, have not been content with such abstractions; they have demanded that wrongdoers suffer a visible and more or less immediate punishment for their bad deeds. The more serious the offense, the more drastic the punishment.

If there is to be a punishment, there must be both a wrongdoer and an authority to impose that punishment. The nature of the authority varies according to the circumstances and the offense. In a family, for example, children who break the rules laid down by the parents are usually punished by the parents. In society at large, punishment is inflicted on those who break the law by the criminal justice system: the police, the courts, and the prisons. In both the family and society at large, the message from the authority to the wrongdoer is clear: Wrongdoing brings consequences; if you do something wrong, you will be made to pay a penalty.

The main reasons for inflicting punishment boil down to two. One is the belief that it is both right and just that a person who has done wrong should suffer for it; the other is the belief that inflicting punishment on wrongdoers discourages others from doing wrong. On some level, these beliefs seem to be instinctive; certainly, they are deeply held and almost universal. They can be found, to some extent at least, in almost every human being

1

and in every human society. Debate over the wisdom and value of punishments—including capital punishment—tends to focus not on basic principles but on the fairness, appropriateness, and effectiveness of specific punishments for specific offenses.

The death penalty rests on the same simple proposition as other punishments. Because of its drastic and irrevocable nature, it is even more open to debate over its fairness, appropriateness, and effectiveness than other punishments. This has not always been the case. At times in the past, certain societies imposed death as the punishment for all sorts of political and criminal offenses. It was, in some places and at some times, virtually the only penalty that the state imposed for crime besides fines and the confiscation of property. In modern times, however, capital punishment is used more sparingly, and many modern nations don't use it at all; those that do, including the United States, usually reserve it for those crimes the society considers most serious.

If you offend those societies deeply enough, you die.

Why Death?

Modern states have many punishments available to inflict on criminals. Ultimately, a state's ability to inflict penalties on those who break its laws is limited only by the laws of that state itself. The state can demand restitution; it can levy fines on wrongdoers, confiscate their property, and/or lay claim to their wages; it can shame them by publicly excoriating them and holding them up to ridicule; it can imprison them, under either a definite or an indefinite sentence, for any length of time, up to and including the remainder of their lives; it can even exact punishment on their families. In addition, states can (and some do) inflict physical and mental pain on wrongdoers through torture. Down through history, and even today, all these and more penalties have been inflicted by various governments on those who have been deemed to have broken the laws of their societies. For the most part, governments have imposed their penalties with the approval and support of the people who make up those societies.

With such a great variety of other punishments available to them, why do some societies still choose to kill at least some of their criminals? Of the millions of criminals who have been tried and convicted of crimes around the world, why are only a relative few taken from their prison cells and executed each year?

On the face of it, the deliberate and cold-blooded killing of a human being seems both brutal and uncivilized, regardless of the identity of the victim (or, for that matter, of the killer). On some level, this seems particularly true when, as in the case of executions by the state, the person who is killed is a defenseless prisoner. Killing is, after all, a violent act, no matter how it is done. As individuals, most of us instinctively shrink from the idea of taking the life of another human being. Killing is forbidden by every major religion, and murder is considered a crime in every civilized human society. How can the government of a civilized society claim the right to kill any of its citizens—and to kill them in the name of the very law that condemns murder?

In reality, the prohibition on killing has never been absolute; even many religions make exceptions to it. Despite the commandment "Thou shalt not kill," for example, most branches of the Jewish and Christian faiths accept at least the occasional need for war, as well as the right of an individual to kill in self-defense or to protect someone else from a murderous attack. And, in practice, these faiths accept capital punishment as well.

Civil governments make even more exceptions than major religions. In time of war, soldiers are not only permitted to kill other human beings, they are required to do so. Many U.S. jurisdictions permit citizens to kill not only in self-defense but (in some circumstances) in defense of their property. Capital punishment, then, is only one of many exceptions that our society makes to the general prohibition against killing.

Still the fundamental question remains: Why? Why does society itself kill some of its members? Why (if at all) *should* society kill? Proponents of the death penalty make various arguments on its behalf: practical, moral, and philosophical.

Controlling the "Uncontrollable Brutes"

The pragmatic reasons put forward for capital punishment have to do with the protection of society. Certain criminals must die, defenders of the death penalty argue, so that the rest of us can be safe—or, at least, safer.

How do the deaths of some criminals protect the rest of us? In several ways, according to the death penalty's proponents. At the most basic level, the execution of dangerous criminals can be seen as a simple matter of self-defense, because, at the very least, death stops executed criminals from ever repeating their crimes.

This is how Judge Alfred J. Talley of New York saw it in a famous debate with the famous defense lawyer Clarence Darrow. "If I, as an individual, have the right to kill in self-defense," asked Talley, "why has not the State, which is nothing more than an aggregation of individuals, the same right to defend itself against unjust aggression and unjust attack?"[1]

Supporters of the death penalty argue that truly vicious criminals are like rabid animals and must be destroyed. Their disease, which makes them attack and kill others, has no cure. Why not simply get rid of them before they kill or injure someone else? As Albert Einstein once suggested, "There is no reason why society should not rid itself of individuals proved socially harmful."[2] The philosopher Jacques Barzun compares such criminals to wolves and calls for them to be dispatched by what he terms *judicial homicide:* "The uncontrollable brute whom I want put out of the way is not to be punished for his misdeeds, nor used as an example or a warning; he is to be killed for the protection of others."[3]

Even some of the "brutes" themselves agree with this prescription. Westly Allan Dodd, who was executed in 1993, asked that the state of Washington kill him. Dodd's crimes had been especially horrible. He raped and murdered three young boys, the youngest of whom was only four years old. He tortured one of the children for two days before killing him, a diary of his atrocities, and taking pictures of the boys to keep with him afterward. When he was arrested, he was in the process of kidnapping yet another young victim from the bathroom of a movie theater. The details of the killings were so awful that some of the jurors who were forced to listen to them went for psychiatric counseling after the trial.[4] Dodd asked to be put to death, insisting that only execution could stop him from continuing his murderous ways. If he were not executed, he told a judge, he would kill a guard in order to escape. Once free, he would seek out more young boys to kill. The state of Washington willingly granted his request, and Dodd was hanged on January 5, 1993.

Westley Allan Dodd is a prime example of the kind of criminal Barzun wants destroyed; yet if the death penalty were limited only to those like him, it would almost never be applied. Obsessive killers like Dodd are rare. They make up only a tiny fraction of the thousands of criminals convicted of murder in the United States each year. Most fall into very different categories. A few are professional killers-for-hire. Many more commit murder in the process of committing robberies or other crimes. Some kill in the throes of a drug- or alcohol-induced frenzy. Most kill in the heat of the moment, unable to control a sudden burst of rage, hatred, or jealousy. Still others act in desperation, like the battered wives and abused children who strike out in their final attempts to free themselves from situations they can no longer endure.

Some murderers, like Dodd, may be determined to kill again and again, but most are not. Many may be no more likely to kill again than the average citizen is to murder someone in the first place. As far as can be proven, it is no more necessary to execute such people to keep them from killing again than it is to execute those of their fellow citizens who have exhibited violent behavior without actually killing anyone. Nonetheless, some supporters of capital punishment believe that society is protected by executing any killer, if only because executions discourage other potential murderers from carrying out their crimes.

Deterrence

Robert E. Crowe, the Illinois state's attorney who demanded the death sentence for the notorious Chicago murderers Nathan Leopold and Richard Loeb, was a great supporter of capital punishment. "I urge capital punishment for murder," he once explained, "not because I believe that society wishes to take the life of a murderer, but because society does not wish to lose its own. . . . It is the finality of the death penalty which instills fear of punishment which protects society."[5]

In other words, Crowe wanted Leopold and Loeb to die, not to protect society from them, but to protect society from others who might come after them. This is probably the most frequent of all the arguments made for the death penalty, the belief that the deaths of some criminals will deter others from committing similar crimes.

It is true that many murderers plan their acts and take the consequences into account when doing so. This is particularly true of professional criminals, but it is often true of others as well, including spouses who kill each other for insurance money and individuals who kill out of long-term hate or revenge. In making their plans, these potential killers must consider many different factors: How good are their plans? How likely are they to succeed in accomplishing what they set out to do? How likely are they to be caught? If they are caught, how likely is it that they will be convicted? If they are convicted, what will the punishment be?

One factor that potential murderers should have to take into account, say proponents of the death penalty, is the likelihood—if not the certainty—that they will be killed if they are caught.

There is a great deal of debate over how powerful a deterrent capital punishment is. Most of us have an instinctive feeling that the death penalty *must* deter, at least to some extent. Deterrence is, after all, one of the fundamental reasons for punishment of any kind. The harsher the punishment, the stronger the deterrent effect.

Since death is considered the harshest punishment available under the law, it seems logical that it must also be the most effective deterrent to crime. "No other punishment deters men so effectually from committing crimes as the punishment of death," remarked the English barrister Sir James Stephen almost two hundred years ago. "In any secondary punishment, however terrible, there is hope; but death is death; its terror cannot be described more forcibly."[6]

Another aspect of the deterrence argument applies to criminals who have already received the harshest punishment available under the law short of death. They are the lifers who have been condemned to spend the rest of their lives in prison.

Without the threat of execution to hold over these prisoners' heads, argue some prison officials, there is nothing to deter them from committing further terrible crimes while in prison. The dangers of this situation were pointed out by Professor Ernest van den Haag of New York University in an interview in 1976—a time when the death penalty had not been carried out in the United States for several years: "The federal prisons now have custody of a man sentenced to life imprisonment, who, since he has been in prison, has committed three more murderers on three separate occasions—both of prison guards and inmates. There is no further punishment that he can receive. In effect, he has a license to murder."[7]

A Sense of Justice

The reasons for the death penalty that have been discussed so far are essentially pragmatic. They assume that the death penalty accomplishes something useful for society; that is, it protects society from criminals who might prey on it in the future if the death penalty is not there to stop them. Not all the reasons for supporting capital punishment are utilitarian, however. In the eyes of many people who support the death penalty, such support is not so much a practical decision as a gut instinct. It does not depend on logical arguments but on a deep sense of justice—a sense that death is the only punishment truly fitting for crimes too monstrous to be dealt with in any other way.

As Professor Ernest van den Haag explains: "Our system of punishment is based not just on deterrence but also on what is called 'justice'—namely that we feel a man who has committed a crime must be punished in proportion to the seriousness of the crime. Since the crime that takes a life is irrevocable, so must be the punishment."[8] It was this sense that caused Judge Alfred J. Talley to refer to the death penalty as the very "symbol of justice."[9]

Lord Justice Denning, Master of the Rolls of the Court of Appeals in England, made the same point in 1949 before a royal commission that was considering whether England should retain capital punishment: "It is a mistake to consider the objects of punishment as being deterrent or reformative or preventive and nothing else. . . . The truth is that some crimes are so outrageous that society insists on adequate punishment because the wrongdoer deserves it, irrespective of whether it is deterrent or not."[10]

The American judge Samuel Hand made a similar point almost seventy years earlier when he tied capital punishment to the Judeo-Christian tradition of U.S. law:

> In truth, there is inherent in all punishment for crime the idea of executing justice, of rewarding the offender according to his misdeeds. It is an idea entirely separate from and independent of any notion of prevention, even of public safety.
>
> "Vengeance is mine, and I will repay, saith the Lord," but vengeance—righteous vengeance—is the right and duty of the state. The state is, in this respect, the representative of the Divine Governor. To it, the sword of justice and retribution is delivered. By it, it must be wielded.
>
> Capital execution upon the deadly poisoner and the midnight assassin is not only necessary for the safety of society, it is the fit and deserved retribution of their crimes. By it alone is divine and human justice fulfilled.
>
> This is the crowning and all-sufficient ground for the destruction of the convicted murderer by the civil power.[11]

The death penalty has always been considered especially appropriate for the crime of murder. No other option so well meets the test of proportionality. To many people, death seems the logical—and even the inevitable—consequence for that particular crime: the only fit retribution. Death is, after all, the only punishment that has the same remorseless finality as murder itself. As Shakespeare had a haunted man proclaim about the murder he had committed, "It will have blood, they say; blood will have blood."[12]

Some supporters of the death penalty believe that it is precisely this appropriateness that justifies capital punishment. The "real reason" for the death penalty, says Los Angeles County District Attorney Ira Reiner, is that "the overwhelming majority of [the American public] feels that it is the appropriate penalty for certain types of limited types of crimes." Those crimes, Reiner specifies, are "the most horrendous of the murder cases."[13]

Historically, the special connection between murder and capital punishment in the United States is emphasized by the fact that when states began cutting back on the use of the death penalty in the nineteenth century, most retained it for murder. Today, not only the United States but most other countries in the world that still impose the death penalty continue to reserve it primarily for murderers.

Here is how one nineteenth-century judge expressed this peculiar appropriateness to a murderer he was sentencing to die:

> By our law, the crime of which you stand convicted is the only one that is punishable with death. Against the murderer, the law has attached the greatest penalty known to criminal jurisprudence. The universal opinion and sanction of all ages has induced our legislature to put this law upon the statute book; and as life is the most sacred boon to man, it is only allowed to be taken for the highest offense which it is considered in the power of man to inflict upon his fellow-man, of this offense you stand convicted.[14]

Some judges in non–capital punishment states feel so strongly about the ultimate penalty that they hunger for the ability to impose death sentences. In 1992, one frustrated Wisconsin judge sentenced a thirty-four-year-old man who had killed three people and wounded another with a machine gun to three life sentences for the killings, plus another twenty-five years for the attempted murder. Since people serving life sentences in Wisconsin eventually become technically eligible for parole, the judge set the killer's potential parole date as the year 2100.[15]

Keeping Order

In ancient times, individuals were expected to take their own revenge on those who had wronged them. If a man robbed or killed another person, or raped a woman, it was up to the victim or the victim's family to exact a price from the wrongdoer. Sometimes that price was paid in money, sometimes in blood.

This practice had some obvious flaws. One of the worst was that it left the weak at the mercy of the strong. More than that, it left justice itself to the strong. Another problem was that it led to social disorder: One act of violence led to another, families developed vendettas against one another, and violence multiplied over the generations.

Down through the centuries, governments took over the job of exacting retribution from wrongdoers and carrying out society's ever-changing view of justice. Laws, police forces, courts, and prisons were developed to find and punish criminals.

No legal system was ever perfect. Some punishments seemed much too harsh, others much too light. Some criminals escaped discovery and punishment altogether. By and large, however, people tended to agree that legal systems worked better than private vengeance. Here in the United States, the majority believed that the legal system worked better than most.

There were times and places, however, when people believed that their legal systems had broken down. They lost faith in the law's version of justice and became dissatisfied with the way the government protected them. In times like these, people frequently took the law into their own hands.

During the time of the American frontier, there were usually too few sheriffs, judges, and other legal officials to oversee and hand out justice throughout a large territory. Some communities had no law enforcement officers at all. Not wanting to be at the mercy of toughs and criminals, local citizens formed groups of vigilantes, or "vigilance committees," private organizations that became their own "law" and took it upon themselves to punish wrongdoers or to chase out of town people they considered dangerous.

In time, every American community of any size organized an official police force of some kind, and federal and state courts extended effective coverage over the entire country. Gradually, the need for regular vigilante organizations disappeared; but even then, there were still individual cases in which outraged citizens became impatient with the law and took it upon themselves to punish criminals—or those they thought were criminals.

Occasional acts of vigilantism were common in parts of the United States in the late nineteenth century, and they continued well into the twentieth. These were not acts of individual vengeance but group actions carried out by self-righteous mobs. Minor criminals were daubed with hot tar, sprinkled with feathers, and escorted to the county line. Accused rapists or murderers were lynched in communities across the country. Lynchings of black men—sometimes men whose worst crime was showing disrespect to a white person—remained almost commonplace in the South into the 1930s. Individual cases continued to occur even into the 1950s and 1960s.

Vigilante lynchings are different from other murders because they are accepted—even condoned—by the community. Although many citizens may have personally disapproved of lynching, and some formal investigations of lynching incidents did occur, it was extremely rare, where vigilantism was common, for vigilante killers to be tried and convicted. Trials and convictions were almost unheard of when vigilantes acted together in mobs. In some sense, vigilantes were seen as trying, however misguidedly, to uphold the community's sense of justice.

The need to control or end vigilantism is an important reason put forward for having the death penalty. In Colorado, for instance, capital punishment for murder was abolished in 1897. Within a few years, Colorado mobs had lynched three accused criminals they believed to be murderers. One victim, a black man, was horribly burned at the stake. The death penalty was quickly reinstated.[16]

U.S. Supreme Court Justice Potter Stewart recognized the lynching problem when he wrote his concurring opinion in the historic *Furman v. Georgia* decision of 1972: "The instinct for retribution is part of the nature of man and channeling that instinct in the administration of criminal justice serves an important purpose in promoting the stability of a society governed by law. When people begin to believe that organized society is unwilling or unable to impose upon criminal offenders the punishment they 'deserve' then there are sown the seeds of anarchy—of self-help, vigilante justice, and lynch law."[17]

Vigilante lynchings have been rare in the United States in recent decades, but the threat is always present. "Most people desire some sort of retribution," warns Richard Samp of the pro–capital punishment public interest group, Washington Legal Foundation. If they don't get it from the criminal justice system, some, at least, will be tempted to take justice into their own hands. "The one way we can prevent vigilantism," says Samp, is to give people "confidence that society is going to mete out justice to people who commit violent crime."[18] For the worst examples of premeditated first-degree murder, Samp would argue, death is the only punishment that potential vigilantes will accept as just.

This reason for the death penalty assumes that there is a fundamental difference between ordinary citizens killing criminals and the state doing the same thing. If the family of a murder victim hangs the killer from a tree, that is a lynching. If the state electrocutes the same killer, that is justice. The murderer is dead in either case. In the first case, social order and the rule of law have broken down; in the second, the supporters of the death penalty insist, they have been reinforced.

The Origins of Capital Punishment

We know the death penalty was prescribed for various crimes in Babylon at least 3,700 years ago, and we can assume that it was used in many parts of the world long before that. Some ancient societies applied it sparingly, and only for the most terrible of crimes. Others imposed it for minor offenses. Under Rome's law of the Twelve Tablets in the fifth century B.C., for example, death was the penalty for publishing "insulting songs" and disturbing the peace of the city at night.[19] Under Greece's Draconian legal code (named for the Athenian lawgiver Draco) in the seventh century B.C., death was the punishment for *every* crime.

The Draconian code was an exception, however, even in the ancient world. Death was rarely the only available punishment, even then. Captured criminals who were not executed were often tortured or maimed. Some primitive societies did not employ the death penalty at all, and many of those that did reserved it either for crimes against the ruler or for religious crimes, such as blasphemy. Punishment for crimes committed against individuals—murder, rape, and robbery—was rarely handed down by a legal authority. It was left up to the victims, or to their families or clans, to exact the appropriate penalty or to carry out the appropriate revenge.[20]

Beginning in ancient times and continuing well into the twentieth century, executions were frequently carried out in public. Execution grounds were set up in spacious town squares or in jail yards—easily accessible places where there was plenty of room for crowds of spectators. Ordinary citizens were not only allowed but encouraged to watch wrongdoers pay for their crimes.

Public executions provided benefits for everyone concerned. For the surviving victims of the condemned criminals, the executions provided the grim satisfaction of witnessing the final punishment of those who had wronged them. For the authorities, executions served as graphic demonstrations of their determination to protect the public safety. With criminals being dispatched before large crowds in the city square, who could doubt that the police and judges were doing their jobs?

Public executions even helped the authorities to do their jobs by serving as grisly object lessons for potential wrongdoers. What better way to strike fear into the hearts of those who might be tempted to take up a life of crime than to show them the fatal consequences that would result if they did? In some places, corpses or body parts of executed criminals were displayed in public places. Bodies were left dangling from gibbets on hillsides outside of town. Decapitated heads were perched on stakes at city gates.

For the crowds who often flocked to them, the awful ceremonies served as a kind of spectacle—a rare opportunity to gather together and share the horror and excitement of watching other men and women die. In some times and places, executions were regarded as a form of public entertainment—a kind of blood sport. This was true in the days of the Roman Empire, when condemned criminals were forced to participate in battles to the death, known as gladiatorial "games."

Even the condemned criminals themselves had something to gain from having their deaths take place in public. This was their last chance to proclaim their innocence publicly, or to cry out their defiance of the society that was executing them. Public execution was also an opportunity to win sympathy from the crowd; there was some honor to be gained by "dying well," and authorities often complained that some execution victims were regarded as heroes by the crowds.

Class Distinctions

Typically, then as now, the extent and nature of criminal punishment depended as much on the social standing of the criminal as on the nature of the crime. Commoners were executed much more often than nobles, the wealthy, and the otherwise influential, and for a wider variety of crimes. Minorities and foreigners were treated more harshly than members of the dominant group. In many European countries, from the seventeenth century on, clergymen could not even be tried, much less put to death, by civil authorities for ordinary crimes.

The method of execution varied. In general, the more socially privileged the criminal, the more merciful the form of execution. (An exception was sometimes made for nobles who committed treason.) As late as 1813, Jews, Christians, and members of other religious minorities who ran afoul of the law were still being impaled alive in at least one corner of the Ottoman Empire—stakes being driven up through their bodies with blows of a heavy mallet; Turks, on the other hand, were swiftly and mercifully decapitated.[21]

Killing Machines: Methods of Execution in England and Europe

Hanging and beheading were the most common methods of execution in Europe and Great Britain. Beheading was usually reserved for members of the upper classes, while hanging was favored for other criminals. When there was a desire to make sure that traitors and other heinous criminals suffered as much as possible, they might be left to dangle for a while, choking at the end of a rope, before being taken down and gutted with a knife. Others were drawn and quartered.

One reason for the relatively frequent use of the death penalty in many countries was the lack of a feasible option. There was nothing in these countries that could have served the function of a modern prison system. There were places where prisoners were held, of course. Paris had the Bastille, London had the

Tower, and other capitals had their equivalents. Many of the castles that overlooked the European countryside had dungeons; but for the most part, these were small, cramped places of confinement, capable of holding only a handful of prisoners at most. Consequently, they were reserved for political enemies and other special cases. Even in the most law-abiding regions, they could never have contained the mass of common criminals.

As for the other punishments that could be imposed on those who broke the law, the confiscation of property was an option only with those who had property to confiscate; it was inappropriate for most thieves, murderers, and other common scoundrels. Short of death, the only other options were such corporal punishments as whipping and the chopping off of hands or other body parts.

During the Middle Ages, the death penalty was used less commonly in England than in most European countries. During much of the eleventh century, it wasn't imposed at all. Neither King Canute (1016–1035) nor William the Conqueror (1066–1087) relied on the executioner to keep order in the kingdom. That didn't mean they dealt gently with criminals, however. Death penalty or no death penalty, it was a violent age. Torture was commonplace, and many prisoners died while being tortured. Nonetheless, few, if any, executions took place.

Later English rulers re-imposed the death penalty, but, for centuries, British law was merciful compared with the laws on the continent. During the late Middle Ages, at a time when several European countries continued to execute people for minor offenses, England reserved the death penalty primarily for such relatively serious crimes as murder, treason, rape, arson, and robbery (although such pesky petty thieves as snatch-purses were still often executed.)

The array of crimes punishable by death in England increased over the years; by the early nineteenth century, more than 200 crimes had become capital offenses. Gypsies could be executed simply for overstaying their welcome in the country. Even the native born could be hanged for stealing a fish from a pond, illegally hunting a deer, or cutting down a growing tree.[22] Passing even one forged bank note could send a counterfeiter to the scaffold; several women as well as men were executed for that crime. In the year of 1820 alone, some forty-six people were hanged for forgery.[23]

The French Revolution spurred the invention of perhaps the most infamous method of execution in history: the guillotine. The guillotine was named after Joseph-Ignace Guillotin, the French doctor who convinced the National Assembly that the use of a beheading machine would be more merciful and more democratic than the mix of inefficient methods the revolutionary government had been using.

Professor Daniel Gerould, author of *Guillotine: Its Legend and Lore,* has called the guillotine "the first modern technological killing machine."[24] It was not, however, the first machine devised for the express purpose of executing criminals, nor was it the first decapitating machine; after all, the ancient sword and the headsman's axe were both machines of a sort. The guillotine wasn't even the first complex machine to be used for decapitation: A device called the Halifax Gibbet was used in Ireland as early as 1307.

The Scottish Maiden, used some centuries later in Scotland and Ireland, possessed the nearly unique feature of allowing community participation in executions. (This was also a feature of the Middle Eastern method of death by stoning.) A large blade was attached to one end of a rope, which was slung over the top of a wooden scaffold. Several members of the community held the other end of the rope, keeping the blade suspended over a block on which the condemned person's neck was placed. When the time came, they let go of the rope, allowing the blade to fall. Thus, the responsibility for dispatching the victim was shared among them, and execution itself became a communal event.

The genius of the guillotine consisted of two improvements over earlier decapitating machines. The first was the introduction of a kind of collar, similar to a pillory, which was secured over the neck of the victim, effectively pinning the head in place below the blade. With earlier decapitation machines, the head would have to be held in place either by the victim him or herself, or by an executioner's assistant. If the condemned prisoner wriggled or attempted to pull away, the falling blade could miss its intended target, hitting either the skull or the victim's back and shoulders. The guillotine's collar, however, assured that the blade would strike the victim in the neck, neatly severing the head from the body. The second improvement was the guillotine's slanted blade, which cut off the victim's head with a reliable slicing action.

The American Colonies

Although English law provided the principal model for the legal codes of Britain's American colonies, they did not imitate the mother country's policies slavishly. In fact, each colony instituted its own laws and its own list of crimes punishable by death. Although these laws flowed from a common legal tradition, there was a significant range of difference among them.

On one end of the American spectrum were two colonies whose laws reflected the Quaker beliefs of their founders: William Penn's Pennsylvania, which prescribed the death penalty only for murder and treason, and West Jersey, which originally had no capital crimes at all. On the other end were colonies like Virginia, which inflicted death even for petty crimes.

Most of the American colonies fell somewhere in between these two extremes. Although the laws were changeable, the average colony made roughly ten crimes subject to the death penalty at any given time. For example, at one time thirteen offenses were punishable by death in Massachusetts; at another, only nine.[25] Pennsylvania eventually went from its original two to fifteen.[26]

Murder was a capital crime in every colony at one time or another, as was treason and rebellion. Other crimes typically punishable by death were rape, robbery, arson, and perjury in a capital case. Some of the colonies also prescribed death for such sexual offenses as adultery, sodomy, and bestiality, as well as for such religious offenses as witchcraft and blasphemy (public disrespect for God). In Massachusetts, at one point, even cursing a parent was a capital crime.[27]

The colonies depended so heavily on the death penalty at least partly because they had no prison systems. Little could be done with serious miscreants—particularly impoverished miscreants who couldn't even be fined—short of killing them.

The Early United States

In the wake of the American Revolution, the U.S. Constitution gave both the states and the federal government the right to set their own criminal penalties. The very first Congress of the United States passed federal laws making death the penalty for rape and murder, and each of the original states declared several other crimes punishable by death as well.

The usual manner of execution in most states was hanging, although Native Americans and slaves were sometimes burned at the stake. In Louisiana, whose legal traditions were French instead of British, beheading was sometimes used, at least for slaves. As in most other parts of the world, executions in the early United States were public affairs, and the bodies of the executed were often put on display for days—and sometimes months—afterwards.

Although the death penalty was widely accepted in the early United States, its approval was not universal. Among those who expressed serious doubts, and even objections, to the practice were some of the men who played important roles in founding the country. The founders were profoundly influenced by the ideas of the European Enlightenment, and one of the most striking of those ideas was the belief that capital punishment might be abolished. This radical notion was proposed by an Italian named Cesare Beccaria in a landmark essay titled *On Crimes and Punishment*, translated into English in 1767. The essay had already played an important part in leading Tuscany to abandon capital punishment, and it encouraged many thoughtful Americans to consider abandoning the practice here.

Some of the most prominent founders of the United States, including Thomas Jefferson, had serious reservations about the death penalty and hoped to see its use severely limited in the new nation. Others—such as Dr. Benjamin Rush, the surgeon general of the American forces during the Revolutionary War—called for the abolition of capital punishment altogether. Although these views did not prevail, and the death penalty was initially established in every state, the practice remained controversial among American intellectuals.

There would be three great waves of anti–death penalty sentiment in the first two centuries of the country's history. The first, which occurred in the mid-nineteenth century, led to important restrictions on the use of the death penalty in several northern states; Michigan, Wisconsin, and Rhode Island abandoned the practice altogether. The movement for the abolition of the death penalty was led by many of the same reformers who called for the abolition of slavery; but as slavery became more and more a central issue, the death penalty receded into the background until it all but disappeared in the smoke and blood of the Civil War. As historian David Brion Davis wrote, "Men's finer sensibilities, which had once been revolted by the execution of a fellow being, seemed hardened and blunted."[28]

The second wave of abolition also broke against the rocks of war. This one rose up toward the end of the nineteenth century and continued until the United States entered World War I. The state of Missouri and the territory of Puerto Rico both abolished the death penalty in 1917; no other state or territory would abolish it for forty years.

Opposition to the death penalty gathered strength again in the mid-twentieth century. Sympathy for the cause was fueled by the controversial executions of Willie Francis, Burton Abbot, Caryl Chessman, and Barbara Graham. Powerful and popular movies about Chessman (*Cell 2455 Death Row*) and Graham (*I Want to Live!*) vividly portrayed both the sufferings of the condemned and the possibilities for irremediable error inherent in putting people to death. Once again, several states either abolished or restricted the use of the death penalty.

In 1972, American abolitionists scored their greatest success yet. In the case of *Furman v. Georgia,* the U.S. Supreme Court declared that the death penalty, as it was then carried out, was "cruel and unusual" punishment under the Eighth Amendment, and, therefore, that it was unconstitutional. For a time, it seemed that the abolitionists might have won the long debate once and for all. However, many state legislatures scrambled to write new laws in the hope that the Court might accept them as constitutional. Four years later, the Court ruled in several cases, the best known being *Gregg v. Georgia;* that death penalties imposed in some states under new laws were constitutional. Once again, the death penalty was declared constitutional in the United States, and it remains so today.

First degree murder is a capital offense in all thirty-eight of the U.S. states that have the death penalty. Many state laws specify that aggravating (or special) circumstances must be present for the death penalty to be imposed, and some spell out specific aggravating circumstances that apply in that state. Whether or not state law requires a finding of aggravating circumstances, the U.S. Supreme Court has made clear that for a death sentence to be constitutional, the jury must have found that the circumstances of the case that aggravate the seriousness of the crime outweigh those that mitigate it. In fact, a separate penalty phase of the trial must be held in which evidence may be considered, both in aggravation and mitigation, that the jury would not be allowed to hear in the guilt phase.

In addition to murder, treason is also a capital offense in Arkansas, California, Georgia, and Louisiana.[29]

Other crimes punishable by death in specific states:

- Train-wrecking, and perjury resulting in the execution of an innocent person, in California
- Felony murder, and "capital drug-trafficking," in Florida
- The hijacking of an aircraft, and kidnapping with bodily injury or in which the victim dies, in Georgia
- Aggravated kidnapping, in Idaho and South Dakota
- Kidnapping with aggravating factors, in Kentucky
- Aggravated rape of a child (below the age of twelve), in Louisiana
- Aircraft piracy, in Mississippi
- Capital sexual assault, in Montana
- "Solicitation by command or threat" in connection with a drug conspiracy, in New Jersey ·

Death is also a penalty for various crimes under federal law, although federal death sentences are relatively infrequent, and actual executions even more so.[30] Of the 3,726 death row inmates in the United States in 2000, only 25 were prisoners of the federal government, and another 7 were held by the U.S. military.[31]

From the time of the reinstatement of the death penalty in 1976 until April 3, 2001, 706 executions took place in the United States. The annual number of executions took eight years to climb out of the single digits, and until 1992 to reach into the thirties. Since then, as the Supreme Court has repeatedly streamlined the appeals process, the pace of executions has been accelerating, although not consistently. For some reason, the number has tended to jump in the odd-numbered years and fall back slightly in the even-numbered years, and then jump to new highs in the next odd year. By 2001, executions were taking place at the rate of about seven per month.[32]

Elsewhere

The international community is divided over the death penalty. Many nations, as represented by their governments, are strongly opposed to it; many others both defend and practice it. Although an increasing majority of the world's countries never, or only rarely, inflict the death penalty, others do so with increasing frequency.

Countries fall into four categories with respect to capital punishment. *Retentionist* countries not only retain the death penalty but use it (albeit, in some cases, only rarely); *abolitionist* countries have formally abolished the death penalty for all crimes, and in all circumstances. Countries that are *abolitionist for ordinary crimes* have abandoned capital punishment for common criminal offenses, such as murder and rape, but retain it as an option for such crimes as treason and desertion from the armed forces in time of war. Countries that are *abolitionist de facto* retain the death penalty in theory but have not carried out an execution for so long that they are considered to have effectively abandoned it.

The number of countries in each category changes frequently as more and more countries abandon the use of the death penalty while a handful who have previously abandoned the practice return to it. On April 1, 2000, according to the Death Penalty Information Center, 87 nations were in the *retentionist* category, 73 fell into the absolute *abolitionist* category, 13 were *abolitionist for ordinary crimes*, and "at least 22" were *abolitionist de facto*, making a total of 108 countries that were "abolitionist in law or practice."[33]

Certain major cultural and geographical patterns become evident when one examines a map of the world. The nations of the Arab Middle East, for example, are uniformly retentionist (as of early 2001). With the notable exceptions of Cambodia and Hong Kong, Asia is also retentionist; and except for Haiti and the Dominican Republic, most of the island nations of the Caribbean also retain the death penalty.

On the other hand, almost all the European countries are abolitionist; among them, only the Federal Republic of Yuogoslavia and certain states of the old Soviet Union are retentionist. (Although Russia itself has committed to abolishing capital punishment, it has carried out at least one execution since doing so.) The bulk of the South American continent is also abolitionist, either in law or in practice; in North America, the retentionist United States is sandwiched between Canada, which is abolitionist, and Mexico, which is abolitionist for ordinary crimes. Africa and Oceania are roughly divided between abolitionist and retentionist nations. (Australia is abolitionist.) Of the ten most populous nations, nine are retentionist, and the position of the tenth (Russia) is equivocal.

Although a great many countries retain the death penalty, only a handful of them impose it on anything like a regular basis, much less an extensive one. According to Amnesty International,

85 percent of the 1,813 executions known to have been carried out in 1999 took place in just five countries: China, the Democratic Republic of the Congo, Iran, Saudi Arabia, and the United States.[34] (Countries are listed alphabetically, not in the order of most executions.) Although the worldwide total was down from 1998, the number of executions in three of the five leading executioners—the United States, Iran, and Saudi Arabia—actually went up.

Conclusion

Capital punishment is a long-established element of the criminal justice systems of many nations, including the United States. In this country, the majority of states retain the option of capital punishment, although fewer have actually carried out executions since the Supreme Court declared the death penalty constitutional in 1976; and of those states, only a handful use it routinely. Federal law also permits the central government to use the death penalty for the most serious federal crimes, although, like several states, the central government rarely exercises this power.

Public opinion polls show that a significant majority of Americans approve of the death penalty under at least some circumstances. Similar sentiment exists in many other countries, including some of those that have abolished the death penalty. And yet, the international trend is clearly against the death penalty. There is a growing consensus among Western governments that the death penalty has no place in the twenty-first century; that it is outmoded, if not barbaric.

Capital punishment has already been abandoned by most of the developed world, and several international organizations, including the United Nations, are pressing for its abolition worldwide. In Chapter 2, we will explore the most common objections made to the death penalty.

Notes

1. "Should Capital Punishment Be Retained?" *Congressional Digest* (August-September 1927): 231.

2. Albert Einstein, *Berliner Tageblatt*, quoted in *Congressional Digest*, 243.

3. Jacques Barzun, "In Favor of Capital Punishment," *American Scholar* (spring 1962); reprinted in *Social Ethics: Morality and Social Policy*, ed.

Thomas A. Mappes and Jane S. Zembaty (New York: McGraw-Hill, 1977), 89.

4. "Washington Sex Offender Dies by Hanging," *Wausau Daily Herald,* 5 January 1993.

5. *Congressional Digest,* "Capital Punishment," 228.

6. Quoted by Leonard A. Stevens in *Death Penalty: The Case of Life vs. Death in the United States* (New York: Coward, McCann & Geoghegan, 1978), 73.

7. "Bring Back the Death Penalty," *U.S. News & World Report* (April 1976); reprinted in *The Death Penalty,* ed. Irwin Isenberg (New York: H. W. Wilson, 1977), 133.

8. Ibid., 135.

9. *Congressional Digest,* "Capital Punishment," 232.

10. Royal Commission on Capital Punishment, Minutes of Evidence (1 December 1949): 207.

11. Samuel Hand, "The Death Penalty," *North American Review* (December 1881): 549.

12. *MacBeth* 3.4. 122.

13. Interviewed on *Crossfire,* CNN Television Network, 20 April 1992.

14. Carrie Cropley, "The Case of John McCaffary," *Wisconsin Magazine of History* (summer 1952): 284.

15. "Fits Crime," *Wausau Daily Herald,* 19 July 1992.

16. J. E. Cutler, "Capital Punishment and Lynching," *Annals* (May 1907): 184.

17. *Furman v. Georgia,* 408 U.S. 238 (1972).

18. Speaking on *Close-Up,* C-SPAN Television Network, 16 November 1992.

19. John Laurence, *A History of Capital Punishment* (New York: Citadel Press, 1960), 2.

20. David L. Sills, ed., "Capital Punishment," *International Encyclopedia of the Social Sciences,* vol. 2 (New York: Macmillan & Free Press, 1968), 290.

21. Charles Lewis Meryon, "Execution by Impalement: Latakia, 1813," a contemporary account published in *Eyewitness to History,* ed. John Carey (New York: Avon, 1987), 284.

22. Lewis E. Lawes, quoted in *Congressional Digest,* 232.

23. Laurence, *Capital Punishment,* 14.

24. "Dr. Guillotin and His Execution Machine," *History's Mysteries,* The History Channel; written by Arthur Drooxer and produced by Susan Frincke.

25. Philip English Mackey, *Voices against Death* (New York: Burt Franklin & Company, 1976), xii.

26. Hugo Adam Bedau, *The Death Penalty in America*, rev. ed. (New York: Alsine, 1968), 6.

27. Mackey, *Voices*, xi.

28. David Brion Davis, "The Movement to Abolish Capital Punishment in America, 1787–1861," *American Historical Review* (October 1957): 46.

29. Information regarding crimes punishable by death under state laws is available in the Bureau of Justice Statistics publication, *Capital Punishment 1999* (December 2000), NCJ 184795.

30. See Chapter 7 for a complete list of federal offenses punishable by death. Bureau of Justice Statistics publication, *Capital Punishment 1999* (December 2000), NCJ 184795.

31. NAACP Legal Defense Fund, *Death Row USA*, 1 January 2001.

32. Numbers provided by the Death Penalty Information Center.

33. These figures were posted on the DPIC Web site at *http://www.death-penaltyinfo.org//dpicintl.html*, where current totals should be available.

34. Amnesty International news release, 18 April 2000.

2

Problems and Controversies

Discussions of the death penalty tend to resolve themselves into debates between retentionists—those who wish to see the death penalty retained—and abolitionists, who wish to see it abolished. This debate is a complicated one. Capital punishment is not merely—or even primarily—a legal question; it is also a practical, philosophical, social, political, and moral question. Each of these elements of the issue has many ramifications, and each affects the others in a variety of ways.

For the sake of simplicity, we will sometimes talk about what the abolitionists believe and what the retentionists believe as though everyone in each of these broadly defined groups thinks alike. In reality, of course, they do not. There is a wide range of belief and nuance within each group.

Some in both camps claim a religious foundation for their views; others approach capital punishment as a practical question; still others consider it a moral issue. Some on both sides focus primarily on questions of social justice, others on the requirements of law enforcement. Some are primarily concerned with the protection of society, others with legal technicalities. And so on.

Some retentionists would like to see capital punishment retained but used as little as possible; they favor reserving the death penalty for such specific and rare offenses as presidential assassination and treason in time of war. Others would like to see the use of the death penalty expanded either by increasing the number of capital crimes or by executing a higher percentage of those convicted of the crimes already punishable by death.

In essence, the complex concerns raised by the death penalty can be boiled down into three distinct questions:

- The first is practical: *Is capital punishment useful?* Put another way, Does the death penalty help to protect society?
- The second is philosophical: *Is capital punishment morally acceptable?* Put another way, Is it right and just?
- The third is political: *Should we continue executing criminals?*

Each of these questions, of course, raises more questions. In this chapter, we will explore some of those questions. Although we will look at them from both sides, we will pay particular attention to the objections raised by the opponents of capital punishment, just as we paid particular attention to the reasons *for* the death penalty discussed in Chapter 1.

The Question of Deterrence

Traditionally, the notion of deterrence has been central to the practical debate over the question of capital punishment. Other beliefs, instincts, and desires may run deeper as personal motives for favoring or opposing the death penalty, but the public argument over the death penalty invariably returns to the question of deterrence.

Most of us assume that we execute murderers primarily because we believe such executions will discourage others from becoming murderers. Retentionists have long asserted that the deterrent power of capital punishment is an obvious fact. As Sir James Stephen wrote in 1804, "This is one of those propositions which it is difficult to prove, simply because they are in themselves more obvious than any proof can make them. It is possible to display ingenuity in arguing against it, but that is all. The whole experience of mankind is in the other direction. The threat of instant death is the one to which resort has always been made when there was an absolute necessity for producing some result."[1]

Still, abolitionists believe that deterrence is little more than an assumption—a naive assumption at that. "Cruelty and viciousness are not abolished by cruelty and viciousness," said publisher William Randolph Hearst, "not even by legalized cruelty and viciousness."[2]

The question is not whether the death penalty could ever be a deterrent to crime; even the most confirmed abolitionist will admit that it could. If everyone caught littering the streets were immediately hanged from the nearest lamppost, most people would pocket their candy wrappers instead of dropping them in the street. The real question is how effective the death penalty can be as a deterrent to such serious crimes as murder.

Littering is a casual offense, usually committed for no better reason than convenience. It's easier to toss a wrapper down in the street than to hang onto it until you come to a litter basket. With such a weak reason for breaking the law, virtually any severe penalty would be enough to convince most people to dispose of their trash more carefully. Murder, however, is rarely casual. It is often committed for the strongest, not the weakest, of motives: passionate hatred, anger, or greed.

Abolitionists argue that most murderers cannot think rationally enough to be deterred by *any* penalty, including death. Most murders are crimes of passion, committed in moments of intense rage, frustration, hatred, or fear when the killers aren't thinking clearly of the personal consequences of what they do. People in such states are incapable of taking such consequences into account.

Most other murderers—those who cold-bloodedly plan and carry out their crimes—think they are too clever to be caught. The death penalty cannot be a deterrent to them because they are convinced they will escape punishment of any kind. "The death penalty never once acted as a deterrent in all the jobs I carried out . . . and I have executed more people than anyone this century," declared Albert Pierrepoint, the legendary British executioner who became an opponent of capital punishment after his retirement in the late 1950s.[3]

Retentionists consider such testimony irrelevant. The threat of capital punishment obviously hasn't deterred those criminals who have committed capital crimes. No one expects the death penalty to deter every criminal and to prevent every terrible crime. It is enough, retentionists argue, that it deters some criminals and prevents some crimes. But even that level of deterrence is difficult to prove with any certainty.

Supporters of capital punishment face an obvious problem when they try to prove that the death penalty deters. How can they establish that someone *would have* committed a crime if that person had not been deterred by the threat of the death penalty? Historically, defenders of the death penalty have brushed aside such problems, relying on arguments based on anecdotes and common sense.

In the early 1970s, the Los Angeles Police Department reported interviews conducted with ninety-nine criminals who had not carried lethal weapons when they committed their crimes. According to the police, roughly half gave fear of the death penalty as the reason for their decision to reject weapons. The others claimed that it had had no effect on them, either because they weren't worried about it or because they would never have carried deadly weapons anyway.[4]

Abolitionists respond with their own anecdotal evidence. "On June 21, 1877," Professor George W. Kirchwey recounted, "ten men were hanged in Pennsylvania for murderous conspiracy. The *New York Herald* predicted the wholesome effect of this terrible lesson. 'We may be certain,' it said, 'that the pitiless severity of the law will deter the most wicked from anything like the imitation of these crimes.' And yet, the night after the large scale execution two of the witnesses at the trial of these men had been murdered, and within two weeks five of the prosecutors had met the same fate."[5]

Abolitionists base most of their argument against deterrence on statistics. As long ago as 1919, American Professor Raymond T. Bye used a statistical study to show that "there is no measurable relation between the existence or nonexistence of capital punishment and the homicide rate."[6] That same conclusion has been reached by dozens of studies since. They have compared all sorts of statistical variations, including murder rates in states that have abolished the death penalty versus those in states that use it extensively; rates of serious crimes in countries that impose the death penalty versus those that do not; and differences in the rates of capital crimes before and after the abolition or reinstatement of the death penalty in a particular state or nation.

After examining the statistical studies available in the 1950s, Thorsten Sellin issued a report for the American Law Institute that concluded that capital punishment did little or nothing to deter crime.[7] A decade later, the *International Encyclopedia of the Social Sciences* could still report that statistical studies "have in general failed to identify any meaningful correlation between the presence of the death penalty and the rates of serious criminality."[8]

If the death penalty really does deter murderers, suggest the abolitionists, then societies that execute murderers should be relatively free of murder. Yet many of the most murder-ridden societies in history have practiced capital punishment. Even today, the four states that make the most use of the death penalty are consistently among those with the highest murder rates.[9] Texas, which has carried out more than one out of every four executions in the entire country since 1976, has one murder for every 6,385 residents. Florida has one per 9,952, Georgia one per 8,997, and Virginia one per 11,249. Compare these statistics to one murder per 20,383 residents and one per 43,750 in the non–capital punishment states of Wisconsin and Minnesota.[10]

Retentionists argue that none of this statistical evidence proves that capital punishment never deters potential criminals. They point out that the murder rate in any given state depends on many things besides whether that state imposes capital punishment. They cite such factors as the proportion of urban residents in the state, the level of economic prosperity, and the social and racial makeup of the population. States like Texas and Florida, they say, would probably have even higher murder rates if they did not have the death penalty to keep things at least partly in check.

Retentionists do have some figures of their own. The most notable statistical study upholding the value of deterrence was conducted by an economist, Isaac Erlich, who examined the possible effects of capital punishment on murder rates in the United States in the mid-twentieth century. Erlich suggested that "an additional execution per year . . . may have resulted, on average, in seven or eight fewer murders."[11] Erlich's methods were scientifically controversial, however, particularly because his results contradicted those of most other studies in the field. A board of experts commissioned by the National Academy of Sciences to examine Erlich's study in 1975 brushed it aside as offering "no useful evidence" on the deterrent effect of capital punishment.[12]

In addition to Erlich's study, retentionists point to events in the United States during the 1950s, 1960s, and 1970s. Throughout the late 1950s and early 1960s, executions in the United States held fairly steady at between forty and sixty-five each year. During that time, the number of murders in the United States remained fairly stable, too, at between 8,060 and 9,140. As the 1960s moved on, the number of executions dropped dramatically, until there were no executions at all during the nine years from 1968 until 1977. (The Supreme Court decision striking down the capital punishment statutes came in 1972, and the ruling allowing executions to resume came in 1976.) As executions dragged to a stop, murders soared, reaching a high of 20,600 in 1974.[13]

Proponents of deterrence take this as evidence that the threat of the death penalty *must* have deterred murders before

1968 because the number of murders rose so sharply when it was removed. Opponents of deterrence protest that there is no evidence showing the rise in murders had anything to do with the absence of the death penalty. They point out that homicides rose again after the death penalty was restored in 1976 and have climbed since, although more slowly. Murders in the United States reached a new high—of 24,040—in 1991.[14] Furthermore, murder rates jumped sharply in two states—Florida and Georgia—during the very next year after executions resumed in the wake of the *Gregg* decision.[15]

If retentionists cannot prove that capital punishment deters crime, abolitionists cannot prove that it doesn't. Even so, the bulk of the statistical evidence has convinced even some retentionists to abandon the deterrence argument. In his famous essay "In Favor of Capital Punishment," Jacques Barzun conceded that he is "ready to believe the statistics tending to show that the prospect of his own death does not stop the murderer."[16] Murderers, Barzun points out, are often "blind egoists" who fully expect to get away with their crimes, and who could not imagine their own deaths in any case. Barzun bases his defense of the death penalty on other arguments, relying primarily on the need to protect society from killers who are considered high risks for killing again.

Two similar conclusions about deterrence were reached by Great Britain's Royal Commission on Capital Punishment in 1953 and by U.S. Supreme Court Justice Potter Stewart in 1976. After examining all the evidence available internationally—both from countries that had abandoned the death penalty and from those where it was still practiced—the Royal Commission concluded that "there is no clear evidence of any lasting increase" in murders resulting from the abolition of the death penalty. Furthermore, "there are many offenders on whom the deterrent effect is limited and may often be negligible."[17] According to Justice Stewart, "Although some of the studies suggest the death penalty may not function as a significantly greater deterrent than lesser penalties, there is no convincing empirical evidence either supporting or refuting this view."[18]

Does the Death Penalty Encourage Crime?

"Of all the arguments against the death penalty," writes Dr. Louis Joylon West, Chairman of the Department of Psychiatry and Behavioral Sciences at the UCLA Medical Center, "there is one that is perhaps least understood and most paradoxical: *Capital punishment breeds murder.*"[19] It does this, the abolitionists argue, in at least three ways.

The first way in which capital punishment may encourage murder is fairly straightforward and even obvious: The threat of capital punishment raises the stakes of getting caught. Anyone already subject to the death penalty has little to lose by killing again and again. Their potential sentence cannot be made any worse than it already is. This means that criminals who already face death for previous crimes are more likely to kill to avoid capture. In particular, the death penalty gives them more reason to silence any potential witnesses against them.

This is a particularly strong argument against making crimes other than murder punishable by death. When kidnapping is a capital crime, for example, kidnappers have little practical reason not to kill their victims. The same is true of rape and other possible capital crimes.

In addition to encouraging criminals to kill to avoid detection or capture, it can be argued that, from the time it is imposed until the time it is carried out, a death sentence removes all practical checks on condemned criminals' behavior. If murderers are going to be executed anyway, why should they refrain from venting their anger and frustration on those around them? Of course, not all condemned convicts are moved to take out their bitterness by committing violence, but for those who are, the fact that they already face what they may consider the ultimate punishment removes a powerful potential reason for restraint. This puts fellow prisoners, guards, and other prison personnel in greater danger than they would be in otherwise.

Those who favor the death penalty argue that if there were no death penalty to hold over the head of prisoners, those who have been sentenced to life without parole would be free to commit whatever crimes they chose without fear of increased punishment.

Abolitionists respond that the conditions of a convict's imprisonment may be altered and privileges may be revoked. A prisoner may be put into solitary confinement or refused the right to smoke or watch television, for example. Such things, they say, may not seem significant to someone in the outside world, but they loom very large in the life of a long-term prisoner.

The third way in which capital punishment may encourage criminals to commit murder is more subtle: Some criminals may use it as a form of suicide.

It is reasonably assumed that most people who break the law don't want to be caught. They want—and usually expect—to get away with their crimes. According to West and other leading psychiatrists, however, this assumption is not true of all criminals. Some not only want to be caught, they want to be punished. At some level, they may even want to die, and, for them, killing others becomes a way to bring about their own deaths.

Gary Gilmore was apparently one of these. Gilmore, the first criminal to be executed after the *Gregg* decision reinstated the death penalty in the mid-1970s, protested the legal efforts abolitionists made to save his life. He insisted that the state *owed* him an execution and claimed to resent the legal efforts made to protect his rights and prevent his death. "I took 'em serious when they sentenced me to death," he once complained. "I thought you were supposed to take 'em serious. I didn't know it was a joke."[20]

Dr. John C. Woods, the chief of forensic psychiatry at Utah State Hospital, who examined Gilmore, was convinced that the killer sought his own death. "He took the steps necessary to turn the job of his own destruction over to someone else," Woods told an interviewer. "[T]hat's why he pulled two execution-style murders he was bound to be caught for. I think it's a legitimate question, based on this evidence and our knowledge of the individual, to ask if Gilmore would have killed if there was not a death penalty in Utah."[21]

In an article originally published in a psychiatric journal, Dr. West described several other cases examples of men who killed in the hope of receiving the death penalty. Whether out of fear or for some other reason, they chose not to kill themselves but to let society do it for them. In one case West cites, a truck driver explained to police that he had killed a total stranger because he (the killer) was "tired of living." In another, a killer-to-be actually left a state that didn't have the death penalty in order to commit his crime in a state that would execute him when he was caught.[22]

Days before his execution in 1992, an Illinois murderer named Lloyd Wayne Hampton explained that he had killed a sixty-nine-year-old man partly because "I had given up trying to make it. What was I going to do? . . . I either had to put myself in a position of being killed by someone else or committing suicide.

At that point, I had strong beliefs about not killing myself. . . . So I put myself in a position to have the state kill me."[23]

It seems that the death penalty probably does deter some potential criminals, as its supporters believe, and it probably does incite others to commit crimes, as some psychiatrists insist. But does it save more lives than it costs, or does it put more lives in jeopardy than it saves? Although neither side in the death penalty debate is content with the answer, the reality seems to be that there is no way to tell. This being so, concerned citizens must decide for themselves where the greater danger lies.

Is the Death Penalty Needed to Protect Society from Those Who Would Kill Again?

Jacques Barzun is far from alone in favoring the death penalty as a way of protecting society from "uncontrollable brutes." One of the most elemental concerns people have about those who have already committed terrible crimes is the fear that they will commit more of them. Most murderers who are not executed eventually get out of prison, and many people believe that these released killers are likely to kill again.

This belief is fostered not only by sensational news reports about murderers who do kill again but by politicians anxious to win votes through the public's natural fear of crime. In 1988, Democratic presidential candidate Michael Dukakis was badly damaged by opposition television ads that reminded the public about the case of a convicted murderer named Willie Horton. Horton had been serving a life sentence in a Massachusetts prison during the time Dukakis was governor of the state. When he was released for a short period on a special program that allowed some Massachusetts prisoners a taste of freedom, Horton committed another brutal murder. The publicity these ads generated about the Horton case solidified a widespread belief that Dukakis was soft on criminals, and it may have intensified the hostility and distrust a frightened public already felt toward released murderers.

Despite the widespread public belief that murderers are likely to be recidivists (repeat criminals), the evidence suggests that most murderers are unlikely to kill again. Various studies, both in the United States and elsewhere, indicate that, apart from professional hit men and a few serial killers, most murderers are good risks never to repeat their crimes compared to other categories of criminals. The United Kingdom Royal Commission on Capital Punishment, which looked into recidivism rates among murderers in the United Kingdom and Europe, found almost no repeat offenders among released murderers.[24] An even more sweeping American study covered all the released murderers in twelve states from the beginning of the twentieth century up to 1976. Of the 2,646 killers released from prison during that time for any reason, only 16 ever returned for committing another murder—barely more than one half of one percent.[25] Recidivism rates for most other serious crimes are much higher.

Even inside prisons, convicted murderers do not seem to be especially high risks to kill again.[26] Many murders do take place in prisons, but most are not committed by prisoners held for murder. Of the sixteen California prisoners who committed murders in a two-year study period in the 1960s, for example, none was serving a sentence for murder at the time.[27]

So far, even the most determined retentionists have not seriously suggested the execution of everyone who kills another human being. This being so, the problem for those who want to protect society by eliminating truly dangerous murderers becomes identifying them. How do we distinguish Barzun's "uncontrollable brutes" from the great majority of murderers who are apparently no more likely to kill again than other members of society are likely to kill at all?

This is no easy task. At the time of his conviction for murder in the 1920s, Nathan Leopold would have seemed to be as much of a risk as any killer of the time. His crime had been a "thrill killing," denounced as cold-blooded and heartless by the prosecution. Leopold expressed no remorse. Released from prison many years later, Leopold led an apparently blameless life and even served as a medical missionary in Puerto Rico.[28]

In some cases, the line seems easy to draw. A few killers, like the child-murderer Westley Allan Dodd, draw it for themselves. They declare themselves uncontrollable, and insist that the only way to stop them is to kill them. But even Dodd later changed his tune. In a final statement, delivered at the time of his execution, he announced that he had "found peace in the Lord, Jesus Christ."[29] Few psychologists believe it's possible to tell with certainty which killers will or will not kill again if eventually released.

What of serial killers who kill obsessively? Killers such as Ted Bundy, John Wayne Gacy, Ed Gein, and Jeffrey Dahmer had already killed over and over again by the time they were caught. It may not be certain that they will repeat their crimes if given a chance, but it's far from certain that they won't. Most of us would feel very uncomfortable if one of them were released and moved in next door to us.

Abolitionists point out that, despite the enormous publicity given to serial killers by the media, such murderers are rare. One reason they get as much attention as they do is because they are so unusual. As horrible as their crimes are and as numerous as they appear to be, serial killings make up only a tiny fraction of the more than 20,000 murders committed in the United States in a given year. If serial killers were the only people executed, we would probably see less than one execution in the United States per year.

Besides, abolitionists argue, history proves that there is no need to execute even relentless killers like these to keep them from repeating their crimes. Few, if any, serial killers, once caught, have ever killed again—mostly, of course, because they were successfully incarcerated. Of those mentioned above, Bundy and Gacy have been executed so far. Gein was imprisoned for many years in Wisconsin, a state that does not have the death penalty, before being released, and he later died without killing again. Dahmer was killed by a fellow prisoner while serving a life sentence in the same state. None of these men was implicated in any killings after his conviction.

If the death penalty is really necessary to protect society from killers who have already been caught and convicted, it seems there should be some evidence of it. States that do not have capital punishment should have more problems with once-convicted murderers than death penalty states do, but there is no evidence to suggest that this is so.

Is Life-without-the-Possibility-of-Parole an Effective Alternative to the Death Penalty?

Abolitionists argue that a sentence of life-without-the-possibility-of-parole would be a morally preferable alternative to the death penalty and would be an equally effective means of protecting society from the worst criminals.

A key element of public support for the death penalty is the fear that, without it, such dangerous offenders will one day be released to menace society once again. On the evidence we have seen, this fear may be overdone, but it is by no means entirely unreasonable. In the past, many murderers who have been given life sentences have eventually been released, whether on parole, to alleviate prison overcrowding or because of some other circumstance.

In recent years, however, several states have passed "'life' means life" laws, which allow sentences that deny any possibility that the convict will ever be released for any reason.

Many people who otherwise support the death penalty consider a life sentence without the possibility of parole an acceptable alternative. Others, however, find it difficult to have faith that these sentences will be enforced. In effect, some believe that there is no such thing as a true sentence of life without any possibility of parole. The legislatures and courts of today cannot bind the legislatures and courts of the future. There is nothing that these institutions can do today that the same institutions cannot overrule at some time in the future—except give and carry out a sentence of death. The only way for the institutions of today to make sure that the punishments they impose are carried out is to carry them out themselves, contemporaneously. Executing murderers, the skeptics feel, is the only certain means of protecting society from the possibility that they will kill again.

Does the Death Penalty Mean Fewer Convictions?

Far from protecting society by eliminating dangerous criminals, abolitionists argue, the death penalty may protect some criminals by making juries reluctant to convict them. "The punishment of murder by death multiplies murders, from the difficulty it creates in convicting people who are guilty of it," wrote Dr. Benjamin Rush in 1798. "Humanity, revolting at the idea of the severity and certainty of capital punishment, often steps in, and collects such evidence in favour of a murderer, as screens him from death altogether, or palliates his crime into manslaughter."[30] In modern times, this reluctance has been translated into the American court's recognition that "death is different." A variety of special procedures and legal technicalities kick into effect in capital cases. Designed to protect the rights of defendants whose lives are on the line, such procedures make it more difficult to convict people accused of capital crimes. As we will see in the next section, these protections also add greatly to the expense of prosecuting cases involving the death penalty.

Even aside from the legal technicalities, capital punishment raises the stakes of a guilty verdict, and jurors know this. The knowledge that death may await the defendant if they convict may well make some jurors more scrupulous than they would be otherwise, and therefore less willing to convict. This is not entirely a bad thing. Certainly a jury *should* be certain of their facts before sending a defendant to the executioner.

If the shadow of the death penalty makes juries more reluctant to find defendants guilty, its absence may encourage them to convict. Three years after the death penalty was abolished in Minnesota, there was no significant change in the number of murders committed in the state. According to the Minnesota Governor A. O. Eberhart, however, the state saw an increase in the percentage of murder *convictions* "to the extent of approximately fifty percent."[31]

To some extent, these arguments must remain speculative. Jurors cannot be compelled to talk about their deliberations, much less to explain their rationale for convicting or acquitting, and many are reluctant to do so. This makes it impossible to determine the degree to which the existence of the death penalty has an effect on jurors' willingness to convict.

The Question of Cost

Among those who applauded the January 1993 execution of Westley Allan Dodd was the popular evangelist minister, television talk show host, and sometime presidential candidate Rev. Pat Robertson. He defended the execution partly on economic grounds. If Dodd had been allowed to live, he told the audience of his program, *The 700 Club,* the state of Washington would have had to support him in a costly prison cell for the rest of his life. "Why should the taxpayers have to pay [to support] this killer?" asked Robertson.[32]

The same question is frequently asked about other murderers. Why should honest citizens have to pay for the food and lodging of killers? Why not simply execute them and be done with them—and save a lot of money into the bargain? (The same question could also be asked about other criminals. Why should honest citizens pay to support rapists, thieves, and embezzlers?)

Many retentionists assume that it is cheaper to execute criminals than to keep them in prison for life, or even for several years. How much does a bullet cost? Or the drugs used for lethal injections? How expensive can it be to build an electric chair and then send a couple of thousand volts of electricity through a criminal's body?

Ironically, cost is also important to the abolitionists, who claim that it costs more to execute criminals than to imprison them. They point out the cost of maintaining capital punishment involves much more than the relatively minor cost of killing the condemned.

Going for the death penalty doesn't just raise the stakes for the defendant whose life is on the line—it raises the financial stakes for the state. Simply charging a defendant with a capital crime escalates the costs of the trial. The U.S. Supreme Court insists that the awesome finality of the death penalty requires a "correspondingly greater degree of scrutiny of the capital sentencing determination."[33] This is why all but two capital punishment states provide for an automatic review of all death sentences.[34]

As the American Civil Liberties Union Foundation of Northern California explains, the possibility of the death penalty raises the costs at every stage: "A capital case requires two trials (one to determine guilt and another to determine penalty), automatic state supreme court review, postconviction proceedings, and Supreme Court appeals, all of which are extremely costly to the state both in terms of money and human resources. Jury selection and pretrial motions are also more lengthy in capital cases, and expert consultants such as psychiatrists often must be retained. The cost of maintaining death rows in state prisons, clemency hearings, and the execution itself must also be added to the price of executions."[35]

That price is very high. A one-time administrator of the California prisons has pointed out that "the actual cost of execution, the cost of operating the super-maximum security condemned unit, the years spent by some inmates in condemned status, and a pro-rata share of the top-level prison officials' time spent in administering the units, add up to a cost substantially greater than the cost to retain them in prison for the rest of their lives."[36]

A 1988 Kansas Legislative Research Department study found that trying a capital case cost the state over $116,00 more than the cost of holding a noncapital trial.[37] In the 1980s, the state of Florida spent six times more per person to execute criminals than to maintain them in prison for life without parole.[38]

It has been estimated that Texas, which has executed more people than any other state since 1976, spent a whopping $183.2 million on expenses related to the death penalty in only six years.[39] "Whether you're for [the death penalty] or against it," declared Chief Criminal Judge James Ellis of Oregon, "I think that the fact is that Oregon simply can't afford it."[40] (Despite this opinion, Oregon has continued to use the death penalty.) According to the *Sacramento Bee* newspaper, California would save $91 million a year by abolishing the death penalty.[41]

The special costs of the death penalty hit the hardest on local governments, and the hardest of all on the governments of small towns and counties that have relatively few resources. Ironically for those who favor the death penalty on the grounds that it helps to maintain law and order, these costs often come out of state and local funds that would otherwise go to building jails and prisons and putting more police officers on the streets. This is one reason why prosecutors and other law enforcement officials are sometimes reluctant to file capital charges.

The Death Penalty Information Center points out that Florida recently had to reduce its Department of Corrections budget by $45 million, although the state had spent more than $57 million on enforcing the death penalty in recent years. The result was that eighteen convicted murderers were permanently removed from society by execution, but 3,000 other convicted criminals had to be released from prison early because Florida didn't have the money to keep them there.[42]

Much of the enormous cost of maintaining the death penalty could be saved if the legal system stopped treating death as "different"—if capital trials and appeals were conducted in the same way that ordinary criminal cases are. Accomplishing this, however, would take a massive transformation in American judicial philosophy. Critics of the way death penalty cases are treated now believe that judges bend over backwards to protect the rights of criminals. When doubts arise, critics charge, the courts tend to err on the side of the defendant. It is time, they say, for the courts to start erring on the side of society. They argue that many savings could be made if judges took a less sympathetic attitude toward the rights of defendants.

The U.S. Supreme Court seems to be moving in that direction. Under Chief Justice William Rehnquist, the Court has been increasingly unsympathetic and even hostile toward repeated appeals to the federal courts (*habeas corpus* appeals) from death row inmates. Even while the Rehnquist Court has been eating away at certain of the special protections granted to capital defendants, however, it has not only reaffirmed but extended others.

It would probably be unrealistic—as well as unfair—to ask judges at any level to cut legal corners or to dispense with the presumed rights of defendants when their lives are at stake. Judges, after all, are human beings, too. They need to feel justified in what they do. Supreme Court Justice William O. Douglas spoke for many of his judicial colleagues when he wrote, in 1953, "As a justice it is also important that before we allow human lives to be snuffed out, we be sure—empathically sure—that we act within the law. If we are not sure, there will be lingering doubts to plague the conscience after the event."[43]

Does the Death Penalty Violate (or Uphold) the Sanctity of Human Life?

If deterrence is at the heart of the practical debate over the death penalty, the sanctity of human life is at the heart of the philosophical and moral debate. Both sides claim to put a high value on human life, but their attitudes toward the death penalty reflect that value in opposite ways.

For many abolitionists, every person's life is equally sacred, and no life should be taken unless absolutely necessary. They have an instinctive feeling, as Minnesota Congressman O. J. Kvale expressed it, that the death penalty "cheapens human life. And human life should be sacred."[44]

Most abolitionists accept the idea that it might be necessary to kill someone—for instance: in battle, in self-defense, or to protect the life of another person. However, they do not accept the argument that it is necessary to kill convicted criminals who can be punished in other ways. The life of the murderer's victim is already lost and cannot be brought back by killing the murderer. Because they see no absolute need to take the life of the prisoner, who is already confined and controlled in jail, abolitionists believe that it is wrong to do so.

Retentionists, on the other hand, are much more concerned with the sanctity of the victim's life than with the murderer's. They are impatient with the arguments based on the value of the life of a killer. Theodore Roosevelt, who ordered men into battle as a colonel in the Spanish-American War, scoffed at the idea that a criminal's life is too precious to destroy: "[I]nasmuch as, without hesitation, I have again and again sent good and gallant and upright men to die, it seems to me the height of folly both mischievous and mawkish to contend that criminals who have deserved death should nevertheless be allowed to shirk it. No brave and good man can properly shirk death and no criminal who has earned death should be allowed to shirk it."[45]

Other supporters of capital punishment turn the abolitionist's value-of-life argument on its head; they insist that it is the sacredness of human life itself that demands the death penalty. "All religions that I'm aware of feel that human life is sacred," Professor Ernest van den Haag told an interviewer, "and that its sacredness must be enforced by depriving of life anyone who deprives another person of life."[46] Van den Haag was overstating his point. Some religions disapprove of the death penalty. Still, he was stating a widely held retentionist belief that instead of cheapening human life, the death penalty affirms its worth.

For those who agree with van den Haag, the execution of a killer is the ultimate proof of the value society puts on the life of the killer's victim. It is not the death penalty but the failure to impose it that "demeans the value of innocent human life," says Paul Kamenar of the Washington Legal Foundation.[47] For Kamenar, unwillingness to execute a vicious murderer puts a higher value on the murderer's life than the victim's.

The famous economist and philosopher, John Stuart Mill, made a similar but more complex argument to the British Parliament over a century ago:

> Much has been said of the sanctity of human life, and the absurdity of supposing that we can teach respect for life by ourselves destroying it. But I am surprised at the employment of this argument. . . . It is not human life only, not human life as such, that ought to be sacred to us, but human feelings. The human capacity of suffering is what we should cause to be re-

spected, not the mere capacity of existing. And we may imagine somebody asking how we can teach people not to inflict suffering by ourselves inflicting it? But to this I should answer—all of us would answer—that to deter by suffering from inflicting suffering is not only possible, but the very purpose of penal justice. Does fining a criminal show want of respect for property, or imprisoning him, for personal freedom? Just as unreasonable is it to think that to take the life of a man who has taken that of another is to show want of regard for human life. We show, on the contrary, most emphatically our regard for it, by the adoption of a rule that he who violates that right in another forfeits it for himself, and that while no other crime that he can commit deprives him of his life, this shall.[48]

Is Death the Ultimate Punishment?

Most people assume that death is the worst possible punishment a civilized society can impose. As Sir James Stephen wrote nearly two centuries ago, "In any secondary punishment, however terrible, there is hope; but death is death; its terrors cannot be described more forcibly."[49]

However, not everyone agrees that death is the worst possible punishment. The mother of a young woman killed in the bombing of the Alfred P. Murrah Building in 1995 expressed a different view. Interviewed following the passage of the death sentence on the bomber, Timothy McVeigh, she expressed disappointment. "There is a lot of pain in living," she told a reporter from the *Washington Post*, "—death is pretty easy."[50]

Some people, including some of those who have been sentenced to spend the rest of their lives in prison, believe that life imprisonment, far from being a mercy, is often a more terrible penalty than a relatively swift and painless execution. As philosopher John Stuart Mill rhetorically asked the British Parliament in 1868, "What comparison can there really be, in point of severity, between consigning a man to the short pang of a rapid death, and immuring him in a living tomb, there to linger out what may be a long life in the hardest and most monotonous toil, without any of its alleviations or rewards—debarred from all pleasant sights and sounds, and cut off from all earthly hope, except a slight mitigation of bodily restraint, or a small improvement of diet?"[51]

The father of Westley Allan Dodd's four-year-old victim insisted that his desire to see Dodd die was not based on the belief that this was the most terrible punishment that Dodd could suffer, only the most final: "If justice were to be served in a vindictive way," he told a reporter, "I'd want him to spend . . . his life in jail. That's the cruel and unusual punishment in this case."[52]

As we have already seen, Gary Gilmore and Lloyd Wayne Hampton not only preferred death but virtually demanded it. Charles Bryant, whose death sentence for aggravated rape was overturned in Louisiana, explained that if given a choice between death and life imprisonment, he would choose death. "Even if they could fry me tomorrow," he said, "that would be preferable to spending the rest of my life here [in Angola State Prison]. This isn't living. It is just existing."[53]

The Gilmores, Hamptons, and Bryants are exceptions. Most condemned criminals battle to the end to have their death sentences overturned.

Hope

For some opponents of capital punishment, the key issue is not that life in itself is sacred, nor that it is always, and in all circumstances, preferable to death. Some abolitionists may even agree that life in prison, without hope of parole, may be a bleaker fate than execution. For them, the key factor is that life offers hope, no matter how remote or farfetched that hope may be.

So long as a prisoner is alive, there is always a chance that he may some day be set free. A variety of future events could free him. If he is innocent, his innocence might be proved. Even if he is not, he can hope that some technicality may be found to free him. A future governor may grant clemency. In his old age, he might be given some form of compassionate release. Other, more general, possibilities exist as well. At some point in the distant future, society's attitude toward sentencing might change to the extent that life-without-parole becomes considered a cruel and barbaric punishment; all life sentences may then be reduced. The prison system may one day become so overcrowded, or so expensive, that it will no longer be feasible to support even the worst prisoners for the rest of their lives.

Even for a convict sentenced to mandatory life-without-possibility-of-parole, such imagined prospects will always stand between him and ultimate despair, offering him hope if he is inclined to take it. They may be unlikely, and the odds against them in any particular case may be long, but such eventualities are within the realm of possibility. Such things have happened in the past, and, for many convicts, life will be a long time. Most people who are convicted of capital crimes are young men who would ordinarily look forward to many decades of life. In that expanse of time, great changes may occur, not only in them but in society at large.

Ironically, the very things that allow a prisoner to hope are the same ones that make proponents of the death penalty reluctant to accept the alternative of life-without-possibility-of-parole. So long as there is hope for prisoners, they will always remain a threat to the public safety in the eyes of those who fear them.

Private Vengeance/Public Retribution

Every murder has other victims besides the person whose life is ended. Family members—children, parents, husbands, wives—and everyone else who loved or valued the murdered person are all victims, too. So, in another way, are the family members and others who love and value the murderer. In a sense, the entire society is a victim.

Whenever a great wrong has been done, people feel the need to do something that puts the wrong right. Murder is a great wrong that can never be put right in the sense that the life, once taken, can never be restored. Even if the wrong cannot be righted, though, it can at least be avenged. For many people, the death of the wrongdoer seems the only medicine that can heal the wound inflicted on society.

For most supporters of capital punishment, the desire for retribution is an impersonal thing—a judgment about what is best for society. For those who knew and loved the murdered person, the wound is an intensely personal one. Their need for healing is not abstract, but real and specific.

Family members and other close survivors often look forward to the deaths of those who victimized their loved ones. Some even ask to attend the execution so that they can have the satisfaction of watching the killer die. Some have a hunger for revenge. Others deny this motive. They simply hope the execution of the murderer will somehow help them close the chapter on their tragedy and get on with their lives. As we have seen, the father of a young boy who was tortured and then murdered by Westley Allan Dodd was impatient for the execution of his son's killer because he believed it would help end the continuing stress his family was suffering.[54] "I'm not vengeful," declared the widow of a policeman as she explained her wish to see the death penalty inflicted on his murderer, "but I feel it's scriptural." The policeman's daughter, who, unlike her mother, did not ask to attend the execution, still expected it to bring "a lot of relief. . . . I feel," she added, "like Daddy will finally be put to rest."[55]

Family members have traditionally been allowed to witness executions, although, since executions ceased to be public events, their numbers have been limited. In 2001, however, U.S. Attorney General John Ashcroft decided that, because of the unique circumstances surrounding the bombing of the Murrah Office Building in Oklahoma City—a crime whose victims, killed, injured, and maimed, numbered in the hundreds—a closed circuit telecast of the execution of the bomber, Timothy McVeigh, would be made available for viewing by victims' relatives. Although this procedure, like the crime, was exceptional, Ashcroft acknowledged that the precedent set would help shape the future policies of the Bureau of Prisons in regard to executions.

Even opponents of capital punishment can understand and sympathize with the pain that causes many loved ones of murder victims to call for the death of the killer. In some ancient societies, it was left to the family of the dead person to exact a price for the wrong that had been done to them—whether that price was an economic penalty or a "life for a life." Punishment by the state is, in an essential way, a substitute for personal vengeance. It was meant not only to replace it but to supersede it.

There is a real question, then, whether the personal feelings of those close to the murdered person have a place in the legal proceedings that decide the killer's fate. One view is that they don't belong in that process at all. Judges and juries are there to inflict punishment, not to satisfy someone's desire for revenge. "Punishment as retribution has been condemned by scholars for centuries," wrote Thurgood Marshall in his opinion in the *Furman* case, "and the Eighth Amendment was adopted to prevent punishment from being synonymous with vengeance."[56] An opposing view is that the pain and trouble a murder causes to other individuals is a valid and aggravating circumstance that should be taken into account when determining the seriousness of the crime.

Even some retentionists make a distinction between society's desire for retribution and the individual citizen's demand for vengeance. The damage done to society and the damage done to individual survivors are very different things, just as public outrage and personal anguish are distinct. No matter how understandable the feelings of individual survivors may be, many people believe they should not be allowed to influence death penalty sentencing.

In June 1991, the U.S. Supreme Court declared that "victim impact" evidence could be allowed in the penalty phase of a capital trial.[57] Juries can now take the suffering of the victim's family into account when deciding whether to inflict the death penalty. In effect, this means they can also take into account the family's desire for revenge.

Opponents of victim impact evidence argue that it inevitably leads to increased hostility and prejudice against the defendant. They also complain that it leads juries to put a higher value on the lives of certain victims than others, assuring that the deaths of victims with many loving friends and family members will be considered more terrible—and so more deserving of the death penalty—than those of victims who died friendless.

Some abolitionists argue that if the feelings of the *victim's* family deserve to be taken into account, so do those of the *defendant's* family. Shouldn't the jury hear from them as well? Shouldn't the jury consider the agony they will suffer if their loved one is executed? Aren't they just as innocent and just as deserving of consideration as the friends and relatives of the victim?

Not all close survivors of murder victims desire the killer's death. Some actively call for mercy, although often only after the trial is over and the defendant has already been sentenced to die. The Franciscan Sisters of Mary Immaculate, of Amarillo, Texas, appealed for mercy on behalf of Johnny Frank Garrett, who had raped and murdered an elderly member of their order, Sister Tadea Benz. Long after the brutal murder and as Garrett's execution day approached, the nuns issued a statement protesting Garrett's death sentence: "[W]e are still convinced, ten years later, that faithfulness to Jesus Christ and to our founder, St. Francis, requires of us that we forgive Johnny Frank Garrett. . . . [A]s the family of Sister Tadea Benz we respectfully submit that justice would not be served by executing [him]," they pleaded.[58] The sisters went on to ask the Texas State Board of Pardons and the governor to commute Garrett's sentence to life imprisonment. The board refused, however, and Johnny Frank Garrett was executed in February 1992.[59]

If the use of the victim impact evidence harks back to the ancient tradition of family vengeance, then the wishes of the survivors should be considered whatever they may be. Although it is true that in some ancient cultures the family members were free to destroy the killer who had wronged their relative, they were equally free to let the killer live. In modern times, juries, judges, governors, and pardons boards are more influenced by relatives' calls for death than by their calls for leniency. It is as though the desire for vengeance is somehow more understandable and easier to sympathize with than the desire for mercy. In any event, many abolitionists and retentionists alike are uncomfortable about the state's basing decisions about who should die on the personal wishes of individuals. Even for an expansionist such as Paul Kamenar of the Washington Legal Foundation, the anger and anguish of family members is not the main point: "What's at work here is not the personal feelings of vengeance that may come up in some cases," he declares. "What's important is that there's a societal interest of retribution, which is a collective self-expression of society's revulsion about the heinousness of the crime that was committed."[60]

Questions of Fairness

Abolitionists complain that the death penalty is almost exclusively reserved for those who are the weakest and most disadvantaged in life: the outcasts, the unpopular minorities, and the poor. There is no question that the death penalty falls unequally on different groups within society, although retentionists insist that this has more to do with the different behaviors of the groups than with the built-in bias of the criminal justice system.

The Indigent

"Execution," remarked Clinton Duffy, an ex-warden of San Quentin prison, is a "privilege of the poor."[61] On the other side of the social coin, as Supreme Court Justice William O. Douglas once pointed out, "One searches our chronicles in vain for the execution of any member of the affluent strata of this society."[62]

There may be many reasons why the death penalty is imposed primarily on poor and lower-class defendants. One reason, at least, is glaringly obvious: They can't afford good lawyers. Under the American legal system, a death sentence is never inevitable, even for defendants convicted of the most terrible of crimes. Therefore, what happens in the preparation of a case, at trial, and during the appeal is vital. The better the case is handled, the lower the risk the defendant will be put to death. A good, experienced lawyer improves the defendant's chances at every stage of the.process. This means that, all else being equal, the better the lawyer, the better the defendant's chances of escaping execution.

Indigent (poor) defendants simply cannot afford to hire the best lawyers, particularly in the most important early stages of their cases. Once murderers have been sentenced to death, they may receive the help of competent pro bono attorneys who donate their services because they are opposed to capital punishment. In the crucial earlier stages of the case, however—when the decisions of guilt or innocence, life or death, are being made—the poor defendant is virtually alone. According to Amnesty International, the lawyer for one poor defendant in Louisiana apparently spent only eight hours preparing his case. The lawyer for another was working on three hundred cases simultaneously. Not surprisingly, both of these defendants were convicted and executed. Furthermore, "a recent study found that capital defendants in Texas with court-appointed lawyers were more than twice as likely to receive a death sentence" as those who were able to hire their own lawyers.[63] It's hardly surprising, then, that the poor have always made up the majority of inhabitants on death rows in the United States.

Race

Historically, says John Healey of Amnesty International, the death penalty "has been primarily used against the black community [and] primarily in the South."[64] Until the end of the Civil War, slaves could be executed for many more crimes than their masters, and, even after slavery was abolished, African Americans continued to be executed at a much higher rate than other Americans until late in the twentieth century.

African Americans made up more than half of all the people executed from 1930 (when the government started keeping records) until 1972, although they made up little more than 10 percent of the population during than time. When the Supreme Court authorized the resumption of executions in 1976, it assumed that the new laws passed since 1972 had corrected the problem; indeed, the proportion of black defendants sentenced to death has dropped dramatically. As of January 1, 2001, the National Association for the Advancement of Colored People (NAACP) Legal Defense Fund knew of 1,595 black convicts awaiting execution, or 42.81 percent of the total, compared to 1,719 whites (46.014 percent).[65] This means that black people are no longer a majority on the nation's death rows, although they still make up a much higher percentage of death row residents than of the population at large.

Despite this apparent improvement, abolitionists insist that the application of the death penalty is still heavily influenced by race—often not the race of the defendant, but the race of the victim. In the words of Henry Schwartzchild of the American Civil Liberties Union (ACLU) Capital Punishment Project, "We reserve the death penalty in this country essentially only for people who kill whites, irrespective of their own race."[66]

Schwartzchild was exaggerating, but there was some truth in what he said. Of the fourteen people (all male) executed in 1991, for instance, only three (one of whom was white) died for killing black people. The other eleven had killed whites.[67] This proportion of black victim cases (21 percent) may seem reasonable enough, until it's remembered that roughly as many blacks as whites are murdered each year.

In the 1980s, Professor David C. Baldus, made an extensive study of more than 2,000 murders that had occurred in Georgia in the previous decades. Even allowing for 230 separate nonracial factors, the study concluded that the race of both victim and defendant helped determine whether the defendant would be condemned to death or would receive a lighter sentence. Baldus's study didn't claim that race was always decisive. In the case of the most atrocious murders, defendants tended to be sentenced to death regardless of their race or that of the victim. Similarly, in cases where there were mitigating circumstances, the defendants almost always escaped death. In less obvious cases, death was imposed in 34 percent of those involving white victims, but only 14 percent of those in which the victims were black—a disparity of more than 2 to 1. If the other, nonracial factors were ignored, the difference was 11 to 1.[68]

The Baldus study was an important piece of evidence in a 1987 appeal to the U.S. Supreme Court in which a black Georgia defendant, Warren McClesky, argued that the death sentence had been influenced by his race and the race of his white victim. Despite accepting the validity of Baldus's figures, the Court rejected McClesky's appeal.

The majority of the justices were clearly worried that accepting McClesky's statistical claim might lead to the abolition of the death penalty altogether. It might even lead to unanswerable questions about jury decisions in other kinds of cases. If the Court accepted the Baldus study as proof that Georgia law and practice were biased, it might have to accept other "claims based on unexplained discrepancies that correlate to the membership in other minority groups, and even to gender. Similarly, since McClesky's claim relates to the race of his victim, other claims could apply with equally logical force to statistical disparities that correlate with the race or sex of other actors in the criminal justice system, such as defense attorneys or judges."[69]

In a strong dissent, Justice Harry Blackmun complained that the decision "seems to give a new meaning to our recognition that death is different. Rather than requiring 'a correspondingly greater degree of scrutiny of the capital sentencing determination,' the Court relies on the very fact that this is a case involving capital punishment to apply a *lesser* standard of scrutiny under the Equal Protection Clause."[70]

An equally distressed Justice William Brennan complained that the Court's unwillingness to accept the Baldus study's evidence as "sufficient is based in part on the fear that the recognition of McClesky's claim would open the door to all aspects of criminal sentencing." Taken on its face, Brennan continued, "such a statement seems to suggest a fear of too much justice."[71]

For abolitionists like Brennan, the central fact of racial discrimination in sentencing is clear and unmistakable. "At some point in this case," he wrote in his dissent, "Warren McClesky doubtless asked his lawyer whether a jury was likely to sentence him to die. A candid reply to this question would have been disturbing. First counsel would have to tell McClesky that few of the details of the crime or of McClesky's past criminal conduct were more important than the fact that his victim was white."[72]

Brennan's concerns were confirmed by a 1990 report from the U.S. government's General Accounting Office (GAO). Evaluating twenty-eight different studies of death penalty sentencing, the GAO determined that there have, in fact, been "racial disparities in the charging, sentencing, and imposition of the death penalty after *Furman*."[73] One reason seems to be that prosecutors tend to seek the death penalty more often against black defendants, and particularly against black defendants accused of killing white people.

Retentionists argue that many of the supposed disparities are more apparent than real. Those that do exist, they argue, are coincidental, caused by factors other than racism. Retentionists point to conditions of poverty, drugs, and social unrest that make crimes of violence more common in black neighborhoods than in most other places. Furthermore, says George C. Smith of the pro–capital punishment Washington Legal Foundation, "Felony murders—those committed in the course of a rape or robbery— are the chief crimes eligible for capital punishment under the post-*Furman* statutes. The available data demonstrates that whites constitute between 77 percent and 89 percent of rape and robbery victims. It follows inescapably that whites would represent a comparable percentage of murder victims killed during a rape or robbery. In other words, the seemingly disproportionate number of capital sentences involving white victims is nothing more than a statistical proxy for the established facts that murders of whites are more likely to be felony murders involving robbery or rape—i.e., capital murders."[74]

Abolitionists respond that, although murder in the course of rape or robbery may be the "chief crimes" that result in the death penalties, they are not the only ones. Further, the disproportionate percentage of murderers executed for killing whites cannot be explained by the numbers of white versus black murder victims. Those numbers are roughly equal. Yet, as of 1985 (the year the figures Smith cites were published), 89 percent of all those who had been executed since the *Gregg* decision had murdered whites.[75]

According to the abolitionists, it makes little difference whether racism is the direct cause of disparities in death penalty sentencing. No matter what the cause of the phenomenon may be, the result is racial discrimination—and racial discrimination is unacceptable in a highly multiracial society such as ours.

Underrepresented Groups

Application of the death penalty does not seem to discriminate against all minorities. If the poor and the black are drastically overrepresented on death row, certain other groups are drastically underrepresented. Hispanics, for example, make up only about 7.3 percent of those sentenced to death, although they constitute about 9 percent of the population. Even more striking, Native Americans, Asian Americans, and Pacific Islanders make up roughly 3.7 percent of the population, but only 1.6 percent of the residents of death rows.[76]

Women of all races are by far the most underrepresented group on death rows in the United States. Although they are over 51 percent of the American population—and roughly 14 percent of those convicted of homicide,[77] they made up only 1.53 percent of the 3,669 people on death row in January 2001.[78]

Summary

Retentionists contend that some disparities are probably inevitable. People from different groups tend to commit different kinds and numbers of crimes. It follows that a higher proportion of criminals from those groups that tend to commit the most deplorable crimes will inevitably be subject to the death penalty.

Abolitionists respond that these differences are not coincidental. They stem from and reflect a variety of prejudices and hostilities at every stage of the criminal justice process. This seems fundamentally unjust. If the death penalty has any legitimacy at all, they argue, it must be applied equally and fairly across the social spectrum; but this has never been the case in the United States, and is still not the case today.

Inconsistency

Both opponents and supporters of capital punishment complain about the capricious way in which death sentences seem to be imposed and carried out. Only a small minority of those who commit capital crimes are sentenced to death for them, and only a tiny minority of that minority are ever actually executed. Even when comparing only similar murders, committed by members of a single racial and economic group, we see the death penalty is still being applied inconsistently in the United States today.

This is an old problem, and one that is getting worse. In the two decades before the *Furman* decision halted executions in 1972, only about 20 percent of the people sentenced to die were executed.[79] In the time since the *Gregg* decision led to the resumption of executions in 1976, the rate has dropped to under 4 percent.[80]

Some of this inconsistency is built into the American judicial system, with its fifty state and two federal (civilian and military) jurisdictions. Some of these fifty-two jurisdictions have capital punishment; others do not. Some, Texas and Florida among them, use the death penalty regularly and frequently; others rarely, if at all. Even within a single jurisdiction, people who commit virtually identical crimes receive death or prison terms unpredictably. Even criminals who commit the same crime may receive different punishments. Charles Brooks was executed for murder in Texas in 1982, but his accomplice received only forty years in prison, even though it was not established which of them had actually killed the victim.[81]

Some of this inconsistency is deliberate. "Discretion in the criminal justice system is unavoidable," writes Hugo Adam Bedau. "Society clearly wishes to mitigate the harshness of capital punishment by allowing mercy for some persons. But when discretion is used, as it has always been, to mark for death the poor, the friendless, the uneducated, the members of racial minorities, the despised, the discretion become injustice." Ironically, it is the desire for mercy in principle that often leads to discrimination in practice. Consequently, argues Bedau, "Thoughtful citizens, who in contemplating capital punishment in the abstract might support it, must condemn it in actual practice."[82]

For any punishment to be truly just, say the critics, it must be dispatched in a fair and even-handed manner. The more severe the punishment, the greater the need to apply it consistently. If the great majority of those who theoretically deserve to die are spared, it seems manifestly unjust that a handful of others are not. This unfairness is made worse, opponents of capital punishment say, when the small number of those who are forced to suffer the ultimate penalty are so often black, poor, or mentally ill.

Supporters of capital punishment have other objections to the haphazard way in which it is administered as well. In particular, they complain that inconsistency undermines death's value as a deterrent. They insist that to make capital punishment a truly effective deterrent, it should be carried out swiftly and certainly—if not in every case, at least in most of them. This is far from true today.

If the execution rate is a mere 4 percent of those sentenced to die, it is practically insignificant for those who *might* have been sentenced to die had they been caught and effectively prosecuted. Richard Samp, of Washington Legal Foundation, puts the odds at 1,000 to 1 that someone who commits a capital crime will be executed for it. This troubles retentionists because, says Samp, "We have so few executions that it is really not possible to say definitively that the death penalty is a deterrent."[83] How could such long odds be expected to deter anyone?

In theory, one solution to the manifest unfairness of executing only a handful of the people liable to the death penalty would be to execute many more of them; however, applying the death penalty to everyone already condemned would mean proceeding with thousands of executions. Opponents of capital punishment view the idea of wholesale executions with horror: "If we kill everybody on death row," argues John Healey, "we'll kill more people than Khomeini did when he took over Iran."[84] To do this, Healey warns, would mean losing for the United States all claim to moral leadership in the eyes of the other nations of the world. (Healey has some knowledge of the way the United States is regarded by other nations, having once served as director of the Peace Corps.)

Most observers doubt that such an unprecedented slaughter will ever happen. Even in the past, when executions were much more common in the United States then they have been in recent decades, only a relatively small proportion of first degree murderers were ever executed. "People say that capital punishment might deter if it were enforced," wrote Warren Lawes of Sing Sing Prison almost seventy-five years ago, when executions were more common than they have been in recent decades. "The point is that until the characteristics of mankind change, it will never be enforced. . . . Capital punishment has never been and can never be anything but an uncertainty."[85]

Charles L. Black, Jr., the author of an important book on the administration of the death penalty, agrees. No matter how the laws are written, says Black, "No society is going to kill everybody who meets certain preset verbal requirements, out on the statute books without awareness or coverage of the infinity of special factors the real world can produce."[86]

Discretion in death penalty sentencing may lead to discrimination in many cases; but removing discretion would lead to a kind of ruthlessness totally outside the British American tradition. Ever since colonial days, the death penalty's bark has always been worse than its bite. The laws of the colonies that prescribed death for a wide variety of offenses were often ignored or softened by judges and juries alike. As Philip Mackey has written, "[D]espite the severity of colonial criminal laws and practices, there is evidence of an underlying leniency toward criminals in American society of the mid-nineteenth century."[87]

Although historically many countries have been more relentless in applying the death penalty than the United States, none has ever executed everyone guilty of murder, regardless of the circumstances of the case, without review and without opportunity for a condemned person to appeal. It is hardly likely that the United States will be the first.

Even some supporters of the death penalty caution against applying the death penalty too widely. As attorney Howard Friedman warned other supporters of capital punishment, "An indiscriminate application of the death penalty will ultimately result in such public revulsion that [the death penalty] will not survive."[88]

Shame and Excitement — the Public's Response

Most ordinary citizens can no longer attend executions in the United States. Although a handful of press and public witnesses are permitted, and even required by law, they are limited to a small number of people who are well screened in advance. Although sketch artists are allowed in some jurisdictions, photographs are forbidden. This means the only visual records we have of modern executions are drawings.

Some critics suggest that the official fog cast over the event is a sign that society feels a sense of shame about holding executions at all. If we are really at ease with the practice of executing criminals, and even proud of it, why do we refuse to look at it directly? Why don't we let the country see exactly what we do to those whom we decide must die?

As far back as 1872, the famous newspaper editor Horace Greeley commented on the growing trend in some states of holding executions away from the public eye. "When I see any business or vocation sneaking and skulking in dark lanes and little by-streets which elude observation, I conclude that those who follow such business feel at least doubtful in its utility and beneficence. They may argue that it is a 'necessary evil,' but they can hardly put faith in their own logic."[89]

Modern critics of the death penalty suggest that conducting executions behind the closed doors of prisons is not only cowardly but hypocritical. On the one hand, we claim to need executions to frighten potential criminals out of committing terrible crimes; on the other, we protect the same potential criminals—along with the rest of us—from witnessing the very events whose horrors are supposed to frighten them.

In 1962, author William Styron suggested that if society were really serious about deterrence, executions would be held on television. "Until by legislative mandate, all executions are carried on the television networks of the states involved (they could be sponsored by the gas and electric companies), in a dramatic fashion which will enable the entire population—men, women, and all the children over the age of five—to watch the final agonies of those condemned, even the suggestion that we inflict the death penalty to deter people from crime is a farcical one."[90]

Some abolitionists support the idea of making executions public again because they believe it would arouse revulsion against the death penalty. If large numbers of citizens had to face the reality of putting their fellow citizens to death, they say, the public would soon clamor for an end to capital punishment once and for all.

Historically, there is some reason to believe that some people would be appalled. Certainly many witnesses of past public executions were repulsed by what they saw. James Boswell, the eighteenth-century Scottish lawyer and biographer of Samuel Johnson, was so overcome by the "gloomy terrors" he felt after witnessing a man being hanged in London in 1763 that he didn't dare to sleep alone that night.[91] Nearly a century later, another famous author, William Makepiece Thackeray, reported that the sight of an execution "left on my mind an extraordinary feeling of terror and shame. It seems to me that I have been abetting an act of frightful wickedness and violence."[92]

Reactions like these were far from universal; indeed, many people enjoyed attending executions in the days when they were public. In ancient Rome, executions were public entertainment. In revolutionary France, executions became a kind of patriotic celebration. One revolutionary wrote to his brother, "What pleasure you would have experienced if, the day before yesterday, you had seen national justice meted out to two hundred and nine villains. What majesty! What imposing tone! How completely edifying."[93]

In less revolutionary times and places, the audiences at executions were usually less triumphant, but often equally entertained. Thackeray reported that a crowd of 40,000 Londoners attending an execution were apparently thrilled to "give up their natural quiet night's rest, in order to partake of this hideous debauchery . . . more exciting than sleep, or than wine, or the last new ballet, or any other amusement they have."[94] Charles Dickens described the crowd attending a public execution in Rome as "resign[ing] all thoughts of business, for the moment, and abandoning themselves wholly to pleasure" as they jockeyed for good positions in the throng. After the young man's severed head was displayed for all to see, Dickens continued, "Nobody cared, or was at all affected. There was no manifestation of disgust, or pity, or indignation, or sorrow."[95]

Would it be any different today? We might like to think that civilization has passed beyond the point where we would eagerly gather to watch fellow human beings be killed, but there is little evidence to show that we really have.

The idea of televising executions may have seemed far-fetched when Styron proposed it in 1962, but it is a real possibility today. Public television station KQED-TV in San Francisco unsuccessfully sued to be allowed to televise the execution of Robert Alton Harris in 1991. An anti–capital punishment group in California, Death Penalty Focus, passed a resolution supporting the idea, "providing the condemned agrees," in the belief that "faced with the grisly horror of watching an individual put to death—the people of California will be moved to abolish executions."[96]

A small step in the direction of televising executions took place in April 2001, when it was announced that the execution by lethal injection of Timothy McVeigh would be transmitted via closed circuit television. The televised execution would not be truly public, however. McVeigh, who had left the bomb that killed or maimed hundreds of people in the Murrah Office Building in Oklahoma City, was to die in Terra Haute, Indiana; the telecast would be carried to Oklahoma City, where it would be available for viewing only by McVeigh's victims and relatives of victims.

In any case, it is not at all clear that the abolitionists' assumption that televising executions would lead to public revulsion is correct. If the past is a guide, it is probably wrong. Accounts of the crowds at executions from different countries at different historical periods are surprisingly similar. Although some spectators were sickened by what they saw, others were titillated, and the crowds kept coming back for more. Finally, it was not the public indignation but the squeamishness of politicians that drove executions behind closed doors.

What is more, the adoption of lethal injection as the main method of execution has had the effect of eliminating the most visibly horrific aspects of executions. When things go as planned, the condemned prisoner is already drugged into unconsciousness by the time the deadly chemicals are introduced into his bloodstream. The purpose of televising this quasi-medical procedure may be to relieve some of the presumptive unease and revulsion many now feel at the thought of the death penalty. The reaction of many viewers may well be, "That's not so terrible, after all. It's not nearly as bad as I thought it would be." Such a reaction would presumably please neither those who want capital punishment abolished nor those who want executions televised as a deterrent to potential criminals. Both groups would prefer a publicly viewed execution to be as awe-inspiringly horrible as possible.

The Risk of Mistake

No issue is more troubling to abolitionists and retentionists alike than the possibility that the state might execute an innocent person. This possibility alone is frightening enough to convince some people that capital punishment should be abolished. Retentionists argue, however, that capital punishment saves lives as well as takes them; the risk that an innocent life may inadvertently be lost is worth taking if many others are saved.

There is no serious question that the risk exists. As Supreme Court Justice William O. Douglas once wrote: "[O]ur system of criminal justice does not work with the efficiency of a machine—errors are made, and innocent as well as guilty people are sometimes punished. . . . [T]he sad truth is that a cog in the machine often slips; memories fail; mistaken identifications are made; those who wield the power of life and death itself—the police officer, the witness, the prosecutor, the juror, and even the judge—become overzealous."[97] Judges know this, and juries know this, too. Even the most confirmed defenders of the death penalty know this.

In 1987, Hugo Adam Bedau and Michael L. Radelet published the results of a study in which they named 350 people they said had probably been wrongfully convicted of capital crimes between 1900 and 1987.[98] Although the authors are both abolitionists, they have solid reputations for integrity. For the most part, the cases they reported involved prisoners who either had been pardoned or had seen their convictions overturned after the presentation of new evidence. As we have already seen, however, once prisoners are convicted, their guilt is accepted as legal fact. It is extremely hard, once that legal fact has been established, for a defendant to get a court to consider new evidence. We can only guess at how many innocent people may have been executed before new evidence could surface or be heard.

Retentionists who take comfort from the Bedau-Radelet study might argue that most of the cases involved defendants who were not, after all, executed. The system may have made some mistakes, but ultimately, it seems, the system worked. Nonetheless, it is not always the system that works, according to Diann Rust-Tierney, director of the Capital Punishment Project of the ACLU. She cites several "recent examples of people who were on death row in Georgia [and] Texas who were released—who were found to be innocent—not by the normal [legal] process but by some chance."[99]

One of the lucky ones was Randall Dale Adams, who was convicted and sentenced to death for killing a Dallas policeman in 1976. His sentenced was commuted to life imprisonment three days before he was to die. Years later, a former private investigator who had turned filmmaker made a documentary movie about Adams's case, alleging that Adams had been convicted on perjured evidence encouraged by the prosecution in the case. The film *The Thin Blue Line* received enough attention to reopen the case. After reviewing the evidence, a Texas appeals court judge ruled that the prosecution "had been guilty of suppressing evidence favorable to the accused, deceiving the trial court . . . and knowingly using perjured testimony."[100] Adams was eventually cleared and released in 1989.

Although he admits the theoretical possibility that an innocent person might be executed, Richard Samp of the Washington Legal Foundation insists, "I don't think anybody seriously contends that anybody who's been executed in the past fifteen years in this country had any legitimate claim of innocence."[101]

The American Civil Liberties Union and others concerned with the rights of criminal defendants disagree. They point to a number of recent cases in which they claim serious doubts exist about the guilt of those who were executed. Among them was the case of Willie Darden, who was on death row in the Florida State Prison at Starke so long before being executed in 1988 that he was known as the Dean of Death Row. "If ever a man received an unfair trial," declared Supreme Court Justice Harry Blackmun, "Darden did."[102]

The Darden execution does not meet Samp's arbitrary fifteen-year time frame, but at least five other cases in which allegedly innocent men were executed do. In 1992 Roger Keith Coleman was executed for the rape and murder of his sister-in-law largely because of incompetence on the part of his attorneys; Joseph O'Dell, who was refused his request for DNA tests, which he hoped would clear him, was executed in 1997; David Spence was executed in 1997 even though the police who investigated the crime believed that he was innocent; Leo Jones was executed in 1998 despite evidence that he had confessed only under torture; and Gary Graham was executed in 2000 despite shaky evidence and affidavits from some jurors declaring they would have acquitted him if they had seen all the evidence.

Safeguards are built into the system to assure that miscarriages of justice never result in the execution of an innocent person. Perhaps the most important is the right of convicted prisoners to make habeas corpus appeals to the federal courts; but, as we have also seen, these safeguards are far from foolproof, and in recent years even the Supreme Court has been eating away at the right to habeas corpus. It has become harder and harder for those convicted of capital crimes to receive a new trial.

After adding to the protections against wrongful conviction in capital cases in the wake of the *Gregg* decision, the Supreme Court has proceeded to crack down on what Chief Justice William Rehnquist and some other justices consider unnecessary delays and frivolous appeals. Since more than a decade ago, the Court has done what it can to speed up the appeals processes in death penalty cases. In the process, the Court has launched what three of its own justices have attacked as an "unjustifiable assault on the Great Writ [of habeas corpus]."[103]

The Court has undercut the same Eighth and Fourteenth Amendment protections that it has upheld by refusing to consider potentially valid constitutional claims on the grounds that the defendant has raised them improperly, raised them too late in the appeals process, or has simply come to the Court too often.[104] In addition, the Court has denied poor death row inmates free legal assistance to prepare their appeals.[105]

The Court's impatience with death sentence appeals was exhibited most dramatically in the 1992 case of Roger Keith Coleman, whose otherwise valid appeal was turned down on the grounds that Coleman's incompetent attorney had been a day late in filing a petition in the state court of Virginia. In Coleman's case, the Supreme Court virtually ordered the lower courts to stop granting stays and to proceed with his execution.[106]

In January 1993, the Court made what may be its most controversial death penalty ruling yet. By a vote of 6 to 3, it refused to block the execution of Leonel Herrera, who was scheduled to die for killing a Texas policeman in 1981, despite new evidence that someone else, not Herrera, had committed the murder. Three of the judges who voted against Herrera believed that this new evidence was not persuasive enough to warrant a hearing. The other three concurring justices indicated that it didn't matter how persuasive the evidence was. Innocence was no reason for the court to step in to stop the execution so late in the process. In effect they were saying it is not unconstitutional in the United States to execute an innocent person. This so outraged Justice Harry Blackmun that he spoke from the bench to emphasize his dissent. "Execution of a person who can show that he is innocent," protested Blackmun, "comes perilously close to simple murder."[107]

Despite the enormous odds against them, and the increasing reluctance of the courts to consider new evidence after someone has been convicted, ninety-five death row convicts in twenty-two states have been released since 1973. Eight such releases occurred in each of the past two years (1999 and 2000).[108] The circumstances of these cases differ, but, in each case, the releases came about because authorities were convinced that the convicts were innocent of the crimes for which they had been sentenced to die. The major factor in many of these releases has been the introduction of DNA evidence.

In addition to those death row inmates who have been released on the grounds of innocence, several other inmates have had their death sentences reduced because of serious doubts about their guilt.

As long as there is a death penalty, it is clear that some risk of executing innocent people will continue to exist. It is also clear that the risk is limited. The real question becomes this: Is *any* risk worth taking?

Confirmed opponents of the death penalty argue that it is not. Any risk that the state might kill an innocent man or woman is far too high. Defenders of the death penalty respond that the possibility that an innocent person might die is no reason to abandon capital punishment altogether. They say that the potential for injustice could be used as an argument against any kind of punishment at all if it were taken to extremes. There is always some chance that an innocent person might be convicted of any type of crime by mistake.

Abolitionists insist that the death penalty is fundamentally different from all other punishments. As Diann Rust-Tierney puts it, "[T]he death penalty, unlike other punishments, does not give us the chance to correct mistakes."[109] Other injustices can be alleviated. If they cannot always be set right, they can at least be amended. Society can try to make up for its error. Prisoners serving life sentences who are found not guilty after all can be released and their reputations can be restored. Apologies can be made. If the injustice was gross enough, money can be awarded to make up for the shame and suffering they have endured. Once a person has been executed, though, society can do nothing to make up for its mistake.

Clemency: The Potential for Mercy

In its rejection of Herrera's appeal, the Court advised that if he really were innocent, the proper place for him to seek help was no longer the courts but the executive authorities of his own state. Rather than seek a new trial so late in the process, he should appeal to the state of Texas for clemency.

Clemency is the traditional last resort, not only for wrongly convicted defendants but for those seeking some special mercy on humanitarian grounds. In most states, the governor has the power to pardon and release a convicted criminal, or to commute (reduce) his or her sentence from death to a lesser punishment. In some states, Texas being one, that power is at least partly vested in a state board or agency.

Even if all else fails and the judicial system makes a terrible mistake, the defenders of the death penalty comfort themselves with the thought that the mistake is correctable by political authorities. The governor or pardons board is there to step in and set things right before it's too late. Even while reinstating the death penalty in *Gregg*, the Supreme Court emphasized the need to keep open the possibility of executive clemency. Not to provide that potential remedy, the Court declared, "would be totally alien to our notions of criminal justice."[110]

The last-minute phone call from the governor is more than a staple of dramatic movies and television comedy routines. It happens. As far back as 1824, the hanging of four white men for the murder of several Native Americans in Indiana was interrupted by the governor's arrival on horseback, come to spare the youngest of the four.[111] Unfortunately, the correction may not always come in time. In 1957, California's Governor Goodwin J. Knight's phone call to the San Quentin gas chamber came just moments too late to save convicted murderer Burton Abbott.[112]

Death penalty opponents argue that clemency is too thin a reed on which to risk an innocent person's life. Governors are political officeholders, and the public that elects them favors the death penalty. Many if not most governors are reluctant to grant clemency because they fear being considered soft on crime. Far from being eager to exercise clemency, some governors win election by emphasizing their eagerness to sign as many death warrants as possible. As one observer put it, the central issue in the 1990 race for governor of Texas between the Republican Clayton Williams and Democrat Ann Richards was "Who can kill the most Texans?"[113]

The reluctance to grant clemency is so great that the practice is extremely rare. During the 1980s, only twenty-three clemencies were granted in the United States, an average of less than two and a half per year. That compares to a total of 2,724 death sentences handed down during that time, or just under 275 per year. In 1991, the number of clemencies rose to ten, thanks to the eight granted in Ohio alone. (Legal challenges have since been launched to seven of the Ohio clemencies, however.)[114]

"Cruel and Unusual Punishment"

In *Gregg*, the Supreme Court ruled that capital punishment, as such, does not violate the Eighth Amendment's ban on cruel and unusual punishment. But are some methods of execution so painful or so liable to go wrong that they violate modern standards of decency and humanity? This possibility was raised by Supreme Court Justice Stanley Reed, who declared in his opinion in a 1947 case that "[t]he traditional humanity of modern Anglo-American law forbids the infliction of unnecessary pain in the execution of the death sentence."[115]

Even the most fervent modern supporters of capital punishment would balk at drawing and quartering criminals, burning them at the stake, or boiling them in oil; yet, all these methods have been common in some countries in the past. What about the methods used in the United States today—lethal injection, electrocution, gas, hanging, and the firing squad? Each was originally proposed as being more humane than the methods used before it. Each has been hailed as quick and virtually painless by its defenders. And each has been protested as cruel and unusual.

None of these methods is foolproof. Electrocution may or may not be relatively painless when death is virtually immediate; but several electrocutions in the 1980s—in at least three different states—required more than one charge to kill, and at least one victim took ten minutes to die.[116]

Opponents of the gas chamber argue that such a death is "excruciatingly painful and slow."[117] One expert compared the experience of being asphyxiated by cyanide gas to the "pain felt by a person during a massive heart attack."[118] When James Autry was executed in Texas in 1984, *Newsweek* magazine reported that he "took at least ten minutes to die and throughout much of that time was conscious, moving about and complaining of pain."[119]

Some of the worst problems involved in recent executions have occurred with the most modern and most frequent method of execution in the United States—lethal injection. In 1985, a Texas executioner spent forty minutes poking the victim twenty-three times before finding a vein that could be used to insert the needle.[120] Arkansas authorities took a full hour trying to insert the needle into the arm of Rickey Ray Rector in 1992. In desperation, they even dug into his arm with a scalpel in their search for a useable vein. Even after they were successful and the first of the chemical solutions began entering Rector's bloodstream, the massive prisoner took nineteen minutes to die.[121]

Ironically, the two oldest methods of execution may still be the most efficient. British hangman Albert Pierrepoint once pronounced a modern hanging "the fastest, the quickest method in the world bar nothing. It is quicker than shooting, and cleaner."[122] Most recent hangings have gone fairly smoothly. There have been no recent problems with executions by firing squad, either, although these rarely take place in the United States today. So far, the Supreme Court has rejected the argument that any of the current methods are "cruel and unusual."

For most retentionists, and many abolitionists as well, debates over the relative cruelty of this method versus that method are irrelevant. For supporters of the death penalty, they are red herrings that abolitionists try to throw in the way of particular executions; defenders of the death penalty insist that abolitionists who complain about particular methods of executions are hypocrites. Abolitionists, they say, will never admit that any form of execution is *not* cruel and unusual. Whichever form of execution is threatened will always be the one they complain is unusually cruel. If the condemned prisoner is about to be hanged, then hanging is barbaric compared to lethal injection. When lethal injection is the method in question, it becomes a torturous experiment compared to the time-tested practice of hanging, and so on.

Some retentionists argue that it doesn't really matter whether particular methods of execution are painful or not. So what if it hurts? Why shouldn't vicious criminals sentenced to death suffer some moments of pain for the atrocities they have committed? George C. Smith of the Washington Legal Foundation insists that "[t]here is no suggestion in the [Eighth] Amendment or in its historical context that the government is required to make the punishments for crime as painless and inoffensive as possible. Pain and discomfort are an inherent and necessary aspect of legal punishment for crime. Were this not so, the deterrent aspect of legal punishment would be drastically undercut."[123] Even those retentionists who prefer executions to be as painless as possible accept the idea that some pain is probably inevitable. However unfortunate it may be, argues Paul Kamenar of the Washington Legal Foundation, condemned criminals "are not entitled to die with no pain whatsoever."[124]

Some abolitionists agree that debates over execution methods are irrelevant. They believe, along with Supreme Court Justice

Brennan, that "arguments about the 'humanity' and 'dignity' of any method of officially sponsored execution are a constitutional contradiction in terms."[125] Whatever the method, they believe that execution is a form of torture. "The whole process, not just what happened in the death chamber, is torturous," insists the Reverend Joe Engle. "Imagine someone placing you in a large closet, telling you how you are going to be killed in a few years . . . taking you out to kill you . . . stopping . . . finally one day slaughtering you."[126] If that is not torture, the abolitionists ask, what is?

Brutalization

"A government that persists in retaining these horrible punishments," wrote nineteenth-century English philosopher Jeremy Bentham, "can only assign one reason in justification of their conduct: that they have already so degraded and brutalized the habits of the people, that they cannot be restrained by any moderate punishments."[127] Lewis E. Lawes, who presided over many executions as the warden of Sing Sing Prison, agrees. "Executions, like war, brutalize men," wrote Lawes. "[T]he more that take place, the greater the number there is to execute."[128] George Bernard Shaw, in his play *Man and Superman*, echoed Lawes's statement: "It is the deed that teaches, not the name we give it. Murder and capital punishment are not opposites that cancel one another, but similars that breed their kind."

If Bentham, Lawes, and Shaw were miraculously brought back to life, they would not be surprised to learn that the United States—the only one of the five largest western nations that retains the death penalty for ordinary crimes—has a much higher murder rate than any of the others. Each year, the United States sees roughly three times as many murders as Canada, France, Germany, and the United Kingdom combined, although those four countries together have almost as many people as the United States.[129] Nor would Bentham, Lawes, and Shaw be surprised to hear that the localities producing the most executions are consistently among those having the highest murder rates. Texas has executed more people since 1977 than any other state, as we have seen. Still, despite the supposed deterrent effect of the death penalty, three Texas cities—Houston, Dallas, and Fort Worth—have murder rates among the top twenty-five in the country.[130]

On the other side of the coin, New York City, located in a state that did not impose the death penalty until 1995, has sentenced only six people to death since then, and in early 2001 had not yet executed any of them. Despite its reputation for violent crime, New York is not even among the top twenty-five cities in terms of its murder rate. Furthermore, while the murder rate in most large American cities (including the three Texas cities named above) was going up, New York City's rate was going down.[131]

Abolitionists would say this all demonstrates something Bentham pointed out nearly two hundred years ago: "[T]he most savage banditti are always to be found under laws the most severe, and it is no more than what might be expected. The fate with which they are threatened hardens them to the suffering of others as well as their own. They know that they can expect no lenity, and they consider their acts of cruelty as retaliations."[132]

Retentionists argue that the high execution rates in the United States in general, and in Texas in particular, are the results of high murder rates—not the other way around. Abolitionists respond that they are not making a which-came-first argument. Their point is that the two forms of death tend to go together.

Whether or not capital punishment brutalizes society, it is certainly a burden on those who have to carry it out. "Execution is an abominable thing," declared Canon Popot, a French priest and prison chaplain who comforted seventy-nine condemned prisoners in their last moments, "a vast comedy in which everyone lies, hides his feelings, and is deeply ashamed."[133]

Those who do not become brutalized by carrying out the death penalty often join the abolitionist cause. Historically, many prominent opponents of capital punishment came from the ranks of prison wardens, executioners, and others who have assisted in the application of the death penalty. Among them were Lewis E. Lawes and Thomas Mott Osborne, both of whom served as wardens of Sing Sing, and Clinton Duffy, the legendary warden of San Quentin. In Britain, even Albert Pierrepoint, who bragged about being the most prolific executioner in modern British history, eventually became convinced that the death penalty was a mistake.

"Why, then, execution?" asked Tom Teepen, writing about the execution of the vicious child-killer Westley Allan Dodd. "Because," he answered, "killing him felt good—so much so a crowd outside the prison partied raucously, chanting and firing Roman candles. At the end, we are reduced to holding that it is all right to execute just because the killing is, well, satisfying. Shouldn't it give us pause, at least, that Westley Dodd would understand?"[134]

Executing the Incompetent

Even some confirmed retentionists are troubled by the executions of those who are not fully responsible for their actions: the mentally ill, the retarded, and young people under eighteen.

The Mentally Ill

There has always been a reluctance to execute those criminals most lay people would consider lunatics, no matter how horrible their crimes. This tradition remains alive in American law today. Insanity is, in and of itself, a defense against a criminal charge, even a charge of murder. In most jurisdictions, defendants so mentally ill at the time of the crime that they were unable to understand the nature and consequences of their actions will be found innocent "by reason of insanity."

"Innocent" in such cases, is a technical term. Defendants found innocent for this reason can still find themselves confined for long periods. Those who are considered likely to repeat their atrocities are usually committed to an institution for the dangerously insane, where their imprisonment often lasts longer than an ordinary prison sentence for the same crime. Even so, this technicality angers many members of the public, who find it absurd that someone who has clearly committed a terrible act can be found innocent.

When it comes to capital punishment, the defendant's mental condition at the time of the crime is not the only issue. Even a defendant who was legally sane when he or she committed a crime cannot be executed if he or she is found to be insane at the time set for execution.[135] In theory, then, no one who is insane should ever be executed in the United States. That is the theory, but the reality is different. Legal insanity is more a legal technicality than a medical diagnosis. Many people have been executed despite being what any layman would consider raving lunatics. Amnesty International claims that at least three such people were executed during the 1980s alone.[136] Other abolitionists would argue that this is a conservative estimate.

One of those people was Morris Mason, a black man who had raped and murdered a white woman in Virginia. He was executed in 1985 when he was thirty-two, even though he had been diagnosed as a paranoid schizophrenic on three occasions by three state mental institutions. (Schizophrenia is considered the most extreme class of mental illness; schizophrenics often cannot distinguish between reality and fantasy.) In addition, Mason was severely mentally retarded, and was an active drug addict and alcoholic as well. He had specifically asked for help dealing with his mental conditions at least twice in the days leading up to his fatal crime.

Despite all of the above, Mason was unable to plead insanity at his trial because he had no money to pay for psychiatrists to examine him and testify on his behalf. He could only plead guilty and rely on the mercy of the court. The court, however, showed no mercy and sentenced him to death.[138]

Not long before Mason's execution, the Supreme Court ruled that states had to provide psychiatric help to indigent defendants in cases where the court is convinced that sanity is a real issue. The Court's ruling might have helped Mason if it had been made earlier, but the Court refused to apply it to cases, like Mason's, in which verdicts had already been reached.

The 1985 decision should help mentally ill defendants in the future, but even though it will be easier for them to plead insanity, that is no guarantee that their pleas will succeed. The definition of legal insanity remains imprecise and extremely difficult to meet, and juries are notoriously wary of insanity pleas. It is also no guarantee that, once found guilty, they will not be sentenced to death and executed.

The Young

The United States is one of very few countries that execute people for crimes committed when they were under eighteen years old. Indeed, eighteen seems to be something like an internationally accepted minimum age for the imposition of capital punishment. More than seventy countries have laws setting eighteen as the minimum; several others have signed treaties agreeing not to execute people below that age. What is more, most of the countries that have no formal age restriction nonetheless refrain from executing people under eighteen. According to Amnesty International, the only countries known to have executed people under eighteen in recent years are Iran, Iraq, Bangladesh, Pakistan—and the United States.[139]

As of January 2001, two hundred people had been sentenced to death in the United States for crimes committed when they were juveniles; seventeen of them had been executed, the majority in Texas. Juvenile offenders continue to be sentenced to death at the rate of roughly ten a year in the United States, on average, although only six were so sentenced in 2000. Although this suggests that the frequency of juvenile death sentences is declining, the number of executions is speeding up. Four such executions took place in the year 2000.[140]

By executing juvenile offenders, the United States violates at least two international agreements: the International Covenant on Civil and Political Rights and the American Convention on Human Rights. The United States signed both these agreements, although it has not ratified either of them.[141]

Several prominent American organizations—not all of them abolitionist in other respects—have come out against the execution of juveniles. Organizations such as the American Bar Association's House of Delegates, the National PTA (Parent-Teacher Association), the American Society for Adolescent Psychiatry, and the Child Welfare League of America make two arguments: first, that adolescents are not fully responsible for their actions; and second, that they are peculiarly subject to reform and rehabilitation. What's more, juvenile offenders often commit their crimes under the influence of adult criminals. To punish adolescents equally with—or, in some cases, even more harshly than—the older offenders seems unfair and excessive.

Nonetheless, since 1972 over ninety young people have received death sentences for crimes committed when they were under eighteen. The youngest was fourteen at the time of the crime, and the oldest seventeen. Four had been executed by the beginning of 1991.

The Supreme Court has ruled that the youth "of a minor is itself a relevant mitigating factor of great weight" when deciding whether to impose the death penalty.[142] Still, it remains just one mitigating factor to be weighed with others against whatever aggravating factors there may be. Despite the Court's ruling, evidence suggests that, in some cases, judges and juries have largely discounted age as a factor.

In 1988, the Supreme Court overturned the death sentence of a young man who had been sentenced to death under Oklahoma law for taking part in a murder when he was fifteen. Four of the nine justices ruled that the execution of a fifteen-year-old was cruel and unusual punishment; but Justice Sandra Day O'-Connor, who provided the fifth vote to overturn, gave a different reason. She ruled that the Oklahoma law was too vague because it set no specific minimum age for receiving the death penalty. This, she argued, violated the need to take special care in imposing the death penalty.[143] The ruling was taken by some to mean that sixteen was now, in effect, the minimum constitutional age for imposing the death penalty. That hasn't stopped Alabama and Florida from sentencing young men to death for murders committed when they were fifteen (the Florida sentence came as recently as 1991). Like the Oklahoma law, the Alabama law has no minimum age limit.

The laws of all ten states and the federal government specify eighteen-at-the-time-of-the-offense as the youngest at which a defendant may be sentenced to death. Sixteen states specify some lower age, ranging as low as fourteen. In Montana, defendants theoretically can be tried as adults and sentenced to death as young as ten. It is extremely unlikely, however, that such a sentence would be upheld. Nine of the death penalty states set no minimum age, despite Justice O'Connor's attack on the vagueness of the Oklahoma law.

Although American public opinion favors retaining the death penalty in general, it opposes executing those under eighteen.[144] Nonetheless, there is no sign that those states that still execute juveniles intend to bring the United States in line with most of the world by elimination the practice any time soon.

The Retarded

Some condemned criminals who are no longer children in a physical or chronological sense are still children mentally and emotionally. Their mental retardation—even severe mental retardation—is not necessarily considered a disqualification for execution.

Some death row inmates are so retarded that they are virtually unable to understand their situation. "Am I going with you?" one asked hopefully when a visitor rose to leave after interviewing him.[145] Another, who was scheduled to die on a Friday evening, put aside the dessert he was given along with his traditional last meal because he intended to eat it later. "[H]e thinks he'll be back in his cell on Saturday morning," his lawyer explained.[146]

Both of these men were considered competent enough to be executed. This means that they were presumed to be competent enough to aid their attorneys in preparing their defenses and appeals. James Bowden was considered competent, too. Although he was thirty-three years old chronologically when he was executed in Georgia in 1986, he was estimated to have a mental age of about twelve.

Shortly before Bowden's execution, a state-hired psychiatrist gave him a three-hour test to determine how retarded he really was. The test determined that he had an IQ of 65, which is 35 points below that of the average adult. The Georgia Board of Pardons and Paroles decided this score was too high too keep him from execution. One member of the board remarked that he would have needed a score lower than forty-five to escape death. "Ultimately," the *Atlanta Constitution* editorialized in disgust, "the difference between life and death for James Bowden boiled down to a few numbers . . . toted up by state-paid professionals. . . . If anyone doubts the role of brutal whimsy as states apply the death penalty, this wretched tale offers convincing proof."[147]

If Bowden's IQ test proved nothing else, it proved that he was not smart enough to cheat on the test by failing it badly enough to save his life. It is not unusual, however ironic, for death row residents to try their hardest to do well on such tests.

Judeo-Christian Beliefs

The Capitall Lawes of New-England, established in the Massachusetts Bay Colony in 1636, cited specific Old Testament passages as authority for each of the thirteen separate crimes it made punishable by death.[148] The American political debate over the death penalty has been entangled with religious beliefs—and particularly with Judeo-Christian religious beliefs—ever since.

Many abolitionist and retentionist leaders alike have testified that their positions on the death penalty flow from their religious beliefs. Both quote biblical passages to defend their views. God, as described in the Old Testament, meted out death to those who offended him in the form of plagues, wars, and natural disasters. Religious supporters of the death penalty look to society to follow God's prescriptions: "Whoso sheddeth man's blood, by man shall his blood be shed."[149] They also point to several other biblical passages that seem to mandate death for fifteen different offenses, including murder, witchcraft, working on the Sabbath day, and having sexual relations with animals, among others.

Most religiously motivated retentionists acknowledge that not all the offenses proclaimed to deserve death in the Old Testament ought to be capital offenses today. They insist, however, that such passages make it clear that the Judeo-Christian God favors the practice of putting at least some kind of evildoers to death.

Religious abolitionists, on the other hand, argue that "Whoso sheddeth man's blood, by man shall his blood be shed" is not a command to execute evildoers but a warning to the evildoers to reform. They take comfort in the commandment, "Thou shalt not kill," and note that, in the case of the first act of murder recorded in the Bible, God Himself refused to condemn the killer to death. After Cain killed Abel, God not only declined to kill Cain in return but put a mark on him as a warning to others not to harm him.

For the most part, Christian abolitionists look to the New Testament for support, while defenders of capital punishment look to the Old Testament and point to such prescriptions as "an eye for an eye, and a tooth for a tooth." Thomas Mott Osborne and other opponents respond by pointing out that Jesus Christ specifically rejected that formula in the Sermon on the Mount.[150]

Christian abolitionists also point out that, on the only occasion the Bible reports Christ as being present at an execution (other than his own), he put a stop to it. When a crowd was about to stone an adulterous woman to death, as prescribed by law, Jesus turned them away with the admonishment that only someone "who is without sin among you" should cast the first stone.[151]

Abolitionists dispute Ernest van den Haag when he states that "[a]ll religions that I am aware of feel that human life is sacred, and that its sacredness must be enforced by depriving of life anyone who deprives another person of life."[152] They point out that Quakers and other religious pacifists have historically opposed the taking of any human life, even that of the most vicious criminals. According to Amnesty International USA, the leading bodies of at least twenty major religious denominations in the USA have passed resolutions opposing the death penalty on religious, moral, humanitarian, and social grounds."[153] Among them are the Gen-

eral Conference of the United Methodist Church, the General
Synod of the United Church of Christ, the General Synod of the Re-
formed Church in America, the General Assembly of the Unitarian
Universalist Association, the General Assembly of the Presbyterian
Church (USA), the All-American Council of the Orthodox Church
in America, the Governing Board of the National Council of the
Churches of Christ in the U.S.A., the Mennonite Central Commit-
tee U.S. of the Mennonite Church, the Biennial Convention of the
Lutheran Church in America, the Five Year Meeting of Friends, the
General Association of General Baptists, the Fellowship of Recon-
ciliation, General Convention of the Episcopal Church, the Synod
of the Christian Reformed Church in North America, the General
Assembly of the Christian Church (Disciples of Christ), and the
General Board of American Baptist Churches. What is more, the
Roman Catholic Church, the largest Christian body both in the
United States and in the world as a whole, also opposes the death
penalty in virtually all circumstances.

It is also true, however, that many traditional American
Protestant sects and ministers do strongly support the death
penalty, and others do not oppose it. This is true of the authorities
of the Jewish faith as well. On the other hand, the major rabbini-
cal organizations have not been vocal supporters of the practice,
either. Rabbi Israel J. Kazis of Massachusetts has argued that "to
understand the Jewish attitude toward capital punishment," it is
necessary to look beyond the many death penalty prescriptions
in the Bible. "It is quite clear that the many restrictions and provisions imposed by the Rabbis made it very difficult to inflict capital punishment," writes Kazis. "[I]t is reasonable to maintain that
[the Rabbis] did not look with favor upon capital punishment."[154]
In 1969, Roman Catholic authorities removed the Vatican from
the capital punishment provisions of the Italian criminal code;[155]
more recently, several Catholic bishops have spoken out in opposition to the death penalty. Visiting death row at California's San
Quentin prison in 1987, Mother Teresa warned the world to
"[r]emember, what you do to these men, you do to God."[156]

Ultimately, religious belief is a matter of faith, and the faiths
of individuals and churches differ greatly. There is no single Jewish, Protestant, or Catholic position on the death penalty. As one
professor of Christian ethics has explained, "all the above viewpoints will be found among thoughtful and conscientious Christians of every denomination."[157] The same could be said of many
other religious faiths.

The Political Question

Once all of the practical and moral arguments have been explored, the political question remains. Should we continue to execute people in the United States? For some of us, a particular moral or practical argument may be decisive. If I believe that it is always wrong to kill, then I must be against the death penalty. If I believe that fundamental justice demands a life for a life, then I must favor it.

For many people, if not most, the answer is not that clearcut. They find themselves undecided, sympathetic to some arguments on each side of the issue, but not absolutely persuaded by any of them. They would like to see the death penalty abolished, but wonder if it is really right—or safe—to do so. For these people, an important consideration is what we can do instead. Is there an equally effective alternative or combination of alternatives to retaining the death penalty?

Put this way, the answer depends on what you consider the purpose of the death penalty. If the purpose of capital punishment is simply retribution—an eye for an eye—then no other penalty seems to fit the crime so well. If, however, you believe the real purpose of capital punishment is to protect society from criminals, then it is reasonable to consider alternatives.

Life Imprisonment

A poll conducted in Florida in the 1980s indicated that 84 percent of Floridians favored the death penalty over the alternatives then being practiced, but 70 percent said they would support sentencing murderers to a lifetime of prison labor instead if the money they earned went to family members of their victims.[158] In a sense, they would hark back to the ancient practice of family members' demanding financial penalties from those who killed their relatives.

As has already been mentioned, many members of the public mistrust life sentences because in many jurisdictions prisoners sentenced to life eventually become eligible for parole. But this is not true everywhere, and even where it is, not all lifers who become eligible for parole receive it. Many "lifers" do, in fact, die in prison.

In defense of parole, abolitionists point out that some criminals do reform. It is generally true, as well, that there is less and less need to protect society against particular individuals as time goes by. For whatever reason, criminals usually become less violent as they get older. Murder, in particular, seems to be a young person's crime. There are relatively few middle-aged murderers, and almost no elderly ones. Almost 52 percent of the people on the nation's death rows at the end of 1990 had been between the ages of twenty and thirty when they were sentenced to death. Only 0.05 percent were sixty or older.[159]

Although most abolitionists would prefer to keep the possibility of parole open even for lifers, many would gladly surrender the possibility of eventual release in return for an end to capital punishment. For this reason, they join in efforts to pass "life means life" bills that assure that defendants who receive life sentences will never get out of prison.

Prison officials harbor a certain amount of wariness about combining "life means life" laws with the abolition of capital punishment. The hope is that prisoners might eventually be released if they maintain a good record of behavior; this can be a powerful motivation for them to behave themselves. Prisoners who know they will never get out, but cannot be executed, have little to lose and no incentive to behave. For this reason, some prison officials believe that "life means life" should be accompanied by a potential death sentence for those who commit murder while in captivity.

Rehabilitation

For some abolitionists, the most promising alternative to death is rehabilitation. For many people, and for Christians in particular, the idea of redemption has a special attraction, even aside from the social benefits of turning a destructive criminal into a reliable and productive member of society.

Thomas Mott Osborne reported a conversation he had with a twenty-year-old condemned prisoner. The young man told Warden Osborne he was "sorry to go" without "the chance to do enough good in the world to balance the harm I've done." Osborne was moved by the doomed man's complaint. "He had the right idea," said Osborne. "The only way to balance a debit is by a credit. Resist not evil, but overcome evil with good. Balance wrong by right. Give the man a chance to redeem himself after his sin by doing good to make things balance. That can be done, even in prison."[160]

Some retentionists, even among those who accept that rehabilitation is possible, consider it an unacceptable option to retribution. "If rehabilitation were our aim," admits the pro–death
penalty psychologist Ernest van den Haag, "most murderers
could be released. Quite often, they are 'rehabilitated' by the very
murder they committed. They are unlikely to commit other
crimes." That is not the real point, though, he argues. "We punish
[murderers] not for what they may or may not do in the future
but for what they have done," he insists.[161]

Retentionists insist that, at the most, rehabilitation is only a
hope, not a plan of action, and a hope, they say, is not enough on
which to base a criminal justice system. "Nobody knows how to
rehabilitate," insists van den Haag. "There seems to be little difference in the behavior of people who have been subjected to rehabilitation programs compared to those who have not been. The
recidivism rate is about the same."[162] That being so, it is always a
risk to release once-vicious criminals, no matter how rehabilitated they might appear to be.

Abolitionists respond that rehabilitation does not necessarily mean release. Although it may be preferable to release those
who are truly reformed, if there is any doubt, they can continue
to be confined. As Warden Osborne has pointed out, it is possible
for a criminal to do good "to make things balance . . . even in
prison."

Improved Law Enforcement

Most ordinary citizens favor the death penalty primarily because
they believe it protects them from violent criminals. Abolitionists
argue that it does a poor job of that—a fact they claim is demonstrated by the high murder rates in many capital punishment
states.

Even some law enforcement officials who have no moral
objection to the death penalty believe that there are more effective ways of maintaining law and order. They argue that society
would be safer if the enormous resources spent on maintaining a
capital punishment system were used to put more police on the
nation's streets and more judges in the nation's courtrooms. According to a past president of a prosecutor's association in Massachusetts, most district attorneys in that state oppose reinstating
the death penalty there. These district attorneys are neither soft
on crime nor sympathetic to violent criminals. They simply be-

lieve that the state's resources are more efficiently spent on prosecutions and prison cells.[163]

On balance, Norman Kinne, the district attorney of Dallas County, Texas, agrees. "Even though I'm a firm believer in the death penalty," says Kinne, "I also understand what the cost is. If you can be satisfied with putting a person in the penitentiary for the rest of his life . . . I think maybe we have to be satisfied with that as opposed to spending $1 million to try and get them executed."[164]

Summary

Are there alternatives to the death penalty? Certainly there are. After all, the United States abandoned capital punishment for a decade not long ago. The murder rate did not soar, society did not collapse, city streets were no less safe than before.

Several states do not have the death penalty even now, and of those that do, most use it sparingly, if at all. Ultimately, then, the real question cannot be whether we *need* the death penalty. Capital punishment is not the core of our criminal justice system; it is only one aspect of it—and a relatively minor aspect at that. As we have seen, only a small percentage of murderers are sentenced to death, and only a small percentage of that percentage are executed. The real question is whether we will insist on keeping the death penalty even though we don't need it—whether, in Norman Kinne's words, we can be satisfied without it.

Notes

1. *1953 Report*, Great Britain, Royal Commission on Capital Punishment, 1949–1953 (London: H.M. Stationery Office, 1953), 19.

2. "Should Capital Punishment Be Retained?" *Congressional Digest* (August-September 1927): 243.

3. "British Hangman Albert Pierrepoint," *Chicago Tribune*, 13 July 1992.

4. Frank Carrington, "Inconclusive Evidence Does Not Invalidate Deterrence," in *The Death Penalty: Opposing Viewpoints*, ed. David L. Bender and Bruno Leone (St. Paul, MN: Greenhaven, 1986), 124–125.

5. *Congressional Digest*, "Capital Punishment," 228.

6. Ibid., 242.

7. Thorsten Sellin, *The Death Penalty: A Report for the Model Penal Code Project of the American Law Institute* (Philadelphia: American Law Institute, 1959).

8. David L. Sills, ed., "Capital Punishment," *International Encyclopedia of the Social Sciences* (New York: Macmillan & Free Press, 1968), 293.

9. Amnesty International, *The United States of America Death Penalty Developments in 1991* (New York: Amnesty International, February 1992), 5.

10. The murder rates quoted here are based on 1990 census figures compared to 1991 murders as reported by the Senate Judiciary Committee and reported on a chart, "Slayings Set Record in '91; No End in Sight," by Tom Squitieri, *USA Today,* 7 January 1992.

11. Isaac Erlich, "The Deterrent Effect of Capital Punishment: A Question of Life and Death," *American Economic Review* (June 1975): 398–414.

12. Alfred Blumstein and Jacqueline Cohen, eds., *Deterrence and Incapacitation: Estimating the Effects of Criminal Sanctions on Crime Rates* (Washington, DC: National Academy of Science, 1978), 62.

13. The figures in the paragraph are taken from "The Death Penalty Deters Murder," by Karl Spence, in *The Death Penalty: Opposing Viewpoints,* ed. David L. Bender and Bruno Leone (St. Paul, MN: Greenhaven, 1986), 99–100.

14. Squitieri, "Slayings Set Record."

15. Amnesty International, *United States of America, The Death Penalty: Briefing* (New York: Amnesty International, October 1987), 18.

16. In *The Death Penalty in America,* ed. Hugo Bedau (New York: Oxford University Press, 1997), 156.

17. *1953 Report,* 274.

18. *Gregg v. Georgia,* 428 U.S. 153, 96 S.Ct. 2909 (1976).

19. Louis Joylon West, M.D., "Psychiatric Reflections on the Death Penalty," *American Journal of Orthopsychiatry* 45, 4; reprinted in Bender and Leone, *Opposing Viewpoints,* 102.

20. *American Justice,* Nugus/Martin Productions, 1992.

21. Jon Nordheimer, "Gilmore Is Executed," *New York Times,* 18 January 1977.

22. Bender and Leone, *Opposing Viewpoints,* 101–106.

23. Rob Karwath, "Death—His Own—Was Killer's Goal," *Chicago Tribune,* 7 November 1992.

24. Amnesty International, *When the State Kills . . . The Death Penalty: A Human Rights Issue* (London: Amnesty International, 1989), 15.

25. Amnesty International, *Briefing,* 19.

26. Sellin, *The Death Penalty,* 70–72.

27. Amnesty International, *Briefing,* 16.

28. See Nathan Leopold's *Life Plus 99 Years* (Garden City, NY: Doubleday, 1958).

29. "Washington Sex Offender Dies by Hanging," AP news story, *Wausau Daily Herald*, 5 January 1993.

30. From Benjamin Rush's "An Enquiry into the Consistency of the Punishment of Murder by Death, with Reason and Revelation," reprinted in Philip English Mackey's *Voices against Death* (New York: Burt Franklin, 1976), 4.

31. *Congressional Digest*, "Capital Punishment," 243.

32. *The 700 Club*, CBN Television Network, 5 January 1996.

33. *California v. Ramos*, 463 U.S. 992, 998–999 (1983).

34. U.S. Department of Justice, "Capital Punishment 1990," Bureau of Justice Statistics Bulletin, 7.

35. "Misconceptions About the Cost of the Death Penalty" (San Francisco: American Civil Liberties Union Foundation, October 1992), unnumbered.

36. Richard McGee, *Federal Probation*, quoted by Hugo Adam Bedau, "The Case against the Death Penalty" (New York: American Civil Liberties Union, 1984), 22.

37. D. Von Drehle, "Bottom Line: Life in Prison One-Sixth as Expensive," *Miami Herald*, 10 July 1988.

38. Ibid.

39. *Millions Misspent* (Death Penalty Information Center, Washington, DC, October 1992), 4. For more on Texas, see D. Grothaus, "Death, Dollars, and Scales of Justice," *Houston Post*, 7 December 1986.

40. J. Painter, "Death Penalty Seen as Too Costly for Oregon's Pocketbook," *Oregonian*, 7 July 1987.

41. American Civil Liberties Union Foundation, "Misconceptions."

42. Death Penalty Information Center, *Millions Misspent*, 6.

43. Ira Gray and Moira Stanley, *A Punishment in Search of a Crime* (New York: Avon, 1989), 323.

44. *Congressional Digest*, "Capital Punishment," 227.

45. Ibid., 243.

46. Ernest van den Haag, "Bring Back the Death Penalty?" *U.S. News & World Report* (26 April 1976); reprinted in *The Death Penalty*, Irwin Isenberg, ed. (New York: H. W. Wilson, 1977), 135.

47. Interviewed on C-SPAN, 21 April 1992.

48. Bender and Leone, *Opposing Viewpoints*, 34.

49. *1953 Report*, as quoted by Justice Thurgood Marshall, in *Furman*.

50. Tom Kenworthy and Lois Romano, "McVeigh Condemned to Die," *Washington Post*, 14 June 1997.

51. John Stuart Mill, *Hansard's Parliamentary Debate,* Third Series, 21 April 1868; reprinted in Bender and Leone, *Opposing Viewpoints,* 31.

52. Deeann Glamser, "The Spectacle of Death on the Gallows," *USA Today,* 4 January 1993.

53. "Death Row Interviews," *U.S. News & World Report* (12 July 1976), reprinted in Isenberg, *The Death Penalty,* 6.

54. Glamser, "The Spectacle of Death."

55. Marshall Frady, "Death in Arkansas," *New Yorker* (22 February 1993): 122.

56. *Furman v. Georgia,* 408 U.S. 238 (1972).

57. *Payne v. Tennessee,* 501 U.S.—, 115 L Ed 2d 720, 111 S Ct. 2597 (1991).

58. Amnesty International, *The United States of America: The Death Penalty and Juvenile Offenders* (New York: Amnesty International, October 1991), 24–25.

59. Amnesty International, *Death Penalty Developments,* 30–31.

60. Interview on C-SPAN Television Network, 21 April 1992.

61. Bedau, "The Case against the Death Penalty," 13.

62. Ibid., 13.

63. Amnesty International, *Briefing,* 6.

64. John Healey, *Close-Up,* C-SPAN, 16 November 1993.

65. "Death Row, USA," NAACP Legal Defense Fund information bulletin (1 January 2001), unnumbered.

66. Henry Schwarzchild of the ACLU Capital Punishment Project, appearing on *Crossfire,* CNN, 20 April 1992.

67. Amnesty International, *Death Penalty Developments,* 5.

68. *McCleskey v. Kemp* (dissent of Justice Brennan).

69. Ibid. (majority opinion).

70. Ibid. (Blackmun dissent).

71. Ibid. (Brennan dissent).

72. Ibid.

73. See *Death Penalty Sentencing: Research Indicates Pattern of Racial Disparities,* report to Senate and House Committee on the Judiciary, 26 February 1990 (Washington, DC: Government Accounting Office, 1990).

74. George C. Smith, *Capital Punishment 1986: Last Lines of Defense* (Washington, DC: Washington Legal Foundation, 1986), 14.

75. Amnesty International, *Briefing,* 8.

76. Figures on death row populations at the end of 1990 are taken from "Capital Punishment 1990"; U.S. population figures are from Bureau of the Census reports, 1990 census.

77. Bedau, "The Case against the Death Penalty," 13.

78. "Death Row, USA," NAACP Legal Defense Fund information bulletin (January 1, 2001), unnumbered. Also see Victor L. Streib's *Capital Punishment for Female Offenders* available on the Death Penalty Information Web site: http://www.deathpenaltyinfo.org

79. *Gregg v. Georgia.*

80. U.S. Department of Justice, "Capital Punishment 1990," 12.

81. Ibid., 2.

82. Bedau, "The Case against the Death Penalty," 15.

83. *Close-Up*, C-SPAN Television Network, 16 November 1992.

84. Ibid.

85. *Congressional Digest*, "Capital Punishment," 232.

86. Charles L. Black, *Capital Punishment: The Inevitability of Caprice and Mistake* (1982), quoted by Bedau in the "Case against the Death Penalty," 15.

87. Mackey, *Voices*, xiii.

88. Appearing on *Nightline*, ABC-Television, 15 April 1992.

89. Horace Greeley, *Hints Toward Reforms in Lectures, Addresses, and Other Writings* (New York: Harper & Brothers, 1850); reprinted in Bender and Leone, *Opposing Viewpoints*, 42.

90. William Styron, "The Death-in-Life of Benjamin Reid," *Esquire* (February 1962); reprinted in Mackey, *Voices*, 260.

91. James Boswell, *Boswell's London Journal, 1762–1763*, the Yale Editions of the Private Papers of James Boswell (New York: McGraw-Hill, 1950), 253.

92. William Makepeace Thackeray, "Going to See a Man Hanged," *Fraser's Magazine* (August 1840): 156.

93. Simon Schama, *Citizens* (New York: Knopf, 1989), 783.

95. Thackeray, "Going to See a Man Hanged," 156.

95. Charles Dickens, *Pictures from Italy, 1846*; reprinted in *Eyewitness to History* (New York: Avon, 1987), 315–316.

96. "Capital Report," March/April 1991, no. 18, National Legal Aid & Defender Association, 2.

97. Quoted Justice Marshall, *Furman*, concurring opinion.

98. Hugo Adam Bedau and Michael L. Radelet, "Miscarriages of Justice in Potentially Capital Cases," *Stanford Law Review* (November 1987): 21–179.

99. Interviewed on the C-SPAN Television Network, 21 April 1992.

100. James N. Baker and Frank Girney, Jr., "A Movie for the Defense," *Newsweek* (13 March 1989): 27.

101. *Close-Up,* C-SPAN Television Network, 16 November 1992.

102. Gray and Stanley, *A Punishment,* 188.

103. *McCleskey v. Zant,* 111 S.Ct. 1454 (1991).

104. *Dugger v. Adams;* also *McCleskey v. Zant.*

105. *Murray v. Giarratano,* 492 U.S. 1 (1989).

106. *Coleman v. Thompson.*

107. Dennis Cauchon, "Court: Late Evidence May Not Halt Execution," *USA Today,* 26 January 1993.

108. Death Penalty Information Center, "Innocence and the Death Penalty": http://www.deathpenaltyinfor.org/innoc.html.

109. Diann Rust-Tierney, Director of the ACLU's Capital Punishment Project, C-SPAN, 21 April 1992.

110. *Gregg v. Georgia,* 428 U.S. 153 (1976).

111. Jessamyn West, *The Massacre at Fall Creek* (New York: Harcourt Brace Jovanovich, 1975), 313.

112. James Avery Joyce, *Capital Punishment: A World View* (New York: AMS Press), reprint of 1961 edition, 162.

113. Death Penalty Information Center, *Millions Misspent,* 13.

114. Amnesty International, *Death Penalty Developments,* 27.

115. *Louisiana ex rel. Francis v. Resweber,* 329 U.S. 459 (1947).

116. Amnesty International, *When the State Kills,* 58.

117. Rust-Tierney, C-SPAN.

118. Declaration of Richard J. Traystman, Ph.D., "Exhibits in Support of Motion for Temporary Restraining Order in No. 92–70237 (ND Cal.)," quoted by Justice Stevens in his dissent in *Gomez v. District Court For N.D. of California,* 112 S.Ct. 1652 (1992).

119. Quoted in Amnesty International, *When the State Kills,* 59.

120. Ibid., 59.

121. Marshall Frady, "Death in Arkansas," *New Yorker* (22 February 1993): 131.

122. "British Hangman."

123. Smith, *Capital Punishment 1986,* 30.

124. *Today,* NBC-TV, 5 January 1993.

125. Smith, *Capital Punishment 1986*, 31.

126. Maria Goodavage, "Death Penalty Cruelty Debated," *USA Today*, 20 April 1992.

127. Jeremy Bentham, *The Opinions of Different Authors on the Punishment of Death* (1809), quoted in Bender and Leone, *Opposing Viewpoints*, 26.

128. *Congressional Digest*, "Capital Punishment," 232.

129. Squitieri, "Slayings Set Record."

130. Death Penalty Information Center, *Millions Misspent*, 9.

131. Ibid., 8–9.

132. Bender and Leone, *Opposing Viewpoints*, 26.

133. Joyce, *Capital Punishment*, 93.

134. Tom Teepen, "Even Dodd No Case for Executions," *Atlanta Journal/Atlanta Constitution* (10 January 1993).

135. *Ford v. Wainwright*, 477 U.S. 339 (1986).

136. Amnesty International, *When the State Kills*, 299.

137. Amnesty International, *Briefing*, 11–12.

138. Amnesty International, *When the State Kills*, 38.

139. Amnesty International, *Juvenile Offenders*, 1.

140. Victor L. Streib, *The Juvenile Death Penalty Today: Death Sentences and Executions for Juvenile Crimes, January 1, 1973–December 31, 2000*, February, 2001; available at: http://www.law.onu.edu/faculty/streib/juvdeath.htm.

141. Ibid.

142. *Eddings v. Oklahoma*, 455 U.S. 104 (1982).

143. *Thompson v. Oklahoma*, 487 U.S. 815 (1988).

144. Amnesty International, *Juvenile Offenders*, 77.

145. Healey, *Close-Up*.

146. Frady, "Death in Arkansas," 105.

147. Editorial, *Atlanta Constitution* (1 July 1986).

148. Bedau, *The Death Penalty in America*, 5.

149. Genesis 9:6.

150. *Congressional Digest*, "Capital Punishment," 228 (citing Matthew 5:38–39).

151. John 8:7.

152. Ernest van den Haag, "Bring Back the Death Penalty?" *U.S. News and World Report* (26 April 1976); reprinted in *The Death Penalty*, Irwin Isenberg, ed. (New York: H. W. Wilson, 1977), 135.

153. Amnesty International, *Briefing*, 19.

154. Israel J. Kazis, "Judaism and the Death Penalty," a pamphlet reprinted in Bedau, *The Death Penalty in America*, 171–175.

155. Amnesty International, *When the State Kills*, 230.

156. Gray and Stanley, 93.

157. Charles S. Milligan, "A Protestant's View of the Death Penalty," reprinted from *Social Action* (April 1961), with additions and revisions in Bedau, *The Death Penalty in America*, 175.

158. Amnesty International, *Briefing*, 19.

159. U.S. Department of Justice, "Capital Punishment 1990," 8.

160. *Congressional Digest*, "Capital Punishment," 227.

161. Ernest van den Haag and John P. Conrad, *The Death Penalty: A Debate* (New York: Plenum, 1983), 261.

162. Ibid.

163. Death Penalty Information Center, *Millions Misspent*, 8–9.

164. Ibid., 6.

3

The International Perspective

There was a time when the death penalty was employed more or less universally.[1] Some societies used it more and some less often than others, and individuals may have viewed the practice with distaste, but the overwhelming consensus of governments and populations alike was that death was a necessary, if not inevitable, element of any system of dealing with criminals. Indeed, over the many centuries before nations built large prison systems to house their malefactors, few alternatives were available for the punishment of criminals. A thief might have his hands cut off, or a wealthy miscreant might have his property confiscated; but how could a community protect itself from its worst criminals and from habitual offenders unless it permanently removed them, either by exile or by death? (Exile was impractical as a means of eliminating common, largely anonymous criminals, as there was no way to prevent their return.) Serious opposition to the death penalty began to appear in the Western world in the eighteenth century, and a significant abolition movement developed in the nineteenth. The movement's momentum gained force throughout the twentieth century, by the end of which most Western nations had either abolished the death penalty altogether or restricted its use to the most rare and exceptional cases. In other parts of the world, the death penalty continued to be employed as a routine part of the criminal justice system, as well as a weapon of repression by some governments.

The World Divided

Today, the world is almost equally divided over the issue of capital punishment. Depending on what measure is used, both defenders and opponents of capital punishment can fairly argue that most of the world agrees with them. By purely numerical count, the nations that have abolished the death penalty either in law or in practice (ninety-five) edge out those that retain it (eighty-seven). Of the former, seventy-five have formally abolished capital punishment altogether, and twenty have not executed anyone for so long that they are considered abolitionist *de facto*. Another thirteen nations have abolished the death penalty for "ordinary" crimes such as murder, rape, kidnapping, and drug offenses, but retain it for such extraordinary crimes as treason and certain military offenses.[2]

Thirty-eight countries have gone so far as to enshrine the abolition of the death penalty in their national constitutions, each of which includes an absolute statement such as "there shall be no death penalty," "the death penalty is abolished," "there is no death penalty," "the death penalty is prohibited," or "the death penalty may not be imposed." The restrictive constitutional provisions are less sweeping: Argentina's forbids "the penalty of death for political offenses"; Brazil's prohibits "penalties of death, except in cases of declared war"; Greece's provides that "the death penalty shall not be imposed for political crimes, unless these are composite"; and so on. The most elaborate is Mexico's, which prohibits the death penalty for "political crimes, and, in relation to other crimes, [the death penalty] can only be imposed for treason during international war, parricide, murder that is committed treacherously, with premeditation or against a defenseless person, arson, kidnapping, banditry, piracy and grave military offenses."[3]

One way or another, a substantial majority of the world's governments have, at the very least, stopped using the death penalty for those crimes for which it has most often been imposed. This means that the majority of the world's nations no longer use death as a routine criminal punishment.

When population is taken into account, the worldwide bias becomes less clear. This is because most of the world's population lives in countries that retain—and at least occasionally employ—the death penalty; indeed, some of the most heavily populated nations, including China and the United States, not only continue to employ the death penalty but are among its most enthusiastic practitioners. Furthermore, the available evidence suggests that the majority of world popular opinion, even in many of those countries where the death penalty has been abolished, still favors the use of capital punishment—at least to some extent, and in some circumstances.

Almost all the Eastern European governments that came to power after the fall of the Berlin Wall in 1989 have either abolished the death penalty or placed moratoria on it. (The lone exception is Albania, which not only retains the death penalty but continues to carry out executions.) The nearly universal abandonment of capital punishment in Eastern Europe has gone forward in the face of strong public opinion in favor of retention, exacerbated by the rising crime rates associated with the dislocations brought about by the rapid political and social changes in that area of the world.[4]

Although the world as a whole is more or less evenly divided over capital punishment, the same cannot be said about each of the world's regions. Geographically, the distribution of retentionist nations is neither random nor regular. With a few significant exceptions, a world map with the retentionist areas colored black and the abolitionist areas colored red would look more like a map of the continents than a checkerboard.

For the most part, the nations of Asia and both the Near and the Middle East retain the death penalty; Australia, Europe, and South America have abandoned it. (The overwhelming majority of the world's executions take place in Asia.) There are maverick nations within these continents, but they are few enough to constitute the exceptions that prove the rule, or at least that draw attention to it.

Two continents do not fit this overall pattern: Africa, which is roughly divided between retentionist and abolitionist countries, and North America, where Canada and Mexico have effectively abandoned capital punishment, but the United States remains one of the most active practitioners of it. Despite these exceptions, capital punishment is very much a regional phenomenon in the modern world.

When it comes to individual nations, China is far and away the world's chief executioner. China was responsible for 1,077 of the 1,813 executions known to have been carried out in the world in 1999 (the last year for which official figures are available).[5] The actual number of executions in the world, and perhaps in China as well, was certainly much higher. Some countries, including Iran, Iraq, and Cuba, are notorious for failing to report executions. (Even if the highest estimates of executions that may have taken place elsewhere are true, China still leads the world.)

China does not reserve death for the crime of murder, or for what most of the world would recognize as extraordinary offenses. In fact, the majority of executions in China in 1999 were for drug offenses or corruption and other economic crimes.[6]

Religious Influence on National and International Attitudes toward the Death Penalty

One factor that correlates strongly with regional attitudes toward the death penalty—and one that may well influence national policies with respect toward capital punishment—is religion.

Although capital punishment raises significant moral questions, several of the world's religions have refrained from taking definitive stands on the death penalty. Authorities within particular religions frequently disagree among themselves, and the members are left without spiritual guidance on the issue. But the positions taken by certain major religions are clear, and, in areas where one of these religions is the dominant faith, national laws regarding the death penalty tend to reflect those views.

The Judeo-Christian traditions that most influence American attitudes on the death penalty have been discussed in some detail in Chapter 2. To recap: the American Christian denominations are divided, with the leadership of the Roman Catholic Church in the United States (as elsewhere) opposing the death penalty, but what seems to be a majority of the American Protestant denominations supporting it, either directly or tacitly (by taking no stand on the issue).

The main branches of Judaism also remain divided on the question. Several Reform and Conservative Jewish organizations seem to be developing a consensus of sorts against capital punishment, although their objections fall sort of an absolute prohibition. Speaking before the Massachusetts state legislature in 1999, Jerome Somers, chairman of the board of trustees of the Union of American Hebrew Congregations, talked about the historical Jewish search for justice in explaining the changing nature of mainstream Jewish attitudes toward the death penalty: "In biblical times, capital punishment was a search for justice when justice seemed impossible to reach. As rabbis did years ago when they considered the use of the death penalty, let us take time to ask ourselves some relevant questions. Is justice reached when we are taking the chance of killing an innocent person? Is justice reached when we are discriminating against minorities in our death sentences? 'See that justice is done,' the prophet Zachariah proclaims. If justice is not done by legalizing the death penalty—and it is not—human decency and biblical values that stress the sanctity of life require that we put an end to this grisly march of legalized death."[7]

Although it is fair to say that there is no Christian consensus on the death penalty, the largest of the Christian sects, both in the United States and worldwide, has recently taken a strong and clear stand against the practice. With roughly 1 billion members worldwide, the Roman Catholic Church is not only the largest of the Christian religions, but the world's largest religious sect of any kind. For most of its 2,000 years of existence, the Roman Church effectively supported capital punishment; in the Middle Ages, representatives of the Church went so far as to condemn people to death for heresy. In recent times, the Church has undergone a slow but radical evolution in regard to the death penalty. That evolution has reached the point where the latest edition of the definitive *Catechism of the Roman Catholic Church* was revised to make clear that the Church's position has changed. An earlier qualified endorsement of capital punishment was removed, and a statement that the death penalty can be justified only in cases of "absolute necessity," which are "very rare, if not practically nonexistent" was added.[8] The message was further clarified by Cardinal Joseph Ratzinger, the head of the Vatican's Congregation for the Doctrine of the Faith who explained that "it would be very difficult to meet [this condition] today."[9]

Several national organizations of bishops—the bodies that most authoritatively speak for the Church within particular countries—have called for an end to capital punishment. In 1999, for example, the Bishop's Conference of the Philippines appealed for an end to the death penalty in that country, declaring that "[k]illing . . . people on death row diminishes all of us and is a sign of disrespect for human life."[10] Similar positions, which reflect that of the Vatican, have been taken by bishops in many other countries, including New Zealand and the United States.

When speaking for—and to—the worldwide Church, Pope John Paul II has frequently denounced capital punishment, most definitively in the encyclical *Evangelum Vitae* (*The Gospel of Life*), in which he uses the account of the murder of Abel by his brother

Cain in the *Book of Genesis* to refute both Christian and Jewish supporters of the death penalty who justify their positions by an appeal to the Biblical demand for justice.[11]

On a visit to the United States in 2000, John Paul expressed his conviction that "[m]odern society has the means of protecting itself without definitively denying criminals the chance to reform" and appealed "for a consensus to end the death penalty, which is both cruel and unnecessary."[12] Nor does the Pope stop with theoretical objections to the death penalty; he frequently appeals to governments around the world to commute the death sentences of particular prisoners.

Although the potential exceptions that the Roman Catholic Church would make to a total ban on the death penalty have not been spelled out in detail, they would seem to amount to two. The first would apply only to a society that has extremely limited resources and no means of confining an unrepentant killer determined to repeat his crime. The second would be in a case such as that of the fictional Hannibal Lecter, a brilliant and relentless human killing machine who could not be stopped from killing even when he was confined in total isolation in a prison cell. It is doubtful that such an unstoppable creature could be found in real life.

Despite their Church's strong opposition to the death penalty, many individual Catholics continue to support capital punishment, either because they don't know about their Church's stand on the issue or because they do not consider capital punishment a question on which they look to religion for guidance.

Authoritative bodies of some of the other traditional Christian churches have also taken stands against the death penalty. The Council of Bishops of the Russian Orthodox Church, for example, meeting in Moscow in August 2000, called for an end to the death penalty on the grounds that it could make a judicial error uncorrectable.

Islamic tradition supports the death penalty. Sharia (or Islamic law) specifically prescribes the death penalty for a wide variety of offenses. Unlike Jewish and Christian religious laws, Sharia is secularly enforced in several countries, including Saudi Arabia and Afghanistan; this leads to the relatively large number of executions in those countries.

In the Islamic world, the exercise of the death penalty is closely associated with private vengeance—a concept of justice in which murder is a crime that engenders a debt owed by the murderer to the family of the victim. This concept is spelled out in the holy *Qur'an*, which calls for death as the fitting punishment for murder—but which at the same time provides a potential for mercy: "(Y)e who believe! the law of equality is prescribed to you in cases of murder: the free for the free, the slave for the slave, the woman for the woman. But if any remission is made by the brother of the slain, then grant any reasonable demand, and compensate him with handsome gratitude, this is a concession and a Mercy from your Lord. After this whoever exceeds the limits shall be in grave penalty."[13]

In those religiously conservative Islamic nations whose legal systems are based on Sharia, it is often left to the relatives of a murder victim to decide the punishment of the murderer. The family may be permitted to choose between three alternative punishments for the malefactor: They may accept a payment of *diya*, or "blood money," which is usually used for the support of the victim's dependents, or, in the case of especially devout survivors, for a disinterested religious purpose; a term of imprisonment; or death. Once forgiven by the family, the murderer may be, and often is, released into the community without further punishment.

In some cases, not only the sentence but the execution of a murderer may be left to the family. This is true, for example, in Afghanistan, where the religiously conservative Taliban controls most of the country.

Like China, Islamic countries do not reserve the death penalty exclusively, or even primarily, for murder. In Saudi Arabia, for example, death may also be imposed for rape, drug trafficking, armed robbery, and several offenses that are regarded as serious breaches of sexual morality.

The forms of execution used in some of these countries seem exotic by Western standards. Decapitation by sword is the standard means of execution in Saudi Arabia. Stoning is still practiced there for adultery, and, in Afghanistan, people are occasionally executed by being placed under a brick or stone wall and then having the wall toppled over on them. (If they survive, the death sentence is commuted.)

Other, lesser Islamic punishments, which can include whippings and dismemberment, often seem extremely harsh by Western standards. They should not be seen, however, as an indication of either bloodthirstiness or special callousness on the part of the followers of Islam. Nor should the fact that executions are frequently held in public and that large crowds sometimes attend them. The easy assumption is that such crowds are motivated by bloodlust. This is sometimes true, but by no means always. A crowd gathered to witness a killer's execution in Saudi Arabia in 1999 was far from disappointed when the sons of the victim accepted the killer's word that he had not meant their father to die. They not only pardoned the man but renounced their right to *diya*. According to observers, cries of "God is great" sounded from the crowd and "some people fainted with emotion and others praised the brothers for their clemency."[14]

Thousands of Afghanis who attended the execution of a murderer in 1998 pleaded with the victim's family for mercy[15]—something that was rarely if ever seen from the crowds that once regularly attended executions in the Western world.

No authority speaks for world Buddhism, but the Dalai Lama, the exiled Vajrayana Buddhist leader of Tibet, perhaps the best known Buddhist in the world, has expressed unequivocal opposition to the death penalty. "I am against the death penalty," he declared in a public address in London in 1999. "I think it is bad, and it makes me very sad. Whenever I see photographs of convicted prisoners who are condemned to death row I feel very disturbed and uncomfortable."[16]

A commission of the Tendai school of Buddhism in Japan studied and debated the issue before coming out in 1997 with a report declaring that the death penalty was not compatible with the Buddhist tenet that no one living should kill any other living beings. Despite this tenet, several other Buddhist leaders have expressed support and even enthusiasm for capital punishment. What is more, the death penalty is employed in many of those nations where the influence of Buddhism is strongest.

Except for Islamic theocracies and quasi-theocracies, it is difficult to gauge the extent to which a religion's support or opposition to the death penalty affects national policies regarding it. Logic would suggest that the opinion of a religion that enjoys the allegiance of an overwhelming majority of the population must have some effect, and that such an effect would be greatest in those countries where the population is most religiously homogeneous. In that respect, although the Roman Catholic Church's opposition cannot be said to have been directly responsible for the abolition of the death penalty in any country, it is nonetheless true that most of the South American and European countries with overwhelmingly Catholic populations have abandoned the death penalty. Conversely, the heavily Catholic nation of the Philippines, which had abandoned the death penalty in 1987, reinstated it in 1994, and, following a long national debate, resumed executions in 1999.

Legitimacy of the Death Penalty in the Modern World

Opponents of capital punishment believe that, if the death penalty has not already lost its legitimacy in the modern world, it is in the process of doing so. Considering how many countries continue to execute criminals, that belief is open to argument; but it is given credence by the fact that several prestigious and authoritative international organizations have issued either hard-to-meet standards for the imposition of the death penalty or outright condemnations of it. By the same token, it is hard to find any such organization that has come out in favor of capital punishment.

The effort to delegitimize the death penalty has been led by the largest and most inclusive of all international bodies, the United Nations (UN). The official UN attitude toward capital punishment was set forth in a resolution passed by the General Assembly in December 1977: "Having regard to Article 3 of the Universal Declaration of Human Rights, which affirms everyone's right to life," and to "Article 6 of the International Covenant on Civil and Political Rights, which also affirms the right to life as inherent to every human being," the resolution "[r]eaffirms that . . . the main objective to be pursued in the field of capital punishment is that of progressively restricting the number of offenses for which the death penalty may be imposed with a view to the desirability of abolishing this punishment."[17]

In 1984, the General Assembly endorsed a resolution that called for "safeguards guaranteeing protection of the rights of those facing the death penalty." Resolution 39/118 stopped short of condemning capital punishment outright, but it was clear that the authors of the resolution decried the practice (although not every delegation that voted for it did so).

Among other provisions, Resolution 39/118 mandated that

- In countries which have not abolished the death penalty, capital punishment may be imposed only for

the most serious crimes, it being understood that their
scope should not go beyond intentional crimes, with
lethal or other extremely grave consequences
- Persons below eighteen years of age at the time of the
commission of the crime shall not be sentenced to
death, nor shall the death penalty be carried out on
pregnant women, or on new mothers or persons who
have become insane
- Capital punishment may be imposed only when the
guilt of the person charged is based upon clear and
convincing evidence leaving no room for an alternative
explanation of the facts
- Capital punishment may only be carried out pursuant
to a final judgment rendered by a competent court after
legal process which gives all possible safeguards to
ensure a fair trial
- Anyone sentenced to death shall have the right to
appeal to a court of higher jurisdiction . . . [and] to seek
pardon, or commutation of sentence
- Capital punishment shall not be carried out pending
any appeal or other recourse procedure . . . relating to
pardon or commutation of the sentence
- Where capital punishment occurs, it shall be carried
out so as to inflict the minimum possible suffering[18]

Year after year, the UN Human Rights Commission passes
its own resolution calling for a worldwide moratorium on capital punishment as a step toward its ultimate abolition. The resolution passed in the year 2000 called on all countries that
choose to retain the death penalty to severely restrict its use.
Sponsored by sixty-eight nations, the 2000 resolution received
the votes of twenty-seven of the commission's members;
twelve members abstained, and thirteen voted against it, including the United States. Fifty-one members of the United Nations formally objected to the resolution, insisting in their de-
murrer that it was "inappropriate to make a universal decision
on this question or to propose such action in the forum of an international organization."[19]

The United States—which routinely voted against such resolutions in the commission—was deprived of a chance to vote
against yet another in the year 2001. That year, for the first time
since the commission had been established fifty-seven years be-

fore (largely through the efforts of Eleanor Roosevelt), the United States failed to receive enough votes to retain its seat.

In discussing the exclusion of the United States, deeply offended American politicians and media commentators focused on international displeasure over longtime refusal by the United States to pay certain funds it owed the UN and what was seen as generalized and widespread anti-Americanism among that organization's members. These may have been factors in the UN's decision; but, as the swing votes that kept the U.S. off the commission were those of America's European friends, all of which have abolished the death penalty and pressed the United States to do the same, it seems likely that the U.S. insistence on retaining the death penalty may also have played a part, even if a minor one. For the Europeans, the death penalty is not only a major human rights issue but a settled one. Added to their other reasons for voting against the United States, the irony of having one of the world's most frequent executioners sitting on the body that oversees compliance with human rights standards may have been one final, and, in some cases, determining one. If any of the nations that voted to remove the United States from the commission were trying to send a message involving the death penalty, that message apparently failed to get through, either to the U.S. government or the American public.

Binding Treaties

The above resolutions were hardly more than declarations of intention. Critics of the UN might well say that they were even less than that, mere expressions of pious hopes for an unrealistically idealized future. Certainly, the resolutions were not binding on UN members, even on those members who voted for them.

In 1982, another international organization had already adopted a protocol that made abolition of the death penalty binding on all who signed it. That was Protocol No. 6 to the European Convention for the Protection of Human Rights and Fundamental Freedoms (also known as the European Convention on Human Rights), which had been signed in Rome in 1950. Opened for signature in April 1983, Protocol No. 6 cited the "evolution" that had been occurring in "several member states of the Council of Europe [expressing] a general tendency in favour of the abolition of the death penalty." Article 1 of the protocol was unequivocal, stating flatly that "[t]he death penalty shall be abolished. No one shall be condemned to such penalty or executed." Article 2 allowed for an exception to this blanket ban, granting member states the right to "make provision" for the death penalty "in respect of acts committed in time of war or of imminent threat of war."[20] Even in such cases, the death penalty "shall be applied only in the instances laid down in the law and in accordance with its provisions."[21]

In September 2000, Albania became the thirty-eighth nation to ratify Protocol No. 6, the first international treaty ever to require that its signatories abolish the death penalty for ordinary crimes.

The Council of Europe has made the abolition of capital punishment a condition of membership. By the turn of the millennium, the council had forty-three members, all of whom had effectively abolished the death penalty. If anything, the Council of Europe has become even more adamant in its opposition to capital punishment over the years. Its Parliamentary Assembly has expressed the view that "the death penalty has no legitimate place in the penal system of modern civilized societies," and equated its use with torture.[22]

In 1989, another treaty requiring its signatories to abolish the death penalty was passed by the UN General Assembly. This was the Second Optional Protocol to the International Covenant on Civil and Political Rights. "Convinced that all measures of abolition of the death penalty should be considered as progress in the enjoyment of the right to life," the signatories to this protocol agreed that, "[n]o one within the jurisdiction of a State Party to the Protocol shall be executed," and that "[e]ach State Party [would] take all necessary measures to abolish the death penalty within its jurisdiction." Once again, a sole exception was made to this binding agreement in the case of "a reservation made at the time of ratification or accession that provides for the application of the death penalty in time of war pursuant to a conviction for a most serious crime of a military nature committed during wartime."[23]

In May 2001, forty nations were State Parties to the Second Optional Protocol, and four others had signed but not yet ratified it.

Another treaty binding its signatories to abolish the death penalty is the Protocol to the American Convention on Human Rights to Abolish the Death Penalty, which was adopted by the General Assembly of the Organization of American States in 1990. By 1999, only six countries (Brazil, Costa Rica, Ecuador,

Panama, Uruguay, and Venezuela) had ratified the protocol; two more signatories (Nicaragua and Paraguay) were in the process of ratifying it. Needless to say, the United States is not a full party to any of these binding international agreements.

Near Unanimity on the Execution of Juveniles

Although the world is divided on the issue of capital punishment in general, it is close to unanimous in its opposition to the execution of juvenile offenders—defined as those who were under the age of eighteen at the time they committed their crimes.

Indeed, it can be said that the execution of juveniles is against international law because it is expressly forbidden by a number of international instruments: Among them are the Convention on the Rights of the Child, the American Convention on Human Rights, the Geneva Convention Relative to the Protection of Civilian Persons in Time of War, and the International Covenant on Civil and Political Rights. The last document explicitly states that "[s]entence of death shall not be imposed for crimes committed by persons below eighteen years of age and shall not be carried out on pregnant women."[24]

The United States has signed and ratified the International Covenant on Civil and Political Rights, but it did so with expressed reservations in regard to the articles that outlaw the execution of juvenile offenders. A serious question in international law is whether the United States ever had the right to make such a reservation as such reservations are not allowed for in the treaty itself. Furthermore, the Inter-American Court of Human Rights, the highest legal authority to take a position on the issue, has held that it did not. The United States does not seem to take this judgment seriously. In 2001, the U.S. Supreme Court denied certiorari to (refused to hear) an appeal of a Nevada death row inmate named Michael Domingues; Domingues, who was under sentence of death for a murder committed when he was sixteen, claimed that his execution would violate U.S. obligations under the convenant.[25]

(As for other treaties forbidding the execution of juvenile offenders, the United States has also signed the American Convention on Human Rights, although it has not ratified it. And in 2000, the United States and Somalia were the only two countries that had not ratified the Convention on the Rights of the Child.)[26]

Despite both international law and the force of worldwide opinion, the United States continues not only to execute juvenile offenders but to execute more of them than any other nation. A 1999 resolution passed by the UN Sub-commission on the Promotion and Protection of Human Rights named six countries (Iran, Nigeria, Pakistan, Saudi Arabia, the United States, and Yemen) known to have executed nineteen juvenile offenders in the previous ten years. Of the nineteen known executions, ten had been carried out in the United States.[27] (The last of these, a young man named Sean Sellers, was executed in Oklahoma in February 1999 for a crime committed when he was sixteen years old.)[28]

The reasons the execution of juvenile criminals is so troubling to so many governments and ordinary citizens around the world were summarized in a European Union memorandum on the death penalty that was addressed to the United States:

> All the EU Member States reject the idea of incorrigibility of juveniles. These States hold the view that the problem of juvenile delinquency should be addressed bearing in mind that young offenders are in the process of full development, facing several difficulties of adaptation. In addition, poor backgrounds, lack of success at school and dependence on drugs are just some of the social problems affecting them and fostering their criminal behavior. As a result, they are less mature, and thus less culpable, and should not be treated as adults, deserving a more lenient criminal sanctions system. This implies, among other things, rejection of the death penalty for juveniles.[29]

It is not clear whether the United States (or, for that matter, any of the other countries that continue to execute juvenile offenders) considers incorrigibility a major factor in determining whether the death penalty should be imposed. The notions of punishment and retributive justice may be equally, if not more, important.

International Pressures

Differing national policies and attitudes toward capital punishment often result in controversies, and sometimes in legal disputes, between nations. As a leading exponent of the death penalty, the United States in particular has been carrying on a running dispute with much of the international community, including virtually all of its closest friends and neighbors.

As Felix Rohatyn, the Clinton administration's ambassador to France, has pointed out, the international chagrin with U.S. policy goes beyond governments: "People in France admire the United States, and much of what passes for anti-Americanism is limited to the intellectual milieu of Paris. Not so in the case of the death penalty," Rohatyn has said. "You hear opposition to the death penalty in Bordeaux, you hear it in Toulouse, everywhere. When I speak to audiences the question always comes up. And I don't believe this is just a French phenomenon. I recently spoke to . . . our ambassador to Germany, and he told me the death penalty is the single most recurring question there."[30]

The most common disputes involve the extradition of criminals (or accused criminals) from an abolitionist country to a retentionist one. Countries that have abolished the death penalty—whether completely or for the particular crime with which a foreign visitor is charged by another country—typically refuse to extradite an accused criminal if extradition could result in the person's being sentenced to death. Such countries typically ask for guarantees from the country requesting extradition that it will not seek the death penalty.

Canada, which has not had the death penalty for ordinary crimes for over a quarter of a century, has, in the past, been somewhat more willing than most other abolitionist nations to extradite, even when the death penalty was a possibility. In February 2001, however, the Canadian Supreme Court ruled that two Canadians wanted for murder in the state of Washington could not be extradited without a guarantee that they would not be liable to a death sentence. In a unanimous decision, the Court ruled that "such assurances are constitutionally required in all but exceptional cases."[31]

The United States has been extremely reluctant to grant such guarantees; it regards criminal charges and punishments as internal matters, not to be negotiated with other governments. Indeed, the United States has been determined to resist all forms of international pressure when it comes to this issue.

Retentionist nations, the United States included, also frequently find themselves embroiled in international disputes when they impose the death penalty on foreign nationals, particularly when they are citizens of countries that do not employ capital punishment. The United States has found itself in this position many times in the years since it reinstated the death penalty.

In 1999, for example, when the state of Arizona executed two German citizens, the German government was angered, not merely by the executions themselves, but by what it saw as the U.S. disregard of international norms and obligations in dealing with foreign nationals accused of crimes. The LeGrand brothers, Walter and Karl, were tried, convicted, and sentenced to death before the German government was even informed that two of its citizens had been arrested for murder. They were subsequently executed despite German protests that they had not received their rights under international law.

In the wake of the executions, the outraged German justice minister, Herta Daeubler-Gmelin, announced that his government planned to sue the United States for flouting international law. "The obligation to respect international laws is valid for everyone," Daeubler-Gmelin declared. "Respecting international law cannot be a one-way street."[32] (Other countries that have sued the United States in international courts in death penalty cases include Mexico and Paraguay.)

The United States is not the only government to face international disapproval for executing foreign nationals. The African nation of Botswana found itself in a similar controversy when it executed a South African woman for murder in April 2001. The controversy was exacerbated because the death sentence was carried out without informing either the woman's husband or the South African embassy when the execution was to take place. South Africa protested both the execution and the secrecy with which it had been conducted. After the fact, the nation's president, Festus Mogae, insisted that Botswana was committed to the death penalty. When reporters asked him whether he was worried about the negative international reaction to the execution, Mogae answered, "That is a price Botswana is prepared to pay, and I represent Botswana."[33]

Like Botswana, the United States government is apparently willing to pay the price in international disapproval for its retention of the death penalty. In fact, the United States seems determined to resist, and even to ignore, all kinds of pressure from foreign governments on the issue. In 1999, the state of Arizona went ahead with the execution of Walter LaGrand (which took place several days after the execution of his brother) despite a nonbinding order from the International Court of Justice to suspend the execution process until the Court had a chance to rule on Germany's objections. In a unanimous opinion, the Court declared that "[t]he United States of America should take all measures at its disposal to ensure that Walter LaGrand is not executed pending the final decision in these proceedings, and should inform the Court of all measures it has taken in implementation of this Order."[34] For all intents and purposes, the United States ignored this order.

International criticism has been directed both to the United States as a whole and to the individual states, which are, after all, responsible for the great majority of the executions that take place in the United States. At least one U.S. state has been warned that continuing executions may result in economic consequences. Writing to George W. Bush, then governor of Texas, the state that has executed more people than any other since 1976, Alan Donnelly, an official of the European Parliament, cautioned that "[m]any companies, under pressure from shareholders and public opinion to apply ethical business practices, are beginning to consider the possibility of restricting [their] investment in the U.S. to states that do not apply the death penalty."[35] This warning did not dampen Texas' enthusiasm for the death penalty.

Unsuccessful in many attempts to apply pressure on the United States to abandon the death penalty, the nations of the European Union recently took the unusual step of addressing the United States directly in a memorandum on the death penalty issue:

> The EU is deeply concerned about the increasing number of executions in the United States of America (USA), all the more since the great majority of the executions since reinstatement of the death penalty in 1976 have been carried out in the 1990s.
>
> Offenders are human beings who committed a crime but who also enjoy an inherent and inalienable dignity, the very same dignity claimed by rationalist philosophy, all relevant religions and by law, the death penalty being a denial of human dignity.
>
> The criminal justice system of a country, and in particular its sanctions system, may reflect traditions and specific historical aspects of a society. However, the death penalty issue is, above political, legal or crimi-

nal considerations, a question of humanity. Human-
ization of the problem of capital punishment should
be a decisive aspect of a people's life.

Long ago European countries, either in practice or
in law, made a choice for humanity, abolishing the
death penalty and thus fostering respect for human
dignity. And this is an ultimate principle that the EU
wishes to share with all countries, as it shares other
common values and principles such as freedom, democracy, and the rule of law and safeguard of human
rights. . . . The EU thus invites the USA to equally embrace this cause.[36]

This is in an invitation that, so far at least, the United States
has been unwilling to accept.

Notes

1. See Keith F. Otterbein, *The Ultimate Coercive Sanction: A Cross-Cultural Study of Capital Punishment* (New Haven, CT: HRAF Press, 1986).

2. As of 21 April 2001. Current figures can be found on the Web site of the Death Penalty Information Center at http://www.deathpenaltyinfo.org//dpicintl.html.

3. Amnesty International, *Constitutional Prohibitions of the Death Penalty*, report, ACT 50/05/99, p. 6.

4. Stephanie Grant, "A Dialogue of the Deaf? New International Attitudes and the Death Penalty in America," *Criminal Justice Ethics* 17 (22 June 1998): 4.

5. *Patto Internazionale Sui Diritti Civili E Politici* (third annual Hands Off Cain report on the status of the death penalty worldwide); with an introduction by Sergio D'Ella, www.handsoffcain.org.

6. Ibid., 4.

7. *To End the Death Penalty*, a report of the National Jewish/Catholic Con-
sultation.

8. *Catechism of the Catholic Church*, nos. 1867 and 2268.

9. "Catechism Takes a Harder Line on Death Penalty," *National Catholic Reporter* (19 September 1997): 12.

10. Amnesty International, *The Death Penalty Worldwide: Developments in 1999*, report, April 2000, 27.

11. See Chapter 7, *Evangelum Vitae* (excerpt).

12. Amnesty International, *The Death Penalty Worldwide: Developments in 1999*, report, April 2000, 26.

13. *The Qur'an* 2:178.

14. *Patto Internazionale Sui Dirritti Civili E Politici*, 5.

15. Abdullah Zahefruddinn, "Thousands Watch Afghan Execution," Associated Press, 13 March 1998.

16. Amnesty International, *The Death Penalty Worldwide: Developments in 1999*, report, April 2000, 26.

17. UN General Assembly Resolution 32/61, passed 8 December 1977.

18. UN Nations General Assembly Resolution 39/118, adopted 14 December 1984.

19. Amnesty International, "Death Penalty News," June 2000.

20. Amnesty International, "Death Penalty News," March 2000.

21. Amnesty International, "Death Penalty News," September 2000.

22. Grant, "Dialogue," 2.

23. General Assembly Resolution 44/128, adopted 15 December 1989; Office of the United Nations High Commissioner for Human Rights, Geneva, Switzerland, 1997.

24. International Covenant on Civil and Political Rights, adopted 16 December 1966; Office of the United Nations High Commissioner for Human Rights, Geneva, Switzerland, 1997.

25. Death Penalty Information Center, "The Death Penalty: An International Perspective," 2001.

26. Amnesty International, "Death Penalty Facts: Juveniles," 8 August 2000.

27. United Nations press release, 24 August 1999.

28. Amnesty International, "Death Penalty Facts: Key Topics: Execution of Child Offenders (as of 20 July 2000)," 8 August 2000.

29. See Chapter 7, "European Union Memorandum on the Death Penalty."

30. *Newsweek*, 29 May 2000.

31. Canadian Press (service), 15 February 2001.

32. Reuters, 16 September 1999.

33. Reuters, 16 April 2001.

34. International Court of Justice, no. 104, 3 March 1999.

35. "Catholics against Capital Punishment News Notes," 20 July 1998.

36. See Chapter 7, "European Memorandum."

4

Chronology

18th century B.C.	The Code of King Hammurabi of Babylon prescribes the death penalty for twenty-five crimes. Interestingly, murder is not among them.
16th century B.C.	The Assyrian Laws contain references to death as a punishment.
	The first death sentence of which a record survives is handed down in Egypt. There have probably been others before this, in Egypt and elsewhere, but no record of them now exists. The wrongdoer in this case is obliged to carry out his own sentence, a common requirement in many societies when the condemned is a member of the nobility. Members of the lower classes are dispatched by government officials or mercenaries.
14th century B.C.	The Hittite Code contains references to the death penalty.
7th century B.C.	In the so-called Draconian Code, promulgated by Dracon of Athens, death is prescribed as the punishment for every crime.
5th century B.C.	The Roman Law of the Twelve Tablets calls for death as the penalty for several crimes. It makes distinctions by social station. Certain offenses call for

5th century B.C. (cont.)	death only when they are committed against free-men, or only when they are committed by slaves.
	At this time, executions are being carried out in Britain.
c. 399 B.C.	The Greek philosopher Socrates is made to drink poison for the offenses of heresy and corruption of the young.
c. A.D. 29	In the most infamous execution in history, Jesus Christ is crucified on a hill outside Jerusalem.
c. A.D. 315	The Emperor Constantine abolishes crucifixion in the Roman Empire.
A.D. 438	The Code of Theodosius makes more than eighty crimes punishable by death.
11th century	Under William the Conqueror, hanging is reserved for murderers.
1500	Eight crimes are officially punishable by death in England. They are murder, treason (treachery against the state), petty treason (murder of a husband by his wife), larceny, robbery, burglary, rape, and arson.
1509–1547	Despite the relatively small number of capital crimes in England, the reign of Henry VIII may be the bloodiest in English history. Estimates of how many Englishmen (and women) executed range as high as 72,000.
1608	In the first known execution in British America, George Kendall, an ex-councilor in the colony of Virginia, is executed for plotting to betray the British colony to Spain.
1612	Under Governor Thomas Dale, Virginia institutes the Divine, Moral, and Martial Laws, the most unrelenting criminal code in any of Britian's Ameri-

can colonies. It prescribes death for, among other things, trading with Indians, killing chickens, and stealing grapes.

1619   Virginia softens the Divine Laws because it has become clear that fear of the executioner is discouraging people from settling in Virginia.

1632   Jane Champion is the first woman to be executed in the American colonies.

1636   The Capitall Lawes of New-England go into effect in the Massachusetts Bay Colony. Among the "Capitall" crimes enumerated are murder, witchcraft, sodomy, adultery, blasphemy, idolatry, assault in sudden anger, rape, statutory rape, manstealing, perjury (in a capital trial), and rebellion.

1665   New York colony institutes the Duke's Laws, which make death the penalty for a wide variety of crimes, including sodomy and denial of the true God.

1682   William Penn's Great Act makes only two crimes—treason and murder—punishable by death in Pennsylvania. West Jersey soon passes a similar law. These two colonies, both settled by Quakers, are the most lenient of England's American colonies. Most others prescribe death for at least eleven or twelve separate crimes.

1689   The English Parliament adopts a Bill of Rights that, among other provisions, forbids cruel and unusual punishments.

1692   *10 June.* The first woman to be convicted of witchcraft and sentenced to die in what have become known as the Salem Witch Trials is hanged in Massachusetts.

22 September. The last eight of the Salem "witches" to be executed—two men and six women—are hanged. Altogether, there have been nineteen executions of

1692 (*cont.*)	convicted witches of both sexes, and one man has been crushed to death for refusing to stand trial.
1747	*9 April.* Simon, the Lord of Lovat, is the last person executed by decapitation in England.
1754	Russia abandons the death penalty for ordinary criminal offenses, including murder. It retains capital punishment for use against political criminals.
1756	Pennsylvania, once the most lenient of the American colonies, now mandates death for fourteen crimes.
1764	Cesare Beccaria's *Essay on Crimes and Punishments* is published in Italy. It calls for an end to capital punishment.
1767	Beccaria's *Essay on Crimes and Punishments*, which is already having a great impact in European intellectual circles, is translated into English and begins to influence American abolitionists.[1]
1777	A group of reformers led by Thomas Jefferson proposes abolishing capital punishment in Virginia, except for treason and murder. The proposed retention of the death penalty for treason is ironic considering that the Virginia reformers are currently engaged in what England regards as treason against the mother country.
1780–1790	During this decade, the anti–death penalty arguments of Cesare Beccaria, Jeremy Bentham, Voltaire, and others begin to take hold in some of the more enlightened courts of Western Europe. Tuscany and Austria abolish the death penalty.
1785	A bill to abolish capital punishment fails by one vote in the Virginia legislature.
1787	*9 March.* Speaking in the home of Benjamin Franklin, Dr. Benjamin Rush delivers an address

opposing capital punishment. It is the first time that a prominent American has called for the total abolition of the death penalty.

1789   Dr. Joseph-Ignace Guillotin proposes using a beheading machine (later dubbed a "guillotine") for all executions in France. The idea of executing nobles and peasants in the same way is a radical notion. It is the democratic ideal of the French Revolution applied to the death penalty. Even the revolutionary National Assembly is reluctant to go this far.

1790   The first Congress to meet after the adoption of the Constitution of the United States passes laws that prescribe death by hanging as the punishment for the crimes of rape and first degree murder.

1791   The first nine amendments to the Constitution of the United States, known collectively as the American Bill of Rights, come into effect. Although none of them is primarily concerned with the death penalty, the Eighth Amendment prohibits "cruel and unusual punishments" (as does the English Bill of Rights), and the Fifth Amendment forbids the government from depriving anyone of their lives without due process of law.

1792   *25 April.* A highwayman named Nicolas Pelletier becomes the first victim of the French guillotine.

21 August. Louis Collot d'Angremont, the secretary of the administration of the National Guard of France, becomes the first political victim of the guillotine. D'Angremont is executed for his supposed involvement in a royalist plot. Although first proposed to the National Assembly as a more humane method of execution by two prominent doctors, Joseph-Ignace Guillotin and Antoine Louis, the guillotine is fast becoming the most feared symbol of the revolutionary Terror that is sweeping France.

1793   *An Enquiry into How Far the Punishment of Death Is Necessary in Pennsylvania,* by Pennsylvania Attorney General William Bradford, finds no strong evidence to support the need for capital punishment. Bradford (later the attorney general of the United States) recommends abandoning the death penalty for all crimes except murder and treason, at least until the question can be studied further.

1794   *27 April.* Pennsylvania becomes the first state to abolish the death penalty for all crimes except murder in the first degree.

1812   Sixteen slaves who had participated in a slave rebellion are beheaded in New Orleans.

1820   Roughly 200 crimes are punishable by death in England. They include stealing fish and cutting down a growing tree.

1824   Three white men are hanged for the murder of nine Native Americans at Fall Creek, Indiana. Three of their victims were women and two were children. So far as it is known, this is the first time in American history that a white person has been executed for the murder of a Native American.

1829   One thousand English bankers present a petition to the British Parliament requesting that it remove death as punishment for forgery. The bankers argue that the death penalty is encouraging counterfeiting by making jurors reluctant to convict forgers. Jurors don't want to be party to executing a man for such a relatively minor and nonviolent crime.

1833   Edward Livingston, who has been commissioned by the state legislature to suggest penal reforms for Louisiana, presents his "Introductory Report to the System of Penal Law Prepared for the State of Louisiana," which calls for an end to capital punishment in that state.[2] Although the legislature rejects his recommendation, Livingston's ideas are widely discussed, not only in America but in Europe as well.

1834   Pennsylvania becomes the first of the United States to ban public executions and carry them out only in correctional facilities. In practice, some other states, including New York, have also stopped conducting executions in public, although doing so remains legal there. In most states, executions are still watched by large and often rowdy crowds.

1835   Over 10,000 people flood the streets of the state capital of Maine, jockeying for position to watch the second execution in the state's history. Fights break out, and the police have to step in to prevent what threatens to become a riot.

1837   Tennessee gives juries the option of imposing lesser sentences than death for capital crimes. Until now, death has been mandatory (required) in all states for anyone convicted of a crime that carries the death penalty.

Still shocked by the near riot that took place at an execution two years before, Maine passes what will become known as the Maine Law; this law requires the governor to wait one full year after a person is convicted of a capital crime before signing the death warrant. It is intended to make governors think twice before ordering an execution.

In 1832, capital punishment had been prescribed for 222 crimes in England. By the end of this year, the death penalty has been removed from more than 100 of them.

1838   A new Tennessee law makes the death penalty discretionary there.

1844   By almost two to one, New Hampshire's voters turn down a referendum calling for an end to the death penalty in the state.

1845   Reformers from several states meet in Philadel-
                  phia to establish a national organization to op-
                  pose the death penalty. The new body will be
                  known as the American Society for the Abolition
                  of Capital Punishment. Its first president is
                  George Mifflin Dallas, the vice president of the
                  United States.

1846   Michigan becomes the first state to abolish capital
                  punishment formally; the crime of treason against
                  the state is the exception.

1848   *November.* In France, the constitution of the newly
                  established Second Republic outlaws the death
                  penalty for political crimes.

                  The tiny European nation of San Marino abolishes
                  the death penalty for ordinary crimes.

1852   Rhode Island abolishes the death penalty.

                  Ecuador abandons the death penalty for political
                  crimes.

1853   Wisconsin abolishes the death penalty.

1862   *26 December.* Thirty-eight Native Americans are
                  hanged in what may be the largest mass execution
                  in American history.

                  Greece abolishes the death penalty for criminal
                  offenses.

                  For the first time, the U.S. Congress provides an al-
                  ternative punishment for treason. From now on,
                  treason will be punishable either by death, as be-
                  fore, or by a term in prison of at least five years,
                  and a fine of at least $10,000.

1863   Colombia becomes the first nation in the Western
                  Hemisphere to abolish the death penalty for ordi-
                  nary crimes.

1865	San Marino abolishes the death penalty for all offenses.
1868	The Fourteenth Amendment to the Constitution of the United States extends the Fifth Amendment's protections to the states, forbidding them to "deprive any person of life, liberty or property without due process of law."
1870	The Netherlands abolishes the death penalty.
1872	Iowa abolishes the death penalty.
1874	Executioner William Marwood introduces "the long drop" in England. When done correctly, this method of hanging, which drops the victim at the end of a long rope, kills instantaneously of a broken neck. Before this, most hanging victims had been left to choke slowly to death as they dangled at the end of short ropes.
1875	The U.S. Congress amends the federal capital punishment laws of 1790 to give federal juries the option of convicting defendants of rape or first degree murder "without capital punishment."
1876	Maine abolishes the death penalty.
	Portugal abolishes the death penalty for ordinary crimes.
1877	Costa Rica abolishes the death penalty.
1878	Iowa becomes the first state to re-institute the death penalty after having abolished it.
1879	The U.S. Supreme Court decides *(Wilkerson v. Utah)* that the public execution of a murderer named Wilkerson does not violate the Eighth Amendment's ban on cruel and unusual punishment. It is the first time that the Court has ruled on the question of how the Eighth Amendment applies to a

1879 *(cont.)*	capital case. For the next century and more, the legal debate over the death penalty will center on this amendment.
1883	Maine reinstates the death penalty, having abandoned it only seven years before.
1887	*11 November.* Four men convicted of taking part in a bombing that killed seven Chicago policemen and wounded over sixty more during a labor rally in Chicago's Haymarket Square the year before are hanged in Illinois. Many observers were convinced that the men had been railroaded. Changing its mind once again, Maine abolishes the death penalty for the second time in eleven years.
1889	*1 January.* New York becomes the first state to adopt the electric chair as a method of execution.
1890	The U.S. Supreme Court rules *(In re Kemmler)* that "the punishment of death is not cruel within the meaning of that word as used in the Constitution." As used in the Eighth Amendment, the Court says, "cruel" implies "something inhuman and barbarous, something more than mere extinguishment of life." *6 August.* William Kemmler, whose case prompted an important Supreme Court decision on the meaning of "cruel and unusual punishment," becomes the first person to die in the electric chair. The event takes place in Auburn Prison, at Auburn, New York.
1895	The American Federation of Labor adopts a resolution calling for the abolition of capital punishment, which it terms a "revolting practice."[3]
1897	The number of federal crimes punishable by death is dropped from sixty to three: treason, murder, and rape. Of these, only treason carries a

mandatory death sentence. In effect, this brings the federal laws more in line with the laws of most states.

Colorado abolishes the death penalty.

Ecuador abolishes the death penalty for ordinary crimes.

1901   Alarmed by a rash of lynchings in the wake of the state's abolition of the death penalty in 1897, Colorado reinstates capital punishment.

1903   Panama abolishes the death penalty.

1905   Norway becomes the first European nation in the twentieth century to abolish capital punishment for ordinary crimes.

1906   Ecuador abolishes the death penalty for all offenses.

1907   Uruguay abolishes the death penalty.

Kansas, which has not carried out an execution in thirty-five years, formally abolishes the death penalty.

1910   The Supreme Court holds (*Weems v. United States*) that the meaning of "cruel and unusual punishment" may change over the years due to an "enlightened" public opinion.

The criminal laws of the federal government are revised and reassembled under the title of the U.S. Criminal Code. It provides that "[e]very person guilty of murder in the first degree shall suffer death" and that "[w]hosoever shall commit the crime of rape shall suffer death. Jurors are, however, given the option of qualifying their verdict with the words "without capital punishment," thereby prescribing a sentence of life imprisonment instead of death.

1910 *(cont.)*	Colombia abolishes the death penalty for all offenses.
1911	Minnesota abolishes the death penalty.
1913	The state of Washington abolishes the death penalty.
1914	Oregon abolishes the death penalty.
1915	*19 November.* Joe Hill, a Swedish immigrant and labor organizer for the Industrial Workers of the World (IWW), or Wobblies, is executed by a Utah firing squad. Hill was convicted of armed robbery in a trial that many observers believed was tainted by antilabor prejudice. As he goes to his death, Hill is regarded as a dangerous radical by the state of Utah, but is regarded as a martyred hero by the American labor movement.
	North and South Dakota abolish the death penalty.
	Tennessee abolishes the death penalty for all crimes except rape.
1916	By a margin of only 252 in a statewide referendum, Arizona votes to abolish the death penalty.
1917	The first Mexican state to do so abolishes the death penalty for ordinary crimes.
	Puerto Rico abolishes the death penalty.
	Missouri abolishes the death penalty.
	South Dakota reinstates the death penalty.
	Tennessee reintroduces the death penalty for crimes other than rape.
1918	After only two years of abolition, Arizona reinstates the death penalty.

1919	Puerto Rico reinstates the death penalty.
	The states of Washington and Missouri reintroduce the death penalty.
1920	Following the lead of the neighboring state of Washington, which reintroduced the death penalty in 1919, Oregon does the same.
1924	*8 February.* In Nevada, a gang killer named Gee Jon becomes the first person executed by cyanide gas.
	10 September. Judge John R. Caverly, chief justice of the Criminal Court of Cook County, Illinois, sentences Nathan Leopold, Jr., and Richard Loeb to life plus ninety-nine years in prison for the kidnap-murder of a fourteen-year-old boy named Bobby Franks. The judge's decision not to condemn the young killers to death is considered a victory by opponents of the death penalty, but it outrages millions of other Americans who believe that they "got off" because of their families' wealth.
1924	*23 September.* In the wake of the controversial Leopold and Loeb sentencing, the New York League for Public Discussion sponsors a debate on the subject "Is Capital Punishment a Wise Policy?" at New York's Metropolitan Opera House. Speaking in favor of the death penalty is a prominent New York judge, Alfred J. Talley, who has publicly attacked the leniency shown Leopold and Loeb. Opposed is Clarence Darrow, whose appeal for mercy on their behalf is widely considered one of the strongest emotional arguments ever made against capital punishment.
1925	Clarence Darrow, Lewis E. Lawes, and others found the American League to Abolish Capital Punishment. The league, which establishes itself as the most influential abolition organization in the United States, attracts the support of such other notable abolitionists as Kathleen Norris and Hugo Adam Bedau.

1927	*22 August.* For the first time, an execution in the United States prompts a storm of protest from abroad. Nicola Sacco and Bartolomeo Vanzetti are executed in the electric chair at the prison in Charleston, Massachusetts, for the killing of a guard and a paymaster during the course of a robbery at Braintree, Massachusetts, seven years before. The two are Italian immigrants and political anarchists, who claim they are innocent of the crime. Thousands, if not millions, of people around the world believe them to be the victims of political and anti-immigrant prejudice, and consider their execution a travesty of justice.
1928	Iceland abandons the death penalty.
1929	Puerto Rico abolishes the death penalty for the second time.
1930	*21 February.* Mrs. Eva Dugan becomes the first woman ever executed by the state of Arizona. The execution does not go well. The hangman misjudges the drop, and Mrs. Dugan's head is ripped from her body.
1930–1940	During this decade, an annual average of 167 people are executed in the United States, a new record.
1935	Kansas reinstates the death penalty.
1936	*August.* An estimated 20,000 Kentuckians gather to watch a hanging in Owensboro, Kentucky.
1938	*13 June.* A rapist named Harold B. Van Venison is hanged in the yard of a Kentucky county jail. It is the last public hanging to take place in the United States.
1939	A drunken crowd attends the public execution of a multiple murderer in Versailles, France. Following his decapitation, members of the crowd dip their handkerchiefs in the deceased's blood. Newspaper

accounts of the crowd's behavior arouse indignation and disgust, causing the French government
to announce that future guillotinings will be held
behind prison walls, and that the public will no
longer be able to attend.

1942
With the carnage of World War II all around, neu-
tral Switzerland abolishes the death penalty for ordinary crimes.

1943–1944
During the German occupation of France, roughly
20,000 opponents of the Nazi occupiers are guil-
lotined.

1944
Italy abolishes the death penalty for all crimes except military offenses in wartime.

1945
The death penalty is suspended, although not
abolished, in England and the rest of the United
Kingdom.

1946
The new constitution of Brazil bans the death
penalty except for military crimes in wartime.

1947
The U.S. Supreme Court turns down the appeal
(*State ex rel. Francis v. Resweber*) of a young black
murderer named Willie Francis who argued that
the state of Louisiana had already tried and failed
once to electrocute him (at the age of only seventeen), causing him great pain and suffering, and
should not be allowed to try again. In rejecting his
appeal, the Court insists that the Constitution does
not protect a convicted man from "the necessary
suffering involved in any method employed to extinguish life humanely." [4]

1948
25 June. Caryl Chessman, whose case will become
an international cause célèbre, is sentenced to die
for kidnapping in California.

The United Nations recognizes a "right to life" in
the UN Declaration of Human Rights.

1949   The newly formed nation of West Germany abolishes the death penalty for all crimes.

1953   *19 June.* Another execution in the United States prompts protest, both there and abroad. It is the double execution of Julius Rosenberg and his wife, Ethel, for turning over information about atomic weapons to the Soviet Union. It is the first time that American civilians have been executed for espionage, and the first time an American married couple have been executed together. The press and much of the public blame the Rosenbergs for making it possible for the Soviet Union to build atomic weapons. In sentencing them to death, the trial judge admonishes them that "millions . . . of innocent people may pay the price of your treason."[5] Others, both in the United States and abroad, are convinced that the Rosenbergs are the victims of Cold War hysteria. Even as the switch is thrown, some 2,000 sympathizers gather in New York's Union Square to protest the executions.

1954   The still-young nation of Israel abolishes the death penalty for ordinary crimes. It is retained for treason and for crimes against the Jewish people, crimes against humanity, war crimes, and genocide.

1957   *15 March.* Burton Abbott, who has been sentenced to die for the kidnapping and murder of a fourteen-year-old girl is brought to the gas chamber in California's San Quentin state prison. It is eleven in the morning as Abbot is strapped into one of two chairs in the small, green execution chamber. Abbott has steadfastly maintained his innocence, but the courts have denied his appeals. His only hope for life is a stay of execution from California's governor, Goodwin J. Knight. Knight has decided to grant him the stay, but word of the governor's decision has not reached the prison by 11:18, when cyanide pellets are dropped into the acid bath that will release deadly gas into the chamber. At 11:20, the phone rings at San Quentin. It is the call from the governor with the order that Abbott should be spared. Abbott may well still be alive when the call comes, although perhaps already severely injured by the toxic fumes. The warden decides that it would be too dangerous for anyone from the prison staff to enter the room full of cyanide gas to rescue him, and the execution is completed.[6] News of the botched reprieve helps reignite opposition to the death penalty.

Alaska, Hawaii, and the Virgin Islands abolish capital punishment. This marks the first time in forty years that any American jurisdiction has abandoned the death penalty.

1958   *20 February.* Nathan Leopold, who, along with Richard Loeb, was sentenced to life plus ninety-nine years for his part in the 1924 murder of Bobby Franks, receives parole. Loeb had been killed by a fellow prisoner some years before.

The U.S. Supreme Court rules *(Trop v. Dallas)* that the death penalty remains constitutional. At the same time, it declares that the standard for what is and what is not cruel and unusual punishment under the constitution is subject to change because the Eighth Amendment "must draw its meaning from the evolving standards of decency that mark the progress of a maturing society."

Delaware abolishes the death penalty.

1959   *June.* The infamous killer Charles Starkweather is executed. His accomplice, Caril Ann Fugate, has been given a life sentence because of her extreme youth. At the time of their killing spree, she was only fourteen.

Susan Hayward receives the Academy Award as Best Actress for her portrayal of a real-life condemned murderess named Barbara Graham in the film *I Want to Live!* The movie, released the

1959 (cont.)	year before, shocks audiences with its graphic depiction of the procedures leading up to the doomed woman's execution in San Quentin's gas chamber. It also raises questions in many people's minds about the justice of Graham's death sentence.
1960	*2 May.* The convicted kidnapper Caryl Chessman is finally put to death in the gas chamber at San Quentin. Chessman has fought to evade this moment since his death sentence was first imposed in 1948. In the twelve long years he has spent on San Quentin's death row, he has written several books that have won him support from around the world. Eight previous dates have been set for his execution, but each time he has won a stay from the courts. A ninth stay has been granted, but the call ordering the warden to halt the execution comes fifteen seconds too late.
1961	*December.* Alarmed by a brutal murder in the state, the Delaware legislature re-institutes capital punishment less than three years after abolishing it.
1962	After studying the available evidence, the United Nations issues its first report on the deterrent value of the death penalty. Titled *Capital Punishment*, it concludes that removal of the death penalty from a particular crime "has never been followed by a notable rise" in the number of such crimes that are then committed.[7]
1963	The U.S. Supreme Court decides not to consider the case (*Rudolph v. Alabama*) of a man condemned to death for rape in Alabama. Justice Arthur Goldberg, however, urges the Court to take the case so that it can examine the question of whether the death penalty is still constitutional for crimes that do not take or endanger another's life. Goldberg's argument in respect to this case has been credited with beginning a process that will result in the

Court's overturning all existing capital punishment statutes a decade later.[8]

1964   Oregon abolishes the death penalty for the second
time.

1965   The British House of Commons launches a five-
year experiment during which executions will be
suspended in the United Kingdom.

West Virgina abolishes capital punishment, as does
Iowa, which had abolished it in 1872, only to rein-
troduce it six years later.

Vermont and New York abolish capital punishment for most crimes.

1967   Class action suits brought by the National Association for the Advancement of Colored People
(NAACP) Legal Defense Fund help persuade
many states to put moratoria on further executions
until certain issues surrounding the death penalty
can be resolved.

1968   For the first time since the nation was founded, no
one is executed in the United States during the cal-
endar year.

The U.S. Supreme Court rules against using the
death penalty to force defendants to plead guilty,
overturning a law that provides a maximum penalty of death for a defendant who pleads innocent
to a capital crime and is convicted, but only a maximum penalty of life imprisonment for one who
pleads guilty *(United States v. Jackson)*. The law is
designed to encourage guilty people to admit their
guilt and avoid long and costly trials; but its effect,
the Court declares, is to "discourage the Fifth
Amendment right not to plead guilty, and to deter
the exercise of the Sixth Amendment right to demand a jury trial." The Court rules that laws designed to "chill the assertion of constitutional

1968 *(cont.)*	rights by penalizing those who choose to exercise them" are unconstitutional. By an overwhelming 1,159,348 to 730,649, Massachusetts voters pass a referendum to retain the death penalty.
1969	The Abolition of the Death Penalty Act passes the British Parliament. It renews the general abolition of the death penalty established on an experimental basis in 1965, and makes it permanent. Death is retained as a possible punishment for treason, piracy, and certain military crimes.
1970	*December.* A United States Court of Appeals rules that a law calling for the death penalty in cases of rape in which there has been no threat to the life of the victim is cruel and unusual punishment. This is the first time an appeals court has ever ruled a death penalty unconstitutional under the Eighth Amendment. Illinois voters turn down a proposal to abolish the death penalty by a vote of almost two to one: 1,218,791 to 676,302. The U.S. Supreme Court refuses to consider the claim of an Arkansas rapist that his death sentence was unduly influenced by his being black *(Maxwell v. Bishop)*. The condemned prisoner presents a study showing that a black man convicted of raping a white woman in Arkansas is more than three and a half times as likely to receive a death sentence as someone convicted of raping members of their own race. Although the Court is unwilling to examine what seems to be a purely statistical claim of racial discrimination in death sentencing, it vacates the sentence on other grounds.
1971	*January.* The National Commission on the Reform of Federal Criminal Laws recommends that the federal government remove the death penalty from all federal statutes.

The U.S. Supreme Court rules *(McGautha v. California)* that a jury is free to sentence a defendant to death even when the judge fails to present legal guidelines for imposing the death penalty. Lawyers for a man condemned by a jury that has received no guidance from the trial judge argue that it is unconstitutional to allow juries to set their own conditions for who would live and who would die. The Court disagrees, ruling that trial judges need not spell out standards for juries to use in making their decisions. Justice Harlan even goes so far as to suggest that it may be "beyond present human ability" to design such guidelines.

1972 *29 June.* In by far its most important death penalty ruling to date *(Furman v. Georgia)*, the U.S. Supreme Court declares that the death penalty—as currently administered in the United States—is cruel and unusual punishment under the Eighth Amendment. In doing so, it overturns all the death sentences in effect in the United States, and throws out all current state and federal laws that prescribe the death penalty. (Although hundreds of death sentences have been passed, there has not been an execution carried out in the United States since 1967.)

The ruling involves three cases and three condemned prisoners, all of whom are African American. One, William Furman, has been convicted of murder, the others of rape. The vote of the justices is 5 to 4, but each of the five who make up the majority give somewhat different reasons for their decision. All agree that the death penalty has been unfairly and arbitrarily applied.

1972–1976 State legislatures around the country work to frame new capital punishment statutes they hope will meet the objections the Supreme Court raised to the old laws in *Furman.*

1973 The death penalty is abolished for ordinary crimes in most of Australia. It is retained in the state of

1973
(cont.)

New South Wales and elsewhere for the crimes of treason and piracy.

Kansas and the District of Colombia abolish the death penalty.

1976

2 July. On the most significant day in the legal history of capital punishment in the United States since 19 June 1972, the U.S. Supreme Court hands down several death penalty decisions. The most important, *Gregg v. Georgia,* declares that death is not necessarily a cruel and usual punishment under the Eighth Amendment after all. Gregg had been convicted of armed robbery and murder under a Georgia capital punishment law written after the Supreme Court's 1972 *Furman* decision, which struck down all the then-current death penalty laws. After examining the procedures set by the new law to determine when a murderer should be sentenced to death in Georgia, the Court determines that the new law does not violate the Eighth Amendment and Georgia may proceed to execute Gregg. This is the first time that the Supreme Court has approved a death penalty since the *Furman* decision. Several other important capital punishment cases are handed down on the same day as the *Gregg* decision. Together, they are the Court's effort to clarify what amounts to a new constitutional standard in applying the death penalty. In *Jurek v. Texas,* the Court affirms the death sentence of Jerry Lane Jurek, who had been convicted of strangling a ten-year-old girl after trying to rape her. The Texas statute under which Jurek was sentenced to die required that the jury answer yes to at least two of a list of specific questions establishing aggravating circumstances, which the jury was able to do. The Court rules that the Texas law, like the Georgia law, meets the new constitutional standard. In *Proffitt v. Florida,* the Court affirms a Florida death sentence that was imposed after a judge found four aggravating circumstances. Along with the *Gregg* decision, these cases mean that executions, which had been halted in the United States since 1967, can now begin again.

1976   *13 December.* The U.S. Supreme Court agrees that a condemned prisoner in Utah, Gary Gilmore, is competent to decide not to appeal his death sentence. Gilmore's mother, Bessie, has appealed to have the sentence vacated on her son's behalf, but Gilmore himself has insisted that he wants to have it carried out. Three justices dissent from the Court's ruling, arguing that the Court should first decide whether Utah's new death penalty law is constitutional.

Portugal abolishes capital punishment, and Canada ends the practice except for certain military offenses in wartime.

1977   *17 January.* Gary Mark Gilmore is executed by firing squad in Utah. It is the first execution permitted by the U.S. Supreme Court since the *Furman* decision in 1972, and the first carried out in the United States since 1967. Gilmore's execution is unusual in other ways. For one thing, it is remarkably quick by modern standards, coming less than four months after Gilmore's murder conviction on 7 October 1976. Also, unlike most condemned criminals, Gilmore has not only refused to appeal his death sentence in federal courts, but has pleaded for the death sentence to be carried out. There have been no executions in Utah for so long that there is no place set aside for them. Gilmore is taken to a prison warehouse where a makeshift execution chamber is set up. "Let's do it," he says before being shot to death by a four-man firing squad.[9]

Oklahoma becomes the first state to adopt lethal injection as a means of execution.

The U.S. Supreme Court forbids the imposition of the death penalty for the crime of rape. The case *(Coker v. Georgia)* involves a convicted rapist, mur-

1977
(cont.)

derer, and kidnapper who committed another rape while an escapee from a Georgia prison. Before overturning Coker's death sentence, the Court examines the usual practice of courts and juries in rape cases and finds that death is rarely prescribed for this crime. Partly as a result of this finding, the Court declares: "We have concluded that a sentence of death is grossly disproportionate for the crime of rape and is therefore forbidden by the Eighth Amendment as cruel and unusual punishment."

The Court rules (Dobbert v. Florida) that Florida may execute John Dobbert Jr., for the torture murders of two of his own children, even though the capital punishment law in effect in Florida at the time of the killings was unconstitutional. By the time Dobbert came to trial, a new and constitutional death penalty law was in effect. Ordinarily, people cannot be tried and punished under laws passed after the crime of which they are accused was committed; but in this case, the Court rules that Dobbert has no valid complaint. Both the old, unconstitutional law and the new law under which he was tried provides for capital punishment. Therefore, Dobbert had "fair warning" that he would be liable to the death penalty if he committed such crimes. What's more, the law in effect at the time of his trial gave him more safeguards than he would have had under the old law, not fewer.

1978

The U.S. Supreme Court (Lockett v. Ohio) strikes down Ohio's capital punishment statute because it does not permit juries to consider the defendant's character, record, or even the circumstances of the case as mitigating factors in the sentencing phase of the trial. In essence, the Court rules that lawyers for the defendant must be allowed to present virtually any mitigating factors they wish during the sentencing phase of a capital trial.

Denmark abolishes capital punishment for all offenses. Spain abolishes it as well, except for military crimes in time of war.

1979

25 May. John A. Spenkelink is executed in the electric chair at the Florida State Prison at Starke. It is the first time since 1972 that a death sentence has been enforced in the United States over the legal appeals of the condemned criminal.

Brazil, Fiji, and Peru abolish the death penalty for ordinary crimes, and Norway, Nicaragua, and Luxembourg abolish it altogether.

1980

The U.S. Supreme Court *(Beck v. Alabama)* rules that juries inclined to convict in capital cases must be allowed to consider the alternative of convicting on any lesser included offense that is not subject to the death penalty.

1981

September. Ninety-nine years after the execution of Nicolas Pelletier, France retires the guillotine and abolishes the death penalty.

The U.S. Supreme Court *(Bullington v. Missouri)* rules that the prosecution cannot ask for a second death sentence in the case of a defendant who has won a new trial after already being convicted and sentenced to death for the same crime.

1982

2 December. Charles Brooks, Jr., is executed by lethal injection. It is the first time this new and presumably more humane method has been used in an execution. The execution takes place in the Texas Penitentiary at Huntsville, with both pro– and anti–capital punishment demonstrators gathered outside. The deadly solution is a mixture of sodium thiopental, pavulon, and potassium chloride. Although a doctor who works for the Texas prison system is present, both the mixing of the drugs and the injection are done by nonphysicians. Even so, the use of a traditionally medical

1982
(cont.)

procedure to kill raises concerns about medical ethics.

The last Mexican state abolishes the death penalty for ordinary crimes. Capital punishment has now been abandoned throughout Mexico, except for military crimes and treason.

The Netherlands, which abolished the death penalty in 1870 but re-instituted it in the wake of World War II, abolishes it again.

1983

Protocol Number 6 is added to the European Convention for the Protection of Human Rights and Fundamental Freedoms (ECHR) requiring the thirty-three parties to the ECHR to abolish the death penalty in peacetime. It is the first legally binding international instrument to hold states to the abolition of capital punishment.

The new 1983 Constitution of El Salvador abolishes the death penalty for ordinary crimes.

1984

July. The U.S. Supreme Court approves streamlined procedures for federal appeals courts to use in handling habeas corpus proceedings in capital cases. Under the new guidelines, processes that used to take weeks or even months can now be rushed through in days or hours. Defense attorneys protest that the new procedures drastically reduce the amount of time and consideration such appeals will receive.[10]

1984

2 July. The United States Supreme Court *(Endmund v. Florida)* overturns the death sentence of a man convicted of the robbery and murder of an elderly couple in Florida. Endmund had not directly participated in the murders, but he had driven the getaway car. This is enough under Florida law to make him a "constructive aider and abettor" in the killings and liable to the death penalty. A majority of five of the Supreme Court justices rule that this is not enough to subject him to the death penalty because, they find, Endmund had no intent to kill.

27 July. The Human Rights Committee of the United Nations issues a commentary on the International Covenant on Civil and Political Rights declaring that, while "parties [to the Covenant] are not obliged to abolish the death penalty totally, they are obliged to limit its use, and, in particular, to abolish it for other than the 'most serious crimes.'"[11]

Velma Barfield is executed by the state of North Carolina. She is the first woman executed in the United States since executions were resumed in 1977.

Argentina, the Australian state of Western Australia, and the American state of Massachusetts abolish the death penalty.

1985   The Australian state of New South Wales abolishes the death penalty for piracy, treason, and arson at military and naval establishments—the last offense still punishable by death there. New South Wales had been the only Australian jurisdiction that still imposed the death penalty for any crime.

1985   *February.* The U.S. Supreme Court rules that states must provide financial assistance to pay for psychiatric help in preparing the defense of indigent defendants who wish to plead insanity as a defense. Before this ruling, defendants who couldn't pay for psychiatrists to examine them and testify on their behalf had little or no chance of convincing a judge or jury that they were legally insane. The ruling will not be retroactive, even in capital cases; that is, the executions of indigent defendants who have already been convicted and sentenced to death without the benefit of psychiatric help in preparing their defense can go ahead.

1985   *September.* Charles Rumbaugh is executed in Texas, becoming the first person in more than twenty

1985
(cont.)

years to be executed in the United States for a crime committed when he was under eighteen. Rumbaugh had killed a man during a robbery more than ten years before, when he was seventeen.

1985

November. President Ronald Reagan signs the Department of Defense Authorization Act of 1986. Among its provisions is an amendment to the U.S. Code of Military Justice that permits the death penalty for members of the U.S. military who commit espionage in peacetime. Until now, the code has prescribed the death penalty only for murder and for military crimes committed while the country is at war.

1986

April. The U.S. Supreme Court establishes new standards granting defendants a better opportunity to challenge the exclusion of people of their own race from juries *(Batson v. Kentucky)*.

May. By a vote of 6 to 3, the U.S. Supreme Court upholds the practice of "death-qualifying" juries *(Lockhart v. McCree)*. Ardia McCree had appealed his Arkansas murder conviction on the grounds that prosecutors excluded potential jurors who had admitted that they were opposed to the death penalty. McCree's lawyers presented several studies they claimed showed that death-qualified juries, like McCree's, are more likely to convict, and so argued that McCree had not received a fair trial. The Arkansas Court of Appeals agreed, and voted to overturn McCree's conviction. Writing for the Supreme Court majority, Justice William Rehnquist admits that death-qualified juries are "somewhat more conviction prone," but insists that there is no constitutional requirement that a jury have a mix of opinions on the question of capital punishment. In a strong dissenting opinion, Justice Thurgood Marshall objects that the ruling means "[t]he State's mere announcement that it intends to seek the death penalty . . . [will] give the prosecution license to empanel a jury especially likely to return that very verdict." That is because, in Marshall's view, death-qualified jurors are less likely to be concerned with the defendant's rights and with "the danger of erroneous convictions" than other jurors would be.

June. The U.S. Supreme Court *(Ford v. Wainright)* rules that the state of Florida cannot execute an insane convict, Alvin Ford. A thirty-three-year-old black man, Ford murdered a Florida police officer in 1974. The question before the Court did not involve Ford's sanity when he committed the crime, or at the time of his trial. During his years in prison, his mental condition reached the point where a psychiatrist determined that he had "at best, only minimal contact with the events of the external world." The Court's ruling means that states cannot execute prisoners who are legally insane at the time of their scheduled executions, regardless of whether they were sane at the time of their crimes.

1987   Haiti, the Philippines, Liechtenstein, and the German Democratic Republic all abolish capital punishment.

In the United States, the U.S. Supreme Court upholds the death sentence of a black man named Warren McCleskey for the murder of a white policeman *(McCleskey v. Kemp)*. The vote is 5 to 4. McCleskey argued that the Georgia jury that sentenced him to die had been unfairly influenced both by his race and by the race of his victim. In support of his argument, McCleskey's lawyers presented a major statistical study showing that, in Georgia, murderers whose victims are white receive death sentences four times as often as those whose victims are black. This is true even when the murderers are white. Black murderers whose victims are white are condemned to death even more often. Speaking for the majority of the Court, Justice Powell agrees that the study shows a clear "discrepancy that appears to correlate with race."

1987
(cont.)

Even so, the Court will not assume that racism is the reason for the imbalance. Before it would overturn McCleskey's sentence, says Powell, the Court would need proof that the particular jury that sentenced him was influenced by race, and it had received no such proof. The four dissenters (who include Justice Stevens and Justice Blackmun, as well as the Court's two longtime foes of capital punishment, Justice Brennan and Justice Marshall) argue that it is not necessary for a defendant to show specific prejudice on his own jury. The pattern showing the taint of racism on death sentences is obvious. The *McCleskey* decision comes as a great blow, not only to abolitionists but to civil rights campaigners across the country.

1988

April. Georgia bans the use of the death penalty against defendants whom the jury has found "guilty but mentally retarded."[12] No other state has such a law.

June. The U.S. Supreme Court *(Thompson v. Oklahoma)* overturns the death sentence given to William Wayne Thompson by the state of Oklahoma for his part in the murder of his former brother-in-law. Thompson's sentence was appealed on the grounds that it would be cruel and unusual punishment to execute him because he was only fifteen years old when he committed the crime. Although five of the nine Supreme Court justices vote to vacate the sentence, only four do so on those grounds. Justice Sandra Day O'Connor finds the sentence inappropriate because the Oklahoma statute sets no minimum age at all. The divided ruling still leaves open the question of whether fifteen is constitutionally too young to be sentenced to death.

A new law is enacted in the United States subjecting drug "kingpins" to the death penalty for murders committed during the course of drug conspiracies.

1989
28 February. In an important procedural case *(Dugger v. Adams)*, the U.S. Supreme Court turns down an appeal on behalf of a Florida defendant who argues that the judge at his trial misinformed the jury about its role in sentencing. A federal district court had already ruled that the judge's mistake violated the Eighth Amendment. In any case, the Court rules that it is too late for the defendant to raise the claim in federal court because he failed to raise it in an earlier state court proceeding in which it would have been in order. In essence, the Court seems to be saying that unless a constitutional claim is raised at the earliest opportunity, the defendant looses the right ever to raise it.

May. The United Nations Economic and Social Council passes a resolution recommending the abolition of the death penalty for mentally retarded people or others with severely "limited mental competence."[13]

23 June. The U.S. Supreme Court turns down a class action suit *(Murray v. Giarratano)* filed on behalf of impoverished residents of Virginia's death row who claim a constitutional right to free counsel to help them with appeals.

26 June. The Court declares *(Penry v. Lynaugh)* that it is not unconstitutional to impose the death penalty on a mentally retarded person. The case involves an adult murderer named John Paul Penry, whose IQ is between 50 and 63. His ability to learn is that of a typical six-and-a-half-year-old child and his social maturity is that of a ten-year-old. The Court does rule that juries need to be instructed that they can consider mental retardation as a mitigating factor when deciding whether to impose the death penalty. Since Penry's jury was been so informed, Penry's death sentence is overturned. Nonetheless, the Court's decision clears the way for states to execute other retarded criminals.

1989
(cont.)

26 June. Ruling in the cases of two young men (*Stanford v. Kentucky and Wilkins v. Missouri*) convicted of brutal murders committed when they were sixteen and seventeen years old, the U.S. Supreme Court rules that their proposed executions are not cruel and unusual punishment, despite their youth. Lawyers for the defendants argued that the community's "standards of decency" had evolved to the point where the execution of people that young was no longer acceptable. Writing for the majority, Justice Antonin Scalia disagrees. Among other things, he points out that most states that have capital punishment permit it to be applied to sixteen-year olds.

13 July. The Indiana Supreme Court sets aside the death sentence of a young woman named Paula Cooper. Cooper, who was sixteen at the time she was sentenced in 1986, was only fifteen when she and some accomplices killed a seventy-eight-year-old woman with a knife. The Court rules that death would be a disproportionate punishment, considering her youth at the time of the crime.

In *South Carolina v. Gathers*, the Court expands its 1987 ruling in *Booth v. Maryland* by declaring it unconstitutional under the Eighth Amendment for prosecutors to praise the murder victim's character when trying to persuade jurors to impose the death penalty on a killer. *Gathers* is an effort to protect the rights of a defendant in a capital trial, but in several other important cases, the Court continues to move away from the concerns it expressed in 1972 in *Furman*. Taken together, these cases have the effect of drastically limiting the avenues of appeal available to condemned prisoners. In the eyes of abolitionists, the Court is rapidly stripping away the safeguards that protect prisoners from being put to death unfairly. In the eyes of pro–capital punishment forces, the Court is merely limiting the ability of guilty criminals to delay their moments of reckoning by abusing legal technicalities.

1990   *10 July.* Bulgaria establishes a moratorium on the death penalty.

15 December. By a vote of 59 to 26, the General Assembly of the United Nations adopts the Second Optional Protocol to the International Covenant on Civil and Political Rights, calling on all member nations to take steps toward abolishing the death penalty. Forty-eight nations abstain from the vote.[14]

A protocol is added to the American Convention on Human Rights forbidding its members to apply the death penalty.

A meeting of the Conference on the Human Dimension of the Conference on Security and Cooperation in Europe agrees "to exchange information . . . on the question of the abolition of the death penalty and keep that question under consideration."

1991   *April.* Ray Copeland is sentenced to death in Missouri for a murder committed when he was seventy-one years old. He is the only person in the United States to be given a death sentence for a crime committed after the age of seventy.

16 April. The U.S. Supreme Court sets strict new limits on the right of condemned prisoners to appeal their sentences more than once to federal courts. The case *(McCleskey v. Zant)* involves a new appeal by the same Warren McCleskey whose claim that his death sentence was influenced by race was turned down by the Court in 1987 *(McCleskey v. Kemp).* In effect, the Court is severely limiting the right of the writ of habeas corpus; historically, the writ has protected citizens from acts of injustice by the government by allowing them to challenge the constitutionality of those acts in federal court. In the future, the Court rules, a prisoner can no longer file more than one habeas corpus petition unless exceptional circumstances require it. A constitutional

<table>
<tr>
<td>

1991
(cont.)

</td>
<td>

issue not raised in the initial writ cannot be raised in a later one. To have another writ considered, the prisoner must be able to show that there was a good reason the issue or issues contained in it weren't raised before and that he or she has suffered "actual prejudice" from the claimed abuse of constitutional rights. Three justices (Marshall, Blackmun, and Stevens) file an angry dissent in which they attack the decision as an "unjustifiable assault on the Great Writ."

May. David Chandler becomes the first person sentenced to death under the only current federal law that meets the safeguards required by the 1972 U.S. Supreme Court decision that struck down all the then-existing capital punishment laws. The law is the 1988 Anti-Drug Abuse Act, which makes participation in a murder either committed by or solicited by large-scale drug dealers a federal crime punishable by death.

June. Reversing its recent policy, the U.S. Supreme Court rules *(Payne v. Tennessee)* that juries can take into account the character of the victim and the impact on the victim's family when deciding whether to sentence a killer to death.

24 June. The U.S. Supreme Court refuses to consider an appeal from convicted murderer Roger Keith Coleman on the grounds that his attorney was a day late in filing a petition in the state court of Virginia. The Court rules *(Coleman v. Thompson)* that failure to file an appeal at the proper time in a state court rules out any future consideration of the appeal in a federal court. The 6 to 3 vote is a reversal of a policy established by the Court back in 1963, and it is one more in a series of recent rulings that limits the right of habeas corpus.

30 June. The Canadian Parliament votes 148 to 127 against the reintroduction of the death penalty, outlawed in Canada since 1976. The vote is some-

</td>
</tr>
</table>

thing of a surprise, since the Progressive Conservative Party was elected with a large parliamentary majority in 1984 partly on the promise that it would bring the issue to a new vote.

6 September. Donald Gaskins is executed in South Carolina's electric chair for the 1982 contract murder of a fellow prison inmate. Gaskins, previously convicted of killing nine white people, is the first white man executed in the United States for killing a black person since 1944.

25 September. The state of Georgia electrocutes Warren McCleskey. McCleskey's conviction was the basis for two appeals that have reached the U.S. Supreme Court, resulting in two landmark death penalty decisions—*McClesky v. Kemp* (1987) and *McCleskey v. Zant* (1991). Both appeals were rejected.

October. By a vote of 4 to 3, the Supreme Court of Canada rules that accused kidnapper, rapist, and murderer Charles Ng and convicted murderer Joseph Kindler can be extradited to the United States. The ruling is controversial because Kindler is already under sentence of death in Pennsylvania, and Ng is accused of several murders in California, a death penalty state. Canada, which abolished its death penalty, has refused to extradite people to countries where they were liable to be put to death. Kindler's and Ng's lawyers argued that their clients should not be extradited unless the Canadian government first obtained assurances that their lives would be spared. Apparently not wanting Canada to become a refuge for fugitives from foreign death sentences, the Canadian justice department refuses to ask for such assurances and immediately dispatches the two men to the United States.[15]

25 October. Jerome Allen is sentenced to death in Florida for the murder of a gas station attendant during a robbery committed when he was fifteen

1991
(cont.)

years old. The case is unusual because the recent trend in court decisions is not to execute people for crimes committed before they were sixteen. In this case, the prosecutor insists that Allen is "juvenile in age only."[16]

The year passes without the Comprehensive Violent Crime Control Act of 1991 becoming law. The bill, which was intended as a part of President George Bush's war on drugs, would have had an enormous effect on the administration of the death penalty in the United States. It called for extending the number of federal crimes punishable by death to more than fifty and formally restricting a condemned prisoner to one habeas corpus appeal in the federal courts. (In effect, the U.S. Supreme Court seems determined to do this by its own rulings.) The bill passed both houses of Congress in 1991, but President Bush refused to sign it because it did not eliminate the right of habeas corpus altogether.[17]

1992

21 April. Robert Alton Harris is executed in the gas chamber at San Quentin State Prison. He is the first person to be executed in California in twenty-five years. Harris was sentenced to die for the merciless killing of two sixteen-year-old boys in 1978. His efforts to escape execution received the kind of public attention previously granted only to the likes of Caryl Chessman, Roger Keith Coleman, and others who seemed to have serious claims to innocence. Harris launched a variety of appeals in state and federal courts, including seven to the U.S. Supreme Court. Harris's last stay is granted by the 9th District Court of Appeals minutes after he is strapped into a chair in the gas chamber around 2:00 A.M. He is then unstrapped and led back to his cell on death row. The U.S. Supreme Court, which demonstrated its intolerance of multiple appeals in *McCleskey v. Zant* (1991), loses all patience. In an unprecedented move, it sends a fax message to authorities in California: "No further stays of Robert Alton Harris's execution shall be entered by federal courts except upon order of this court," it declares.[18] In effect, the Court is forbidding lower federal courts to interfere and ordering the execution to proceed. Harris is led back into the gas chamber and strapped into the chair again. At roughly 6:05 in the morning, the cyanide pellets are dropped. Within seven minutes, witnesses report, Harris appears to be unconscious. At 6:21, a doctor pronounces him dead.

May. Roger Keith Coleman is executed in Virginia for the murder of his sister-in-law, despite protests and appeals for mercy from around the world. Coleman has claimed that he is innocent of the brutal murder, and many people believe him.

June. The U.S. Supreme Court rules *(Sawyer v. Whitley)* that condemned prisoners may raise certain constitutional claims in federal appeals, even when they have failed to raise them in state proceedings.

3 November. Voters in Washington, D.C., overwhelmingly reject a referendum calling for the introduction of the death penalty in the District of Columbia.

1993

5 January. Three-time child killer Westley Allan Dodd is hanged in Washington State Prison at Walla Walla, Washington. His execution is the first hanging in the United States since 1965. It comes after an unsuccessful attempt by opponents of capital punishment to block the execution on the grounds that hanging is cruel and unusual punishment. Dodd has refused to cooperate with the effort to block his execution; indeed, he virtually demands to die, declaring that if he is not killed, he will do everything he can to escape and return to his murderous ways. Furthermore, he has chosen hanging (over lethal injection) as the method of execution because he strangled the youngest of his victims, a four-year-old child, and considers it fit-

1993
(cont.)

ting that he should die by a similar method. The execution has been set for just after midnight. Both pro– and anti–death penalty demonstrators gather outside the prison as the time approaches. Despite the cold, the supporters of capital punishment are in a festive mood. One carries a sign reading "Hang 'em High." Chanting together, they count down the final seconds to the appointed time, then cheer and set off fireworks as it arrives. The opponents stand silently, holding candles in the dark. Inside, as witnesses later report, the execution is carried out with remarkable speed. Dodd is ushered briskly into the execution chamber. Two men slip a kind of bag over him, then place the noose around his neck and tighten it. A trap door opens beneath his feet and he drops seven feet to the end of the rope, dying instantly.

25 January. The U.S. Supreme Court refuses *(Herrera v. Collins)* to allow a federal court to review new evidence in the case of Leonel Herrera, convicted of murdering a Texas policeman in 1981. Herrera's attorney has argued that new evidence proves that Leonel's brother committed the crime. Nonetheless, by a 6 to 3 majority, the Court rules that the deadline has long since passed for Herrera to appeal on the basis of actual innocence. His only hope is to appeal to the governor of Texas for execution clemency. Justices Blackmun, Stevens, and Souter angrily dissent from the ruling, charging that "[e]xecution of a person who can show that he is innocent comes perilously close to simple murder."[19]

2 March. All charges are dropped against Walter McMillen who has spent the past six years on death row in Alabama. McMillen, who is black, was convicted in 1988 of killing a white teenager in a trial badly tainted by racism. Even so, the jury that convicted him recommended a life sentence, only to be overruled by the judge who sentenced him to die. Evidence that has surfaced since the trial shows that key witnesses against McMillen—one whom had apparently been told that he would be spared all risk of the death penalty himself if he incriminated McMillen—lied during the trial, perhaps with the prosecution's knowledge.

1994   *October.* The government of Azerbaijan abolishs capital punishment for women.

The Violent Crime Control and Law Enforcement Act, which significantly expands the federal death penalty in the United States, is signed into law by President Bill Clinton.

The Council of Europe makes abolition of the death penalty in peacetime a treaty requirement for any nation wishing to join.

The Philippines reinstates the death penalty, which it had abolished in 1987.

1995   *March.* The Congress of Guatemala approves Decree 14–95, extending the death penalty to kidnapping and other crimes; but the president of Guatemala takes no action either to ratify or to veto the decree, leaving its legal status uncertain.

The South African Constitutional Court rules that the death penalty is contrary to that country's new interim constitution.

1996   *January.* The Committee of Ministers of the Council of Europe calls for a moratorium on executions in all member states.

24 April. President Bill Clinton signs an act to shorten the time available for inmates sentenced to death under the Anti-Terrorism and Effective Death Penalty Act to appeal. In recent years, the U.S. Supreme Court has also shown an increasing impatience with the ability of many death row inmates to fend off their executions with lengthy appeals processes.

1996
(cont.)

28 June. The Parliamentary Assembly of the Council of Europe passes a resolution declaring that any state joining the council must issue an immediate moratorium on the use of the death penalty and assert its intention to ratify Protocol #6 to the ECHR. The resolution also calls on those member states that have yet to ratify Protocol #6 to do so; it also asks those member states who maintain statutes allowing for use of the death penalty (but without having recourse to them, which would violate the conditions of their membership in the council) to rescind those laws or to amend them to eliminate the potential imposition of the death penalty.

June. A new law reduces the number of crimes punishable by death in Azerbaijan from thirty-three to twelve, and sets sixty-five as the maximum age at which the death sentence may be imposed.

June. The General People's Congress of Libya holds a televised session in which it extends the death penalty to the crimes of trading illegally in foreign currencies and the smuggling of drugs and alcohol.

June. Citing a rising crime rate, Bulgaria's minister of the interior writes to the National Assembly asking for an end to the moratorium on executions, which had been put in place in July 1990. The National Assembly declines to act.

August. Russia suspends all executions. The Council of Europe has agreed to admit the Russian Federation on the condition that the newly established nation, formed in the wake of the dissolution of the Soviet Union, abolishes the death penalty.

August. Belgium abandons the death penalty.

September. President Guntis Ulmanis of Latvia announces his intention to grant clemency to all those condemned who asked for it until such time as the legislature renders a final decision on abolition of the death penalty. The Saeima is in the midst of considering a new criminal code that would replace the death penalty with life imprisonment.

10 December. President Nelson Mandela promulgates a new and permanent South African Constitution that retains the wording of the interim constitution effectively banning capital punishment in the new South Africa.

Bahrain carries out an execution for the first time since 1997.

Comoros carries out its first execution since before achieving independence in 1975.

1997   *13 June.* A U.S. federal jury sentences Timothy McVeigh to death for the 19 April 1995 bombing of the Alfred P. Murrah federal office building in Oklahoma City; 168 people were killed and hundreds more injured. McVeigh, who was tried under a federal antiterrorism statute enacted in 1994, hates what he considers the repressive U.S. government and committed the bombing as revenge for the government's destruction of the David Koresh compound and its inhabitants in Waco, Texas, on 19 April 1993.

July 24. The president of the ex-Soviet state of Georgia, Eduard Shevardnadze, announces the commutation of the death sentences of all condemned prisoners in that country.

The 1997 Legislative Assembly of El Salvador fails to ratify a constitutional amendment that was passed by the 1996 Legislative Assembly; the amendment would have reintroduced the death penalty for certain homicides and for rape and kidnapping. The amendment is effectively killed.

1998   *10 February.* The execution of Manuel Martinez Coronado, the first person to be executed by lethal injection in Guatemala, is televised there.

1998
(cont.)

February. Azerbaijan, which abolished the death penalty for women in 1994, abolishes it for men as well.

14 April. The state of Virginia executes a Paraguayan citizen named Angel Francisco Beard despite protests from the Paraguayan government that the Vienna Convention on Consular Relations was violated when Beard was arrested and held without being told of his right to contact the Paraguayan consulate.

October. Trevor Fisher and Richard Woods are executed in the Bahamas even though a petition to the Inter-American Commission on Human Rights on their behalf is pending, and despite requests from the commission and the European Council that the executions be postponed at least until the commission could issue its conclusions.

November. Thirty individuals who were sentenced to death and subsequently released because they were shown to be innocent attend the first National Conference of Wrongful Convictions and the Death Penalty, which is held by Northwestern University.

Karla Faye Tucker is executed by the state of Texas. By the time of her execution, Tucker, who has been condemned for a vicious murder, is by all accounts thoroughly rehabilitated, and her fate has aroused a great deal of national and international sympathy. Her status as an apparently sincere "born again" Christian has even led to appeals on her behalf to Texas Governor George W. Bush from several prominent Christian fundamentalists who usually favor the execution of condemned criminals. These appeals are to no avail.

A moratorium on executions is declared in Malawi.

The Rome Diplomatic Conference decides that the International Criminal Court, which has been established to try cases involving the most serious international crimes, including war crimes and genocide, will not have the power to impose the death penalty.

A United Nations Human Rights Commission resolution calls on those countries that retain the death penalty to limit the number of capital offenses and to establish a moratorium on executions. Fifty UN members respond with a statement insisting that there is no international consensus in favor of abolition.[20]

In Tajikistan, the number of crimes punishable by death is decreased from forty-four to fifteen.

1999   *January.* On a visit to St. Louis, Missouri, Pope John Paul II publicly calls for the abolition of the death penalty.

5 February. Leo Echegaray becomes the first person to be executed by the government of the Philippines since 1976.

3 March. The state of Arizona executes Walter LaGrand. He is the second LeGrand brother, both of whom were German nationals, to be executed in a case that has caused a great deal of international controversy. The executions take place despite strong protests from the German government, and, in the case of Walter, a unanimous but nonbinding opinion from the International Court of Justice asking the United States to suspend the execution until the Court could issue a final decision in the matter.

22 March. The Ukraine formally abolishes the death penalty.

April. A resolution calling for a moratorium on the death penalty, sponsored by sixty-three nations, was adopted by the UN Commission on Human Rights. Prominent among those nations voting

1999
(cont.)

against the resolution were the United States, China, South Korea, and Rwanda.

June. President Boris Yeltsin of Russia commutes all death sentences in Russia.

Nepal abolishes the death penalty.

Oman expands the death penalty for drug crimes.

26 October. Following the bloody electrocution of Allen Lee Davis in Florida, the U.S. Supreme Court agrees to reconsider whether the electric chair constitutes "cruel and unusual" punishment, a question the Court originally decided in 1890 in the case of *In re Kemmler.*

22 December. Bermuda abolishes the death penalty.

29 December. Turkmenistan becomes the first of the former Soviet Central Asian Republics to abolish the death penalty.

Over the objections of several nations, the UN Subcommission on the Promotion and Protection of Human Rights adopts a resolution that calls for an end to the execution of people for crimes committed when they were under eighteen. Among those countries named in the resolution as having executed juvenile offenders are the United States, Iran, Nigeria, Pakistan, Saudi Arabia, and Yemen.

Several groups opposed to the death penalty join together this year to celebrate steps toward the elimination of the death penalty by illuminating the Roman Coliseum for forty-eight hours every time a government abandons capital punishment or a death sentence is commuted anywhere in the world.

2000

15 January. A fourteen-year-old soldier is executed by military authorities in the Democratic Republic of Congo, despite the public stance of the Congolese government that it will abide by a moratorium on executions.

21 March. After being passed by Malta's House of Representatives, with the support of both the governing party and the opposition, and being approved by the nation's president, the Armed Forces (Amendment) Act 2000 is promulgated. The act removes the death penalty, which Malta had abolished for ordinary criminal offenses in 1971, from all offenses under the military law. The promulgation makes Malta the first nation to abolish the death penalty for all crimes in the new millenium.

24 March. The Philippines announces a year-long moratorium on all executions. The step is in response to a proposal by the Catholic Bishops Conference of the Philippines, which has asked for the moratorium to honor the 2,000th anniversary of the birth of Christ.

27 April. The UN Commission on Human Rights adopts a resolution calling for a worldwide moratorium on executions. Fifty-one nations dissociate themselves from the resolution.

May. The corpse of a man beheaded for a particularly horrendous murder in Saudi Arabia is publicly crucified to serve as an example to others.

June. The Nebraska state legislature calls for a two-year moratorium on executions.

22 July. One hundred and ten delegates from fifteen Indian states attend the first National Conference of the Campaign Against the Death Penalty in New Delhi.

23 July. The new constitution of Cote d'Ivoire, which forbids the imposition of the death penalty, is adopted by referendum.

2000
(cont.)

5 *August.* In Pakistan, a Sufi man is sentenced to death, to be preceded by thirty-five years at hard labor, for blasphemy.

12 *September.* The Judicial Committee of the Privy Council, which acts as the last court of appeal for the Commonwealth countries in the Caribbean, commutes the death sentences of six prisoners in Jamaica, ruling that convicts must not be executed while their appeals are pending before international bodies.

27 *November.* The U.S. Supreme Court agrees to hear the appeal of John Paul Penry, whose earlier death sentence had been overturned by the Court in 1989 on the grounds that the jury had not been allowed to consider his mental retardation as a mitigating circumstance when sentencing him to death. Penry has since been retried and again sentenced to death.

2001

31 *March.* A South African woman named Mariette Bosch is executed by hanging in Botswana for the murder of a woman whose husband she later married. Bosch was the first white person to be executed in Botswana since the country achieved its independence from Great Britain in 1966.

2 *April.* The U.S. Supreme Court refuses to hear an appeal by David Paul Hammer, who had filed, then waived, several previous appeals before they could be decided. Hammer, who was convicted of murder in 1998, has vacillated over whether he wanted his death sentence to be appealed. In August 2000, after Hammer expressed a desire to be executed, a U.S. district court dismissed his then-pending appeal. Then, in October 2000, Hammer decided that he wanted to go ahead with the appeal process after all. In making the appeal, his lawyers argued that society's interest in assuring that it did not execute some-

one for whom capital punishment was not legally warranted required at least one appellate review of every death sentence. The Court rejected this argument, ruling in effect that a condemned person has the right to waive all appeals, and that Hammer had done so.

4 April. The lower house of the Chilean Congress votes to abolish the death penalty; the upper house has already done so. "This is an historic day," declares Chile's justice minister, Jose Antonio Gomez. "We have removed from our codes an irrational and inhuman law."

10 April. Laos, which has not imposed the death penalty in more than a quarter of a century, announces that henceforth it will be applied to such serious drug offenses as the possession of more than 6.6 pounds of metamphetamines, or the possession, distribution, or manufacture of more than 17.6 ounces of heroin.

11 April. In a "strike-hard" campaign against crime, China executes eighty-nine people in one day.

12 April. U.S. Attorney General John Ashcroft announces that a closed circuit telecast of Oklahoma City bomber Timothy McVeigh's death by lethal injection will be transmitted to Oklahoma City, where it will be available for viewing by members of the victims' families.

11 June. Timothy McVeigh is executed by lethal injection in the federal penetentiary at Terre Haute, Indiana for the terrorist bombing of the Alfred P. Murrah Building in Oklahoma City, which killed 168 people in 1995. McVeigh, who is the first person executed under federal law since 1963, decides not to make a final statement, leaving behind instead a handwritten copy of the 1875 poem "Invictus," by William Ernest Henley, which concludes

2001
(cont.)

with the famous lines, "I am the master of my fate, I am the captain of my soul."

18 June. Texas Governor Rick Perry vetoes a bill, passed by the Texas State Legislature, which would have prevented the execution of the mentally retarded in the state.

15 August. The Federal Court of Appeals in Texas blocks the execution of a Texas inmate whose lawyer had slept through much of his trial.

Notes

1. Cesare Beccaria, *On Crimes and Punishment*, translated by Henry Paolucci (Indianapolis, IN: Bobbs-Merrill, 1963).

2. Edward Livingston, "Report on the Plan of a Penal Code," in *Complete Works of Edward Livingston on Criminal Jurisprudence*, vol. 1 (New York: National Prison Association, 1873).

3. *Congressional Digest* (August–September 1927): 242.

4. Kurt Anderson, et al., "An Eye for an Eye," *Time* (24 January 1983): 32.

5. Quoted in James Avery Joyce, *Capital Punishment: A World View* (New York: Thomas Nelson & Sons, 1961), 189.

6. Ibid., 161–162.

7. United Nations, *Capital Punishment* (New York: United Nations Department of Economic and Social Affairs, 1962), 54.

8. Ellen Alderman and Caroline Kennedy, *In Our Defense* (New York: Morrow, 1991), 406.

9. *Chronicle of the 20th Century* (Mount Kisco, NY: Chronicle, 1987), 1120.

10. Amnesty International, *United States of America, The Death Penalty: Briefing* (New York: Amnesty International, October 1987), 13.

11. Amnesty International, *When the State Kills . . . The Death Penalty: A Human Rights Issue* (London: Amnesty International, 1989), 244.

12. Ibid., 229.

13. Amnesty International, *United States of America: Death Penalty Developments in 1992* (New York: Amnesty International, 1992), 32.

14. "Death Penalty Protocol Adopted." *UN Chronicle* (March 1990): 85.

15. D'Arcy Jenish and John Howse, "A Momentous Ruling," *Maclean's* (7 October 1991): 62.

16. Amnesty International, *United States of America: Death Penalty Developments in 1991* (New York: Amnesty International, 1992): 21.

17. Ibid., 13.

18. "Execution Witnesses Say Harris Died with Dignity," *Wausau Daily Herald,* 22 April 1992.

19. Dennis Cauchon, "Court: Late Evidence May Not Halt Execution," *USA Today,* 26 January 1993.

20. "ECOSOC Statement on the Question of the Death Penalty," July 29, 1998.

5

People and Events

In the end, most public issues boil down to events and people: the events that frame and focus the issue in the public mind, and the people whose actions and arguments galvanize support for one side or another. What is true of most issues is true of the death penalty. For many centuries, capital punishment was not an issue at all, in the sense that there was no real public controversy about it. It was a fact of life—as accepted by most members of society as the changing of the seasons and the divine right of kings. It took individuals such as Cesare Beccaria in Europe and Dr. Benjamin Rush in the United States to challenge the inevitability of capital punishment—to transform it from an accepted fact of life into a social and moral issue that had to be examined and debated. We have been wrestling with that issue ever since the eighteenth century, and we are still wrestling with it today.

Some people regard capital punishment primarily as an intellectual question, as framed by philosophers such as Jeremy Bentham or social scientists such as Walter Berns. Others react to the death penalty in more human terms. Our beliefs on the subject are formed not so much by rational arguments as by personal and often emotional responses to particular people and events. Gary Mark Gilmore, or someone like him, commits a horrible murder, and we instinctively want to see him punished—eradicated, wiped away, removed from society in the most immediate and final way possible. On the other hand, Sacco and Vanzetti are convicted and executed on questionable and perhaps politically contaminated evidence, we begin to doubt whether even society has the right to impose such an irrevocable punishment.

The individuals discussed here are representative of the many kinds of people—philosophers and activists, judges and criminals, politicians and executioners—who have helped form modern attitudes toward the death penalty. It should be said that, of those who have taken a strong stand on the death penalty, there are more abolitionists than retentionists. This may seem odd, considering that the majority of Americans favor the death penalty; but more abolitionists than retentionists are prominent for their stand on the death penalty.

Why does this imbalance exist? At least part of the reason abolitionists have been the most active side of the battle is that they have had to be on the offensive. For most of our history, retentionism has been the entrenched position. The majority of states have had death penalty statutes on their books, and the majority of the people have supported the practice. Capital punishment, therefore, has not needed a particularly large or powerful force to defend it. As a result of this bias in favor of the death penalty, abolitionists have been forced to launch assault after assault on a position that has often seemed invulnerable. It is an old military axiom that it takes a larger and more determined force to overrun a well-entrenched position than it does to defend it. So it has been the abolitionists who have made the most noise, firing the artillery and lobbing the grenades. All retentionists have to do is batten down their legal fortress and weather the occasional firestorm. It is not surprising that they have been relatively content to let the law and public opinion speak for them.

People

Anthony Guy Amsterdam (1935–)

Prominent attorney who played a leading role in the legal battle to abolish the death penalty in the 1960s and 1970s.

Amsterdam received his law degree from the University of Pennsylvania Law School in 1960, at the threshold of a decade of intense struggle over civil rights of all kinds. A brilliant student, Amsterdam edited the *Pennsylvania Law Review,* for which he wrote at least one article that later influenced the U.S. Supreme Court. Upon graduation, he was picked to serve as law clerk to the legendary Supreme Court Justice Felix Frankfurter. After his clerkship, he served briefly as assistant U.S. attorney in Washington, D.C., before taking a teaching job at his old law school.

In 1963, Amsterdam agreed to help out in the case of a black man sentenced to death for intended rape, although he had not physically injured his victim. This led the young lawyer into the struggle to overturn the death penalty, a pursuit that would engage much of his attention for decades. Working with such anti–capital punishment groups as the NAACP Legal Defense Fund, the National Coalition to Abolish the Death Penalty, and the Southern Poverty Law Center, Amsterdam quickly established himself as one of the most able legal minds working on the issue.

Before long, he was managing the NAACP Legal Defense Fund's growing schedule of capital punishment cases. He played a major role in preparing the brief attacking the constitutionality of the death penalty in the historic *Furman* case. When it came time for oral arguments before the U.S. Supreme Court, it was Amsterdam who led the way.

Among his legal honors, Amsterdam was the recipient of the first Distinguished Service Award of the Pennsylvania Law School in 1968, and in 1973 he was named lawyer of the year by the California Trial Lawyer's Association. In 1969, he took a position as a law professor at Stanford University in California. He stayed there until moving to New York University in 1981.

Cesare Beccaria (1738–1794)

The first prominent European to call for an end to the death penalty, Beccaria is considered the founder of the modern abolition movement.

Born into the minor Italian aristocracy, Beccaria was trained in the law. He was strongly influenced by the Enlightenment ideas that were sweeping intellectual circles in Europe during his young manhood. In 1764, Beccaria published his famous *Essay on Crimes and Punishments*. It was the first major study of the criminal justice system as it operated in eighteenth-century Europe, as well as the first call for the abolition of capital punishment. It remains the most influential attack on the death penalty ever published.

"The useless profusion of punishments, which has never made men better, induces me to enquire, whether the punishment of death be really just or useful in a well governed state?" he asked. His answer was that it was not.

He was aware that, in taking on the death penalty, he was challenging thousands of years of accepted practice, but that neither impressed nor daunted him. "If it be objected, that almost all the nations in all ages have punished certain crimes with death, I answer, that the force of these examples vanishes, when opposed to truth, against which prescription is urged in vain. The history of mankind is an immense sea of errors, in which few obscure truths may here and there be found. But human sacrifices have also been common in almost all nations. That some societies only, either few in number or for a very short time, abstained from the punishment of death, is rather favorable to my argument, for such is the fate of great truths, that their duration is only as a flash of lightning in the long and dark night of error."

Beccaria argued that criminal punishments should be just harsh enough to protect society, and no harsher. He attacked several common practices of the time, including the holding of criminal proceedings in secret and the torture of suspects. He was one of the first—if not the first—men of his age to make the progressive argument that education is a way of combating crime.

Although he was only twenty-six years old when his *Essay* was published, it immediately established him as a significant figure in the European Enlightenment. In addition to his contributions to penology, Beccaria was an important economist, who anticipated to some extent the theories of Adam Smith.

Ironically for someone who had attacked the penal policies of virtually every government of the time, Beccaria was showered with honors by many of those same governments. Austria even founded a prestigious chair in economics to lure him to that country.

More important than the personal honors was the effect his ideas had on penal reform—not just then, but long after his death. Translations of the *Essay* were quickly published in several languages. The first English translation came out in 1767, and the first American edition was published ten years later. The abolition of capital punishment in Tuscany and Austria in the 1780s has been credited largely to Beccaria's arguments. Catherine the Great of Russia, where the death penalty had already been abolished for most crimes in the 1750s, summoned Beccaria to help her establish a new criminal code.

Beccaria was not the only Enlightenment figure who favored penal reform. Voltaire, for example, published a detailed commentary on the *Essay*. It was Beccaria, though, who focused the attention of philosophers and political leaders on the issue. In addition to its effect in Europe, the *Essay* also had a significant effect on the thinking of abolitionists in America, including Dr. Benjamin Rush.

For Further Reading:
Beccaria, Cesare. *On Crimes and Punishments and Other Writings* (Cambridge Texts in the History of Political Thought). Richard Bellamy, ed. (Paperback). New York: Cambridge University Press, 1995. ISBN: 0521479827

Phillipson, Coleman. *Three Criminal Law Reformers: Beccaria, Bentham, Romilly.* (Paperback reprint). Montclair, NJ: Patterson Smith, 1970. ISBN: 0875859046

Hugo Adam Bedau (1926–)

University professor and author, the most prominent contemporary academic opponent of the death penalty.

Hugo Adam Bedau holds the Austin Fletcher Chair in Philosophy at Tufts University, where he was previously chairman of the Department of Philosophy. Professor Bedau was born in Portland, Oregon. He received his undergraduate education at the University of Redlands and went on to obtain a master's degree from Boston University, and another, as well as a Ph.D., from Harvard.

Bedau has served as the president of the American League to Abolish Capital Punishment. His extensive writings on the question include several books, including *The Death Penalty in America* (1964), which has been called "[t]he first completely comprehensive overview on the death penalty attempted by a scholar in this century"[1] (new and revised editions of which have since come out); *The Courts, the Constitution and Capital Punishment* (1977); and *Death Is Different: Studies in the Morality, Law and Politics of Capital Punishment* (1987); as well as innumerable studies, essays, and articles.

Although the bulk of Bedau's published writings have dealt with the death penalty, he has many other interests as well. They are demonstrated by his editorship of such books as *Civil Disobedience* (1969) and *Justice and Equality* (1971).

For Further Reading:
Bedau, Hugo Adam. *The Death Penalty in America: Current Controversies.* New York: Oxford University Press, 1997.

Jeremy Bentham (1748–1832)

British social philosopher, legal reformer, and economist who pressed for the restriction of the death penalty.

Bentham was a child prodigy with a genius for academic studies and a talent for the violin. As a young man, he attended Oxford University and was admitted to the bar. Instead of entering legal practice, however, he devoted himself to the study of ethics and the law. His book, *Introduction to the Principles of Morals and Legislation* (1789), is considered one of the most important philosophical works of the eighteenth century.

Bentham is best known as the cofounder and leading exponent of the philosophical doctrine known as utilitarianism. He believed that social and economic measures should be judged by the happiness or pleasure they produced. The best measures were the ones that produced the greatest happiness for the greatest number of people. Like Beccaria, who influenced his thinking, Bentham believed that a kind of moral arithmetic could be used to determine the utility—or usefulness—not only of social policies and institutions, but of the actions of individuals as well.

Also like Beccaria, he believed that the legal systems of his age needed reform. Among the reforms he suggested was the restriction, if not abolition, of capital punishment. Together with Sir Samuel Romilly, who pressed for similar reforms in the British parliament, Bentham helped lay the foundation for the massive reduction in the number of capital crimes in Britain that would occur in the decades following his death.

For Further Reading:

Bentham, Jeremy. *The Principles of Morals and Legislation* (Great Books in Philosophy). (Paperback). Lanham, MD: Prometheus Books, 1988. ISBN: 0879754346

Phillipson, Coleman. *Three Criminal Law Reformers: Beccaria, Bentham, Romilly.* (Reprint). Montclair, NJ: Patterson Smith, 1970. ISBN: 0875859046

Walter Berns (1919–)

A political scientist and educator, Berns is one of the leading contemporary spokesmen for the retentionist cause.

Born in Chicago, Illinois, Walter Berns received his undergraduate education at the University of Iowa and his postgraduate education at Reed College, the London School of Economics and Political Science, and the University of Chicago. He has served on the faculties of Yale and Cornell universities, among others. From 1979 to 1986 he was a resident scholar of the American Enterprise Institute, where he is currently the John M. Olin Distinguished Scholar, as well as a professor at Georgetown University.

Berns is the author of what has been described as "the land-mark book on the death penalty,"[2] *For Capital Punishment: Crime and the Morality of the Death Penalty* (1979). One of the nation's best-known constitutional scholars, Berns challenges the idea that the death penalty should be considered cruel and unusual punishment under the Eighth Amendment. What's more, he ar-gues that the death penalty is justified as an expression of soci-ety's moral outrage at certain heinous crimes.

For Further Reading:
Berns, Walter. *For Capital Punishment.* (Paperback reprint). Lanham, MD: University Press of America, 2000. ISBN: 0819181501

Marvin H. Bovee (1827–1888)

Nineteenth-century champion of the abolitionist cause.

Born and raised in a political family in the state of New York, Bovee moved to the Wisconsin Territory while still a teenager. The territory became a state in 1848, and four years later, Bovee won election as a Democrat to the state legislature.

Bovee led the fight to end the death penalty in Wisconsin. His efforts, helped by a gruesomely botched hanging in the Wis-consin city of Kenosha, were successful in 1853. Not willing to stop there, Bovee determined to carry the abolitionist fight throughout the country. From Nebraska to New Jersey, and from Missouri to Massachusetts, Bovee spent the rest of his life in largely unsuccessful efforts to deprive hangmen of their jobs. Al-though he did help to impose some restrictions on the use of the death penalty in several places, he was never again as successful as he'd been in Wisconsin.

In addition to his political efforts, Bovee published *Christ and the Gallows*, an important collection of anti–capital punish-ment letters and essays by prominent Americans.

For Further Reading:
Bovee, Marvin H. *Christ and the Gallows: Or, Reasons for the Abolition of Cap-ital Punishment.* (Reprint). New York: AMS Press, 1983. ISBN: 0404624030

William Joseph Brennan, Jr. (1906–1997)

Associate justice (1956–1990) of the U.S. Supreme Court, and op-ponent of the death penalty.

William Brennan was born and raised in Newark, New Jersey. The son of an Irish immigrant brewery worker and union leader, he grew up with a strong sense of social injustice and a desire to make a difference in the world.

An excellent student, Brennan graduated from the Wharton School and attended the prestigious Harvard Law School on scholarships. He practiced law in New Jersey until World War II broke out. He joined the army, where his background as the son of a union activist was put to wartime use when he was assigned to be a troubleshooter with defense industry unions for the undersecretary for war. After demobilization, he returned to his legal practice in New Jersey; soon, he was appointed to the state supreme court.

When Senator Joseph McCarthy began making wild and apparently unfounded charges that hundreds of American scholars, government employees, and ordinary citizens were communists, Brennan spoke out against him. This was considered a brave thing to do at a time when McCarthy had the power to destroy almost any young man's career. But Brennan wasn't damaged by his courageous stand; indeed, when President Dwight Eisenhower appointed him to the U.S. Supreme Court in 1956, McCarthy's vote was the only one cast against him.

Eisenhower, who was a Republican, would consider Brennan's appointment a big mistake when the new justice turned out to be much more of a "broad constructionist" than Eisenhower had expected him to be. In other words, Brennan tended to view broadly the rights and protections the Constitution grants to individuals, and he was very much at home in the liberal Court under Chief Justice Earl Warren. He played a leading role in the Warren Court's expansion of the Constitution's protections into areas where they had not been enforced before. These included rulings that encouraged racial desegregation, affirmative action, and civil rights in general. Brennan was particularly strong in upholding the rights of criminal defendants against the power of police and prosecutors.

Over the years, Brennan earned a reputation as a negotiator within the Court because he found ways for justices with differing views to reach consensus on important decisions. Almost a moderate by Warren Court standards, Brennan was considered increasingly liberal as the Burger and Rehnquist Courts of the late 1970s and 1980s became more and more conservative.

Brennan was never moderate when it came to the death penalty. He concurred in the *Furman* decision, although he wished it had gone further and unequivocally banned capital punishment forever. He was a bitter dissenter from *Gregg* in 1976 and from all the other decisions that followed upholding various state capital punishment statutes. Together with Justice Thurgood Marshall, he continued to vote against the death penalty in every case. Time and again, they dissented from Court decisions upholding death penalty statutes by repeating what retentionists regarded as a kind of abolitionist mantra: "[T]he death penalty is in all circumstances cruel and unusual punishment prohibited by the Eighth and Fourteenth Amendments."

Brennan retired from the Court in 1990, and died on 24 July 1997.

For Further Reading:

Mello, Michael. *Against the Death Penalty: The Relentless Dissents of Justices Brennan and Marshall.* Evanston, IL: Northwestern University Press, 1996. ISBN: 1555532616

Michelman, Frank I. *Brennan and Democracy.* Princeton, NJ: Princeton University Press, 1999. ISBN: 0691007152

Woodward, Bob, and Scott Armstrong. *The Brethren: Inside the Supreme Court.* New York: Simon and Schuster, 1979. ASIN: 0380521830

Rev. George Cheever (1807–1890)

Nineteenth-century clergyman, reformer, and advocate of the death penalty.

The son of a publisher in Hallowell, Maine, George Cheever attended Bowdoin College and Andover Seminary. He was ordained into the Congressional ministry in 1833 and took a post in Salem, Massachusetts. He later became pastor of a Presbyterian church in New York, and eventually of the Church of the Puritans in the same city.

A great believer in the power of the pen, Cheever once attacked a rival religion for its failure to produce great literature. Beginning with his stint in Salem, Cheever depended on his writings as much as his preaching to persuade the public to the rightness of his uncompromising beliefs. Combative by temperament and a reformer by conviction, Cheever was ardent in his published calls for an end to slavery and equally ardent in his defense of capital punishment. Early in his career, his printing press was destroyed by a mob angry with something he had written. As though that weren't bad enough, he was sued for libel, forced to pay a fine of $1,000, and thrown into jail for a month.

Undeterred, Cheever continued to pour out his convictions in print and eventually produced twenty-three books and some fifty pamphlets, speeches, and other literary works. He defended the death penalty on biblical grounds, and his *Defense of Capital Punishment* (1846) is considered the classic presentation of the American Protestant case for the death penalty.

For Cheever, the word of God, as set down in the Bible, was the final word on the matter. "The basis of argument for the death penalty against murder," he wrote in his *Defense*, "is found, along with the reason given for it, in *Gen. v. 6*: 'Whoso sheddeth man's blood, by man shall his blood be shed; for in the image of God made he man.'"

Although Cain, in *Genesis*, was not killed by God for murdering his brother Abel, "God himself would make Cain's own dread of being murdered, through all men's sense of justice, inextinguishable, by having it established as the first law of humanity that, if any man destroyed another another's life, his own life should go for it. And all the fiends of remorse, detection, and a righteous vengeance, with all the energies and vigilance of human selfishness itself, aghast with horror, should combine to arrest and exterminate the miscreant. This uproar of indignation and wrath was what Cain himself expected, when driven forth from the presence and protection of God."

"The penalty is restricted to murder," continued Cheever, "though some crimes against personal rights are equivalent to murder and produce it, and even worse, as, for example, slavery, and, in consequence, all the infinite horrors of the slave trade. And, therefore, there shines forth, illuminating and illustrating the law against murder, like another sun risen on midnoon, that other and later unparalleled Hebrew law in behalf of the enslaved: 'He that stealeth a man and selleth him, or if he be found in his hands, he shall surely be put to death.'"

Cheever argued that the death penalty was not only acceptable in the eyes of God but required. "Malice aforethough once proved, the crime is demonstrated, and nothing shall save the murderer, not even the city of refuge provided by God himself for a just trial, nor the intervention of any pardoning or interceding power, nor the altar of God. 'Thou shalt take the murderer from mine altar, that he may die.' (Ex. xxi. 14.) If not, if the murderer is let off with his life, then the whole land remains guilty, and the blood of the murdered man crieth unto God from the ground; for the primal curse is on this crime against God's image in mankind, and no atonement or restitution can be made for it by man; none shall be accepted."

But it was not only God's authority that made capital punishment a good idea. The abolition of capital punishment would invite all sorts of criminals to become murderers to evade capture. "But the certainty that a murderer cannot at any rate be punished with death would inevitably increase the crime, presenting such a powerful temptation to murder in self-defense, during the commission of any other crime whatever. This would make murderers out of common villains. It would tempt the midnight burglar even to begin his work of robbery even with assassination for security in the process, and then to complete it, double-locked from discovery by the death of all the witnesses. The law of God says to the criminal, Become a murderer and you are lost. The abolition of the penalty says, Murder, and you are saved."

The key to a just and effective exercise of the death penalty was inevitability. It must be made certain that "[t]he man who murders another kills himself. When the most hardened villain is made sure of that, who will strike the blow?

"In the United States . . . the proposed abolition of the divine law [calling for death for murderers] . . . would be more inhuman, reckless, and unjust than it would be to make a breach in one of the dikes in Holland, letting in the sea. God proposes to abolish the crime; man to abolish the penalty. God seeks our deliverance from sin; man our evasion of its consequences. Self-government under God is Heaven. Self-government without God is anarchy and Hell. Which will we choose?"

There was never any question which form of self-government the Reverend Cheever would choose.

At his death, Cheever left his excellent library to Howard University, the nation's leading black college at the time.

Newton M. Curtis (1835–1910)

Abolitionist congressman.

A native of upstate New York, Curtis distinguished himself as a soldier in the Union Army during the Civil War. He not only achieved the rank of brigadier general but won the Congressional Medal of Honor, the highest military award the United States can bestow.

Curtis served with the Reconstruction forces in Virginia for a time after the war before returning to his home state. Back in New York, he took up a series of jobs before entering the state assembly as a Republican in 1884. As a legislator, he championed the causes of prison reform, humane treatment for the mentally ill, and the abolition of the death penalty. He persuaded his colleagues in the assembly to pass a bill calling for the end to capital punishment, but the state senate refused to go along and the measure never became law.

In 1890, Curtis won election to the U.S. Congress, where he took up the cause of abolition on the national level by introducing a bill to end the death penalty in 1892. Although he never succeeded in persuading his colleagues to ban capital punishment outright, in 1897 he did convince them to lower the number of federal crimes punishable by death from sixty to only three.

George Mifflin Dallas (1792–1864)

A politician and statesman, Dallas was one of the most prominent American political figures of the early nineteenth century to take an active stand against the death penalty.

Dallas was born in Philadelphia, the son of Alexander James Dallas, one of the most important secretaries of the treasury in the history of the United States. George Dallas attended the College of New Jersey (now Princeton) before entering the bar in 1813. He began his distinguished career in public service as secretary to Albert Gallatin (the financier who had been secretary of the treasury under Thomas Jefferson) on an important peace mission to Moscow.

After his stint abroad, Dallas returned to Pennsylvania, where he became active in Republican politics and served in a series of legal and political offices. Shifting political allegiances, he became a supporter of Andrew Jackson. After Jackson's election as president, Dallas was first named district attorney in Philadelphia, and then, in 1831, appointed to fill out a term in the U.S. Senate. Retiring from the Senate when that term was over, Dallas served briefly as attorney general of Pennsylvania, only to lose that job when his party was turned out in 1835. Two years later,

Dallas returned to Russia, this time as U.S. minister, appointed by President Martin van Buren.

Dallas, a political enemy of James Buchanan, was nominated to run for vice president of the United States with James Polk. He and Polk were elected in 1844. Not long after, Dallas agreed to address the founding convention of the American Society for the Abolition of Capital Punishment, which picked him to be its first president. He served in both offices at the same time.

In his later years, Dallas was appointed U.S. minister to Great Britain by President Pierce, holding that office until the Republican Abraham Lincoln was elected president and the Civil War began. It was said of Dallas that he "hated abolition [of slavery] and secession both, as he hated all extremes."[3] It might have been added that he also hated the extreme punishment of death. To this day, Dallas remains the highest ranking official in the history of the United States to take an active and absolute stand against the death penalty.

For Further Reading:
Belohlavek, John M. *George Mifflin Dallas: Jacksonian Patrician.* University Park, PA: Pennsylvania State University Press, 1977. ISBN: 0271005106

Clarence Darrow (1857–1938)

Defense attorney and prominent opponent of capital punishment.

Darrow was a product of rural America. Born in Kinsman, Ohio, he passed his law examination in 1878 without having earned a university degree. He began practicing law in Ashtabula, Ohio, but moved to the big city of Chicago, Illinois, in 1888.

Darrow worked as an attorney for the city of Chicago and later for big business corporations, including the Chicago and Northwestern Railroad. Because he had always felt a natural sympathy with ordinary workers, he never felt entirely comfortable with the way most big companies treated their employees. When Eugene V. Debs, the head of a striking railroad workers union, was thrown into jail in 1894, Darrow resigned his job with Chicago and Northwestern and went to work defending Debs. He quickly established himself as the nation's best-known legal champion of underdogs, from political radicals to ordinary citizens, charged with capital crimes.

Darrow hated the death penalty and took on many cases just to save defendants from the gallows. He prided himself on the fact that he had defended more than 100 people who faced the death penalty, and he never lost one defendant to the executioner. Among them were Big Bill Haywood, the union leader accused of conspiring in the murder of Governor Steuenberg of Idaho in 1905; James and John McNamera, brothers charged with planting a bomb in the offices of the *Los Angeles Times* in 1911; and—the most infamous of all his defendents—Richard Loeb and Nathan Leopold.

A year after his success in saving Leopold and Loeb from the gallows, Darrow joined with Lewis E. Lawes and others to found the American League to Abolish Capital Punishment. For the next several decades, the League provided the main base for the agitation against the death penalty in the United States.

Darrow's last famous client was John Scopes, a schoolteacher accused of violating a Tennessee law against teaching the theory of evolution. Scopes was prosecuted by the frequent presidential candidate, William Jennings Bryan. Because of the presence of these renowned antagonists, the case generated enormous national interest. Parts of it were even broadcast on live radio. Scopes was found guilty, but the verdict was later overturned on a technicality.

Darrow retired from the law in 1927, although he spent much of his later years writing. Among his published writings are an early novel, *Farmington* (1904), *Crime: Its Cause and Treatment* (1922), and his autobiography, *The Story of My Life* (1932). A collection of several of Darrow's summations, edited by Arthur Weinberg, was published under the title *Attorney for the Damned* in 1957.

For Further Reading:

Attorney for the Damned: Clarence Darrow in the Courtroom. Edited and with notes by Arthur Weinberg; foreword by William O. Douglas. Chicago: University of Chicago Press, 1989. ISBN: 0226136493

Darrow, Clarence. *Clarence Darrow on Capital Punishment.* Evanston, IL: Chicago Historical Bookworks, 1991. ISBN: 9990800251

———. *The Story of My Life.* Introduction by Alan M. Dershowitz. New York: Da Capo Press, 1996. ISBN: 0306807386

Joseph-Ignace Guillotin (1738–1814)

The French doctor who designed and gave his name to the guillotine.

Guillotin was a professor of the medical sciences at the Paris Faculty of Medicine at the time of the French Revolution, and he was also an influential member of the revolutionary National Assembly. Guillotin was deeply interested in penal reform in general and in the death penalty in particular. At the time of the French Revolution, members of the aristocracy were executed in a different way from members of the lower classes. A democratic idealist, Guillotin believed that legal punishments should be identical for all, regardless of their wealth, power, or social standing.

In December 1789, Guillotin proposed to the National Assembly that a beheading machine should be used for all executions in France. Not only would such a machine be more democratic, he argued, but it would be quicker and more humane than any method currently being used. The Assembly was not immediately convinced by his arguments, but in 1792 it did authorize a decapitating machine to be the sole method of executing people in France.

By that time, Dr. Guillotin had given up his campaign for *la machine*, and the device was originally dubbed the *louisette* or *louison*, after another prominent physician, Dr. Antoine Louis, who had picked up Guillotin's proposal. In later years, the machine became known as the guillotine, after its first sponsor in France. Despite his support for the machine, the idealistic Dr. Guillotin was always uncomfortable with the fact that a death device was known by his name.

Dr. Guillotin died in Paris, of natural causes, on 26 March 1814.

For Further Reading:
Gerould, Daniel. *Guillotine: It's Legend and Lore*. (Paperback). New York: Blast Books, 1992. ISBN: 0922233020

Rev. Joe Ingle (1948–)

Minister, abolitionist, and prison reformer.

Joe Ingle is a minister of the United Church of Christ and one of the nation's most vocal opponents of the death penalty. He lives in Nashville, Tennessee, but works throughout the South— the heartland of the American death penalty. He is the first, and so far the only, director of the Southern Coalition on Jails and Prisons, founded in the mid-1970s to promote prison reform and the abolition of capital punishment. Ingle does what he can to minister to the spiritual needs of the hundreds of prisoners on death row in the southern states while working to remove the threat of execution that hangs over them.

Ingle is fiercely and uncompromisingly opposed to capital punishment, which he believes has made the United States a society of murderers. He stresses the need for all Americans to take responsibility for the executions that are carried out in their names. He believes that U.S. use of the death penalty—directed primarily against the poor, black people, and those of all races who kill white people—parallels the situation in the early days of Nazi rule in Germany.

Ingle's tireless opposition to the death penalty has attracted international attention. He was nominated for the Nobel Peace Prize in 1988 and 1989.

Jack Ketch (?–1686)

A legendary executioner in seventeenth-century England.

Jack (or John) Ketch is the most famous—or infamous—executioner in history. He reigned over the English scaffold in the days when victims were either hanged or beheaded, and sometimes quartered after death. Because of his varied duties, Ketch is sometimes pictured with a rope in one hand and an axe or hatchet in the other.

The most famous of Ketch's victims was James Scott, the Duke of Monmouth and pretender to the throne of England. Monmouth's beheading on 15 July 1685 was not only the most important execution of Ketch's career but the most trying. For some reason, Ketch found it much harder than usual to sever the head from the body. After a few blows, he tried to give up the effort entirely and had to be threatened into returning to complete the job.

In Britain, the name "Jack Ketch" means "executioner" in much the same way that "Benedict Arnold" means "traitor" in the United States. But Ketch may not have been the infamous executioner's real name. Tyburn Prison, where criminals were held in Ketch's time, had long been leased to a family named Jacquet; it is thought that Jack Ketch might be a mispronunciation of that name. Whatever his real name, the executioner known as Jack Ketch died in 1686.

Lewis E. Lawes (1883–1947)

The warden of Sing Sing Prison who became a leading advocate for prison reform and the abolition of capital punishment.

Born and raised in upstate New York, Lawes went into the army as a young man. Mustered out in 1904, he got a job as a guard in the New York state prison at Dannemora. As he worked his way up in the penal system, he served in a variety of posts at several state institutions; in 1920, he was appointed to the top job at Sing Sing prison in Ossining, New York.

At that time, Sing Sing was regarded as the toughest state prison in New York. It housed many of the state's most hardened prisoners, as well as the electric chair, which had been moved there from its original home at Auburn.

Lawes was a hard-headed penologist who would run Sing Sing effectively for more than twenty years. He was also a man of compassion and sympathy, even for the worst of the criminals he confined. Both sides of his nature led him to institute a variety of reforms aimed at increasing efforts to rehabilitate prisoners and making the prison experience more humane.

His belief in reform and rehabilitation led him to change his mind about the death penalty. Initially a firm supporter of capital punishment, within three years of his appointment to Sing Sing he came to see executions as primitive, futile, and cruel. He quickly became the nation's most prominent example of an advocate of the death penalty who was converted into an opponent by being required to take part in carrying it out.

In 1925, Lawes helped found the American League to Abolish Capital Punishment, and he remained an active spokesperson for the abolitionist cause, even while continuing to supervise executions in his job as warden. He explained his opposition to the death penalty in *Man's Judgment of Death* in 1923 and again in *Life and Death in Sing Sing* in 1928. Other books by Lewis Lawes include *Twenty-Thousand Years in Sing Sing* (1932) and *Meet the Murderer!* (1940).

For Further Reading:
Lawes, Lewis Edward. *Man's Judgement of Death: An Analysis of the Operation and Effect of Capital Punishment Based on Facts.* Montclair, NJ: Patterson Smith, 1969. ASIN 0875850626

Edward Livingston (1764–1836)

A distinguished American lawyer and statesman and the author of an influential argument against capital punishment.

Livingston was born in Clermont, New York. In 1804, he moved west to the territory of Orleans, which had just been purchased from France. He served on Andrew Jackson's staff during the war of 1812, and later represented Louisiana in the U.S. House of representatives (1823–1829) and the Senate (1829–1831). Under the presidency of his old commander, Andrew Jackson, Livingston served first as secretary of state (1831–1833) and later as minister to France (1833–1835).

In the 1820s, the Louisiana legislature asked Livingston to draft a new penal code for the state. His "Introductory Report," which was originally written in 1824 and published in 1833, presented a detailed argument against capital punishment, providing what Supreme Court Justice Thurgood Marshall would later describe as "a tremendous impetus to the abolition movement for the next half century."[4]

Thurgood Marshall (1908–1993)

Associate justice (1967–1991) of the U.S. Supreme Court and opponent of the death penalty.

First as a civil rights attorney and later on the U.S. Supreme Court, Thurgood Marshall was a champion of the rights of minorities and a bitter enemy of the death penalty.

Born and raised in Baltimore, Maryland, in the days of segregation, Marshall attended the kind of public schools he would later play a major role in desegregating. He received his higher education in the black college system, earning his A.B. from Lincoln University in 1930 and his law degree from Howard in 1933.

He worked in private practice in Maryland for a while, then moved to New York, where he did legal work for the National Association for the Advancement of Colored People (NAACP). By the late 1930s, he had joined the NAACP full time, becoming the director of its Legal Defense and Education Fund in 1940. His position with the fund put him at the center of the legal battle to end segregation, which would come to a head in the 1950s.

Marshall fought and won the historic *Brown v. Board of Education* (1954) case that put an end to legal segregation in public schools. Even more importantly, *Brown* signaled an end to the doctrine of "separate but equal" in society at large.

Marshall was appointed to the United States Circuit Court in 1961 and to the position of solicitor general of the United States—sometimes called the government's lawyer—in 1965. Two years later, President Lyndon Johnson appointed him associate justice of the United States Supreme Court. He was the first black justice ever to sit on the nation's highest court.

Both his personal experience as a black man in the Middle South and his work with the NAACP had made Marshall bitterly aware of the injustices in American society—and had also made him more conscious than most of the value of constitutional rights and the need to enforce and expand them. This became his mission on the Court, which he felt was the greatest engine for change in American society.

When it came to the death penalty, Marshall was a committed abolitionist. He opposed capital punishment both as unjust in itself and because he believed that it would inevitably be applied disproportionately to racial minorities, the poor, and the politically unpopular. Marshall's was the leading voice in the 1972 *Furman* decision, which struck down all existing death penalty statutes. Although some of the five concurring justices held out the possibility that new, constitutional death penalty laws could be drafted, Marshall disagreed. He insisted that *any* capital punishment would be cruel and unusual in a modern society.

Marshall was a bitter dissenter when the Court reinstated capital punishment with the *Gregg* decision four years later, and the night the decision was announced, he suffered a heart attack.[5]

Despite his collapsing health, Marshall remained on the Court for another fifteen years. Throughout that time, he and his fellow abolitionist, William Brennan, continued to dissent from every decision that affirmed a death sentence, arguing that "the death penalty is in all circumstances cruel and unusual punishment prohibited by the Eighth and Fourteenth Amendments."

A conservative, retentionist majority dominated the Court during Marshall's last years there. He and Brennan found themselves increasingly isolated as they fought to hold back the Court's drive to facilitate the use of the death penalty. Marshall hoped to remain on the Court until a more liberal president won the White House and replaced him with someone of similar views. By the summer of 1991, this had not happened; Marshall could no longer fulfill his duties, and he retired.

When Bill Clinton, the more liberal president Marshall had hoped for, was finally elected in 1992, he invited Marshall to swear him in at the inauguration ceremony. Unfortunately, when the inauguration day came, Marshall was in the hospital and unable to attend. He died the following week. To the end, he considered his inability to persuade a majority of his colleagues to abolish the death penalty the greatest failure of his career on the Court. President Clinton eulogized Marshall as "a giant in the quest for human rights,"[6] and Lawrence Tribe, the famous law professor, called him "the greatest lawyer of the twentieth century."[7]

Marshall's body was laid in state at the Supreme Court building, the site of his greatest triumphs and his most galling failures. It rested on the same bier that had held the body of Abraham Lincoln more than a century before.

For Further Reading:

Mello, Michael. *Against the Death Penalty: The Relentless Dissents of Justices Brennan and Marshall.* Evanston, IL: Northwestern University Press, 1996. ISBN: 1555532616

Woodward, Bob, and Scott Armstrong. *The Brethren: Inside the Supreme Court.* New York: Simon and Schuster, 1979. ASIN: 0380521830

Albert Pierrepoint (1905–1992)

The most prolific British executioner of the twentieth century.

The son and nephew of hangmen, Albert determined to follow in his relatives' footsteps while he was still a boy. He achieved his ambition when he was in his twenties, eventually attaining the position of Britain's chief executioner in 1946.

Pierrepoint's first victim in his new post would prove to be the most notorious: William Joyce, better known as Lord Haw Haw, the Brooklyn-born British and American citizen condemned as a traitor for broadcasting Nazi propaganda into England during World War II.

Before he retired in 1956, Pierrepoint claimed credit for executing 450 people, including seventeen women. Although he never publicly expressed guilt for what he had done, he did become an opponent of capital punishment in his retirement. His change of heart was based, at least partly, on his long experience in the trade.

An autobiography, *Executioner: Pierrepoint: The Amazing Autobiography of the World's Most Famous Executioner,* was published in 1974 but is out of print and no longer available.

William Hubbs Rehnquist (1924–)

Associate justice (1972–1986) and chief justice of the U.S. Supreme Court (1986–) who has consistently defended the death penalty.

Born in Milwaukee, Wisconsin, William Rehnquist graduated from Stanford Law School in 1951. He served as law clerk for Supreme Court Justice Robert H. Jackson for two years before moving to Phoenix, Arizona, to practice law. While there, he was active in conservative political affairs and opposed efforts to encourage racial integration in the city.

Rehnquist returned to Washington, D.C., in 1969 to serve as assistant attorney general for the Supreme Court's Office of Legal Counsel. President Richard Nixon appointed him associate justice of the Court in 1972, and President Ronald Reagan appointed Rehnquist chief justice in 1986.

In both positions, Rehnquist has been a law-and-order justice, reliably supporting the rights of law enforcement officials over the rights of the accused in most criminal cases. In particular, Rehnquist argues that, although states are required to treat citizens fairly, the restrictions on governmental power laid down in the Bill of Rights do not necessarily apply to them.

Rehnquist has been a staunch and consistent defender of the death penalty. He was a dissenter in the *Furman* decision, and firmly in the majority on *Gregg*. As the more liberal justices aged and left the Court in the 1980s and more conservative justices came onto it, Rehnquist became the head of a solid pro–capital punishment majority. Although he has been enthusiastically joined by fellow justices Antonin Scalia, Byron White, and Sandra Day O'Connor, Rehnquist has been the guiding spirit in the recent drive to see that obstacles to the enforcement of the death penalty are removed.

In recent years, the Rehnquist Court has ruled, among other things, that it is permissible to execute teenagers and the mentally retarded. Convinced that condemned criminals and their attorneys have been abusing the system by taking advantage of technical delays, Rehnquist has led a frequently successful effort to streamline appeal procedures in capital cases.

Under his leadership, the Court has shown increasing reluctance to listen to death sentence appeals. Even when the Court has extended constitutional protections to cover new situations, it has refused to make those protections retroactive and apply them to prisoners already under sentence of death. Writing for the majority, for example, Rehnquist has ordered that defendants may not appeal "good faith interpretations of existing precedents made by state courts even though they are shown to be contrary to later decisions."[8] In addition, the Rehnquist Court has refused to allow inmates to appeal to federal courts on the basis of issues they neglected to raise earlier in state courts, however much merit those issues may have.

It was the Rehnquist Court that fired off an impatient fax to judges in California, ordering them to stop granting stays of execution to Robert Alton Harris in 1992. It was also Rehnquist who led the 7 to 2 majority denying Leonel Herrera the right to a new trial in 1993, despite evidence that the condemned man might have been innocent after all.

Supporters of capital punishment, who feel that criminals are allowed to escape justice for far too long, applaud Rehnquist's determination to remove procedural obstacles to swift and certain execution. Opponents of the death penalty criticize these efforts and see them as a potentially fatal attack on the constitutional right of habeas corpus.

For Further Reading:
Woodward, Bob, and Scott Armstrong. *The Brethren: Inside the Supreme Court*. New York: Simon and Schuster, 1979. ASIN: 0380521830

Yarbrough, Tinsley E. *The Rehnquist Court and the Constitution*. New York: Oxford University Press, 2000.

Sir Samuel Romilly (1757–1818)

The most important legal reformer in the British Parliament in the early nineteenth century and an advocate for reducing the number of crimes punishable by death.

Romilly was admitted to the English bar in 1783. He was deeply influenced by the Enlightenment that was taking place on the continent and was particularly intrigued by the ideas of Rousseau and other French thinkers. His *Letters Containing an Account of the Late Revolution in France* (1792) welcomed the French Revolution; his *Thoughts on Executive Justice* (1786) was heavily influenced by Cesare Beccaria's calls for penal reform. Romilly was appointed solicitor general in 1806 and later, when he became a member of Parliament, he attempted to put Beccaria-inspired reforms into practice.

Romilly was particularly appalled by the excessive use of the death penalty. When he first took office, more than 200 crimes were punishable by death in England, most of them relatively minor offenses. As Jeremy Bentham's chief ally in Parliament, he set out to reduce that number. Although only somewhat successful during his lifetime, his efforts began a legislative process that would lead to the abolition of the death penalty for the vast majority of criminal offenses by the middle of the nineteenth century.

For Further Reading:
Phillipson, Coleman. *Three Criminal Law Reformers: Beccaria, Bentham, Romilly.* (Reprint, paperback). Montclair, NJ: Patterson Smith, June 1970. ISBN: 0875859046

Dr. Benjamin Rush (1745–1813)

"The father of the movement to abolish capital punishment in the United States."[9]

Born in Pennsylvania, Rush was a highly educated man for his time. He received his colonial education at what is now known as Princeton University, then went abroad to complete his studies at the University of Edinburgh in Scotland. Returning to America, he became professor of chemistry at the College of Philadelphia.

Considered the leading American medical man of his time, he had an enormous influence on the development of medicine in the United States. Among other medical distinctions, he is regarded as the founder of American psychiatry, and he authored the first book on the subject to be published in the United States.

A physician by profession, Rush was a crusading reformer by temperament. Active in the movement for American independence, he was a signer of the Declaration of Independence and a member of the Continental Congress. During the Revolution, he was made surgeon general of the Continental Army.

Even compared to many of his fellow revolutionaries, Rush was a fiercely independent thinker. He took pride in attacking popular ideas that he believed were wrong or misguided. Among them was the traditional practice of executing criminals.

In 1787, Rush presented a talk on the reform of the American criminal justice system at the home of his friend, Benjamin Franklin. He proposed that the new nation being formed should deal with its criminals in an entirely new way. He urged the establishment of a new kind of jail, one that would not just imprison criminals but reform them as well. This was a novel idea in the eighteenth-century United States, but Rush believed that such prisons would not just protect law-abiding citizens from criminals, they would redeem the criminals and transform them into decent and useful members of society. Rush urged the abandonment of the death penalty as a central element of his reforms.

Rush's address was published in the foreword of an essay titled *An Enquiry into the Effects of Public Punishments upon Criminals and upon Society.* He published a second essay, which dealt in more detail with the specific issue of capital punishment. Titled *Considerations on the Injustice and Impolicy of Punishing Murder by Death,* it was, in his own words, "the boldest attack" he ever made on a public policy. It aroused a storm of controversy that caused him to publish two revised versions. The final version, titled *An Enquiry into the Consistency of the Punishment of Murder by Death, with Reason and Revelation,* was published in 1798.[10]

Although the main thrust of Rush's quarrel with capital punishment was religious, he also put forth many secular arguments that have a surprisingly modern ring. Several are still being put forward today by people who base their opposition to capital punishment not on Rush but on recent psychological and sociological research. According to Philip Mackey, in his book *Voices against Death,* "Rush apparently invented his argument[s] that capital punishment makes convictions harder to obtain, that murderers are usually not hardened criminals likely to murder again, and that the death penalty invites murders by those who want the state to help them commit suicide."[11]

For Further Reading:

Hawke, David Freeman. *Benjamin Rush, Revolutionary Gadfly.* Indianapolis, IN: Bobbs-Merrill, 1971.

Mackey, Philip. *Voices against Death.* New York: Burt Franklin & Company, 1976. ASIN: 0891020381

Harvey Schwartzchild (1926–)

A leading twentieth-century opponent of the death penalty.

Born in Germany, Henry Schwartzchild fled his native country as a young man at the start of World War II. Like many of his fellow refugees from Naziism, he came to the United States. Here, he attended Colombia University, receiving his degree in time to serve with U.S. counterintelligence during the war. He later served in important research posts with the U.S. Department of State and the Rand School of Social Science, and in various positions with organizations such as the International Rescue Committee and the Anti-Defamation League of B'nai B'rith.

Vitally concerned with social justice, he joined the civil rights movement early, putting his body on the line as well as his professional abilities. He participated in sit-ins in the early 1960s and later served as executive director of the Lawyers Constitutional Defense Committee in the deep South. In the 1970s, he was director of the ACLU's Project on Amnesty for Vietnam War Resisters, an organization that helped make it possible for thousands of young Americans to return to their homes. Despite these many activities, his major work has been the battle against the death penalty.

For years now, Schwartzchild has been one of the nation's most active abolitionists and one of the movement's most prominent voices. He was the founder and first director of the National Coalition to Abolish the Death Penalty (NCADP), which has proven vital to the abolitionist movement in its role as a bridge and clearinghouse for anti–death penalty groups all over the country. Even while staying active with the NCADP, Schwartzchild served as director of the American Civil Liberties Union Capital Punishment Project until 1992, when his place was taken by Diann Rust-Tierney.

Potter Stewart (1915–1985)

Associate justice (1958–1981) of the U.S. Supreme Court, and perhaps the chief architect of the *Gregg* decision.

Potter Stewart was born and bred in Ohio. People said that it was this Midwestern background that nurtured the common-sense attitude and gift for negotiation he brought with him to the U.S. Supreme Court.

The son of an Ohio Supreme Court judge and one-time mayor of Cincinnati, Stewart was all but predestined for the bench. After graduating from college, he won a fellowship at Cambridge University in England. Returning to the United States, he attended the prestigious Yale Law School and entered the bar in 1941. An extremely promising career as a Wall Street lawyer was interrupted by a stint in the navy during World War II. After returning briefly to Wall Street, he moved back to Cincinnati to follow in his father's footsteps, becoming prominent in both politics and the law.

President Dwight Eisenhower appointed Stewart to the Sixth Circuit Federal Court of Appeals in 1954 and to the U.S. Supreme Court in 1958. Stewart was not an ideological judge. He liked to base his rulings on narrow questions of the law rather than on grand constitutional issues. At the same time, he could couch his judicial decisions in no-nonsense language that everyone could understand. Although he might not have been able to define pornography, he admitted in one ruling, "I know it when I see it."[12]

Stewart's lack of ideology earned him a reputation as an important and influential swing vote on the Supreme Court. He sometimes voted with Marshall and the liberals, and sometimes with Rehnquist and the conservatives; he often helped find ways for majorities to solidify in the middle ground between the two. His tendency to be a swing vote was particularly apparent on votes involving the death penalty.

Although Stewart voted with the majority in *Furman*, helping to strike down the capital punishment laws in 1972, he wrote a separate opinion in which he argued that it was primarily the capriciousness and arbitrariness of the laws that made them unconstitutional, not the death penalty itself.

When the majority of the Court was ready to reinstate the death penalty in the *Gregg* case in 1976, it was Stewart's negotiating ability and instinct to find compromise that helped them find the way to do it. More than anyone else, Stewart was the architect of the plurality decision that he announced for the Court.[13] For better or worse, that decision laid the foundation for the approach the Court has taken toward the death penalty ever since.

Events

A Plea for the Lives of the Notorious "Thrill" Killers Leopold and Loeb

Both Richard Loeb and Nathan Leopold were intellectually gifted scions of wealthy Chicago families. As young men, they were drawn together by common backgrounds and interests, but their friendship was unhealthy and insular: They assured each other that they were fundamentally superior to other people and somehow above the moral and criminal laws that bound other members of society. At least partly to prove their supposed superiority, they planned and carried out what they expected to be the perfect crime. This turned out to be a surprisingly slapdash kidnapping and murder of a fourteen-year-old boy. Not nearly as clever as they thought they were, they were soon caught and indicted for their crime.

There was enormous prejudice against the defendants in the city of Chicago. They were not only wealthy in a heavily working class city, but Jewish in a city that was rife with anti-Semitism. What's more, their crime was not only heartless but pointless, and they expressed no remorse for it.

Frightened for their children's lives, the Leopold and Loeb families hired the famous Chicago attorney Clarence Darrow to defend them. Realizing there was no chance to win an acquittal, Darrow pleaded both clients guilty. Waiving their right to a jury trial, Darrow appealed directly to the judge, John R. Caverly, to spare their lives.

The speech that Darrow directed to Judge Caverly was not a legal argument of the facts of the case, but an emotional attack on the death penalty. It is considered one of the greatest pleas ever delivered in an American courtroom.

Darrow made clear that he was pleading not just for the lives of Leopold and Loeb but for the lives of all defendants, for nothing less than an end to the death penalty.

> I know that every step in the progress of humanity has been met and opposed by prosecutors, and many times by the courts. I know that when poaching and petty larceny were punishable by death in England, juries refused to convict. They were too humane to obey the law; and judges refused to sentence . . . I know that every step in the progress of the world in reference to crime has come from the human feelings of man. . . .
>
> Gradually, the laws have been changed and modified, and men look back with horror at the hangings and killings of the past. What did they find in England? That as they got rid of these barbarous statutes, crimes decreased instead of increased; as

the criminal law was modified and humanized, there was less crime instead of more. I will undertake to say, Your Honor, that you can scarcely find a single book written by a student—and I will include all the works on criminology of the past—that has not made the statement over and over again that as the penal code was made less terrible, crimes grew less frequent.

I am not pleading so much for these boys as I am for the infinite number of others to follow, those who perhaps cannot be as well defended as these have been, those who may go down in the storm and the tempest without aid. It is of them that I am thinking, and for them I am begging of this court not to turn backward toward the barbarous and cruel past.

Darrow implored Judge Caverly to ignore public sentiment.

The easy thing and the popular thing to do is to hang my clients. I know it. Men and women who do not think will applaud. The cruel and thoughtless will approve. It will be easy today; but in Chicago, and reaching out over the length and breadth of the land, more and more fathers and mothers, the humane, the kind, and the hopeful, who are gaining an understanding and asking not only about these poor boys, but about their own—these will join in no acclaim at the death of my clients. They would ask that the shedding of blood be stopped, and that the normal feelings of man resume their sway. And as the days and the months and the years go on, they will ask it more and more. But, Your Honor, what they shall ask might not count. I know the easy way. I know Your Honor stands between the future and the past. I know the future is with me, and what I stand for here; not merely the lives of these two unfortunate lads, but for all boys and girls; for all of the young, and, as far as possible, for all of the old. I am pleading for life, understanding, charity, kindness, and the infinite mercy that considers all. I am pleading that we overcome cruelty with kindness, and hatred with love.

Darrow saw the abolition of capital punishment as inevitable. "I know that the future is on my side," he told the judge, inviting him to join in the march toward that future.

Your Honor stands between the past and the future. You may hang these boys; you may hang them by the neck until they are dead. But in doing it you will turn your face toward the past. In doing it you are making it harder for every other boy who, in ignorance and in darkness, must grope his way through the mazes that only childhood knows. In doing it you will make it harder for unborn children. You may save them and make it easier for every child that sometime may stand where these boys stand. You will make it easier for every human being with an aspiration and a vision and a hope and a fate.

I am pleading for the future; I am pleading for a time when hatred and cruelty will not control the hearts of men, when we can learn by reason and judgment and understanding and faith that all life is worth saving, and that mercy is the highest attribute of man.

Clearly moved by Darrow's plea (according to a reporter, tears appeared in Caverly's eyes at one point), the judge sentenced the young men to life plus ninety-nine years in prison.

While still a young man, Richard Loeb was stabbed to death in a dispute with a fellow prisoner in 1936. Nathan Leopold became a model prisoner and was eventually paroled in 1958. The same year, he published *Life Plus 99 Years*, which documented what he claimed was his rehabilitation in prison. Soon after being released, Leopold moved to Puerto Rico, where he would spend the rest of his life working with a religious group.

For Further Reading:

Classics of the Courtroom: Clarence Darrow's Sentencing Speech in State of Illinois vs. Leopold & Loeb. Edited by Irving Younger. Minnetonka, MN: Professional Education Group, 1988. ISBN: 0943380146

Higdon, Hal. *Leopold & Loeb: The Crime of the Century.* Champagne, IL: University of Illinois Press, 1999. ISBN: 0252068297.

Logan, John. *Never the Sinner: The Leopold and Loeb Story.* New York: Penguin, 1999. ISBN: 0879519304

The Futile Struggle of Caryl Chessman (1920–1960)

The highly publicized struggle of thief and kidnapper Caryl Chessman, who tried to avoid execution, aroused public sympathy for him and opposition to the death penalty in the 1950s.

Born on 27 May 1920 in St. Joseph, Michigan, Chessman was always a sickly and disturbed child. Quick to cry and equally quick to fly into a rage, he showed an early streak of cruelty; he later said this trait caused him to strike out even at things he loved.

While he was still very young, the family moved to California. Chessman's early life there was wracked with disaster. His mother was partially paralyzed in an accident, and the resulting medical bills impoverished the family. Chessman's criminal career began with childhood thefts to help feed and support them. Before long, he had progressed to stealing automobiles for thrill rides and other more serious crimes.

In his mid-teens, he was caught and sentenced to a forestry camp for juvenile delinquents. He escaped twice and was twice recaptured. When he was transferred to a more secure reform school, he became even more hardened than he had been before. Almost as soon as he was released, he began a new career: holding up houses of prostitution. He was arrested in the process of committing a burglary on his seventeenth birthday and returned to prison.

Released in 1939, Chessman had ambitions to become a writer, but in the meantime he continued his criminal career. Falling in with a group of other young criminals, he embarked on a string of armed robberies, burglaries, and other crimes. When Chessman and his cohorts were captured in a violent encounter with police, the press referred to them as the Boy Bandit Gang. Except for a brief period during which he escaped, he spent the next several years in various California prisons until he was paroled in December 1947.

Less than two months later, on 23 January 1947, he was arrested in Hollywood, California. Police suspected him of being the notorious "Red Light Bandit" who had been terrorizing couples parked in lovers' lanes in the Los Angeles area. The bandit had a red light in his car, like the ones the police used. He would approach the couples as though he were a policeman, then pull out a gun and rob them. In some cases, he would force the woman to go off with him and sexually attack her. After questioning by the police, Chessman confessed to the crimes, although he later claimed the confession had been beaten out of him.

Chessman was charged with robbery and kidnapping. Under California law at that time, taking a woman anywhere for the purpose of rape was considered kidnapping, so Chessman was liable to the death penalty, although no rape had taken place. At the trial, Chessman chose to defend himself. He was found guilty, and on 25 June 1948 he was sentenced to death. He was sent back to San Quentin prison, this time to a cell on death row.

For the next eleven years and eleven months, Chessman waged a fierce battle to save his life. Teaching himself the ins and outs of the legal system, he used every device he could think of to delay his execution and reverse his sentence. Fulfilling his earlier ambition to be a writer, he published two best-selling books about his case, *Cell 2455 Death Row* and *Trial by Ordeal.* He also wrote another less popular book, *The Face of Justice,* which dealt with the broader issues of life and death.

Altogether, Chessman would file almost fifty appeals against his conviction and sentence, and fifteen of them would reach the Supreme Court of the United Sates. There were many legitimate questions about his conviction. He clearly had not been able to mount a professional defense. The trial judge had shown prejudice against him, and much of the transcript of the trial had been lost. The noted criminologist, Dr. Harry Elmer Barnes, remarked that it would require restraint to describe the trial merely "as one of the most fantastic travesties of justice in the history of civilized criminal jurisprudence."[14]

Thanks to his remarkable talent for publicizing his cause, people around the world were inspired to join in support of Chessman's long battle to escape the executioner. Among the thousands of foreign voices raised in protest were those of the British author J. B. Priestly, humanitarian Albert Schweitzer, and even the official newspaper of the Vatican. Despite the widespread and emotional sympathy for him, Chessman's appeals eventually ran out. He was put to death in the gas chamber at San Quentin on 2 May 1960. It was the eighth official date that had been set for his execution.

A wave of anti–death penalty sentiment swept much of the Western world in the late 1950s and 1960s; revulsion at Chessman's death accelerated that sentiment, which eventually resulted in the abolition of capital punishment in several countries and its temporary abandonment in the United States.

For Further Reading:

Chessman, Caryl. *Cell 2455 Death Row.* Reissue. Westport, CT: Greewood Press, 1969. ISBN: 837116317

Kunstler, William M. *Beyond a Reasonable Doubt?: The Original Trial of Caryl Chessman.* Westport, CT: Greenwood, 1973. ISBN: 0837–1695–18

The Trial and Execution of Sacco and Vanzetti

The execution of Sacco and Vanzetti raised concerns that the U.S. government was using capital punishment to eliminate its enemies.

Nicola Sacco and Bartolomeo Vanzetti were Italian immigrants to the United States in the early part of the twentieth century. Sacco was a shoe worker and Vanzetti a fish peddler. Both were proud and active anarchists who had been under investigation by the police because of their antigovernment political activities even before their 1920 arrest following a bank robbery in South Braintree, Massachusetts. Because two people had been killed in the robbery, the men were charged with murder as well as armed robbery. Both insisted that they were innocent of the crime and that they were being railroaded because of their political beliefs.

Their trial received an enormous amount of attention, not only in the United States but in Europe as well. In many people's minds, here and abroad, it was a test of whether the U.S. government could deal fairly with political radicals accused of crime. People everywhere took sides either for or against Sacco and Vanzetti.

Much of the American public was hostile to the defendants, either because they were immigrants or because they were anarchists, or both. The Russian Revolution had taken place only a few years before, and many Americans feared that "foreign" communists and anarchists were plotting to stage a similar violent uprising here.

Others, both in the United States and abroad, firmly believed that the men were innocent; the two men may have been anarchists, but they did not seem to be the sort of people who would wantonly rob and kill. The left regarded the case less as a criminal prosecution than as a political persecution. To these observers, the trial seemed blatantly unfair and the judge hope-lessly prejudiced against the defendants. The jury took practi-cally no time at all to return a verdict of guilty against the men, and the judge seemed delighted to impose death sentences.

The case was a true cause célèbre. Around the world, not only people of the left but many others who simply believed that the two men had been railroaded, vehemently protested against the planned executions. Among them were several famous and influential figures, including the American poet Edna St. Vincent Millay, who carried a sign in one demonstration that read: "Free them and save Massachusetts! American honor dies with Sacco and Vanzetti!" Among those who worked to overturn the death sentences was a man who would later become one of the cen-tury's most respected Supreme Court justices, Felix Frankfurter.

The men bore their fate with dignity while they waited in prison for their sentences to be carried out. From his cell, Sacco wrote a letter to his thirteen-year-old son, Dante. "But remember always, Dante," he wrote, "in the play of happiness, don't you use all for yourself only, but . . . help the weak ones that cry for help."[15] Vanzetti wrote to the boy as well: "One day you will un-derstand," he told him, "that your father has sacrificed every-thing dear and sacred to the human heart and soul for his fate in liberty and justice for all."[16] When these touching letters were made public, they only served to deepen the conviction of Sacco and Vanzetti's supporters that the pair were innocent. Men capa-ble of such noble sentiments could not be cold-blooded killers, they insisted.

Despite appeals from around the world, the two men were executed by electric chair in 1927. They continued to protest their innocence and proclaim their beliefs to the end. Sacco called out "Long live anarchy!" in Italian from the electric chair.

Sacco and Vanzetti were only two of a great many con-demned prisoners who were executed despite widespread doubts about their guilt. Still, their deaths haunt the American ju-dicial system more stubbornly than any of the others—more than Chessman's, or the Rosenbergs', or, recently, even Roger Keith Coleman's. Part of the reason the memory of Sacco and Vanzetti has such power lies in the interest aroused in their case by the in-fluential writers and artists who took up their cause at the time. Another part of the reason lies in the strength and character of the two men; most other executed criminals, whether guilty of the crimes that bring them to death or not, are shady and unpleasant characters at best. Sacco and Vanzetti, on the other hand, were seen as honorable and even noble—men who were ready to live and to die for a cause they believed in with all their hearts, no matter how misguided their belief might have been.

The thought that men like these might have been killed unjustly is especially troubling, even to many who are relatively unconcerned about the fates of most ordinary death row residents.

For Further Reading:

Russell, Francis. *Tragedy in Dedham*. New York: McGraw-Hill, 1971. ASIN: 0070543429

Young, William, and David E. Kaiser. *Postmortem: New Evidence in the Case of Sacco and Vanzetti*. Boston: University of Massachusetts Press, 1985. ISBN: 087023479X

Gary Mark Gilmore Gets His Wish (1940–1977)

The 1977 execution of Gary Mark Gilmore was the first to take place after the Supreme Court's 1976 ruling permitting executions to resume in the United States.

Gary Gilmore grew up in Portland, Oregon. His father was a criminal, and Gary, who was a troubled child, seemed determined to follow in his father's footsteps. He began stealing while still in elementary school. By the time he was in his early twenties, he had progressed from simple thievery to armed robbery, and from a relatively short stint in a boys' reformatory to a long sentence in state prison.

Gilmore hated life in prison, and attempted to kill himself several times during his incarceration. By the time he was released on parole in 1976, he had lived half his life in prison.

Gilmore moved to Provost, Utah, where he became obsessed with a young woman named Nicole Baker. When Baker ran away from him, frightened by his violence and the threats he made toward her, he became desperate. On 19 July 1976, only three months after he'd been paroled, he held up a gas station. Although the station attendant offered no resistance, Gilmore made him lie down on the floor of the station and shot him twice in the back of the head. The next day, Gilmore held up a motel and killed the clerk. He was soon caught, and three months later, he was found guilty of murder and sentenced to death.

The American Civil Liberties Union and other anti–death penalty groups attempted to overturn Gilmore's sentence. There had been no executions in a decade, and anti–capital punishment organizations did want to see them started up again. Gilmore, however, would have nothing to do with the efforts to save him and he did everything he could to put a stop to them. Even when his mother, Bessie Gilmore, appealed to the U.S. Supreme Court for a stay of execution on her son's behalf, he instructed his lawyers to protest that she had no right to do so. He then filed papers voluntarily waiving all his rights to appeal.

Gilmore was apparently terrified that his sentence would be commuted to life in prison. He was so impatient for the execution order to be carried out that he attempted to kill himself with an overdose of barbiturates that his old girlfriend Nicole Baker had smuggled into prison for him.

Finally, on 17 January 1977, Gilmore got his wish. Taken to a largely unused prison warehouse, he was strapped into a chair that faced a canvas wall that had holes cut into it for the guns of his executioners. Despite his request to face his executioners, a black bag was pulled down over his head. Four riflemen, all police volunteers, opened fire at once. Three bullets (the fourth was blank) struck Gilmore, killing him instantly and assuring him a place in the history of capital punishment.

The Gilmore case was the subject of a popular book by Norman Mailer, as well as a television movie based on the book.

For Further Reading:
Mailer, Norman. *The Executioner's Song.* (Paperback). New York: Random House, 1998. ISBN: 0375700811

Notes

1. Ian Gray and Moira Stanley, *A Punishment in Search of a Crime* (New York: Avon, 1989), 225.

2. David L. Bender et al., eds., *The Death Penalty, Opposing Viewpoints* (St. Paul, MN: Greenhaven, 1986), 68.

3. *Dictionary of American Biography, Vol. III* (New York: Charles Scribner's Sons, 1958), 39.

4. *Furman v. Georgia,* 408 U.S. 238 (1972).

5. Bob Woodward and Scott Armstrong, *The Brethren: Inside the Supreme Court* (New York: Simon and Schuster, 1979), 441.

6. Judy Keen, "A Giant in the Quest for Human Rights," *USA Today,* 25 January 1993.

7. News reports CNN Television, 24 January 1993.

8. *Butler v. McKellar,* 494 U.S. 407 (1990).

9. Hugo Adam Bedau, ed., *The Death Penalty in America* (Chicago: Aldine, 1968), 8.

10. Philip Mackey, *Voices against Death* (New York: Burt Franklin & Company, 1976), 1–2.

11. Ibid., 2.

12. *Jacobellis v. Ohio,* 378 U.S. 184 (1964).

13. Woodward and Armstrong, *The Brethren,* 430–441.

14. James Avery Joyce, *Capital Punishment: A World View* (New York: AMS Press, 1961), 27.

15. Quoted in Francis Russell's *Tragedy in Dedham* (New York: McGraw-Hill, 1971), 438.

16. Ibid., 439.

6

Facts and Statistics

Key Death Penalty Decisions of the United States Supreme Court

*B*atson v. Kentucky, 476 U.S. 79 (1986). The Court limited the use of peremptory challenges of prospective jurors by prosecutors when the use of those challenges would have the effect of eliminating jurors of the same race as the defendant. Although *Batson* was not a capital punishment case, the ruling applied to all criminal trials, including capital trials in which race is often an important, if unacknowledged, issue.

Beck v. Alabama, 447, U.S. 625, 100 S. Ct. 2382 (1980). The Court ruled that juries in capital cases must be allowed to consider the alternative of lesser included offenses that would not carry the death penalty.

Butler v. McKellar, 494 U.S. 4–7 (1990). The Court ruled that defendants could not appeal state court interpretations of precedents provided those interpretations had been both reasonable and made in good faith, even if those interpretations were contradicted by later decisions. For capital case defendants this decision removed another ground of appeal.

Coker v. Georgia, 433 U.S. 584, 97 S. Ct. 2861 (1977). The Court overturned the sentence of a man sentenced to death for rape on the grounds that the death penalty was so disproportionate to the crime as to constitute "cruel and unusual punishment" under the Eighth Amendment.

Coleman v. Thompson, iii S. Ct. 2546 (1991). The Court refused to consider an appeal from the convicted murderer Roger Keith Coleman, whom many observers believed to be innocent of the crime for which he was scheduled to die, on the grounds that his attorney was a day late in filing a petition in the state court of Virginia. In its opinion, the Court declared that failure to file an appeal at the proper time in a state court rules out future consideration of the appeal in a federal court. This reversed a policy established by the Court in 1963, and is one of the most important of a series of recent rulings that limit the right of habeas corpus.

Endmund v. Florida, 458 U.S. 782 (1982). The Court voided the death sentence of man who had driven the getaway car in the robbery and murder of an elderly couple, but who had himself had no intent to kill them. The Court held that, although his participation in the crime was sufficient to make him culpable, it was not sufficient to subject him to the death penalty.

Federal Republic of Germany v. United States, 119 S. Ct. 1016 (1999). The Court turned down an application by the Federal Republic of Germany for an injunction to halt the execution in Arizona of a German citizen named Walter LaGrand.

Ford v. Wainwright, 477 U.S. 399 (1986). The Court ruled that the state of Florida could not execute a man who was legally insane, regardless of whether he was insane at the time he committed the crime, or at the time of his trial.

Furman v. Georgia, 408 U.S. 238 (1972). The Court ruled that the death penalty, as then being administered in the United States, was "cruel and unusual" punishment, and therefore not permitted under the Eighth Amendment to the United States Constitution. This ruling voided all the death sentences then pending in the United States.

Gilmore v. Utah, 429 U.S. 1012, 97 S. Ct. 436 (1976). The Court ruled that convicted killer Gary Mark Gilmore was competent to decide for himself whether to proceed with an appeal of his death sentence, and that, therefore, his mother could not appeal his sentence over his objections.

Gregg v. Georgia, 428 U.S. 153, 96 S. Ct. 2909 (1976). In this and companion cases decided at the same time, the Court found that laws enacted since *Furman* had corrected the problems the Court had found with the administration of the death penalty in that case, and so permitted executions to resume in the United States.

Herrera v. Collins, 112 S. Ct. 1074 (1993). In one of its most internally controversial decisions ever, a bitterly divided Court ruled that, lacking other valid constitutional grounds, newly uncovered evidence of actual innocence does not provide sufficient grounds for the granting of a new trial.

In re Kemmler, 136 U.S. 10 S. Ct. 930 (1890). The Court ruled that "the punishment of death is not cruel within the meaning of that word as used in the Constitution." As used in the Eighth Amendment, the Court declared, "cruel" implies "something inhuman and barbarous, something more than mere extinguishment of life."

Jurek v. Texas, 428 U.S. 262, 96 S. Ct. 2950 (1976). The Court affirmed the death sentence of a man convicted of murdering a child after trying to rape her. The sentence was imposed under a Texas law requiring that jurors answer yes to at least two of a list of questions establishing aggravating circumstances. Decided at the same time as *Gregg* and *Proffitt.*

Lockett v. Ohio, 438 U.S. 586, 98 S. Ct. 2954 (1978). The Court overturned an Ohio capital punishment statute on the grounds that it didn't allow juries to consider all the facts they need to consider in mitigation when determining whether to impose a sentence of death.

Lockhart v. McCree, 476 U.S. 162 (1986). The Court rejected the argument of an Arkansas inmate that his conviction should be overturned because the prosecution had kept potential jurors who expressed opposition to the death penalty off his jury. In effect, the Court endorses the practice of "death-qualifying" juries in capital cases, despite evidence that such juries are not only more likely to impose death sentences but they are more likely to convict.

Maxwell v. Bishop, 398 U.S. 262 (1970). The Court refused to review the case of an Arkansas man sentenced to death for rape. He made the equal protection claim that his sentence was influenced by his being black. His attorneys had supported this claim with a variety of statistical and other evidence, including studies that showed that nearly 90 percent of the men sentenced to death for rape in the United States were black, and that over a recent twenty-year period, a black man convicted of raping a white woman in Arkansas was more than three times as likely to be sentenced to death as the average perpetrator of an interracial rape. Although unwilling to consider this statistically-based argument, the Court did vacate the death sentence on other constitutional grounds unrelated to the claim of racial discrimination.

McCleskey v. Kemp, 481 U.S. 279 (1987). The Court upheld the death sentence of a black Georgia inmate named Warren Mc-

Clesky who had been convicted of killing a white policeman, despite convincing statistical evidence that Georgia defendants convicted of killing whites are sentenced to death at four times the rate of those convicted of killing blacks. The Court held that there was no direct evidence to show that the jury in the McCleskey trial had been influenced by the race of the victim. This is one of several rulings in which the Court has shown itself extremely reluctant to apply statistical evidence to particular death penalty cases.

McCleskey v. Zant, iii S. Ct. 1454 (1991). In one of the most important of a series of rulings limiting the right of habeas corpus in death penalty cases, the Court ruled that an inmate facing death could file a second habeas corpus petition only if he could show that (1) he had suffered "actual prejudice" as a result of the abuse alleged; and (2) that there was good reason the issues raised in the new petition had not been raised before.

McGautha v. California, 402 U.S. 183, 91 S. Ct. 1454 (1971). The Court ruled that a jury is free to sentence a defendant to death, even when the judge fails to give that jury legal guidelines for imposing such a penalty.

Murray v. Giarratano, 492 U.S. 1 (1989). The Court rejected the claim of impoverished inmates on Virginia's death row that they had a constitutional right to be provided with counsel to help them with appeals.

Payne v. Tennessee, 482 U.S. 496, 96 L Ed 2nd 440, 107 S. Ct. 2529 (1987). The Court ruled that victim impact evidence cannot be used in deciding whether to impose the death penalty. (See *South Carolin v. Gathers.*)

Payne v. Tennessee, 501 U.S. 808, 827 (1991). Reversing its earlier positions, taken in *South Carolina v. Gathers* and *Booth v. Maryland,* the Court ruled that juries may take into account both the character of the defendant's victim and the impact of the crime on survivors when deciding whether to impose the death penalty.

Penry v. Lynaugh, 492 U.S. 302 (1989). The Court vacated the death sentence of a mentally retarded man. Although the Court ruled that there is no constitutional bar to imposing the death sentence on someone who is mentally retarded, it insists that juries deciding the fate of a mentally retarded defendant be instructed that they may consider his mental deficiencies as a mitigating factor.

Proffitt v. Florida, 428 U.S. 242, 96 S. Ct. 2960 (1976). The Court upheld a death sentence imposed after a Florida judge found four aggravating circumstances. Decided at the same time as *Gregg* and *Jurek*, *Proffitt* helped establish the new standards that would have to be met for a death penalty to be constitutional.

Sawyer v. Whitley, 112 S. Ct. 2514 (1992). The Court allowed a condemned prisoner to raise an issue in his federal appeal that he had not previously raised at the state level. In effect, the Court modified its 1989 ruling in *Dugger v. Adams*, which forbade claims in federal court that had not already been raised in appropriate state court proceedings. The modification is only a limited one; the exceptional procedure can be used only to establish violations that prevented defendants from proving their innocence of the crime, not by defendants who merely hope to escape death by mitigating their guilt.

Simmons v. South Carolina, 512 U.S. 154 (1994). The Court ruled that juries considering whether to impose a death sentence must be informed when, under state law, if defendants are sentenced to life instead, they would never be eligible for parole.

Slack v. McDaniel, 530 U.S. ____ (2000). The Court held that an inmate whose appeal had been dismissed on procedural grounds, but whose constitutional claims had not been adjudicated, was not barred from raising the constitutional claims in a later federal appeal. Although the case did not involve the death penalty directly, it could apply to capital cases.

South Carolina v. Gathers, 490 U.S. 805, 109 S. Ct. 2207 (1989). The Court ruled that prosecutors may not praise the character of the victim when trying to convince jurors to impose a death sentence; in effect, the Court held that the victim's character was not a permissible aggravating circumstance. (See *Payne v. Tennessee*.)

Stanford v. Kentucky, 492 U.S. 106 L Ed 2nd #06, 109 S. Ct. 2969 (1989). In this case, and in *Wilkins v. Missouri*, which was decided at the same time, the Court ruled that the execution of inmates who were juveniles at the time of their crimes was not necessarily "cruel and unusual punishment" under the Eighth Amendment. As the youngest of the two petitioners in these cases was sixteen, the Court implied that the execution of anyone younger than that would violate the Eighth Amendment ban.

State ex rel. Francis v. Resweber, 329 U.S. 459 (1947). The Court ruled that Louisiana could again attempt to electrocute a murderer named Willie Francis. An earlier attempt had failed, causing the condemned man (who was then only seventeen years old) much pain. In ruling that a second execution attempt would not violate the Eighth Amendment ban on "cruel and unusual punishment," the Court declared that the Constitution does not protect the condemned from "the necessary suffering involved in any method employed to extinguish life humanely."

Thompson v. Oklahoma, 487 U.S. 815 (1988). The Court voided the death sentence of a man convicted of a murder committed when he was fifteen. The ruling is widely regarded as establishing that the execution of prisoners who were as young as fifteen at the time of their crimes is "cruel and unusual punishment," and therefore unconstitutional. Only four of the justices went this far; the fifth, and therefore deciding, justice (Sandra Day O'Connor) ruled only that the Oklahoma law under which the young man had been sentenced was unconstitutionally vague because it specified no minimum age for the death penalty.

Trop v. Dulles, 356 U.S. 86, 100 (1958). The Court ruled that the Eighth Amendment's proscription of cruel and unusual punishment "must draw its meaning from the evolving standards of decency that mark the progress of a maturing society." In effect, this decision reinforces the principle laid down in *Weems*. Like *Weems*, *Trop v. Dulles* was not a capital punishment case (it involved the withdrawal of the defendant's citizenship, or "the right to have rights"); nonetheless, the principle established in these cases is vital to the question of whether the death penalty violates the Eighth Amendment to the Constitution.

United States v. Jackson, 390 U.S. 570 (1968). The United States Supreme Court ruled unconstitutional a law that made a defendant eligible for death who was convicted after pleading not guilty to a capital crime, but provided a maximum sentence of life imprisonment for one who pled guilty. The Court found that the law's effect was to "discourage the Fifth Amendment right not to plead guilty, and to deter the exercise of the Sixth Amendment right to demand a jury trial," and ruled that laws designed to "chill the assertion of constitutional rights by penalizing those who choose to exercise them" violated the Constitution.

Weems v. United States, 217 U.S. 349, 373 (1910). The Supreme Court held that the meaning of "cruel and unusual punishment" should not remain fixed by "impotent and lifeless formulas," but instead be determined according to the "enlightened" public opinion of the time. Although *Weems*, which concerned an American sentenced to hard labor under Philippine law (the United States controlled the Philippines at that time) did not involve capital punishment directly, its establishment of an evolving standard for what constitutes "cruel and unusual punishment" would profoundly affect the constitutional debate over the death penalty.

Wilkerson v. Utah, 99 U.S. 130 (1879). The Court held that the public execution of a murderer did not violate the Eighth Amendment's ban on cruel and unusual punishment. *Wilkerson* was the first Court ruling on the question of how the Eighth Amendment applies to a capital case. For the next century and more, the legal debate over the death penalty would center on this amendment.

Wilkins v. Missouri, 492 U.S. 361 S. Ct. 2969 (1989). See *Stanford v. Kentucky*.

Woodson v. North Carolina, 428 U.S. 280, 96 S. Ct. 2978 (1976). The Court held North Carolina's mandatory death penalty statute unconstitutional, ruling that judges and juries must consider the circumstances of the individual case when determining whether to impose the death penalty.

Common Contemporary Methods of Execution

Shooting

With the invention of the firearm, it became possible to execute criminals more easily than ever before. It even became possible to do it from a distance. There are two main methods of execution by firearm. One involves a single executioner, the other a group, or firing squad. The single executioner typically stands within arm's length of the victim and fires a handgun directly into the victim's brain. This method offers the advantage of simplicity, and (if the executioner has a steady hand) the virtual certainty of an immediate "clean" kill. A firing squad usually involves as least four executioners using rifles and standing some distance away. A firing squad is more impersonal than an individual executioner, and also less accurate. In the state of Utah, executioners shoot through a hole in a canvas barrier that conceals them from the victim's view. To make a good target, the victim is usually seated, stood against a wall, or tied in a standing position to a pole or board. In some places, one of the executioners' rifles contains a blank round, so that no individual is ever sure which rifle fired a fatal shot.

Hanging

It is probable that more criminals have died by hanging than by any other method of execution. Hanging was practiced in the Middle East in biblical times, and it has survived in many countries—including the United States—until today. The first hangings in Europe were not executions but exhibitions. Corpses of criminals killed by other means were dangled from tree branches or the cross beams of makeshift gibbets. Probably the Germanic tribes of Europe first used hanging as a way of executing people. For centuries, most hanging victims were hanged from a short rope and died by agonizingly slow strangulation. In the past century techniques were developed to drop the victim at the end of a rope long enough to break the neck, thus killing more quickly.

The other three methods of execution in the United States (gas, electrocution, and lethal injection) are peculiar to this country—that is, this is the only country that uses any of them.

Gas

The gas chamber was the first new means of execution developed in the twentieth century. The condemned prisoner is strapped into a chair in a small, airtight chamber; windows in its walls allow official witnesses to view the death. Below the death chamber chair is a container of sulfuric acid. At the appointed moment, a white cloth bag containing cyanide pellets is dropped into the acid. A chemical reaction causes the release of the cyanide gas, which rises up around the chair and fills the room and the lungs of the victim. The cyanide interferes with enzymes in the respiratory system that transfer oxygen from the blood to the cells of the body. Starved of oxygen, the brain loses consciousness, and soon the other vital organs give out.

Electrocution

First used in the United States in 1890, electrocution is currently the second most commonly used method of execution in this country. The victim is strapped into a wooden chair, and copper electrodes are attached to his or herhead and legs. At the appropriate time, a massive electrical charge is passed through them, burning the body's internal organs and causing respiratory paralysis and cardiac arrest.

Lethal Injection

First adopted in Kansas in 1977, and by Texas later in the same year, lethal injection has become the most common method of execution in the United States today, prescribed by more states than any other two methods combined. It involves the transmission of deadly chemicals—typically a combination of sodium thiopental, pancuronium bromide, and potassium chloride—directly into the veins of the condemned criminal. An execution by lethal injection mimics a medical procedure, the condemned being strapped down on a hospital gurney. The execution device is similar to the apparatus used to intravenously feed or medicate patients. A flexible tube is attached to a container of chemicals on one end and a needle on the other. The end with the needle extends through a hole in the wall of the execution chamber to the gurney, where the needle is inserted into one of the condemned person's veins. At the appropriate time, the tube is opened and the chemicals are allowed to flow into the victim's bloodstream.

Shooting and hanging remain the most frequently used methods of execution in the world today. Shooting is used in eighty-six nations, hanging in seventy-eight. Both methods are prescribed by the laws of at least one state of the United States, although they are rarely used there. Gas, lethal injection, and electrocution are all used either exclusively or predominantly in the United States.

Less Commonly Used Methods of Execution

The following methods of execution are still legal means of carrying out executions in some countries.

Stoning

One of the most primitive possible methods of execution, stoning dates back at least as far as the law of Moses. Traditionally, a crowd of ordinary citizens would gather around the condemned to act as executioners. The one who had made the accusation against the prisoner threw the first stone, after which everyone picked up stones and pelted the accused until he or she either died from brain damage or was smothered or crushed beneath the weight of the stones. Stoning is still prescribed by law in a few countries, all of which have Islamic traditions. It is typically reserved for crimes involving illicit sexual activities. The only place known to have used it with frequency recently is Iran.

Beheading or Decapitation

This is the means of execution from which "capital punishment" gets its name. (The Latin word *capitalis,* which means "the head," is the root of the English words *capital* and *decapitation.*) Nations differed in the preferred weapon of decapitation—some preferred the sword and others the axe. Whatever the weapon, the condemned person was made to kneel before the executioner, leaning forward with neck extended to receive the blade. In some cases, the victim's head was placed on a chopping block, which made the executioner's job easier. But even with a block, it took a strong and steady arm to lop off a head with a single blow. Expert headsmen were highly prized—by the victim most of all—since a botched blow could result in enormous pain. In time, decapitating machines were invented to replace the unreliable hands and arms of unsteady human executioners. Although not foolproof, these machines helped remove human uncertainty from the beheading process. Beheading was practiced in ancient Greece and Rome, as well as in Japan, China, and throughout Europe, from the late Middle Ages until fairly recent times. Even today, decapitation is an official method of punishment in the Congo, Mauritania, Saudi Arabia, Qatar, the United Arab Emirates, and the Arab Republic of Yemen.

Ancient Methods of Execution

Crucifixion

A slow and tortuous method of execution, crucifixion was used in the Middle East, classical Greece, and the outlying areas of the Roman Empire. Forms of this punishment later appeared in some parts of Europe during the early Middle Ages, and in Japan as recently as the nineteenth century. The victim was hung on a tree or some kind of constructed cross, and left to die of exposure or starvation, whichever came first. At times, however the victim was impaled or pierced with a spear before that happened, which brought a quicker death, if not a less painful one.

Burning

Burning at the stake was a common method of punishment in Europe during the Middle Ages and for some centuries after that; it was also used by certain North American Indian tribes. In Europe, the typical victim was female. In several countries, burning was the prescribed penalty for witches. In England, where witches were usually hanged, it was often used for those guilty of treason—not only "high treason" against the government, but "petty treason," which meant the murder of a husband by his wife. Burning carried a special horror for medieval Christians because it destroyed the body. It was a religious age in which even many of the worst criminals hoped to be forgiven their sins and to spend eternity in paradise. This would not happen, they believed, without a Christian burial. When a body was burnt, and the ashes scattered, a proper burial was impossible.

Breaking on the Wheel

In medieval France and Germany, as well as in some other countries, breaking on the wheel was as much a form of torture as of execution. Condemned criminals were stretched out and splayed on a large wooden wheel. The bones in their arms and legs were smashed with a large iron bar, after which their chests were caved in with the same instrument. A skilled executioner could perform these operations without breaking the skin or rendering the victim unconscious. Victims were then left to hang there, gasping for breath with their shattered bones pressing on their lungs, until they died of thirst, hunger, or exposure. A much messier variation began with the process explained above but with no effort to keep the skin intact. Then the wheel was spun, sending the victim's insides flying.

Drawing and Quartering

A gruesome method of execution in which the victim's body was literally torn limb from limb. Each arm and leg of the victim was tied to a different horse, and the horses spurred to pull in four directions. To make the horses' task easier and to assure that the body was ripped into several pieces, the tendons and large muscles were sometimes cut through in advance. Sometimes the victim was hanged before being drawn and quartered, sometimes not.

Peine forte et dure

Also known as pressing, this was a method of slowly crushing—or pressing—a prisoner to death. It was primarily used in England from the fifteenth to the eighteenth centuries as a way of forcing accused criminals to plead either guilty or not guilty to a crime. If they refused to plead, they would die. Typically the prisoner was stripped and made to lie down on his or her back. A board or other flat object was laid on the prisoner's chest. Iron weights were piled on top of the board, one after another, steadily increasing the weight pressing down on the prisoner. This process often went on for several days, during which food and drink were kept to a minimum. Typically, three scraps of bread might be given on one day, three drinks of water on the next. Pressing was used in colonial America during the 1692 witch trials in Salem, Massachusetts, when an eighty-year-old Salem man named Giles Cory was crushed to death.

Garotting

A garotte is a strangling device. The simplest version consisted of a board with a hole in it. A loop of rope or cord was stuck through the hole and placed around the victim's neck. Two executioners stood behind the board and pulled with all their strength on the ends of the rope, slowly choking the victim to death. Later versions of the garotte used lever and screw mechanisms to make the executioners job easier. One version of the garotte used an iron band that could be tightened, in place of a cord. Another used two collars, one set above the other. Each was placed to surround a different adjoining vertebra in the victim's neck. The collars were operated by a screw that, when turned quickly, would pull one collar forward and the other one back, abruptly snapping the victim's neck. Still another version of the garotte, employed in some Spanish-American countries until well into the twentieth century, used a steel spike attached to a collar. When the collar was tightened, the spike was driven into the back of the victim's neck, slicing the spinal cord.

Other Historical Methods

Over the course of history, governments have been extremely inventive in devising ways of executing people. At one time or another, in one place or another, people have been executed by the following methods:

Flayed, skin cut from the body, strip by strip
Sawed into pieces
Beaten to death
Shot with arrows
Thrown from a high place onto rocks or stakes
Boiled alive in water or oil
Eaten by insects
Bitten by poisonous snakes
Buried alive, or walled up in cement
Drowned
Suffocated in a bog, quicksand, or soft pit of ashes
Whipped to death
Left in a cell to die of starvation or thirst
Left outdoors to die of exposure

Tables and Figures

Number of Abolitionist Countries, 1981–1999

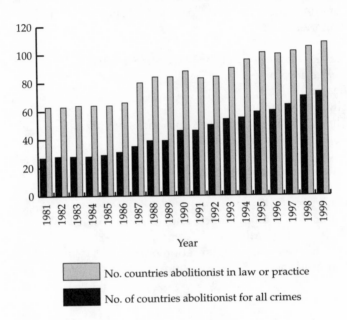

Year

No. countries abolitionist in law or practice

No. of countries abolitionist for all crimes

Source: Amnesty International Report: ACT 50/04/00, April 2000

Abolitionist for All Crimes

Country	Date of Abolition	Country	Date of Abolition
Andorra	1990	Liechtenstein	1987
Angola	1992	Lithuania	1998
Australia	1985	Luxembourg	1979
Austria	1968	Mauritius	1995
Azerbaijan	1998	Moldova	1995
Belgium	1996	Monaco	1962
Bulgaria	1998	Mozambique	1990
Cambodia	1989	Namibia	1990
Canada	1998	Nepal	1997
Cape Verde	1981	Netherlands	1982
Colombia	1910	New Zealand	1989
Costa Rica	1877	Nicaragua	1979
Croatia	1990	Norway	1979
Czech Republic	1990	Paraguay	1992
Denmark	1978	Poland	1997
Dominican Republic	1966	Portugal	1976
East Timor	1999	Romania	1989
Ecuador	1906	San Marino	1865
Estonia	1998	São Tomé and Principe	1990
Finland	1972	Seychelles	1993
France	1981	Slovak Republic	1990
Georgia	1997	Slovenia	1989
Germany	1987	South Africa	1997
Greece	1993	Spain	1995
Guinea-Bissau	1993	Sweden	1972
Haiti	1987	Switzerland	1992
Honduras	1956	United Kingdom	1998
Hungary	1990	Uruguay	1907
Iceland	1928	Vatican City State	1969
Ireland	1900	Venezuela	1863
Italy	1994		

Source: Amnesty International Report: ACT 50/04/00, April 2000

Abolitionist for Ordinary Crimes Only

Country	Date of Abolition	Country	Date of Abolition
Argentina	1984	Fiji	1979
Bolivia	1997	Israel	1954
Bosnia-Herzegovina	1997	Latvia	1999
Brazil	1979	Malta	1971
Cyprus	1983	Peru	1979
El Salvadore	1983		

Source: Amnesty International Report: ACT 50/04/00, April 2000

Abolitionist De Facto

Country	Date of Last Execution	Country	Date of Last Execution
Albania		Maldives	1952*
Bermuda	1977	Mali	1980
Bhutan	1964*	Nauru	None
Brunei Darussalam	1957	Niger	1976*
Central African		Papua New Guinea	1950
Republic	1981	Senegal	1967
Congo (Republic)	1982	Sri Lanka	1976
Cote D'Ivoire		Suriname	1982
Djibouti		Togo	
Gambia	1981	Tonga	1982
Grenada	1978	Turkey	1984
Madagascar	1958*	Western Samoa	None

Source: Amnesty International Report: ACT 50/04/00, April 2000
Notes: *Last known execution
None = None since independence

Recorded Worldwide Executions by Year, 1980–1999

Year	Number of Countries Carrying Out Executions	Number of Executions Recorded	Number of Countries with over 100 Executions 1980–1999	Percentage of All Recorded Executions Carried Out in Countries with over 100 Executions
1980	29	1,229		
1981	34	3,278		
1982	42	1,609		
1983	39	1,399		
1984	40	1,513	4	78
1985	44	1,125	3	66
1986	39	743	3	56
1987	39	769	3	59
1988	35	1,903	3	83
1989	34	2,229	3	85
1990	26	2,029	4	84
1991	32	2,086	2	89
1992	35	1,708	2	82
1993	32	1,831	1	77
1994	37	2,331	3	87
1995	41	3,276	3	85
1996	39	4,272	4	92
1997	40	2,607	3	82
1998	37	2,258	2	72
1999	31	1,813	4	80

Source: Amnesty International Report ACT 50/04/00, April 2000.
Note: *The total for 1999 may be subject to alteration at a later date if further information becomes available.

Countries with the Most Executions in 1998

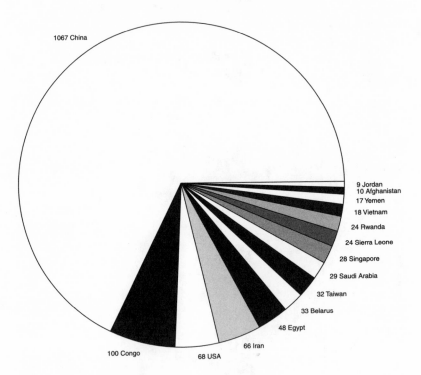

Source: Amnesty International Report: ACT 50/04/00, April 2000
Note: 1988 is the last date for which statistics are available.

Confirmed Executions of Juveniles Worldwide, 1990–1999

Country	Name	Age
Iran	Kazeem Shirafkan	17 at time of execution
	Three young males	One aged 16, two aged 17 at time of execution
	Ebrahim Qorbanzadeh	17 at time of execution
Nigeria	Chiebore Onuoha	15 at time of offense, 17 at time of execution
Pakistan	One juvenile	17 when executed
	Shamun Masih	14 at time of offense, 23 at time of execution
Saudi Arabia	Sadeq Mal-Allah	17 when sentenced to death
USA	Dalton Prejean	17 at time of offense
	Johnny Garrett	17 at time of offense
	Curtis Harris	17 at time of offense
	Frederick Lashley	17 at time of offense
	Christopher Burger	17 at time of offense
	Ruben Cantu	17 at time of offense
	Joseph John Cannon	17 at time of offense
	Robert Anthony Carter	17 at time of offense
	Dwayne Allen Wright	17 at time of offense
	Sean Sellers	16 at time of offense
Yemen	Nasser Munir Nasser al'Kirbi	13 at time of execution

Source: Amnesty International Report: ACT 50/04/00, April 2000

Number of U.S. Executions by Year since 1976

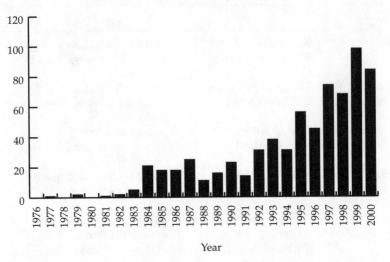

Year

Source: Amnesty International, December 15, 2000

Number of U.S. Executions by Jurisdiction, 1930–1999

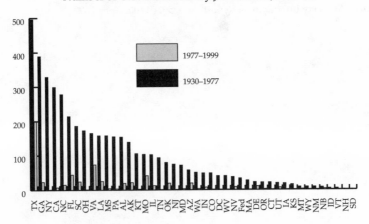

Source: U.S. Bureau of Justice Statistics, National Prisoner Statistics (NPS-8)

Number of U.S. Inmates under Death Sentences on December 31, 1999, by State

State	Number at Year-end	State	Number at Year-end
Florida	365	Missouri	83
California	553	Idaho	21
Texas	460	South Carolina	65
Georgia	116	Utah	10
Tennessee	100	Montana	6
Nevada	86	Delaware	17
Nebraska	9	New Jersey	14
Illinois	156	Virginia	31
Alabama	180	Colorado	4
North Carolina	202	Washington	13
Arizona	116	Connecticut	6
Kentucky	39	Oregon	25
Arkansas	40	Federal system	20
Indiana	43	South Dakota	3
Pennsylvania	230	New Mexico	4
Oklahoma	139	Wyoming	2
Mississippi	60	Kansas	3
Maryland	17	New York	5
Ohio	199	Total	3,527
Louisiana	85		

Source: U.S. Bureau of Justice Statistics, National Prisoner Statistics (NPS-8)
Note: For those persons sentenced to death more than once, the numbers are based on the most recent death sentence.

Number of U.S. Executions by State and Method, 1977–1999

State	Lethal Injection	Electrocution	Lethal Gas	Hanging	Firing Squad
Alabama	0	19	0	0	0
Arizona	17	0	2	0	0
Arkansas	20	1	0	0	0
California	5	0	2	0	0
Colorado	1	0	0	0	0
Delaware	9	0	0	1	0
Florida	0	44	0	0	0
Georgia	0	23	0	0	0
Idaho	1	0	0	0	0
Illinois	12	0	0	0	0
Indiana	4	3	0	0	0
Kentucky	1	1	0	0	0
Louisiana	5	20	0	0	0
Maryland	3	0	0	0	0
Mississippi	0	0	4	0	0
Missouri	41	0	0	0	0
Montana	2	0	0	0	0
Nebraska	0	3	0	0	0
Nevada	7	0	1	0	0
North Carolina	13	0	2	0	0
Ohio	1	0	0	0	0
Oklahoma	19	0	0	0	0
Oregon	2	0	0	0	0
Pennsylvania	3	0	0	0	0
South Carolina	19	5	0	0	0
Texas	199	0	0	0	0
Utah	4	0	0	0	2
Virginia	48	25	0	0	0
Washington	1	0	0	2	0
Wyoming	1	0	0	0	0

Source: U.S. Bureau of Justice Statistics, National Prisoner Statistics (NPS-8)

Methods of Execution in the United States

Lethal Injection	Electrocution	Hanging	Firing Squad	Lethal Gas
Arizona	Alabama	Delaware	Idaho	Arizona
Arkansas	Arkansas	Montana	Oklahoma	California
California	Florida	New	Utah	Maryland
Colorado	Georgia	Hampshire		Mississippi
Connecticut	Kentucky	Washington		Missouri
Delaware	Nebraska			North
Florida	Ohio			Carolina
Idaho	Oklahoma			Wyoming
Illinois	South			
Indiana	Carolina			
Kansas	Tennessee			
Louisiana	Virginia			
Maryland				
Mississippi				
Missouri				
Montana				
Nevada				
New				
Hampshire				
New Jersey				
New Mexico				
New York				
North				
Carolina				
Ohio				
Oklahoma				
Oregon				
Pennsylvania				
South				
Carolina				
South Dakota				
Texas				
Utah				
Virginia				
Washington				
Wyoming				
U.S. Military				

Source: U.S. Bureau of Justice Statistics, Capital Punishment 1996 Bulletin, Table 2 (Dec. 1997); updated by Amnesty International December 15, 2000
Notes: Arizona authorizes lethal injection for persons sentenced after 11/15/92; those sentenced before that date may select lethal injection or lethal gas.

Methods of Execution in the United States *(continued)*

Arkansas authorizes lethal injection for persons committing a capital offense after 7/4/83; those who committed the offense before that date may select lethal injection or electrocution.

Delaware authorizes lethal injection for those whose capital offense occurred after 6/13/86; those who committed the offense before that date may select lethal injection or hanging.

Florida lawmakers agreed to switch the state's primary method of exocution from electrocution to lethal injection. The state will allow prisoners to choose between the two methods.

Georgia authorizes lethal injection for those sentenced after May 1, 2000. Those sentenced before May 1, 2000, will be executed by electrocution.

Idaho authorizes firing squad only if lethal injection is "impractical."

Kentucky authorizes lethal injection for those convicted after March 31, 1998; those who committed the offense before that date may select lethal injection or electrocution.

Maryland authorizes lethal injection for those whose capital offense occurred on or after 3/25/94; those who committed the offense before that date may select lethal injection or lethal gas.

New Hampshire authorizes hanging only if lethal injection cannot be given.

Oklahoma authorizes electrocution if lethal injection is ever held to be unconstitutional and firing squad if both lethal injection and electrocution are held unconstitutional.

Tennessee authorizes lethal injection for those sentenced after Jan. 1, 1999, and those currently on death row will choose between the electric chair and lethal injection.

Wyoming authorizes lethal gas if lethal injection is ever held to be unconstitutional.

The method of execution of Federal prisoners is lethal injection, pursuant to 28 CRR, Part 26. For offenses under the Violent Crime Control and Law Enforcement Act of 1994, the method is that of the state in which the conviction took place, pursuant to 18 USC 3596. If the state has no death penalty, the inmate will be transferred to another state.

Foreign Nationals Executed in the United States since 1976

Name	Citizenship	Jurisdiction	Date Executed
Carlos Santana	Dominican	Texas	March 23, 1993
Ramon Montoya	Mexican	Texas	March 25, 1993
Nicholas Ingram	British/American	Georgia	April 7, 1995
Pedro Medina	Cuban	Florida	March 25, 1997
Irineo Montoya	Mexican	Texas	June 18, 1997
Mario Murphy	Mexican	Virginia	September 18, 1997
Angel Breard	Paraguayan	Virginia	April 14, 1998
Jose Villafuerte	Honduran	Arizona	April 22, 1998
Tuan Nguyen	Vietnamese	Oklahoma	December 10, 1998
Jaturun Siripongs	Thai	California	February 9, 1999
Karl LaGrand	German	Arizona	February 24, 1999
Walter LaGrand	German	Arizona	March 3, 1999
Alvaro Calamvrp	Filipino	Nevada	April 5, 1999
Joseph Stanley Faulder	Canadian	Texas	June 17, 1999

Source: Amnesty International Report: ACT 50/04/00, April 2000

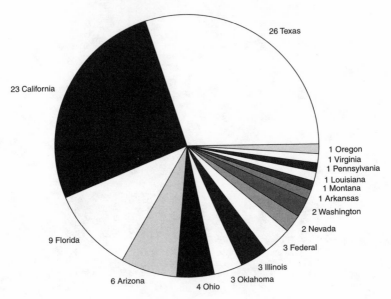

Foreign Nationals on American Death Rows
by Jurisdiction, as of July 20, 2000

26 Texas

23 California

1 Oregon
1 Virginia
1 Pennsylvania
1 Louisiana
1 Montana
1 Arkansas
2 Washington
2 Nevada
3 Federal
3 Illinois
3 Oklahoma
4 Ohio
6 Arizona
9 Florida

Source: Amnesty International Report: ACT 50/04/00, April 2000

Juvenile Offenders Executed in the United States since 1976

Name	State	Date of Execution
Charles Rumbaugh	TX	09/11/85
James Terry Roach	SC	01/10/86
Jay Pinkerton	TX	05/15/86
Dalton Prejean	LA	05/18/90
Johnny Frank Garrett	TX	02/11/92
Curtis Harris	TX	07/01/93
Frederick Laskley	MO	07/28/93
Ruben Cantu	TX	08/24/93
Christopher Burger	GA	12/07/93
Joseph Cannon TX	TX	04/24/98
Robert Anthony Carter	TX	05/18/98
Dwayne Allen Wright	VA	10/21/98
Sean Sellers	OK	02/04/99
Douglas Christopher Thomas	VA	01/10/00
Steve Edward Roach	VA	01/13/00
Glen McGinnis	TX	01/25/00
Gary Graham (Shaka Sankofa)	TX	06/22/00

Source: Amnesty International, December 15, 2000

Minimum Age for Application of the Death Penalty in the United States as of December 15, 2000

Age 16 or Less	Age 17	Age 18	None Specified*
Alabama	Georgia	California	Arizona
Arkansas	New Hampshire	Colorado	Idaho
Delaware	North Carolina	Connecticut	Louisiana
Florida	Texas	Illinois	Montana
Indiana		Kansas	Pennsylvania
Kentucky		Maryland	South Carolina
Mississippi		Nebraska	South Dakota
Missouri		New Jersey	Utah
Nevada		New Mexico	
Oklahoma		New York	
Virginia		Ohio	
Wyoming		Oregon	
		Tennessee	
		Washington	
		Federal government	

Source: Amnesty International, December 15, 2000
Notes: *The U.S. Supreme Court has determined 16 as the minimum age.

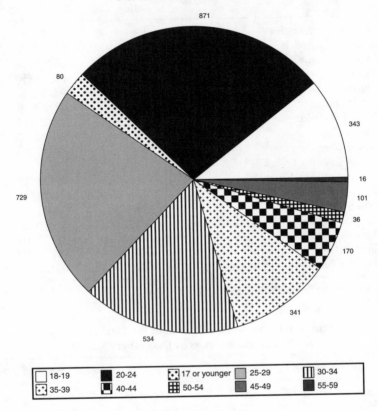

Age at Time of Arrest of Defendants Sentenced to Death, U.S. Statistics for Year-end 1999

Legend: 18-19 | 20-24 | 17 or younger | 25-29 | 30-34 | 35-39 | 40-44 | 50-54 | 45-49 | 55-59

Source: U.S. Bureau of Justice Statistics, National Prisoner Statistics (NPS-8)
Note: Excludes 295 prisoners for whom the date of arrest was not available.

Age at Year-end 1999 of Inmates under Sentence of Death, U.S. Statistics

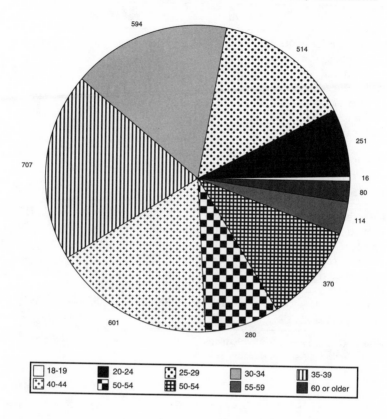

	18-19		20-24		25-29		30-34		35-39
	40-44		50-54		50-54		55-59		60 or older

Source: U.S. Bureau of Justice Statistics, National Prisoner Statistics (NPS-8)
Note: No inmates sentenced to death were 17 or younger at year-end.

Criminal History of U.S. Inmates under Death Sentence, by Race 1999

	All*	White	Black	Latino/a
Inmates under death sentences at year end	3,527	1,651	1,500	325
With prior felony convictions	2,085	949	939	172
Not reported	276			
With prior homicide convictions	290	134	128	22
Not reported	71			

Legal Status at Time of Criminal Offense

	All*	White	Black	Latino/a
Charges pending	228	127	90	11
Probation	311	134	144	27
Parole	554	229	250	65
Prison escapee	39	25	10	3
Incarcerated	86	36	44	5
Other status	21	11	8	1
None	1,860	916	755	161
Not reported	428			

Source: U.S. Bureau of Justice Statistics, National Prisoner Statistics (NPS-8)
Note: *Includes Asian and Native American

U.S. Death Sentences in 1997 Murder Cases
by Race of Defendant and Victim

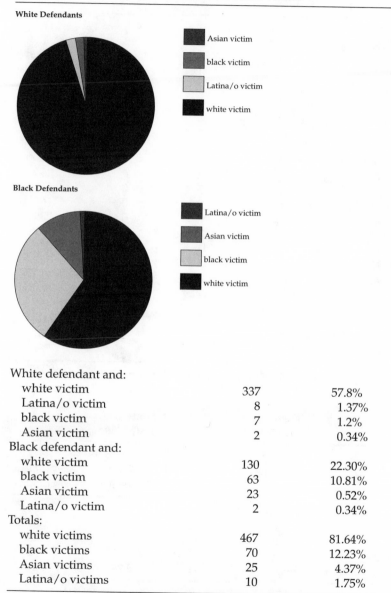

White Defendants

Asian victim

black victim

Latina/o victim

white victim

Black Defendants

Latina/o victim

Asian victim

black victim

white victim

White defendant and:		
white victim	337	57.8%
Latina/o victim	8	1.37%
black victim	7	1.2%
Asian victim	2	0.34%
Black defendant and:		
white victim	130	22.30%
black victim	63	10.81%
Asian victim	23	0.52%
Latina/o victim	2	0.34%
Totals:		
white victims	467	81.64%
black victims	70	12.23%
Asian victims	25	4.37%
Latina/o victims	10	1.75%

Source: Amnesty International Report: ACT 50/04/00, April 2000
Note: According to the U.S. Bureau of Justice Statistics, white and black victims comprise nearly equal proportions of murder victims.

U.S. Executions 1977–1999, by Race (post-*Furman*)

Year	White	Black	Other Races	Total
1977	1	0	0	1
1978	0	0	0	0
1979	2	0	0	2
1980	0	0	0	0
1981	1	0	0	1
1982	1	1	0	2
1983	4	1	0	5
1984	13	8	0	21
1985	11	7	0	18
1986	11	7	0	18
1987	13	12	0	25
1988	6	5	0	11
1989	8	8	0	16
1990	16	7	0	23
1991	7	7	0	14
1992	19	11	1	31
1993	23	14	1	38
1994	20	11	0	31
1995	33	22	1	56
1996	31	14	0	45
1997	45	27	2	74
1998	48	18	2	68
1999	61	33	4	98

Source: U.S. Bureau of Justice Statistics, National Prisoner Statistics (NPS-8)

Disposition of U.S. Death Sentences, 1977–1999, as of December 31, 1999

Race	Under Sentence of Death*	Executed	Other Dispositions**	Remaining on Death Row
White	3,141	334	1,156	1,651
Black	2,633	211	922	1,500
Latino/a	498	43	130	325
Other	93	10	32	51
Totals	6,365	598	2,240	3,527

Source: U.S. Bureau of Justice Statistics, National Prisoner Statistics (NPS-8)
Notes: *Includes 380 persons sentenced to death prior to 1977 whose cases had not been disposed
**Includes death other than execution

Average Time from Sentence to Execution in the United States

Year	All Races*	White	Black
1977–83	51	49	58
1984	74	76	71
1985	71	65	80
1986	87	78	102
1987	86	78	96
1988	80	72	89
1989	95	78	112
1990	96	97	91
1991	116	124	107
1992	114	104	135
1993	113	112	121
1994	122	117	132
1995	134	128	144
1996	125	112	153
1997	133	126	147
1998	130	128	132
1999	143	143	141
Since 1977	118	114	126

Source: U.S. Bureau of Justice Statistics, National Prisoner Statistics (NPS-8)
Notes: Average time was calculated from the most recent sentencing date. Time shown in months.
*includes Native Americans and Asians

Disposition of U.S. Death Sentences by Year of Sentencing, 1973–1999

Year	Sentenced to Death	Executed	Other Death	Overturned	Commuted	Other/ Unknown	Under Death Sentence, 12/31/1999
1973	42	2	0	31	9	0	0
1974	149	10	4	110	22	1	2
1975	298	6	4	262	21	2	3
1976	233	13	5	196	15	0	4
1977	137	19	3	98	7	0	10
1978	185	34	6	118	8	0	19
1979	152	26	12	88	5	1	20
1980	173	40	13	80	7	0	33
1981	227	48	13	118	4	1	43
1982	266	54	13	103	7	1	88
1983	253	53	14	86	7	2	91
1984	285	46	10	99	6	8	116
1985	269	31	5	112	4	3	114
1986	300	41	16	95	6	5	137
1987	290	34	14	96	2	6	138
1988	292	31	11	85	3	0	162
1989	259	19	9	78	3	0	150
1990	253	19	7	67	2	0	158
1991	264	13	9	63	3	0	176

(continues)

Disposition of U.S. Death Sentences by Year of Sentencing, 1973–1999 (continued)

Year	Sentenced to Death	Executed	Other Death	Overturned	Commuted	Other/ Unknown	Under Death Sentence, 12/31/1999
1992	288	15	7	56	4	0	206
1993	290	13	9	35	5	0	228
1994	319	11	7	42	2	0	257
1995	319	10	7	32	1	0	269
1996	316	7	3	32	1	0	273
1997	276	1	3	11	0	0	261
1998	300	2	1	0	0	0	297
1999	272	0	0	0	0	0	272
Totals	6,707	598	205	2,193	154	30	3,527

Source: U.S. Bureau of Justice Statistics, National Prisoner Statistics (NPS-8)

Note: For those persons sentenced to death more than once, the numbers are based on the most recent death sentence.

Removals from U.S. Death Rows by Jurisdction, 1973–1999

Jurisdiction	Executed	Died	Overturned	Commuted	Other
Federal	0	0	2	0	0
Alabama	19	13	100	2	0
Arizona	19	9	73	5	1
Arkansas	21	1	30	2	0
California	7	31	116	15	0
Colorado	1	1	10	1	0
Connecticut	0	0	1	0	0
Delaware	10	0	13	0	0
Florida	44	29	363	18	2
Georgia	23	9	134	6	1
Idaho	1	1	12	2	0
Illinois	12	9	85	3	8
Indiana	7	1	37	2	2
Kansas	0	0	0	0	0
Kentucky	2	2	27	1	0
Louisiana	25	3	76	6	1
Maryland	3	1	24	3	0
Massachusetts	0	0	2	2	0
Mississippi	4	2	94	0	3
Missouri	41	7	25	2	0
Montana	2	0	6	1	0
Nebraska	3	2	8	2	0
Nevada	8	5	25	3	0
New Jersey	0	3	23	0	8
New Mexico	0	1	16	5	0
New York	0	0	3	0	0
North Carolina	15	9	237	5	0
Ohio	1	9	133	9	0
Oklahoma	19	7	128	1	0
Oregon	2	1	18	0	0
Pennsylvania	3	10	80	0	0
Rhode Island	0	0	2	0	0
South Carolina	24	4	67	3	0
South Dakota	0	0	0	0	0
Tennessee	0	9	81	0	2
Texas	199	21	103	45	1
Utah	6	0	9	1	0
Virginia	73	3	6	9	1
Washington	3	1	17	0	0
Wyoming	1	1	7	0	0

Source: U.S. Bureau of Justice Statistics, National Prisoner Statistics (NPS-8)
Note: For those persons sentenced to death more than once, the numbers are based on the most recent death sentence.

7

Documents

A Nineteenth-Century Execution by Guillotine

In the popular imagination, the guillotine is associated primarily, if not exclusively, with France. But France was not the only country to use the guillotine. In 1845, the English author Charles Dickens attended an execution by guillotine in Rome, Italy. Dickens was not only a great novelist but a fine journalist, and his description of the event provides valuable insights into the reality of a public execution in the nineteenth century.

Note in particular the speed with which the condemned man was dispatched. From the movies, we have become conditioned to think of an execution by guillotine as an extremely dramatic, almost stately, event. In reality, however, the brisk and matter-of-fact efficiency with which it acted was one of the prime factors recommending the guillotine as a method of capital punishment.

Note as well the uniquely Italian intermingling of the secular ceremonies attendant on the execution with the religious practices of the Roman Catholic Church.

Dickens' account was published in his book Pictures from Italy in 1846. Some thirteen years later, he would make a fictional guillotining the climactic event of his novel A Tale of Two Cities.

On one Saturday morning (the eighth of March), a man was beheaded here. Nine or ten months before, he had waylaid a Bavarian countess, travelling as a pilgrim to Rome—alone and on foot, of course—and performing, it is said, that act or piety for the fourth time. He saw her change a piece of gold at Viterbo, where he lived;

followed her; bore her company on her journey for some forty miles or more, on the treacherous pretext of protecting her; attacked her, in the fulfillment of his unrelenting purpose, on the Campagna, within a very short distance of Rome, near to what is called (but what is not) the Tomb of Nero; robbed her; and beat her to death with her own pilgrim's staff. He was newly married, and gave some of her apparel to his wife: saying that he had bought it at a fair. She, however, who had seen the pilgrim-countess passing through their town, recognised some trifle as having belonged to her. Her husband then told her what he had done. She, in confession, told a priest; and the man was taken, within four days after the commission of the murder.

There are no fixed times for the administration of justice, or its execution, in this unaccountable country; and he had been in prison ever since. On the Friday, as he was dining with the other prisoners, they came and told him he was to be beheaded the next morning, and took him away. It is very unusual to execute in Lent; but his crime being a very bad one, it was deemed advisable to make an example of him at that time, when great numbers of pilgrims were coming towards Rome, from all parts, for the Holy Week. I heard of this on the Friday evening, and saw the bills up at the churches, calling on the people to pray for the criminal's soul. So, I determined to go, and see him executed.

The beheading was appointed for fourteen and a-half o'clock, Roman time; or a quarter before nine in the forenoon. I had two friends with me; and as we did not know but that the crowd might be very great we were on the spot by half-past seven. The place of execution was near the church of San Giovanni Decollato (a doubtful compliment to Saint John the Baptist) in one of the impassable back streets without any footway, of which a great part of Rome is composed—a street of rotten houses, which do not seem to belong to anybody, and do not seem to have ever been inhabited, and certainly were never built on any plan, or for any particular purpose, and have no window-sashes, and are a little like deserted breweries, and might be warehouses but for having nothing in them. Opposite to one of these, a white house, the scaffold was built. An untidy, unpainted, uncouth, crazy-looking thing of course: some seven feet high, perhaps; with a tall, gallows-shaped frame rising above it, in which was the knife, charged with a ponderous mass of iron, all ready to descend, and glittering brightly in the morning sun, whenever it looked out, now and then, from behind a cloud.

There were not many people lingering about; and these were kept at a considerable distance from the scaffold, by parties of the Pope's dragoons. Two or three hundred foot-soldiers were under arms, standing at ease in clusters here and there; and the officers were walking up and down in twos and threes, chatting together, and smoking cigars.

At the end of the street, was an open space, where there would be a dust heap, and piles of broken crockery, and mounds of vegetable refuse, but for such things being thrown anywhere and everywhere in Rome, and favouring no particular sort of locality. We got into a kind of wash-house, belonging to a dwelling house on this spot; and standing there in an old cart, and on a heap of cartwheels piled against the wall, looked, through a large grated window, at the scaffold, and straight down the street beyond it until, in consequence of its turning off abruptly to the left, our perspective was brought to a sudden termination, and had a corpulent officer, in a cocked hat, for its crowning feature.

Nine o'clock struck, and ten o'clock struck, and nothing happened. All the bells of all the churches rang as usual. A little parliament of dogs assembled in the open space, and chased each other, in and out among the soldiers. Fierce-looking Romans of the lowest class, in blue cloaks, russet cloaks, and rags uncloaked, came and went, and talked together. Women and children fluttered, on the skirts of the scanty crowd. One large muddy spot was left quite bare, like a bald place on a man's head. A cigar-merchant, with an earthen pot of charcoal ashes in one hand, went up and down, crying his wares. A pastry-merchant divided his attention between the scaffold and his customers. Boys tried to climb up walls, and tumbled down again. Priests and monks elbowed a passage for themselves among the people, and stood on tiptoe for a sight of the knife; then went away. Artists, in inconceivable hats of the middle-ages, and beards (thank Heaven!) of no age at all, flashed picturesque scowls among them from their stations in the throng. One gentleman (connected with the fine arts, I presume) went up and down in a pair of Hessian-boots, with a red beard hanging down on his breast, and his long and bright red hair, plaited into two tails, one on either side of his head, which fell over his shoulders in front of him, very nearly to his waist, and were carefully entwined and braided!

Eleven o'clock struck and still nothing happened. A rumor got about, among the crowd, that the criminal would not confess; in which case, the priests would keep him until the Ave Maria (sunset); for it is their merciful custom never finally to turn the crucifix away from a man at that pass, as one refusing to be shriven, and consequently a sinner abandoned of the Saviour, until then. People began to drop off. The officers shrugged their shoulders and looked doubtful. The dragoons, who came riding up below our window, every now and then, to order an unlucky hackney-coach or cart away, as soon as it had comfortably established itself, and was covered with exulting people (but never before), became imperious, and quick tempered. The bald place hadn't a straggling hair upon it; and the corpulent officer, crowning the perspective, took a world of snuff.

Suddenly, there was a noise of trumpets. "Attention!" was among the foot-soldiers instantly. They were marched up to the scaffold and formed round it. The dragoons galloped to their nearer stations too. The guillotine became the centre of a wood of bristling bayonets and shining sabres. The people closed round nearer, on the flank of the soldiery. A long straggling stream of men and boys, who had accompanied the procession from the prison, came pouring into the open space. The bald spot was scarcely distinguishable from the rest. The cigar and pastry-merchants resigned all thoughts of business, for the moment, and abandoning themselves wholly to pleasure, got good situations in the crowd. The perspective ended, now, in a troop of dragoons. And the corpulent officer, sword in hand, looked hard at a church close to him, which he could see, but we, the crowd, could not.

After a short delay, some monks were seen approaching to the scaffold from this church; and above their heads, coming on slowly and gloomily, the effigy of Christ upon the cross, canopied with black. This was carried round the foot of the scaffold, to the front, and turned toward the criminal, that he might see it to the last. It was hardly in its place, when he appeared on the platform, barefooted; his hands bound; and with the collar and neck of his shirt cut away, almost to the shoulder. A young man—six-and-twenty—vigorously made, and well-shaped. Face pale; small dark moustache; and dark brown hair.

He had refused to confess, it seemed, without first having his wife brought to see him; and they had sent an escort for her, which had occasioned the delay.

He immediately kneeled down, below the knife. His neck fitting into a hole, made for the purpose, in a cross plank, was shut down, by another plank above; exactly like the pillory. Immediately below him was a leathern bag. And into it his head rolled instantly.

The executioner was holding it by the hair, and walking with it round the scaffold, showing it to the people, before one quite knew that the knife had fallen heavily, and with a rattling sound.

When it had travelled round the four sides of the scaffold, it was set upon a pole in front—a little patch of black and white, for the long street to stare at, and the flies to settle on. The eyes were turned upward, as if he had avoided the sight of the leathern bag, and looked to the crucifix. Every tinge and hue of life had left it in that instant. It was dull, cold, livid, wax. The body also.

There was a great deal of blood. When we left the window, and went close up to the scaffold, it was very dirty; one of the two men who were throwing water over it, turning to help the other lift the body into a shell, picked his way as through mire. A strange appearance was the apparent annihilation of the neck. The head was taken off so close, that it seemed as if the knife had narrowly escaped crushing the jaw, or shaving off the ear; and the body looked as if there were nothing left above the shoulder.

Nobody cared, or was at all affected. There was no manifestation of disgust, or pity, or indignation, or sorrow. My empty pockets were tried, several times, in the crowd immediately below the scaffold, as the corpse was being put into its coffin. It was an ugly, filthy, careless, sickening spectacle; meaning nothing but butchery beyond the momentary interest, to the one wretched actor. Yes! Such a sight has one meaning and one warning. Let me not forget it. The speculators in the lottery station themselves at favourable points for counting the gouts of blood that spurt out, here or there; and buy that number. It is pretty sure to have a run upon it.

The body was carted away in due time, the knife cleansed, the scaffold taken down, and all the hideous apparatus removed. The executioner: an outlaw ex officio (what a satire on the Punishment!) who dare not, for his life, cross the Bridge of St. Angelo but to do his work retreated to his lair, and the show was over.

Excerpt from Pope John Paul II's Encyclical Letter, *On the Value and Inviolability of Human Life*

In this encyclical letter, also known as Evangelium Vitae, *the Supreme Pontiff of the world's largest Christian sect, the Roman Catholic Church, uses the biblical account of God's response to the killing of Abel by his brother Cain to explain the Church's opposition to using the death penalty as a punishment for crime.*

The Voice of Your Brother's Blood Cries to Me from the Ground

Present Day Threats to Human Life

"*Cain rose up against his brother Abel, and killed him*" (Gn 4:8): *the roots of violence against life.*

"God did not make death, and he does not delight in the death of the living. For he has created all things that they might exist . . .

God created man for incorruption, and made him in the image of his own eternity, but through the devil's envy *death entered the world,* and those who belong to his party experience it" (Wis 1:13–14; 2:23–24).

The *Gospel of life,* proclaimed in the beginning when man was created in the image of God for a destiny of full and perfect life (cf. Gn. 2:7; Wis 9:2–3), is contradicted by the painful experience of *death which enters the world* and casts its shadow of meaninglessness over man's entire existence. Death came into the world as a result of the devil's envy (cf. Gn 3:1,4–5) and the sin of our first parents (cf. Gn 2:17, 3:17–19). And death entered it in a violent way, *through the killing of Abel by his brother Cain:* "And when they were in the field, Cain rose up against his brother Abel, and killed him" (Gn 4:8).

This first murder is presented with singular eloquence in a page of the Book of Genesis which has universal significance: it is a page rewritten daily, with inexorable and degrading frequency, in the book of human history.

Let us re-read together this biblical account which, despite its archaic structure and its extreme simplicity, has much to teach us.

> *Now Abel was a keeper of sheep, and Cain a tiller of the ground. In the course of time Cain brought to the Lord an offering of the fruit of the ground, and Abel brought of the firstlings of his flock and of their fat portions. And the Lord had regard for Abel and his offering, but for Cain and his offering he had not regard. So Cain was very angry, and his countenance fell. The Lord said to Cain, "Why are you angry and why has your countenance fallen? If you do well, will you not be accepted? And if you do not do well, sin is crouching at the door; its desire is for you, but you must master it."*
>
> *Cain said to Abel his brother, "Let us go out to the field." And when they were in the field, Cain rose up against his brother Abel, and killed him. Then the Lord said to Cain, "Where is Abel your brother?" He said, "I do not know; am I my brother's keeper?" And the Lord said, "What have you done? The voice of your brother's blood is crying to me from the ground. And now you are cursed from the ground, which has opened its mouth to receive your brother's blood from your hand. When you till the ground, it shall no longer yield to you its strength; you shall be a fugitive and a wanderer on the earth." Cain said to the Lord, "My punishment is greater than I can bear. Behold, you have driven me this day away from the ground; and from your face I shall be hidden; and I shall be a fugitive and a wanderer on the earth, and whoever finds me*

will slay me." Then the Lord said to him, "Not so! If any one slays Cain, vengeance shall be taken on him sevenfold." And the Lord put a mark on Cain, lest any who came upon him should kill him. Then Cain went away from the presence of the Lord, and dwelt in the land of Nod, east of Eden (Gn 4:2–16).

Cain was "very angry" and his countenance "fell" because "the Lord had regard for Abel and his offering" (Gen. 4:4–5). The biblical text does not reveal the reason why God prefers Abel's sacrifice to Cain's. It clearly shows however that God, although preferring Abel's gift, does not interrupt his dialogue with Cain. He admonishes him, reminding him of his freedom in the face of evil: man is in no way predestined to evil. Certainly, like Adam, he is tempted by the malevolent force of sin which, like a wild beast, lies in wait at the door of his heart, ready to leap on its prey. But Cain remains free in the face of sin. He can and must overcome it: "Its desire is for you, but you must master it" (Gn 4:7).

Envy and anger have the upper hand over the Lord's warning, and so Cain attacks his own brother and kills him. As we read in the *Catechism of the Catholic Church:* "In the account of Abel's murder by his brother Cain, Scripture reveals the presence of anger and envy in man, consequences of original sin, from the beginning of human history. Man has become the enemy of his fellow man."

Brother kills brother. Like the first fratricide, every murder is a violation of the *"spiritual" kinship* uniting mankind in one great family, in which all share the same fundamental good: equal personal dignity. Not infrequently the kinship *"of flesh and blood"* is also violated; for example when threats to life arise within the relationship between parents and children, such as happens in abortion or when, in the wider context of family or kinship, euthanasia is encouraged or practised.

At the root of every act of violence against one's neighbour there is *a concession to the "thinking" of the evil one,* the one who "was a murderer from the beginning" (Jn 8:44). As the Apostle John reminds us: "For this is the message which you have heard from the beginning, that we should love one another, and not be like Cain who was of the evil one and murdered his brother" (1 Jn 3:11–12). Cain's killing of his brother at the very dawn of history is thus a sad witness of how evil spreads with amazing speed: Man's revolt against God in the earthly paradise is followed by the deadly combat of man against man.

After the crime, *God intervenes to avenge the one killed.* Before God, who asks him about the fate of Abel, Cain, instead of showing remorse and apologizing, arrogantly eludes the question: "I do not know; am I my brother's keeper?" (Gn 4:9). "*I do not know*": Cain tries to cover up his crime with a lie. This was and still is the case, when all kinds of ideologies try to justify and disguise the most atrocious crimes against human beings. "*Am I my brother's keeper?*": Cain does not wish to think about his brother and refuses to accept the responsibility which every person has towards others. We cannot but think of today's tendency for people to refuse to accept responsibility for their brothers and sisters. Symptoms of this trend include the lack of solidarity towards society's weakest members—such as the elderly, the infirm, immigrants, children—and the indifference frequently found in relations between the world's peoples even when basic values such as survival, freedom and peace are involved.

But *God cannot leave the crime unpunished:* from the ground on which it has been spilt, the blood of the one murdered demands that God should render justice (cf. Gn 37:26; Is 26:21; Ez 24:7–8). From this text the Church has taken the name of the "sins which cry to God for justice," and, first among them, she has included willful murder. For the Jewish people, as for many peoples of antiquity, blood is the source of life. Indeed "the blood is the life" (Dt 12:23), and life, especially human life, belongs only to God: For this reason *whoever attacks human life, in some way attacks God himself.*

Cain is cursed by God and also by the earth, which will deny him its fruit (cf. Gn 4:12). *He is punished:* he will live in the wilderness and the desert. Murderous violence profoundly changes man's environment. From being the "garden of Eden" (Gn 2:15), a place of plenty, of harmonious interpersonal relationships and of friendship with God, the earth becomes "the land of Nod" (Gn 4:16), a place of scarcity, loneliness and separation from God. Cain will be "a fugitive and a wanderer on the earth" (Gn 4:14): Uncertainty and restlessness will follow him forever.

And yet God, who is always merciful even when he punishes, "*put a mark on Cain,* lest any who came upon him should kill him" (Gn 4:15). He thus gave him a distinctive sign, not to condemn him to the hatred of others, but to protect and defend him from those wishing to kill him, even out of a desire to avenge Abel's death. *Not even a murderer loses his personal dignity,* and God himself pledges to guarantee this. And it is precisely here that the *paradoxical mystery of the merciful justice of God* is shown forth. As Saint Ambrose writes: "Once the crime is admitted at the very inception of this sinful act of parricide, then the divine law of God's mercy should be immediately extended. If punishment is forthwith inflicted on the accused, then men in the exercise of justice would in no way observe patience and moderation, but would straightaway condemn the defendant to punishment. . . . God drove Cain out of his presence and sent him into exile far away from his native land, so that he passed from a life of human kindness to one which was more akin to the rude existence of a wild beast. God, who preferred the correction rather than the death of a sinner, did not desire that a homicide be punished by the exaction of another act of homicide."

The U.S. Supreme Court Allows the Resumption of Executions

In its historic 1972 ruling in the case of Furman v. Georgia, *the U.S. Supreme Court had ruled that the death penalty—as then administered in the United States—was cruel and unusual punishment under the Eighth Amendment. This ruling not only overturned all the death sentences then in effect in the United States, but threw out all the then current state and federal laws prescribing the death penalty. (Although hundreds of death sentences had been imposed, there had not been an execution in the United States since 1967, at least partly because it was anticipated that the Supreme Court was preparing to decide on the constitutionality of the death penalty.)*

The vote by which Furman *was decided was five to four, and each of the five justices who made up the majority gave somewhat different reasons for his decision; all agreed, however, that the death penalty was being unfairly and discriminatorily applied. That unfairness was dramatically demonstrated, historically and contemporaneously, by death sentences that fell almost invariably on the black and the poor and not on the white and elite.*

Although the effect of Furman *was both dramatic and sweeping, it was not necessarily permanent. The Court had not ruled that the punishment of death, in and of itself, was cruel and unusual; it had ruled only that the way in which the death penalty had been applied under the state and federal laws in effect in 1972 was unconstitutional. This left open the possibility that other and fairer death penalty laws could be written and applied in such a way as to pass constitutional muster. Therefore, in the wake of* Furman, *the legislatures of many states immediately set to work framing new death penalty laws they hoped would meet the objections raised in* Furman.

On June 19, 1972, the Supreme Court found, by a vote of 7 to 2, that new laws in Georgia, Florida, and Texas, which provided guidelines for judges and juries to use for the fair and nondiscriminatory imposi-

tion of the death penalty were constitutional. (On the same day, the Court ruled, in the case of Woodson v. North Carolina, that a mandatory death penalty law would be unconstitutional.) The Court explained its reasoning in its decision in the case of Gregg v. Georgia—the most important death penalty decision in the history of the United States. Extensive excerpts from that decision follow, along with others from the dissent of Justice Thurgood Marshall.

For ease of reading, the decision is presented here without the exhaustive footnotes and case citations that lace the published decision. Such information is primarily of interest to lawyers and legal scholars, and tends to interfere with the enjoyment, and even the understanding, of other readers. Readers who are interested in such information will find it in the 1976 edition of United States Reports, in which the decision was originally published, as well as in several other sources, including online at the Electric Law Library Web site—http://www.lect-law.com/files/case26.htm—and elsewhere.

U.S. Supreme Court
GREGG v. GEORGIA **428 U.S. 156 (1976)**
428 U.S. 153
GREGG v. GEORGIA
CERTIORARI TO THE SUPREME COURT OF GEORGIA
No. 74–6257.
Argued March 31, 1976
Decided 2 July 1976
I

The petitioner, Troy Gregg, was charged with committing armed robbery and murder. In accordance with Georgia procedure in capital cases, the trial was in two stages, a guilt stage and a sentencing stage. The evidence at the guilt trial established that on November 21, 1973, the petitioner and a traveling companion, Floyd Allen, while hitchhiking north in Florida were picked up by Fred Simmons and Bob Moore. Their car broke down, but they continued north after Simmons purchased another vehicle with some of the cash he was carrying. While still in Florida, they picked up another hitchhiker, Dennis Weaver, who rode with them to Atlanta, where he was let out about 11:00 P.M. A short time later the four men interrupted their journey for a rest stop along the highway. The next morning the bodies of Simmons and Moore were discovered in a ditch nearby.

On November 23, after reading about the shootings in an Atlanta newspaper, Weaver communicated with the Gwinnett County police and related information concerning the journey with the victims, including a description of the car. The next afternoon, the petitioner and Allen, while in Simmons' car, were arrested in Asheville, N.C. In the search incident to the arrest a .25-caliber pistol, later shown to be that used to kill Simmons and Moore, was found in the petitioner's pocket. After receiving the warnings required by *Miranda v. Arizona*, 384 U.S. 436 (1966), and signing a written waiver of his rights, the petitioner signed a statement in which he admitted shooting, then robbing Simmons and Moore. He justified the slayings on the grounds of self-defense. The next day, while being transferred to Lawrenceville, Ga., the petitioner and Allen were taken to the scene of the shootings. Upon arriving there, Allen recounted the events leading to the slayings. His version of these events was as follows: After Simmons and Moore left the car, the petitioner stated the he intended to rob them. The petitioner then took his pistol in hand and positioned himself on the car to improve his aim. As Simmons and Moore came up an embankment toward the car, the petitioner fired three shots and the two men fell near a ditch. The petitioner, at close range, then fired a shot into the head of each. He robbed them of valuables and drove away with Allen.

A medical examiner testified that Simmons died from a bullet wound in the eye and that Moore died from bullet wounds in the cheek and in the back of the head. He further testified that both men had several bruises and abrasions about the face and head which probably were sustained either from the fall into the ditch or from being dragged or pushed along the embankment. Although Allen did not testify, a police detective recounted the substance of Allen's statements about the slayings and indicated that directly after Allen had made these statements the petitioner had admitted that Allen's account was accurate. The petitioner testified in his own defense. He confirmed that Allen had made the statements described by the detective, but denied their truth or ever having admitted to their accuracy. He indicated that he had shot Simmons and Moore because of fear and in self-defense, testifying they had attacked Allen and him, one wielding a pipe and the other a knife.

The trial judge submitted the murder charges to the jury on both felony murder and non–felony murder theories. He also instructed on the issue of self-defense but declined to instruct on manslaughter. He submitted the robbery case to the jury on both an armed-robbery theory and on the lesser included offense of robbery by intimidation. The jury found the petitioner guilty of two counts of armed robbery and two counts of murder.

At the penalty stage, which took place before the same jury, neither the prosecutor nor the petitioner's lawyer offered any additional evidence. Both counsel, however, made lengthy arguments dealing generally with the propriety of capital punishment under the circumstances and with the weight of the evidence of guilt. The trial judge instructed the jury that it could recommend either a death sentence or a life prison sentence on each count. The judge further charged the jury that in determining what sentence was appropriate the jury was free to consider the facts and circumstances, if any, presented by the parties in mitigation or aggravation.

Finally, the judge instructed the jury that it "would not be authorized to consider [imposing] the penalty of death" unless it first found beyond a reasonable doubt one of these aggravating circumstances:

"One—That the offense of murder was committed while the offender was engaged in the commission of two other capital felonies, to wit the armed robbery of [Simmons and Moore].

"Two—That the offender committed the offense of murder for the purpose of receiving money and the automobile described in the indictment.

"Three—The offense of murder was outrageously and wantonly vile, horrible and inhuman, in that they [sic] involved the depravity of the mind of the defendant."

Finding the first and second of these circumstances, the jury returned verdicts of death on each count.

The Supreme Court of Georgia affirmed the convictions and the imposition of the death sentences for murder. After reviewing the trial transcript and the record, including the evidence, and comparing the evidence and sentence in similar cases in accordance with the requirements of Georgia law, the court concluded that, considering the nature of the crime and the defendant, the sentences of death had not resulted from prejudice or any other arbitrary factor and were not excessive or disproportionate to the penalty applied in similar cases. The death sentences imposed for armed robbery, however, were vacated on the grounds that the death penalty had been rarely imposed in Georgia for that offense and that the jury improperly considered the murders as aggravating circumstances for the robberies after having considered the armed robberies as aggravating circumstances for the murders.

We granted the petitioner's application for a writ of certiorari limited to his challenge to the imposition of the death sentences in this case as "cruel and unusual" punishment in violation of the Eighth and Fourteenth Amendments.

II

Before considering the issues presented it is necessary to understand the Georgia statutory scheme for the imposition of the death penalty. The Georgia statute, as amended after our decision in

Furman v. Georgia, retains the death penalty for six categories of crime: murder, kidnapping for ransom or where the victim is harmed, armed robbery, rape, treason, and aircraft hijacking. The capital defendant's guilt or innocence is determined in the traditional manner, either by a trial judge or a jury, in the first stage of a bifurcated trial.

If trial is by jury, the trial judge is required to charge lesser included offenses when they are supported by any view of the evidence. After a verdict, finding or plea of guilty to a capital crime, a presentence hearing is conducted before whoever made the determination of guilt. The sentencing procedures are essentially the same in both the bench and jury trials. At the hearing: "the judge [or jury] shall hear additional evidence in extenuation, mitigation, and aggravation of punishment, including the record of any prior criminal convictions and pleas of guilty or pleas of nolo contendere of the defendant, or the absence of any prior conviction and pleas: Provided, however, that only such evidence in aggravation as the State has made known to the defendant prior to his trial shall be admissible. The judge [or jury] shall also hear argument by the defendant or his counsel and the prosecuting attorney . . . regarding the punishment to be imposed."

The defendant is accorded substantial latitude as to the types of evidence that he may introduce. Evidence considered during the guilt stage may be considered during the sentencing stage without being resubmitted.

In the assessment of the appropriate sentence to be imposed the judge is also required to consider or to include in his instructions to the jury "any mitigating circumstances or aggravating circumstances otherwise authorized by law and any of 10 statutory aggravating circumstances which may be supported by the evidence. . . ." The scope of the non-statutory aggravating or mitigating circumstances is not delineated in the statute. Before a convicted defendant may be sentenced to death, however, except in cases of treason or aircraft hijacking, the jury, or the trial judge in cases tried without a jury, must find beyond a reasonable doubt one of the 10 aggravating circumstances specified in the statute. The sentence of death may be imposed only if the jury (or judge) finds one of the statutory aggravating circumstances and then elects to impose that sentence.

If the verdict is death, the jury or judge must specify the aggravating circumstance(s) found. In jury cases, the trial judge is bound by the jury's recommended sentence.

In addition to the conventional appellate process available in all criminal cases, provision is made for special expedited direct review by the Supreme Court of Georgia of the appropriateness of imposing the sentence of death in the particular case. The court is directed to consider "the punishment as well as any errors enumerated by way of appeal," and to determine:

"(1) Whether the sentence of death was imposed under the influence of passion, prejudice, or any other arbitrary factor, and

"(2) Whether, in cases other than treason or aircraft hijacking, the evidence supports the jury's or judge's finding of a statutory aggravating circumstance as enumerated in section 27.2534.1 (b), and

"(3) Whether the sentence of death is excessive or disproportionate to the penalty imposed in similar cases, considering both the crime and the defendant."

If the court affirms a death sentence, it is required to include in its decision reference to similar cases that it has taken into consideration.

A transcript and complete record of the trial, as well as a separate report by the trial judge, are transmitted to the court for its use in reviewing the sentence. The report is in the form of a 6 1/2-page questionnaire, designed to elicit information about the defendant, the crime, and the circumstances of the trial. It requires the trial judge to characterize the trial in several ways designed to test for arbitrariness and disproportionality of sentence. Included in the report are responses to detailed questions concerning the quality of the defendant's representation, whether race played a role in the trial, and, whether, in the trial court's judgment, there was any doubt about the defendant's guilt or the appropriateness of the sentence. A copy of the report is served upon defense counsel. Under its special review authority, the court may either affirm the death sentence or remand the case for resentencing. In cases in which the death sentence is affirmed there remains the possibility of executive clemency.

III

We address initially the basic contention that the punishment of death for the crime of murder is, under all circumstances, "cruel and unusual" in violation of the Eighth and Fourteenth Amendments of the Constitution. In Part IV of this opinion, we will consider the sentence of death imposed under the Georgia statutes at issue in this case.

The Court on a number of occasions has both assumed and asserted the constitutionality of capital punishment. In several cases that assumption provided a necessary foundation for the decision, as the Court was asked to decide whether a particular method of carrying out a capital sentence would be allowed to stand under the Eighth Amendment. But until *Furman v. Georgia*, the Court never confronted squarely the fundamental claim that the punishment of death always, regardless of the enormity of the offense or the procedure followed in imposing the sentence, is cruel and unusual punishment in violation of the Constitution. Although this issue was presented and addressed in *Furman*, it was not resolved by the Court. Four Justices would have held that capital punishment is not unconstitutional per se; two Justices would have reached the opposite conclusion; and three Justices, while agreeing that the statutes then before the Court were invalid as applied, left open the question whether such punishment may ever be imposed. We now hold that the punishment of death does not invariably violate the Constitution.

   A

   The history of the prohibition of "cruel and unusual" punishment already has been reviewed at length. The phrase first appeared in the English Bill of Rights of 1689, which was drafted by Parliament at the accession of William and Mary. The English version appears to have been directed against punishments unauthorized by statute and beyond the jurisdiction of the sentencing court, as well as those disproportionate to the offense involved. The American draftsmen, who adopted the English phrasing in drafting the Eighth Amendment, were primarily concerned, however, with proscribing "tortures" and other "barbarous" methods of punishment.

   In the earliest cases raising Eighth Amendment claims, the Court focused on particular methods of execution to determine whether they were too cruel to pass constitutional muster. The constitutionality of the sentence of death itself was not at issue, and the criterion used to evaluate the mode of execution was its similarity to "torture" and other "barbarous" methods. ("It is safe to affirm that punishments of torture . . . and all others in the same line of unnecessary cruelty, are forbidden by that amendment . . ."). *In re Kemmler* ("Punishments are cruel when they involve torture or a lingering death . . ."). See also *Louisiana ex rel. Francis v. Resweber* (second attempt at electrocution found not to violate Eighth Amendment, since failure of initial execution attempt was "an unforeseeable accident" and "[t]here [was] no purpose to inflict unnecessary pain nor any unnecessary pain involved in the proposed execution").

   But the Court has not confined the prohibition embodied in the Eighth Amendment to "barbarous" methods that were generally outlawed in the 18th century. Instead, the Amendment has been interpreted in a flexible and dynamic manner. The Court early recognized that "a principle to be vital must be capable of wider application than the mischief which gave it birth" [*Weems v. United States*]. Thus the Clause forbidding "cruel and unusual" punishments "is not fastened to the obsolete but may acquire meaning as public opinion becomes enlightened by a humane justice."

In *Weems* the Court addressed the constitutionality of the Philippine punishment of *cadena temporal* for the crime of falsifying an official document. That punishment included imprisonment for at least 12 years and one day, in chains, at hard and painful labor; the loss of many basic civil rights; and subjection to lifetime surveillance. Although the Court acknowledged the possibility that "the cruelty of pain" may be present in the challenged punishment, it did not rely on that factor, for it rejected the proposition that the Eighth Amendment reaches only punishments that are "inhuman and barbarous, torture and the like." Rather, the Court focused on the lack of proportion between the crime and the offense:

"Such penalties for such offenses amaze those who have formed their conception of the relation of a state to even its offending citizens from the practice of the American commonwealths, and believe that it is a precept of justice that punishment for crime should be graduated and proportioned to offense."

Later, in *Trop v. Dulles,* supra, the Court reviewed the constitutionality of the punishment of denationalization imposed upon a soldier who escaped from an Army stockade and became a deserter for one day. Although the concept of proportionality was not the basis of the holding, the plurality observed in dicta that "[f]ines, imprisonment and even execution may be imposed depending upon the enormity of the crime."

The substantive limits imposed by the Eighth Amendment on what can be made criminal and punished were discussed in *Robinson v. California.* The Court found unconstitutional a state statute that made the status of being addicted to a narcotic drug a criminal offense. It held, in effect, that it is "cruel and unusual" to impose any punishment at all for the mere status of addiction. The cruelty in the abstract of the actual sentence imposed was irrelevant: "Even one day in prison would be a cruel and unusual punishment for the 'crime' of having a common cold." Most recently, in *Furman v. Georgia,* supra, three Justices in separate concurring opinions found the Eighth Amendment applicable to procedures employed to select convicted defendants for the sentence of death.

It is clear from the foregoing precedents that the Eighth Amendment has not been regarded as a static concept. As Mr. Chief Justice Warren said, in an oftquoted phrase, "[t]he Amendment must draw its meaning from the evolving standards of decency that mark the progress of a maturing society." Thus, an assessment of contemporary values concerning the infliction of a challenged sanction is relevant to the application of the Eighth Amendment. As we develop below more fully, this assessment does not call for a subjective judgment. It requires, rather, that we look to objective indicia that reflect the public attitude toward a given sanction.

But our cases also make clear that public perceptions of standards of decency with respect to criminal sanctions are not conclusive. A penalty also must accord with "the dignity of man," which is the "basic concept underlying the Eighth Amendment." This means, at least, that the punishment not be "excessive." When a form of punishment in the abstract (in this case, whether capital punishment may ever be imposed as a sanction for murder) rather than in the particular (the propriety of death as a penalty to be applied to a specific defendant for a specific crime) is under consideration, the inquiry into "excessiveness" has two aspects. First, the punishment must not involve the unnecessary and wanton infliction of pain. Second, the punishment must not be grossly out of proportion to the severity of the crime.

B

Of course, the requirements of the Eighth Amendment must be applied with an awareness of the limited role to be played by the courts. This does not mean that judges have no role to play, for the Eighth Amendment is a restraint upon the exercise of legislative power.

"Judicial review, by definition, often involves a conflict between judicial and legislative judgment as to what the Constitution means or requires. In this respect, Eighth Amendment cases come to us in no different posture. It seems conceded by all that the Amendment imposes some obligations on the judiciary to judge the constitutionality of punishment and that there are punishments that the Amendment would bar whether legislatively approved or not" [*Furman v. Georgia,* Justice White, concurring.]

But, while we have an obligation to insure that constitutional bounds are not overreached, we may not act as judges as we might as legislators.

"Courts are not representative bodies. They are not designed to be a good reflex of a democratic society. Their judgment is best informed, and therefore most dependable, within narrow limits. Their essential quality is detachment, founded on independence. History teaches that the independence of the judiciary is jeopardized when courts become embroiled in the passions of the day and assume primary responsibility in choosing between competing political, economic and social pressures" [*Dennis v. United States,* Frankfurter, J., concurring in affirmance of judgment]

Therefore, in assessing a punishment selected by a democratically elected legislature against the constitutional measure, we presume its validity. We may not require the legislature to select the least severe penalty possible so long as the penalty selected is not cruelly inhumane or disproportionate to the crime involved. And a heavy burden rests on those who would attack the judgment of the representatives of the people.

This is true in part because the constitutional test is intertwined with an assessment of contemporary standards and the legislative judgment weighs heavily in ascertaining such standards. "[I]n a democratic society legislatures, not courts, are constituted to respond to the will and consequently the moral values of the people" [*Furman v. Georgia,* Burger dissenting]. The deference we owe to the decisions of the state legislatures under our federal system . . . is enhanced where the specification of punishments is concerned, for "these are peculiarly questions of legislative policy." Caution is necessary lest this Court become, "under the aegis of the Cruel and Unusual Punishment Clause, the ultimate arbiter of the standards of criminal responsibility . . . throughout the country" [*Powell v. Texas,* plurality opinion]. A decision that a given punishment is impermissible under the Eighth Amendment cannot be reversed short of a constitutional amendment. The ability of the people to express their preference through the normal democratic processes, as well as through ballot referenda, is shut off. Revisions cannot be made in the light of further experience.

C

In the discussion to this point we have sought to identify the principles and considerations that guide a court in addressing an Eighth Amendment claim. We now consider specifically whether the sentence of death for the crime of murder is a per se violation of the Eighth and Fourteenth Amendments to the Constitution. We note first that history and precedent strongly support a negative answer to this question.

The imposition of the death penalty for the crime of murder has a long history of acceptance both in the United States and in England. The common-law rule imposed a mandatory death sentence on all convicted murderers. And the penalty continued to be used into the 20th century by most American States, although the breadth of the common-law rule was diminished, initially by narrowing the class of murders to be punished by death and subsequently by widespread adoption of laws expressly granting juries the discretion to recommend mercy.

It is apparent from the text of the Constitution itself that the existence of capital punishment was accepted by the Framers. At the time the Eighth Amendment was ratified, capital punishment was a common sanction in every State. Indeed, the First Congress of the United States enacted legislation providing death as the penalty for specified crimes. The Fifth Amendment, adopted at the same time as the Eighth, contemplated the continued existence of the capital sanction by imposing certain limits on the prosecution of capital cases:

"No person shall be held to answer for a capital, or otherwise infamous crime, unless on a presentment or indictment of a Grand Jury; . . . nor shall any person be subject for the same offense to be twice put in jeopardy of life or limb; . . . nor be deprived of life, liberty, or property, without due process of law. . . ."

And the Fourteenth Amendment, adopted over three-quarters of a century later, similarly contemplates the existence of the capital sanction in providing that no State shall deprive any person of "life, liberty, or property" without due process of law.

For nearly two centuries, this Court, repeatedly and often expressly, has recognized that capital punishment is not invalid per se. In *Wilkerson v. Utah*, where the Court found no constitutional violation in inflicting death by public shooting, it said:

"Cruel and unusual punishments are forbidden by the Constitution, but the authorities referred to are quite sufficient to show that the punishment of shooting as a mode of executing the death penalty for the crime of murder in the first degree is not included in that category, within the meaning of the Eighth Amendment."

Rejecting the contention that death by electrocution was "cruel and unusual," the Court in *In re Kemmler*, reiterated:

"[T]he punishment of death is not cruel, within the meaning of that word as used in the Constitution. It implies there something inhuman and barbarous, something more than the mere extinguishment of life."

Again, in *Louisiana ex rel. Francis v. Resweber*, the Court remarked: "The cruelty against which the Constitution protects a convicted man is cruelty inherent in the method of punishment, not the necessary suffering involved in any method employed to extinguish life humanely." And in *Trop v. Dulles*, Mr. Chief Justice Warren, for himself and three other Justices, wrote:

"Whatever the arguments may be against capital punishment, both on moral grounds and in terms of accomplishing the purposes of punishment . . . the death penalty has been employed throughout our history, and, in a day when it is still widely accepted, it cannot be said to violate the constitutional concept of cruelty."

Four years ago, the petitioners in *Furman* and its companion cases predicated their argument primarily upon the asserted proposition that standards of decency had evolved to the point where capital punishment no longer could be tolerated. The petitioners in those cases said, in effect, that the evolutionary process had come to an end, and that standards of decency required that the Eighth

Amendment be construed finally as prohibiting capital punishment for any crime regardless of its depravity and impact on society. This view was accepted by two Justices. Three other Justices were unwilling to go so far; focusing on the procedures by which convicted defendants were selected for the death penalty rather than on the actual punishment inflicted, they joined in the conclusion that the statutes before the Court were constitutionally invalid.

The petitioners in the capital cases before the Court today renew the "standards of decency" argument, but developments during the four years since *Furman* have undercut substantially the assumptions upon which their argument rested. Despite the continuing debate, dating back to the 19th century, over the morality and utility of capital punishment, it is now evident that a large proportion of American society continues to regard it as an appropriate and necessary criminal sanction.

The most marked indication of society's endorsement of the death penalty for murder is the legislative response to *Furman*. The legislatures of at least 35 States have enacted new statutes that provide for the death penalty for at least some crimes that result in the death of another person. And the Congress of the United States, in 1974, enacted a statute providing the death penalty for aircraft piracy that results in death. These recently adopted statutes have attempted to address the concerns expressed by the Court in *Furman* primarily (i) by specifying the factors to be weighed and the procedures to be followed in deciding when to impose a capital sentence, or (ii) by making the death penalty mandatory for specified crimes. But all of the post-*Furman* statutes make clear that capital punishment itself has not been rejected by the elected representatives of the people.

In the only statewide referendum occurring since Furman and brought to our attention, the people of California adopted a constitutional amendment that authorized capital punishment, in effect negating a prior ruling by the Supreme Court of California in *People v. Anderson*, that the death penalty violated the California Constitution.

The jury also is a significant and reliable objective index of contemporary values because it is so directly involved. The Court has said that "one of the most important functions any jury can perform in making . . . a selection [between life imprisonment and death for a defendant convicted in a capital case] is to maintain a link between contemporary community values and the penal system" [*Witherspoon v. Illinois*]. It may be true that evolving standards have influenced juries in recent decades to be more discriminating in imposing the sentence of death. But the relative infrequency of jury verdicts imposing the death sentence does not indicate rejection of capital punishment per se. Rather, the reluctance of juries in many cases to impose the sentence may well reflect the humane feeling that this most irrevocable of sanctions should be reserved for a small number of extreme cases. Indeed, the actions of juries in many States since *Furman* are fully compatible with the legislative judgments, reflected in the new statutes, as to the continued utility and necessity of capital punishment in appropriate cases. At the close of 1974 at least 254 persons had been sentenced to death since *Furman,* and by the end of March 1976, more than 460 persons were subject to death sentences.

As we have seen, however, the Eighth Amendment demands more than that a challenged punishment be acceptable to contemporary society. The Court also must ask whether it comports with the basic concept of human dignity at the core of the Amendment. Although we cannot "invalidate a category of penalties because we deem less severe penalties adequate to serve the ends of penology" [*Furman v. Georgia*], the sanction imposed cannot be so totally without penological justification that it results in the gratuitous infliction of suffering.

The death penalty is said to serve two principal social purposes: retribution and deterrence of capital crimes by prospective offenders.

In part, capital punishment is an expression of society's moral outrage at particularly offensive conduct. This function may be unappealing to many, but it is essential in an ordered society that asks its citizens to rely on legal processes rather than self-help to vindicate their wrongs.

"The instinct for retribution is part of the nature of man, and channeling that instinct in the administration of criminal justice serves an important purpose in promoting the stability of a society governed by law. When people begin to believe that organized society is unwilling or unable to impose upon criminal offenders the punishment they 'deserve,' then there are sown the seeds of anarchy—of self-help, vigilante justice, and lynch law" [*Furman v. Georgia*, Stewart concurring].

"Retribution is no longer the dominant objective of the criminal law" [*Williams v. New York*], but neither is it a forbidden objective nor one inconsistent with our respect for the dignity of men. Indeed, the decision that capital punishment may be the appropriate sanction in extreme cases is an expression of the community's belief that certain crimes are themselves so grievous an affront to humanity that the only adequate response may be the penalty of death.

Statistical attempts to evaluate the worth of the death penalty as a deterrent to crimes by potential offenders have occasioned a great deal of debate. The results simply have been inconclusive. As one opponent of capital punishment has said:

"[A]fter all possible inquiry, including the probing of all possible methods of inquiry, we do not know, and for systematic and easily visible reasons cannot know, what the truth about this 'deterrent' effect may be. . . .

"The inescapable flaw is . . . that social conditions in any state are not constant through time, and that social conditions are not the same in any two states. If an effect were observed (and the observed effects, one way or another, are not large) then one could not at all tell whether any of this effect is attributable to the presence or absence of capital punishment. A 'scientific'—that is to say, a soundly based—conclusion is simply impossible, and no methodological path out of this tangle suggests itself" [C. Black, *Capital Punishment: The Inevitability of Caprice and Mistake* 25–26 (1974)].

Although some of the studies suggest that the death penalty may not function as a significantly greater deterrent than lesser penalties, there is no convincing empirical evidence either supporting or refuting this view. We may nevertheless assume safely that there are murderers, such as those who act in passion, for whom the threat of death has little or no deterrent effect. But for many others, the death penalty undoubtedly is a significant deterrent. There are carefully contemplated murders, such as murder for hire, where the possible penalty of death may well enter into the cold calculus that precedes the decision to act. And there are some categories of murder, such as murder by a life prisoner, where other sanctions may not be adequate.

The value of capital punishment as a deterrent of crime is a complex factual issue the resolution of which properly rests with the legislatures, which can evaluate the results of statistical studies in terms of their own local conditions and with a flexibility of approach that is not available to the courts. Indeed, many of the post-*Furman* statutes reflect just such a responsible effort to define those crimes and those criminals for which capital punishment is most probably an effective deterrent.

In sum, we cannot say that the judgment of the Georgia Legislature that capital punishment may be necessary in some cases is clearly wrong. Considerations of federalism, as well as respect for the ability of a legislature to evaluate, in terms of its particular State, the moral consensus concerning the death penalty and its social utility as a sanction, require us to conclude, in the absence of more convincing evidence, that the infliction of death as a punishment for murder is not without justification and thus is not unconstitutionally severe.

Finally, we must consider whether the punishment of death is disproportionate in relation to the crime for which it is imposed. There is no question that death as a punishment is unique in its severity and irrevocability. When a defendant's life is at stake, the Court has been particularly sensitive to insure that every safeguard is observed. But we are concerned here only with the imposition of capital punishment for the crime of murder, and when a life has been taken deliberately by the offender, we cannot say that the punishment is invariably disproportionate to the crime. It is an extreme sanction, suitable to the most extreme of crimes.

We hold that the death penalty is not a form of punishment that may never be imposed, regardless of the circumstances of the offense, regardless of the character of the offender, and regardless of the procedure followed in reaching the decision to impose it.

IV

We now consider whether Georgia may impose the death penalty on the petitioner in this case.

A

While *Furman* did not hold that the infliction of the death penalty per se violates the Constitution's ban on cruel and unusual punishments, it did recognize that the penalty of death is different in kind from any other punishment imposed under our system of criminal justice. Because of the uniqueness of the death penalty, *Furman* held that it could not be imposed under sentencing procedures that created a substantial risk that it would be inflicted in an arbitrary and capricious manner. MR. JUSTICE WHITE concluded that "the death penalty is exacted with great infrequency even for the most atrocious crimes and . . . there is no meaningful basis for distinguishing the few cases in which it is imposed from the many cases in which it is not." Indeed, the death sentences examined by the Court in *Furman* were "cruel and unusual in the same way that being struck by lightning is cruel and unusual. For, of all the people convicted of [capital crimes], many just as reprehensible as these, the petitioners [in *Furman* were] among a capriciously selected random handful upon whom the sentence of death has in fact been imposed. . . . [T]he Eighth and Fourteenth Amendments cannot tolerate the infliction of a sentence of death under legal systems that permit this unique penalty to be so wantonly and so freakishly imposed."

Furman mandates that where discretion is afforded a sentencing body on a matter so grave as the determination of whether a human life should be taken or spared, that discretion must be suitably directed and limited so as to minimize the risk of wholly arbitrary and capricious action.

It is certainly not a novel proposition that discretion in the area of sentencing be exercised in an informed manner. We have long recognized that "[f]or the determination of sentences, justice generally requires . . . that there be taken into account the circumstances of the offense together with the character and propensities of the offender" [*Pennsylvania ex rel. Sullivan v. Ashe*]. Otherwise, "the system cannot function in a consistent and a rational manner" [American Bar Association Project on Standards for Criminal Justice, Sentencing Alternatives and Procedures 4.1 (a), Commentary, p. 201 (App. Draft 1968)].

The cited studies assumed that the trial judge would be the sentencing authority. If an experienced trial judge, who daily faces the difficult task of imposing sentences, has a vital need for accurate information about a defendant and the crime he committed in order to be able to impose a rational sentence in the typical criminal case, then accurate sentencing information is an indispensable prerequisite to a reasoned determination of whether a defendant shall live or die by a jury of people who may never before have made a sentencing decision.

Jury sentencing has been considered desirable in capital cases in order "to maintain a link between contemporary community values and the penal system—a link without which the determination of punishment could hardly reflect 'the evolving standards of decency that mark the progress of a maturing society.'" But it creates special problems. Much of the information that is relevant to the sentencing decision may have no relevance to the question of guilt, or may even be extremely prejudicial to a fair determination of that question. This problem, however, is scarcely insurmountable. Those who have studied the question suggest that a bifurcated procedure—one in which the question of sentence is not considered until the determination of guilt has been made—is the best answer. The drafters of the Model Penal Code concluded:

"[If a unitary proceeding is used] the determination of the punishment must be based on less than all the evidence that has a bearing on that issue, such for example as a previous criminal record of the accused, or evidence must be admitted on the ground that it is relevant to sentence, though it would be excluded as irrelevant or prejudicial with respect to guilt or innocence alone. Trial lawyers understandably have little confidence in a solution that admits the evidence and trusts to an instruction to the jury that it should be considered only in determining the penalty and disregarded in assessing guilt.

"The obvious solution . . . is to bifurcate the proceeding, abiding strictly by the rules of evidence until and unless there is a conviction, but once guilt has been determined opening the record to the further information that is relevant to sentence. This is the analogue of the procedure in the ordinary case when capital punishment is not in issue; the court conducts a separate inquiry before imposing sentence."

When a human life is at stake and when the jury must have information prejudicial to the question of guilt but relevant to the question of penalty in order to impose a rational sentence, a bifurcated system is more likely to ensure elimination of the constitutional deficiencies identified in *Furman*.

But the provision of relevant information under fair procedural rules is not alone sufficient to guarantee that the information will be properly used in the imposition of punishment, especially if sentencing is performed by a jury. Since the members of a jury will have had little, if any, previous experience in sentencing, they are unlikely to be skilled in dealing with the information they are given. To the extent that this problem is inherent in jury sentencing, it may not be totally correctible. It seems clear, however, that the problem will be alleviated if the jury is given guidance regarding the factors about the crime and the defendant that the State, representing organized society, deems particularly relevant to the sentencing decision.

The idea that a jury should be given guidance in its decision-making is also hardly a novel proposition. Juries are invariably given careful instructions on the law and how to apply it before they are authorized to decide the merits of a lawsuit. It would be virtually unthinkable to follow any other course in a legal system that has traditionally operated by following prior precedents and fixed rules of law. When erroneous instructions are given, retrial is often required. It is quite simply a hallmark of our legal system that juries be carefully and adequately guided in their deliberations.

While some have suggested that standards to guide a capital jury's sentencing deliberation are impossible to formulate, the fact is that such standards have been developed. When the drafters of the Model Penal Code faced this problem, they concluded "that it is within the realm of possibility to point to the main circumstances of aggravation and of mitigation that should be weighed and weighed against each other when they are presented in a concrete case." While such standards are by necessity somewhat general, they do provide guidance to the sentencing authority and thereby reduce the likelihood that it will impose a sentence that fairly can be called capricious or arbitrary. Where the sentencing authority is required to specify the factors it relied upon in reaching its decision, the further safeguard of meaningful appellate review is available to ensure that death sentences are not imposed capriciously or in a freakish manner.

In summary, the concerns expressed in *Furman* that the penalty of death not be imposed in an arbitrary or capricious manner can be met by a carefully drafted statute that ensures that the sentencing authority is given adequate information and guidance. As a general proposition these concerns are best met by a system that provides for a bifurcated proceeding at which the sentencing authority is apprised of the information relevant to the imposition of sentence and provided with standards to guide its use of the information.

We do not intend to suggest that only the above-described procedures would be permissible under *Furman* or that any sentencing system constructed along these general lines would inevitably satisfy the concerns of *Furman,* for each distinct system must be examined on an individual basis. Rather, we have embarked upon this general exposition to make clear that it is possible to construct capital-sentencing systems capable of meeting *Furman*'s constitutional concerns.

B

We now turn to consideration of the constitutionality of Georgia's capital-sentencing procedures. In the wake of *Furman,* Georgia amended its capital punishment statute, but chose not to narrow the scope of its murder provisions. Thus, now as before *Furman,* in Georgia "[a] person commits murder when he unlawfully and with malice aforethought, either express or implied, causes the death of another human being." All persons convicted of murder "shall be punished by death or by imprisonment for life."

Georgia did act, however, to narrow the class of murderers subject to capital punishment by specifying 10 statutory aggravating circumstances, one of which must be found by the jury to exist beyond a reasonable doubt before a death sentence can ever be imposed. In addition, the jury is authorized to consider any other appropriate aggravating or mitigating circumstances. The jury is not required to find any mitigating circumstance in order to make a recommendation of mercy that is binding on the trial court, but it must find a statutory aggravating circumstance before recommending a sentence of death.

These procedures require the jury to consider the circumstances of the crime and the criminal before it recommends sentence. No longer can a Georgia jury do as *Furman*'s jury did: reach a finding of the defendant's guilt and then, without guidance or direction, decide whether he should live or die. Instead, the jury's attention is directed to the specific circumstances of the crime: Was it committed in the course of another capital felony? Was it committed for money? Was it committed upon a peace officer or judicial officer? Was it committed in a particularly heinous way or in a manner that endangered the lives of many persons? In addition, the jury's attention is focused on the characteristics of the person who committed the crime: Does he have a record of prior convictions for capital offenses? Are there any special facts about this defendant that mitigate against imposing capital punishment (e.g., his youth, the extent of his cooperation with the police, his emotional state at the time of the crime) As a result, while some jury discretion still exists, "the discretion to be exercised is controlled by clear and objective standards so as to produce non-discriminatory application" [*Coley v. State* (Georgia)].

As an important additional safeguard against arbitrariness and caprice, the Georgia statutory scheme provides for automatic appeal of all death sentences to the State's Supreme Court. That court is required by statute to review each sentence of death and determine whether it was imposed under the influence of passion or prejudice, whether the evidence supports the jury's finding of a statutory aggravating circumstance, and whether the sentence is disproportionate compared to those sentences imposed in similar cases.

In short, Georgia's new sentencing procedures require as a prerequisite to the imposition of the death penalty, specific jury findings as to the circumstances of the crime or the character of the defendant. Moreover, to guard further against a situation comparable to that presented in *Furman*, the Supreme Court of Georgia compares each death sentence with the sentences imposed on similarly situated defendants to ensure that the sentence of death in a particular case is not disproportionate. On their face these procedures seem to satisfy the concerns of *Furman*. No longer should there be "no meaningful basis for distinguishing the few cases in which [the death penalty] is imposed from the many cases in which it is not."

The petitioner contends, however, that the changes in the Georgia sentencing procedures are only cosmetic, that the arbitrariness and capriciousness condemned by *Furman* continue to exist in Georgia—both in traditional practices that still remain and in the new sentencing procedures adopted in response to *Furman*.

1

First, the petitioner focuses on the opportunities for discretionary action that are inherent in the processing of any murder case under Georgia law. He notes that the state prosecutor has unfettered authority to select those persons whom he wishes to prosecute for a capital offense and to plea bargain with them. Further, at the trial the jury may choose to convict a defendant of a lesser included offense rather than find him guilty of a crime punishable by death, even if the evidence would support a capital verdict. And finally, a defendant who is convicted and sentenced to die may have his sentence commuted by the Governor of the State and the Georgia Board of Pardons and Paroles.

The existence of these discretionary stages is not determinative of the issues before us. At each of these stages an actor in the criminal justice system makes a decision which may remove a defendant from consideration as a candidate for the death penalty. *Furman*, in contrast, dealt with the decision to impose the death sentence on a specific individual who had been convicted of a capital offense. Nothing in any of our cases suggests that the decision to afford an individual defendant mercy violates the Constitution. *Furman* held only that, in order to minimize the risk that the death penalty would be imposed on a capriciously selected group of offenders, the decision to impose it had to be guided by standards so that the sentencing authority would focus on the particularized circumstances of the crime and the defendant.

2

The petitioner further contends that the capital-sentencing procedures adopted by Georgia in response to *Furman* do not eliminate the dangers of arbitrariness and caprice in jury sentencing that were held in *Furman* to be violative of the Eighth and Fourteenth Amendments. He claims that the statute is so broad and vague as to leave juries free to act as arbitrarily and capriciously as they wish in deciding whether to impose the death penalty. While there is no claim that the jury in this case relied upon a vague or overbroad provision to establish the existence of a statutory aggravating circumstance, the petitioner looks to the sentencing system as a whole (as the Court did in *Furman* and we do today) and argues that it fails to reduce sufficiently the risk of arbitrary infliction of death sentences. Specifically, Gregg urges that the statutory aggravating circumstances are too broad and too vague, that the sentencing procedure allows for arbitrary grants of mercy, and that the scope of the evidence and argument that can be considered at the presentence hearing is too wide.

The petitioner attacks the seventh statutory aggravating circumstance, which authorizes imposition of the death penalty if the murder was "outrageously or wantonly vile, horrible or inhuman in that it involved torture, depravity of mind, or an aggravated battery to the victim," contending that it is so broad that capital punishment could be imposed in any murder case. It is, of course, arguable that any murder involves depravity of mind or an aggravated battery. But this language need not be construed in this way, and there is no reason to assume that the Supreme Court of Georgia will adopt such an open-ended construction. In only one case has it upheld a jury's decision to sentence a defendant to death when the only statutory aggravating circumstance found was that of the seventh, and that homicide was a horrifying torture-murder.

The petitioner also argues that two of the statutory aggravating circumstances are vague and therefore susceptible of widely differing interpretations, thus creating a substantial risk that the death penalty will be arbitrarily inflicted by Georgia juries. In light of the decisions of the Supreme Court of Georgia we must disagree. First, the petitioner attacks that part of 27–2534.1 (b) (1) that authorizes a jury to consider whether a defendant has a "substantial history of serious assaultive criminal convictions." The Supreme Court of Georgia, however, has demonstrated a concern that the new sentencing procedures provide guidance to juries. It held this provision to be impermissibly vague in *Arnold v. State,* because it did not provide the jury with "sufficiently 'clear and objective standards.'" Second, the petitioner points to 27–2534.1 (b) (3) which speaks of creating a "great risk of death to more than one person." While such a phrase might be susceptible of an overly broad interpretation, the Supreme Court of Georgia has not so construed it. The only case in which the court upheld a conviction in reliance on this aggravating circumstance involved a man who stood up in a church and fired a gun indiscriminately into the audience. On the other hand, the court expressly reversed a finding of great risk when the victim was simply kidnaped in a parking lot.

The petitioner next argues that the requirements of *Furman* are not met here because the jury has the power to decline to impose the death penalty even if it finds that one or more statutory aggravating circumstances are present in the case. This contention misinterprets *Furman.*

Moreover, it ignores the role of the Supreme Court of Georgia which reviews each death sentence to determine whether it is proportional to other sentences imposed for similar crimes. Since the proportionality requirement on review is intended to prevent caprice in the decision to inflict the penalty, the isolated decision of a jury to afford mercy does not render unconstitutional death sentences imposed on defendants who were sentenced under a system that does not create a substantial risk of arbitrariness or caprice.

The petitioner objects, finally, to the wide scope of evidence and argument allowed at presentence hearings. We think that the Georgia court wisely has chosen not to impose unnecessary restrictions on the evidence that can be offered at such a hearing and to ap-

prove open and far-ranging argument. So long as the evidence introduced and the arguments made at the presentence hearing do not
prejudice a defendant, it is preferable not to impose restrictions. We
think it desirable for the jury to have as much information before it
as possible when it makes the sentencing decision.

3

Finally, the Georgia statute has an additional provision designed to assure that the death penalty will not be imposed on a
capriciously selected group of convicted defendants. The new sentencing procedures require that the State Supreme Court review
every death sentence to determine whether it was imposed under
the influence of passion, prejudice, or any other arbitrary factor,
whether the evidence supports the findings of a statutory aggravating circumstance, and "[w]hether the sentence of death is excessive
or disproportionate to the penalty imposed in similar cases, considering both the crime and the defendant." In performing its sentence-
review function, the Georgia court has held that "if the death
penalty is only rarely imposed for an act or it is substantially out of
line with sentences imposed for other acts it will be set aside as excessive" [*Coley v. State* (Georgia)]. The court on another occasion
stated that "we view it to be our duty under the similarity standard
to assure that no death sentence is affirmed unless in similar cases
throughout the state the death penalty has been imposed
generally . . ." [*Moore v. State* (Georgia)].

It is apparent that the Supreme Court of Georgia has taken its
review responsibilities seriously. In *Coley*, it held that "[t]he prior
cases indicate that the past practice among juries faced with similar
factual situations and like aggravating circumstances has been to
impose only the sentence of life imprisonment for the offense of
rape, rather than death." It thereupon reduced *Coley's* sentence
from death to life imprisonment. Similarly, although armed robbery
is a capital offense under Georgia law, 26–1902 (1972), the Georgia
court concluded that the death sentences imposed in this case for
that crime were "unusual in that they are rarely imposed for
[armed robbery]. Thus, under the test provided by statute, . . . they
must be considered to be excessive or disproportionate to the
penalties imposed in similar cases." The court therefore vacated
Gregg's death sentences for armed robbery and has followed a similar course in every other armed robbery death penalty case to
come before it.

The provision for appellate review in the Georgia capital-
sentencing system serves as a check against the random or arbitrary
imposition of the death penalty. In particular, the proportionality review substantially eliminates the possibility that a person will be

sentenced to die by the action of an aberrant jury. If a time comes when juries generally do not impose the death sentence in a certain kind of murder case, the appellate review procedures assure that no defendant convicted under such circumstances will suffer a sentence of death.

V

The basic concern of *Furman* centered on those defendants who were being condemned to death capriciously and arbitrarily. Under the procedures before the Court in that case, sentencing authorities were not directed to give attention to the nature or circumstances of the crime committed or to the character or record of the defendant. Left unguided, juries imposed the death sentence in a way that could only be called freakish. The new Georgia sentencing procedures, by contrast, focus the jury's attention on the particularized nature of the crime and the particularized characteristics of the individual defendant. While the jury is permitted to consider any aggravating or mitigating circumstances, it must find and identify at least one statutory aggravating factor before it may impose a penalty of death. In this way the jury's discretion is channeled. No longer can a jury wantonly and freakishly impose the death sentence; it is always circumscribed by the legislative guidelines. In addition, the review function of the Supreme Court of Georgia affords additional assurance that the concerns that prompted our decision in *Furman* are not present to any significant degree in the Georgia procedure applied here.

For the reasons expressed in this opinion, we hold that the statutory system under which Gregg was sentenced to death does not violate the Constitution. Accordingly, the judgment of the Georgia Supreme Court is affirmed.

It is so ordered.

A Justice Dissents

Two U.S. Supreme Court Justices dissented to Gregg v. Georgia, *the landmark decision which reinstated the death penalty in the United States. The dissenters were William Brennan and Thurgood Marshall, both of whom were opponents of the death penalty who had concurred in the decision in* Furman v. Georgia, *which had temporarily ended executions in 1972. In his dissent to* Gregg, *Marshall, the first, and at that time still the only black justice ever appointed to the Court, explained why he still believed the death penalty to be cruel and unusual punishment under the Constitution.*

GREGG v. GEORGIA 428 U.S. 156 (1976)
428 U.S. 153
MR. JUSTICE MARSHALL, dissenting.

In *Furman v. Georgia*, 408 U.S. 238, 314 (1972) (concurring opinion), I set forth at some length my views on the basic issue presented to the Court in these cases. The death penalty, I concluded, is a cruel and unusual punishment prohibited by the Eighth and Fourteenth Amendments. That continues to be my view.

I have no intention of retracing the "long and tedious journey," that led to my conclusion in *Furman*. My sole purposes here are to consider the suggestion that my conclusion in *Furman* has been undercut by developments since then, and briefly to evaluate the basis for my Brethren's holding that the extinction of life is a permissible form of punishment under the Cruel and Unusual Punishments Clause.

In *Furman* I concluded that the death penalty is constitutionally invalid for two reasons. First, the death penalty is excessive . . . second, the American people, fully informed as to the purposes of the death penalty and its liabilities, would in my view reject it as morally unacceptable.

Since the decision in *Furman*, the legislatures of 35 States have enacted new statutes authorizing the imposition of the death sentence for certain crimes, and Congress has enacted a law providing the death penalty for air piracy resulting in death. I would be less than candid if I did not acknowledge that these developments have a significant bearing on a realistic assessment of the moral acceptability of the death penalty to the American people. But if the constitutionality of the death penalty turns, as I have urged, on the opinion of an informed citizenry, then even the enactment of new death statutes cannot be viewed as conclusive.

In *Furman* I observed that the American people are largely unaware of the information critical to a judgment on the morality of the death penalty, and concluded that if they were better informed they would consider it shocking, unjust, and unacceptable. A recent study, conducted after the enactment of the post-*Furman* statutes, has confirmed that the American people know little about the death penalty, and that the opinions of an informed public would differ significantly from those of a public unaware of the consequences and effects of the death penalty.

Even assuming, however, that the post-*Furman* enactment of statutes authorizing the death penalty renders the prediction of the views of an informed citizenry an uncertain basis for a constitutional decision, the enactment of those statutes has no bearing whatsoever on the conclusion that the death penalty is unconstitutional because it is excessive. An excessive penalty is invalid under the Cruel and Unusual Punishments Clause "even though popular sentiment may favor" it. The inquiry here, then, is simply whether the death penalty is necessary to accomplish the legitimate legislative purposes in punishment, or whether a less severe penalty—life imprisonment—would do as well.

The two purposes that sustain the death penalty as nonexcessive in the Court's view are general deterrence and retribution. In *Furman* I canvassed the relevant data on the deterrent effect of capital punishment. The state of knowledge at that point, after literally centuries of debate, was summarized as follows by a United Nations Committee:

"It is generally agreed between the retentionists and abolitionists, whatever their opinions about the validity of comparative studies of deterrence, that the data which now exist show no correlation between the existence of capital punishment and lower rates of capital crime."

The available evidence, I concluded in *Furman*, was convincing that "capital punishment is not necessary as a deterrent to crime in our society."

The Solicitor General in his amicus brief in these cases relies heavily on a study by Isaac Ehrlich, reported a year after *Furman*, to support the contention that the death penalty does deter murder. Since the Ehrlich study was not available at the time of *Furman* and since it is the first scientific study to suggest that the death penalty may have a deterrent effect, I will briefly consider its import.

The Ehrlich study focused on the relationship in the Nation as a whole between the homicide rate and "execution risk"—the fraction of persons convicted of murder who were actually executed. Comparing the differences in homicide rate and execution risk for the years 1933 to 1969, Ehrlich found that increases in execution risk were associated with increases in the homicide rate. But when he employed the statistical technique of multiple regression analysis to control for the influence of other variables posited to have an impact on the homicide rate, Ehrlich found a negative correlation between changes in the homicide rate and changes in execution risk. His tentative conclusion was that for the period from 1933 to 1967 each additional execution in the United States might have saved eight lives.

The methods and conclusions of the Ehrlich study have been severely criticized on a number of grounds. It has been suggested, for example, that the study is defective because it compares execution and homicide rates on a nationwide, rather than a state-by-state, basis. The aggregation of data from all States—including those that have abolished the death penalty—obscures the relationship between murder and execution rates. Under Ehrlich's methodology, a decrease in the execution risk in one State combined with an increase in the murder rate in another State would, all other things being equal, suggest a deterrent effect that quite obviously would not exist. Indeed, a deterrent effect would be suggested if, once again all other things being equal, one State abolished the death penalty and experienced no change in the murder rate, while another State experienced an increase in the murder rate.

The most compelling criticism of the Ehrlich study is [428 U.S. 153, 236] that its conclusions are extremely sensitive to the choice of the time period included in the regression analysis. Analysis of Ehrlich's data reveals that all empirical support for the deterrent effect of capital punishment disappears when the five most recent years are removed from his time series—that is to say, whether a decrease in the execution risk corresponds to an increase or a decrease in the murder rate depends on the ending point of the sample period. This finding has cast severe doubts on the reliability of Ehrlich's tentative conclusions. Indeed, a recent regression study, based on Ehrlich's theoretical model but using cross-section state data for the years 1950 and 1960, found no support for the conclusion that executions act as a deterrent.

The Ehrlich study, in short, is of little, if any, assistance in assessing the deterrent impact of the death penalty. The evidence I reviewed in *Furman* remains convincing, in my view, that "capital punishment is not necessary as a deterrent to crime in our society." The justification for the death penalty must be found elsewhere.

The other principal purpose said to be served by the death penalty is retribution. The notion that retribution can serve as a moral justification for the sanction of death finds credence in the opinion of my Brothers STEWART, POWELL, and STEVENS, and that of my Brother WHITE in *Roberts v. Louisiana*. It is this notion that I find to be the most disturbing aspect of today's unfortunate decisions.

The concept of retribution is a multifaceted one, and any discussion of its role in the criminal law must be undertaken with caution. On one level, it can be said that the notion of retribution or reprobation is the basis of our insistence that only those who have broken the law be punished, and in this sense the notion is quite obviously central to a just system of criminal sanctions. But our recognition that retribution plays a crucial role in determining who may be punished by no means requires approval of retribution as a general justification for punishment. It is the question whether retribution can provide a moral justification for punishment—in particular, capital punishment—that we must consider.

My Brothers STEWART, POWELL, and STEVENS offer the following explanation of the retributive justification for capital punishment:

"The instinct for retribution is part of the nature of man, and channeling that instinct in the administration of criminal justice serves an important purpose in promoting the stability of a society governed by law. When people begin to believe that organized society is unwilling or unable to impose upon criminal offenders the punishment they 'deserve,' then there are sown the seeds of anarchy—of self-help, vigilante justice, and lynch law."

This statement is wholly inadequate to justify the death penalty. As my Brother BRENNAN stated in *Furman*, "[t]here is no evidence whatever that utilization of imprisonment rather than death encourages private blood feuds and other disorders." It simply defies belief to suggest that the death penalty is necessary to prevent the American people from taking the law into their own hands.

In a related vein, it may be suggested that the expression of moral outrage through the imposition of the death penalty serves to reinforce basic moral values—that it marks some crimes as particularly offensive and therefore to be avoided. The argument is akin to a deterrence argument, but differs in that it contemplates the individual's shrinking from antisocial conduct, not because he fears punishment, but because he has been told in the strongest possible way that the conduct is wrong. This contention, like the previous one, provides no support for the death penalty. It is inconceivable that any individual concerned about conforming his conduct to what society says is "right" would fail to realize that murder is "wrong" if the penalty were simply life imprisonment. The foregoing contentions—that society's expression of moral outrage through the imposition of the death penalty pre-empts the citizenry from taking the law into its own hands and reinforces moral values—are not retributive in the purest sense. They are essentially utilitarian in that they portray the death penalty as valuable because of its beneficial results. These justifications for the death penalty are inadequate because the penalty is, quite clearly I think, not necessary to the accomplishment of those results.

There remains for consideration, however, what might be termed the purely retributive justification for the death penalty—that the death penalty is appropriate, not because of its beneficial effect on society, but because the taking of the murderer's life is itself morally good. Some of the language of the opinion of my Brothers STEWART, POWELL, and STEVENS in No. 74–6257 appears positively to embrace this notion of retribution for its own sake as a justification for capital punishment. They state:

"[T]he decision that capital punishment may be the appropriate sanction in extreme cases is an expression of the community's belief that certain crimes are themselves so grievous an affront to humanity that the only adequate response may be the penalty of death."

They then quote with approval from Lord Justice Denning's remarks before the British Royal Commission on Capital Punishment:

"'The truth is that some crimes are so outrageous that society insists on adequate punishment, because the wrong-doer deserves it, irrespective of whether it is a deterrent or not.'"

Of course, it may be that these statements are intended as no more than observations as to the popular demands that it is thought must be responded to in order to prevent anarchy. But the implication of the statements appears to me to be quite different—namely, that society's judgment that the murderer "deserves" death must be respected not simply because the preservation of order requires it, but because it is appropriate that society make the judgment and carry it out. It is this latter notion, in particular, that I consider to be fundamentally at odds with the Eighth Amendment. The mere fact that the community demands the murderer's life in return for the evil he has done cannot sustain the death penalty, for as JUSTICES STEWART, POWELL, and STEVENS remind us, "the Eighth Amendment demands more than that a challenged punishment be acceptable to contemporary society." To be sustained under the Eighth Amendment, the death penalty must "compor[t] with the basic concept of human dignity at the core of the Amendment"; the objective in imposing it must be "[consistent] with our respect for the dignity of [other] men." Under these standards, the taking of life "because the wrongdoer deserves it" surely must fall, for such a punishment has as its very basis the total denial of the wrongdoer's dignity and worth.

The death penalty, unnecessary to promote the goal of deterrence or to further any legitimate notion of retribution, is an excessive penalty forbidden by the Eighth and Fourteenth Amendments. I respectfully dissent from the Court's judgment upholding the sentences of death imposed upon the petitioners in these cases.

European Parliament Resolution on the Death Penalty

On 17 December 1998, the European Parliament passed the following "Resolution on the Death Penalty"; the resolution expressed its con-

cerns, not only about the imposition of the death penalty in general but also about certain pending cases in particular. This unusual step, in essence chastising non-European governments as different as those of the United States and China, was an indication of how seriously the European Community takes the issue.

The European Parliament
—having regard to its previous resolutions on the death penalty,

—having regard to the resolution adopted in Geneva by the 53rd session on the UN Commission on Human Rights on the question of the death penalty,

A. having regard to Protocol 6 the European Convention on Human Rights,

B. having regard, in particular, to its resolution of 18 June 1998 on the establishment of a universal moratorium on executions and regretting the fact that the Council has not yet acted thereon,

C. having regard to the continuing use of capital punishment in many countries, often without a free and fair trial,

D. appalled by the number of executions taking place each year in countries such as China, Iran, Saudi Arabia and the United States,

Regarding certain specific cases

E. expressing its deep regret about the fact that, despite international reaction against executions, the United States continues to apply the death penalty,

F. noting that Mumia Abu-Jamal was condemned to death in December 1982 following an unfair trial, that his application for a re-trial was rejected on 30 October by the Supreme Court of Pennsylvania and that an appeal to the Supreme Court is now the only avenue left open,

G. whereas this rejection means that the Governor of Pennsylvania may at any time sign a fresh warrant setting a date for his execution,

H. having regard to the case of the Spanish national Joaquin Jose Martinez, who has been condemned to death and is in Starke Prison, Florida; whereas Martinez' defense lawyer is submitting an appeal to the Supreme Court of Florida,

I. noting that Sarah Jane Dematera, a 24-year-old Filipino woman, was sentenced to death in February 1996 by a Saudi Arabian court, and emphasizing that Mrs. Dematera had only a very limited opportunity to prove her innocence, as she had no access to legal assistance nor any other opportunities to enable her to exercise effectively her right of defense,

J. expressing its concern at the death sentences passed in Turkmenistan on Shaliko Maisuradze, Gulshirin Shykhyeva and her sister, Tylla Garadshayeva,

Regarding certain specific cases

1. Calls for the immediate and unconditional global abolition of the death penalty;

2. Calls on those states still practicing the death penalty to declare an immediate moratorium;

3. Calls, therefore, on the Council and on the Member States of the European Union to promote the tabling at the 1999 session of the United Nations General Assembly in New York, of a motion for a resolution entailing a universal moratorium on executions, with a view to the complete abolition of the death penalty;

4. Calls on the Member States not to agree to extradite individuals for crimes which carry the death penalty to those states which retain it on their statute books;

5. Calls on the Commission and the Council to promote the abolition of the death penalty through their relations with third countries, including when they negotiate agreements; Regarding specific cases

6. Calls once again on all the States within the United States to abandon the death penalty;

7. Issues an urgent appeal to the Governor of Pennsylvania not to sign a fresh warrant setting an execution date and reiterates its call for a re-trial for Mumia Abu-Jamal and for the death sentence passed on him to be commuted;

8. Calls on the Supreme Court of Florida to annul the death sentence passed on the Spanish national Joaquin Jose Martinez and to guarantee his right to prove his innocence through a re-trial;

9. Calls on the Saudi Arabian Government to abolish the death penalty and to commute the sentence on Mrs. Dematera and all other death sentences, and furthermore calls on the Saudi Arabian Government to give all those accused of capital crimes the necessary access to legal assistance during all stages of their trials;

10. Expresses its concern about the high number of death sentences being passed in Turkmenistan, and calls on the President of Turkmenistan to use his constitutional authority and commute the death sentences passed on Shaliko Maisuradze, Gulshirin Shykhyeva and Tylla Garadshayeva, and all other death sentences that come before him;

11. Instructs its President to forward this resolution to the Commission, the Council, the Secretary-General of the United Nations, the President of the UN Commission on Human Rights and

the parliaments and governments of the United States, Saudi Arabia, Turkmenistan, Iran and the People's Republic of China.

South Africa Abolishes the Death Penalty

The decision, written by Court President Arthur Chaskalson, in which the Constitutional Court of South Africa abolished the death penalty as incompatible with South Africa's new interim constitution, dealt with the question of whether the death penalty constitutes "cruel, inhuman, or degrading punishment" from an international perspective. The following discussion of the international precedents, including a controversial extradition from Canada to the United States, is excerpted from that decision. (Internal footnotes excised.)

CONSTITUTIONAL COURT OF THE REPUBLIC OF SOUTH AFRICA:
State v. Makwanyane and Mchunu

Section 11(2)-Cruel, Inhuman, or Degrading Punishment

Death is the most extreme form of punishment to which a convicted criminal can be subjected. Its execution is final and irrevocable. It puts an end not only to the right of life itself, but to all other personal rights which had vested in the deceased under Chapter Three of the *Constitution*. It leaves nothing except the memory in others of what has been and the property that passes to the deceased's heirs. In the ordinary meaning of the words, the death sentence is undoubtedly a cruel punishment. Once sentenced, the prisoner waits on death row in the company of other prisoners under sentence of death, for the process of their appeals and the procedures for clemency to be carried out. Throughout this period, those who remain on death row are uncertain of their fate, not knowing whether they will ultimately be reprieved or taken to the gallows. Death is a cruel penalty and the legal processes which necessarily involve waiting in uncertainty for the sentence to be set aside or carried out, add to the cruelty. It is also an inhuman punishment for it " . . . involves, by its very nature, a denial of the executed person's humanity," and it is degrading because it strips the convicted person of all dignity and treats him or her as an object to be eliminated by the state. The question is not, however, whether the death sentence is a cruel, inhuman, or degrading punishment in the ordinary meaning of these words but whether it is a cruel, inhuman, or degrading punishment within the meaning of section 11(2) of our *Constitution*. . . .

International and Foreign Comparative Law

The death sentence is a form of punishment which has been used throughout history by different societies. It has long been the subject of controversy. As societies became more enlightened, they restricted the offenses for which this penalty could be imposed. The movement away from the death penalty gained momentum during the second half of the present century with the growth of the abolitionist movement. In some countries, it is now prohibited in all circumstances, in some it is prohibited save in times of war, and in most countries that have retained it as a penalty for crime, its use has been restricted to extreme cases. According to Amnesty International, 1,831 executions were carried out throughout the world in 1993 as a result of sentences of death, of which 1,419 were in China, which means that only 412 executions were carried out in the rest of the world that year. Today, capital punishment has been abolished as a penalty for murder either specifically or in practice by almost half the countries of the world including the democracies of Europe and our neighboring countries, Namibia, Mozambique, and Angola. In most of those countries where it is retained, as the Amnesty International statistics show, it is seldom used.

In the course of the arguments addressed to us, we were referred to books and articles on the death sentence, and to judgments dealing with challenges made to capital punishment in the courts of other countries and in international tribunals. The international and foreign authorities are of value because they analyze arguments for and against the death sentence and show how courts of other jurisdictions have dealt with this vexed issue. For that reason alone they require our attention. They may also have to be considered because of their relevance to section 35(1) of the *Constitution*, which states:

"In interpreting the provisions of this Chapter a court of law shall promote the values which underlie an open and democratic society based on freedom and equality and shall, where applicable, have regard to public international law applicable to the protection of the rights entrenched in this Chapter, may have regard to comparable foreign case law."

Customary international law and the ratification and accession to international agreements is dealt with in section 231 of the *Constitution* which sets the requirements for such law to be binding within South Africa. In the context of section 35(1), public international law would include non-binding as well as binding law. They may both be used under the section as tools of interpretation. International agreements and customary international law accordingly provide a framework within which Chapter Three can be evaluated and understood, and for that purpose, decisions of tribunals dealing with comparable instruments, such as the United Nations Committee on Human Rights, the Inter-American Commission on Human Rights, the Inter-American Court of Human Rights, the European Commission on Human Rights, and the European Court of Human Rights, and in appropriate cases, reports of specialized agencies such as the International Labour Organization may provide guidance as to the correct interpretation of particular provisions of Chapter Three.

Capital punishment is not prohibited by public international law, and this is a factor that has to be taken into account in deciding whether it is cruel, inhuman, or degrading punishment within the meaning of section 11(2). International human rights agreements differ, however, from our *Constitution* in that where right to life is expressed in unqualified terms they either deal specifically with the death sentence, or authorize exceptions to be made to the right to life by law. This has influenced the way international tribunals have dealt with issues relating to capital punishment, and is relevant to a proper understanding of such decisions.

Comparative "bill of rights" jurisprudence will no doubt be of importance, particularly in the early stages of the transition when there is no developed indigenous jurisprudence in this branch of the law on which to draw. Although we are told by section 35(1) that we "may" have regard to foreign case law, it is important to appreciate that this will not necessarily offer a safe guide to the interpretation of Chapter Three of our *Constitution*. This has already been pointed out in a number of decisions of the Provincial and Local Divisions of the Supreme Court, and is implicit in the injunction given to the Courts in section 35(1), which in permissive terms allows the Courts to "have regard to" such law. There is no injunction to do more than this.

When challenges to the death sentence in international or foreign courts and tribunals have failed, the constitution or the international instrument concerned has either directly sanctioned capital punishment or has specifically provided that the right to life is subject to exceptions sanctioned by law. The only case to which we were referred in which there were not such express provisions in the *Constitution*, was the decision of the Hungarian Constitutional Court. There the challenge succeeded and the death penalty was declared to be unconstitutional.

Our *Constitution* expresses the right to life in an unqualified form, and prescribes the criteria that have to be met for the limitation of entrenched rights, including the prohibition of legislation that negates the essential content of an entrenched right. In dealing with comparative law, we must bear in mind that we are required to construe the South African Constitution, and not an international instrument or the constitution of some foreign country, and that this has to be done with due regard to our legal system, our history and circumstances, and the structure and language of our own *Constitution*. We can derive assistance from public international law and foreign case law, but we are in no way bound to follow it.

Capital Punishment in the United States of America

  The earliest litigation on the validity of the death sentence seems to have been pursued in the courts of the United States of America. It has been said there that the "Constitution itself poses the first obstacle to [the] argument that capital punishment is *per se* unconstitutional." From the beginning, the United States *Constitution* recognized capital punishment as lawful. The Fifth Amendment (adopted in 1791) refers in specific terms to capital punishment and impliedly recognizes its validity. The Fourteenth Amendment (adopted in 1868) obliges the states, not to "deprive any person of life, liberty or property, without due process of law" and it too impliedly recognizes the right of states to make laws for such purposes. The argument that capital punishment is unconstitutional was based on the Eighth Amendment, which prohibits cruel and unusual punishment. Although the Eighth Amendment "has not been regarded as a static concept" and as drawing its meaning "from the evolving standards of decency that mark the progress of a maturing society, the fact that the Constitution recognizes the lawfulness of capital punishment has proved to be an obstacle in the way of the acceptance of this argument, and this is stressed in some of the judgments of the United States Supreme Court.

  Although challenges under state constitutions to the validity of the death sentence have been successful, the federal constitutionality of the death sentence as a legitimate form of punishment for murder was affirmed by the United States Supreme Court in *Gregg v. Georgia*. Both before and after *Gregg's case*, decisions upholding and rejecting challenges to death penalty statutes have divided the Supreme Court, and have led at times to sharply-worded judgments. The decisions ultimately turned on the votes of those judges who considered the nature of the discretion given to the sentencing authority to be the crucial factor.

  Statutes providing for mandatory death sentences, or too little discretion in sentencing, have been rejected by the Supreme Court because they do not allow for consideration of factors peculiar to the convicted person facing sentence, which may distinguish his or her case from other cases. For the same reason, statutes which allow too wide a discretion to judges or juries have also been struck down on the grounds that the exercise of such discretion leads to arbitrary results. In sum, therefore, if there is no discretion, too little discretion, or an unbounded discretion, the provision authorizing the death sentence has been struck down as being contrary to the Eighth Amendment; where the discretion has been "suitably directed and limited so as to minimize the risk of wholly arbitrary and capricious action," the challenge to the statute has failed.

Arbitrariness and Inequality

Basing his argument on the reasons which found favour with the majority of the United States Supreme Court in *Furman v. Georgia*, Mr. Trengove contended on behalf of the accused that the imprecise language of section 227, and the unbounded discretion vested by it in the Courts, make its provisions unconstitutional.

Section 277 of the Criminal Procedure Act provides:

"Sentence of death

"(1) The sentence of death may be passed by a superior court only and only in the case of a conviction for—(a) murder; (b) treason committed when the Republic is in a state of war; (c) robbery or attempted robbery, if the court finds aggravating circumstances to have been present; (d) kidnapping; (e) child-stealing; (f) rape.

"(2) The sentence of death shall be imposed—

(a) after the presiding judge conjointly with the assessors (if any), subject to the provisions of s 145(4)(a), or, in the case of a trial by a special superior court, that court, with due regard to any evidence and argument on sentence in terms of section 274, has made a finding on the presence or absence of any mitigating or aggravating factors; and

(b) if the presiding judge or court, as the case may be, with due regard to that finding, is satisfied that the sentence of death is the proper sentence.

"(3) (a) The sentence of death shall not be imposed upon an accused who was under the age of 18 years at the time of the commission of the act which constituted the offense concerned.

(b) If in the application of paragraph (a) the age of accused is placed in issue, the onus shall be on the State to show beyond a reasonable doubt that the accused was 18 years of age or older at the relevant time."

Under our court system questions of guilt and innocence and the proper sentence to be imposed on those found guilty of crimes, are not decided by juries. In capital cases, where it is likely that the death sentence may be imposed, judges sit with two assessors who have an equal vote with the judge on the issue of guilt and on any mitigating or aggravating factors relevant to the sentence; but sentencing is the prerogative of the judge alone. The *Criminal Procedure*

Act allows a full right of appeal to persons sentenced to death, including a right to dispute the sentence without having to establish an irregularity or misdirection on the part of the trial judge. The Appellate Division is empowered to set the sentence aside if it would not have imposed such sentence itself, and it has laid down criteria for the exercise of this power by itself and other courts. If the person sentenced to death does not appeal, the Appellate Division is nevertheless required to review the case and to set aside the death sentence if it is of the opinion that it is not a proper sentence.

Mitigating and aggravating factors must be identified by the Court, bearing in mind that the onus is on the State to prove beyond a reasonable doubt the existence of aggravating factors and to negative beyond a reasonable doubt the presence of any mitigating factors relied on by the accused. Due regard must be paid to the personal circumstances and subjective factors which might have influenced the accused person's conduct, and these factors must then be weighed up with the main objects of punishment, which have been held to be: deterrence, prevention, reformation, and retribution. In this process "[e]very relevant consideration should receive the most scrupulous care and reasoned attention," and the death sentence should only be imposed in the most exceptional cases, where there is no reasonable prospect of reformation and the objects of punishment would not be properly achieved by any other sentence.

There seems to me to be little difference between the guided discretion required for the death sentence in the United States, and the criteria laid down by the Appellate Division for the imposition of the death sentence. The fact that the Appellate Division, a court of experienced judges, takes the final decision in all cases is, in my view more likely to result in consistency of sentencing, than will be the case where sentencing is in the hands of jurors who are offered statutory guidance as to how that discretion should be exercised.

The argument that the imposition of the death sentence under section 277 is arbitrary and capricious does not, however, end there. It also focuses on what is alleged to be the arbitrariness inherent in the application of section 277 in practice. Of the thousands of persons put on trial for murder, only a very small percentage are sentenced to death by a trial court, and of those, a large number escape the ultimate penalty on appeal. At every stage of the process there is an element of chance. The outcome may be dependent upon factors such as the way the case is investigated by the police, the way the case is presented by the prosecutor, how effectively the accused is defended, the personality and particular attitude to capital punishment of the trial judge and, if the matter goes on appeal, the particu-

lar judges who are selected to hear the case. Race and poverty are
also alleged to be factors.

Most accused facing a possible death sentence are unable to afford legal assistance, and are defended under the *pro deo* system.
The defending counsel is more often than not young and inexperi-
enced, frequently of a different race to his or her client, and if this is
the case, usually has to consult through an interpreter. *Pro deo* counsel are paid only a nominal fee for the defense, and generally lack
the financial resources and infrastructural support to undertake the
necessary investigations and research, to employ expert witnesses to
give advice, including advice on matters relevant to sentence, to as-
semble witnesses, to bargain with the prosecution, and generally to
conduct an effective defense. Accused persons who have the money
to do so, are able to retain experienced attorneys and counsel, who
are paid to undertake the necessary investigations and research, and
as a result they are less likely to be sentenced to death than persons
similarly placed who are unable to pay for such services.

It needs to be mentioned that there are occasions when senior
members of the bar act *pro deo* in particularly difficult cases—indeed
the present case affords an example of that, for Mr. Trengove and his
juniors have acted *pro deo* in the proceedings before us, and the
Legal Resources Centre who have acted as their instructing attorneys, have done so without charge. An enormous amount of research has gone into the preparation of the argument and it is highly
doubtful that even the wealthiest members of our society could
have secured a better service than they have provided. But this is
the exception and not the rule. This may possibly change as a result
of the provisions of section 25(3)(e) of the *Constitution,* but there are
limits to the available financial and human resources, limits which
are likely to exist for the foreseeable future, and which will continue
to place poor accused at a significant disadvantage in defending
themselves in capital cases.

It cannot be gainsaid that poverty, race and chance play roles
in the outcome of capital cases and in the final decision as to who
should live and who should die. It is sometimes said that this is understood by the judges, and as far as possible, taken into account by
them. But in itself this is no answer to the complaint of arbitrariness
on the contrary, it may introduce an additional factor of arbitrariness
that would also have to be taken into account. Some, but not all accused persons may be acquitted because such allowances are made,
and others who are convicted, but not all, may for the same reason
escape the death sentence.

In holding that the imposition and carrying out of the death
penalty in the cases then under consideration constituted cruel and

unusual punishment in the United States, Justice Douglas, concurring in *Furman v. Georgia*, said that "[a]ny law which is nondiscriminatory on its face may be applied in such a way as to violate the Equal Protection Clause of the Fourteenth Amendment." Discretionary statutes are: "pregnant with discrimination and discrimination is an ingredient not compatible with the idea of equal protection of the laws that is implicit in the ban on "cruel and unusual" punishments."

It was contended that we should follow this approach and hold that the factors to which I have referred, make the application of section 277, in practice, arbitrary and capricious and, for that reason, any resulting death sentence is cruel, inhuman and degrading punishment.

The differences that exist between rich and poor, between good and bad prosecutions, between good and bad defense, between severe and lenient judges, between judges who favor capital punishment and those who do not, and the subjective attitudes that might be brought into play by factors such as race and class, may in similar ways affect any case that comes before the courts, and is almost certainly present to some degree in all court systems. Such factors can be mitigated, but not totally avoided, by allowing convicted persons to appeal to a higher court. Appeals are decided on the record of the case and on findings made by the trial court. If the evidence on record and the findings made have been influenced by these factors, there may be nothing that can be done about that on appeal. Imperfection inherent in criminal trials means that error cannot be excluded; it also means that persons similarly placed may not necessarily receive similar punishment. This needs to be acknowledged. What also needs to be acknowledged is that the possibility of error will be present in any system of justice and that there cannot be perfect equality as between accused persons in the conduct and outcome of criminal trials. We have to accept these differences in the ordinary criminal cases that come before our courts, even to the extent that some may go to gaol when others similarly placed may be acquitted or receive non custodial services. But death is different, and the question is, whether this is acceptable when the difference is between life and death. Unjust imprisonment is a great wrong, but if it is discovered, the prisoner can be released and compensated; but the killing of an innocent person is irremediable.

In the United States, the Supreme Court has addressed itself primarily to the requirement of due process. Statutes have to be clear and discretion curtailed without ignoring the peculiar circumstances of each accused person. Verdicts are set aside if the defense has not been adequate, and persons sentenced to death are allowed wide rights of appeal and review. This attempt to ensure the utmost procedural fairness has itself led to problems. The most notorious is the "death row phenomenon" in which prisoners cling to life, exhausting every possible avenue of redress, and using every device to put off the date of execution, in the natural and understandable hope that there will be a reprieve from the Courts or the executive. It is common for prisoners in the United States to remain on death row for many years, and this dragging out of the process has been characterized as being cruel and degrading. The difficulty of implementing a system of capital punishment which on the one hand avoids arbitrariness by insisting on a high standard of procedural fairness, and on the other hand avoids delays that in themselves are the cause of impermissible cruelty and inhumanity, is apparent. Justice Blackmun, who sided with the majority in *Gregg's case* ultimately came to the conclusion that it is not possible to design a system that avoids arbitrariness. To design a system that avoids arbitrariness and delays in carrying out the sentence is even more difficult.

The United States jurisprudence has not resolved the dilemma arising from the fact that the Constitution prohibits cruel and unusual punishments, but also permits, and contemplates that there will be capital punishment. The acceptance by a majority of the United States Supreme Court of the proposition that capital punishment is not *per se* unconstitutional, but that in certain circumstances it may be arbitrary, and thus unconstitutional, has led to endless litigation. Considerable expense and interminable delays result from the exceptionally high standard of procedural fairness set by the United States courts in attempting to avoid arbitrary decisions. The difficulties that have been experienced in following this path, to which Justice Blackmun and Justice Scalia have both referred, but from which they have drawn different conclusions, persuade me that we should not follow this route.

The Right to Dignity
Although the United States Constitution does not contain a specific guarantee of human dignity, it has been accepted by the United States Supreme Court that the concept of human dignity is at the core of the prohibition of "cruel and unusual punishment" by the Eighth and Fourteenth Amendments. For Justice Brennan this was decisive of the question in *Gregg v. Georgia*. The fatal constitutional infirmity in the punishment of death is that it treats "members of the human race as nonhumans, as objects to be toyed with and discarded. [It is] thus inconsistent with the fundamental premise of the Clause that even the vilest criminal remains a human being possessed of common human dignity."

Under our constitutional order the right to human dignity is specifically guaranteed. It can only be limited by legislation which passes the stringent test of being 'necessary.' The weight given to human dignity by Justice Brennan is wholly consistent with the values of our Constitution and the new order established by it. It is also consistent with the approach to extreme punishments followed by courts in other countries.

In Germany, the Federal Constitutional Court has stressed this aspect of punishment. Respect for human dignity especially requires the prohibition of cruel, inhuman, and degrading punishments. [The state] cannot turn the offender into an object of crime prevention to the detriment of his constitutionally protected right to social worth and respect.

That capital punishment constitutes a serious impairment of human dignity has also been recognized by judgments of the Canadian Supreme Court. *Kindler v. Canada* was concerned with the extradition from Canada to the United States of two fugitives, Kindler, who had been convicted of murder and sentenced to death in the United States, and Ng, who was facing a murder charge there and a possible death sentence. Three of the seven judges who heard the case expressed the opinion that the death penalty was cruel and unusual:

"It is the supreme indignity to the individual, the ultimate corporal punishment, the final and complete lobotomy and the absolute and irrevocable castration. [It is] the ultimate desecration of human dignity."

Three other judges were of the opinion that:

"[t]here is strong ground for believing, having regard to the limited extent to which the death penalty advances any valid penological objectives and the serious invasion of human dignity it engenders, that the death penalty cannot, except in exceptional circumstances, be justified in this country."

In the result, however, the majority of the Court held that the validity of the order of extradition did not depend on the constitutionality of the death penalty in Canada, or the guarantee in its Charter of Rights against cruel and unusual punishment. The Charter was concerned with legislative and executive acts carried out in Canada, and an order for extradition neither imposed nor authorized any punishment within the borders of Canada.

The issue in *Kindler's case* was whether the action of the Minister of Justice, who has authorized the extradition without any assurance that the death penalty would not be imposed, was constitutional. It was argued that this executive act was contrary to section 12 of the Charter which requires the executive to act in accordance with fundamental principles of justice. The Court decided by a majority of four to three that in the particular circumstances of the case the decision of the Minister of Justice could not be set aside on these grounds. In balancing the international obligations of Canada in respect of extradition, and another purpose of the extradition legislation—to prevent Canada from becoming a safe haven for criminals, against the likelihood that the fugitives would be executed if returned to the United States, the view of the majority was that the decision to return the fugitives to the United States could not be said to be contrary to the fundamental principles of justice. In their view, it would not shock the conscience of Canadians to permit this to be done.

The International Covenant on Civil and Political Rights
Ng and Kindler took their cases to the Human Rights Committee of the United Nations, contending that Canada had breached its obligations under the *International Covenant on Civil and Political Rights*. Once again, there was a division of opinion within the tribunal. In *Ng's case* it was said:
"The Committee is aware that, by definition, every execution of a sentence of death may be considered to constitute cruel and inhuman treatment within the meaning of article 7 of the covenant."
There was no dissent from that statement. But the *International Covenant* contains provisions permitting, with some qualifications, the imposition of capital punishment for the most serious crimes. In view of these provisions, the majority of the Committee were of the opinion that the extradition of fugitives to a country which enforces the death sentence in accordance with the requirements of the *International Covenant*, should not be regarded as a breach of the obligations of the extraditing country. In *Ng's case*, the method of execution which he faced if extradited was asphyxiation in a gas chamber. This was found by a majority of the Committee to involve unnecessary physical and mental suffering and, notwithstanding the sanction given to capital punishment, to be cruel punishment within the meaning of article 7 of the *International Covenant*. In *Kindler's case*, in which the complaint was delivered at the same time as that in *Ng's case*, but the decision was given earlier, it was held that the method of execution which was by lethal injection was not a cruel method of execution, and that the extradition did not in the circumstances constitute a breach of Canada's obligations under the *International Covenant*.
The Committee also held in *Kindler's case* that prolonged judicial proceedings giving rise to the death row phenomenon does not *per se* constitute cruel, inhuman or degrading treatment. There were dissents in both cases. Some Commissioners in *Ng's case* held that

asphyxiation was not crueler than other forms of execution. Some in *Kindler's case* held that the provision of the *International Covenant* against the arbitrary deprivation of the right to life took priority over the provisions of the *International Covenant* which allow the death sentence, and that Canada ought not in the circumstances to have extradited Kindler without an assurance that he would not be executed.

It should be mentioned here that although articles 6(2) to (5) of the *International Covenant* specifically allow the imposition of the death sentence under strict controls "for the most serious crimes" by those countries which have not abolished it, it provides in article 6(6) that "[n]othing in this article shall be invoked to delay or to prevent the abolition of capital punishment by any State Party to the present Covenant." The fact that the *International Covenant* sanctions capital punishment must be seen in this context. It tolerates but does not provide justification for the death penalty.

Despite these differences of opinion, what is clear from the decisions of the Human Rights Committee of the United Nations is that the death penalty is regarded by it as cruel and inhuman punishment within the ordinary meaning of those words, and that it was because of the specific provisions of the *International Covenant* authorizing the imposition of capital punishment by member states in certain circumstances, that the words had to be given a narrow meaning.

The European Convention of Human Rights

Similar issues were debated by the European Court of Human Rights in *Soering v. United Kingdom*. This case was also concerned with the extradition to the United States of a fugitive to face murder charges for which capital punishment was a competent sentence. It was argued that this would expose him to inhumane and degrading treatment or punishment in breach of Article 3 of the *European Convention on Human Rights*. Article 2 of the *European Convention* protects the right to life but makes an exception in the case of "the execution of a sentence of a court following [the] conviction of a crime for which this penalty is provided by law." The majority of the Court held that Article 3 could not be construed as prohibiting all capital punishment, since to do so would nullify Article 2. It was, however, competent to test the imposition of capital punishment in particular cases against the requirements of Article 3—the manner in which it is imposed or executed, the personal circumstances of the condemned person and the disproportionality to the gravity of the crime committed, as well as the conditions of detention awaiting execution, were capable of bringing the treatment or punishment received by the condemned person within the proscription.

On the facts, it was held that extradition to the United States to face trial in Virginia would expose the fugitive to the risk of treatment going beyond the threshold set by Article 3. The special factors taken into account were the youth of the fugitive (he was 18 at the time of the murders), an impaired mental capacity, and the suffering on death row which could endure for up to eight years if he were convicted. Additionally, although the offense for which extradition was sought had been committed in the United States, the fugitive who was a German national was also liable to be tried for the same offense in Germany. Germany, which has abolished the death sentence, also sought his extradition for the murders. There was accordingly a choice in regard to the country to which the fugitive should be extradited, and that choice should have been exercised in a way which would not lead to a contravention of Article 3. What weighed with the Court was the fact that the choice facing the United Kingdom was not a choice between extradition to face a possible death penalty and no punishment, but a choice between extradition to a country which allows the death penalty and one which does not. We are in a comparable position. A holding by us that the death penalty for murder is unconstitutional, does not involve a choice between freedom and death; it involves a choice between death in the very few cases which would otherwise attract that penalty under section 277(1)(a), and the severe penalty of life imprisonment.

Capital Punishment in India

In the amicus brief of the South African Police, reliance was placed on decisions of the Indian Supreme Court, and it is necessary to refer briefly to the way the law has developed in that country.

Section 302 of the Indian *Penal Code* authorizes the imposition of the death sentence as a penalty for murder. In *Bachan Singh v. State of Punjab*, the constitutionality of this provision was put in issue. Article 21 of the Indian *Constitution* provides that:

"No person shall be deprived of his life or personal liberty except according to procedure established by law."

The wording of this article presented an obstacle to a challenge to the death sentence, because there was a "law" which made provision for the death sentence. Moreover, Article 72 of the *Constitution* empowers the President and Governors to commute sentences if death, and Article 134 refers to the Supreme Court's powers on appeal in cases where the death sentence has been imposed. It was clear, therefore, that capital punishment was specifically contemplated and sanctioned by the framers of the *Indian Constitution,* when it was adopted by them in November 1949.

Counsel for the accused in *Bachan Singh's case* sought to overcome this difficulty by contending that Article 21 had to be read with Article 19(3), which guarantees the freedoms of speech, of assembly, of association, of movement, of residence, and the freedom to engage in any occupation. These fundamental freedoms can only be restricted under the Indian Constitution if the restrictions are reasonable for the attainment of a number of purposes defined in sections 19(2) to (6). It was contended that the right to life was basic to the enjoyment of these fundamental freedoms, and that the death sentence restricted them unreasonably in that it served no social purpose, its deterrent effect was unproven and it defiled the dignity of the individual.

The Supreme Court analyzed the provisions of Article 19(1) and came to the conclusion, for reasons that are not material to the present case, that the provisions of section 302 of the Indian *Penal Code* did "not have to stand the rest of the test of Article 19(1) of the Constitution." It went on, however, to consider "arguendo" what the outcome would be if the test of reasonableness and public interest under Article 19(1) had to be satisfied.

The Supreme Court had recognized in a number of cases that the death sentence served as a deterrent, and the Law Commission of India, which had conducted an investigation into capital punishment in 1967, had recommended that capital punishment be retained. The court held that in the circumstances it was "for the petitioners to prove and establish that the death sentence for murder is so outmoded, unusual, or excessive as to be devoid of any rational nexus with the purpose and object of the legislation."

The Court then dealt with international authorities for and against the death sentence, and with the arguments concerning deterrence and retribution. After reviewing the arguments for and against the death sentence, the court concluded that:

"the question whether or not [the] death penalty serves any penological purpose is a difficult, complex and intractable issue [which] has evoked strong, divergent views. For the purpose of testing the constitutionality of the impugned provisions as to the death penalty . . . on the grounds of reasonableness in the light of Articles 19 and 21 of the Constitution, it is not necessary for us to express any categorical opinion, one way or another, as to which of these antithetical views, held by the Abolitionists and the Retentionists, is correct. It is sufficient to say that the very fact that persons of reason, learning and light are rationally and deeply divided in their opinion on this issue, is ground among others, for rejecting the petitioners' argument that retention of the death penalty in the impugned provision, is totally devoid of reason and purpose."

It accordingly held that section 302 of the Indian *Penal Code* "violates neither the letter nor the ethos of Article 19."

The Court then went on to deal with Article 21. It said that if Article 21 were to be expanded in accordance with the interpretive principle applicable to legislation limiting rights under Article 19(1), Article 21 would have to be read as follows:

"No person shall be deprived of his life or personal liberty except according to fair, just and reasonable procedure established by a valid law."

And thus expanded, it was clear that the State could deprive a person of his or her life, by "fair, just and reasonable procedure." In the circumstances, and taking into account the indications that capital punishment was considered by the framers of the constitution in 1949 to be a valid penalty, it was asserted that "by no stretch of the imagination can it be said that the death penalty . . . either *per se* or because of its execution by hanging constitutes an unreasonable, cruel or unusual punishment" prohibited by the *Constitution*.

The wording of the relevant provisions of our *Constitution* are different. The question we have to consider is not whether the imposition of the death sentence for murder "is devoid of any rational nexus" with the purpose and object of section 277(1)(a) of the *Criminal Procedure Act*. It is whether in the context of our *Constitution*, the death penalty is cruel, inhuman or degrading, and if it is, whether it can be justified in terms of section 33.

The Indian *Penal Code* leaves the imposition of the death sentence to the trial judge's discretion. In *Bachan Singh's case* there was also a arbitrariness, along the lines of the challenges that have been successful in the United States. The majority of the Court rejected the argument that the imposition of the death sentence in such circumstances is arbitrary, holding that a discretion exercised judicially by persons of experience and standing, in accordance with principles crystallized by judicial decisions, is not an arbitrary discretion. To complete the picture, it should be mentioned that long delays in carrying out the death sentence in particular cases have apparently been held in India to be unjust and unfair to the prisoner, and in such circumstances the death sentence is liable to be set aside.

The Right to Life

The unqualified right to life vested in every person by section 9 of our *Constitution* is another factor crucially relevant to the question whether the death sentence is cruel, inhuman or degrading punishment with the meaning of section 11(2) of our *Constitution*. In this respect our *Constitution* differs materially from the Constitutions of the United States and India. It also differs materially from the *European Convention* and the *International Covenant.* Yet in the cases decided under these constitutions and treaties there were judges who dissented and held that notwithstanding the specific language of the constitution or instrument concerned, capital punishment should not be permitted.

In some instances the dissent focused on the right to life. In *Soering's case* before the European Court of Human Rights, Judge de Meyer, in a concurring opinion, said that capital punishment is "not consistent with the present state of European civilization" and for that reason alone, extradition to the United States would violate the fugitive's right to life.

"The value of life is immeasurable for any human being, and the right to life enshrined in Article 6 of the Covenant is the supreme human right. It is an obligation of the States [P]arties to the Covenant to protect the lives of all human beings on their territory and under their jurisdiction. If issues arise in respect of the protection of the right to life, priority must not be accorded to the domestic laws of other countries or to (bilateral) treaty articles. Discretion of any nature permitted under an extradition treaty cannot apply, as there is no room for it under Covenant obligations. It is worth repeating that no derogation from a State's obligations under Article 6, paragraph 1, is permitted. This is why Canada, in my view, violated Article 6, paragraph 1, by consenting to extradite Mr. Kindler to the United States, without having secured assurances that Mr. Kindler would not be subjected to the execution of the death sentence."

An individual's right to life has been described as "[t]he most fundamental of all human rights," and was dealt with in that way in the judgments of the Hungarian Constitutional Court declaring capital punishment to be unconstitutional. The challenge to the death sentence in Hungary was based on section 54 of its *Constitution* which provides:

"(1) In the Republic of Hungary everyone has the inherent right to life and to human dignity, and no one shall be arbitrarily deprived of these rights.

"(2) No one shall be subjected to torture or to cruel or inhuman or degrading punishment."

Section 8, the counterpart of section 33 of our *Constitution*, provides that laws shall not impose any limitations on the essential content of fundamental rights. According to the finding of the Court, capital punishment imposed a limitation on the essential content of the fundamental rights to life and human dignity, eliminating them irretrievably. As such it was unconstitutional. Two factors are stressed in the judgment of the Court. First, the relationship between the rights of life and dignity, and the importance of these rights taken together.

Together they are the source of all other rights. Other rights may be limited, and may even be withdrawn and then grated again, but their ultimate limit is to be found in the preservation of the twin rights of life and dignity. These twin rights are the essential content of all rights under the *Constitution*. Take them away, and all other rights cease. I will deal later with the requirement of our *Constitution* that a right shall not be limited in ways which negate its essential content. For the present purposes it is sufficient to point to the fact that the Hungarian Court held capital punishment to be unconstitutional on the grounds that it is inconsistent with the right to life and the right to dignity.

Our *Constitution* does not contain the qualification found in section 54(1) of the Hungarian constitution, which prohibits only the arbitrary deprivation of life. To that extent, therefore, the right to life in section 9 of our *Constitution* is given greater protection that it is by the Hungarian *Constitution*.

The fact that in both the United States and India, which sanction capital punishment, the highest courts have intervened on constitutional grounds in particular cases to prevent the carrying out of a death sentence, because in the particular circumstances of such cases, it would have been cruel to do so, evidences the importance attached to the protection of life and the strict scrutiny to which the imposition and carrying out of death sentences are subjected when a constitutional challenge is raised. The same concern is apparent in the decisions of the European Court of Human Rights and the United Nations Committee on Human Rights. It led the Court in *Soering's case* to order that extradition to the United States, in the circumstances of that case, would result in inhuman or degrading punishment, and the Human Rights Committee to declare in *Ng's case* that he should not be extradited to face a possible death by asphyxiation in a gas chamber in California.

Public Opinion

The Attorney General argued that what is cruel, inhuman or degrading depends to a large extent upon contemporary attitudes within society, and that South African society does not regard the death sentence for extreme cases of murder as a cruel, inhuman or degrading form of punishment. It was disputed whether public opinion, properly informed of the different considerations, would in fact favor the death penalty. I am, however, prepared to assume that it does and that the majority of South Africans agree that the death sentence should be imposed in extreme cases of murder. The question before us, however, is not what the majority of South Africans believe a proper sentence for murder should be. It is whether the Constitution allows the sentence.

Public opinion may have some relevance to the enquiry, but in itself, it is no substitute for the duty vested in the Courts to interpret the *Constitution* and to uphold its provisions without fear or favor. If public opinion were to be decisive there would be no need for constitutional adjudication. The protection of rights could then be left to Parliament, which has a mandate from the public, and is answerable to the public for the way its mandate is exercised, but this would be a return to parliamentary sovereignty, and a retreat from the new legal order established by the 1993 *Constitution*. By the same token the issue of the constitutionality of capital punishment cannot be referred to a referendum, in which a majority view would prevail over the wishes of any minority. The very reason for establishing the new legal order, and for vesting the power of judicial review of all legislation in the courts, was to protect the rights of minorities and others who cannot protect their rights adequately through the democratic process. Those who are entitled to claim this protection include the social outcasts and marginalized people of our society. It is only if there is a willingness to protect the worst and the weakest amongst us, that all of us can be secure that our own rights will be protected.

This Court cannot allow itself to be diverted from its duty to act as an independent arbiter of the *Constitution* by making choices on the basis that they will find favor with the public. Justice Powell's comment in his dissent in *Furman v. Georgia* bears repetition:

"The weight of the evidence indicates that the public generally has not accepted either the morality or the social merit of the views so passionately advocated by the articulate spokesmen for abolition. But however one may assess amorphous ebb and flow of public opinion generally on this volatile issue, this type of inquiry lies at the periphery—not the core—of the judicial process in constitutional cases. The assessment of popular opinion is essentially a legislative, and not a judicial, function."

So too does the comment of Justice Jackson in *West Virginia State Board of Education v. Barnette:*

"The very purpose of a Bill of Rights was to withdraw certain subjects from the vicissitudes of political controversy, to place them beyond the reach of majorities and officials and to establish them as legal principles to be applied by the courts. One's right to life, liberty, and property, to free speech, a free press, freedom of worship and assembly and other fundamental rights may not be submitted to vote; they depend on the outcome of no elections."

Cruel, Inhuman and Degrading Punishment

The United Nations Committee on Human Rights has held that the death sentence by definition is cruel and degrading punishment. So has the Hungarian Constitutional Court, and three judges of the Canadian Supreme Court. The death sentence has also been held to be cruel and unusual punishment and thus unconstitutional under the state constitutions of Massachusetts and California.

The California decision is *People v. Anderson*. Capital punishment was held by six of the seven judges of the Californian Supreme Court to be "impermissibly cruel" under the California Constitution which prohibited cruel or unusual punishment. Also, it degrades and dehumanizes all who participate in its processes. It is unnecessary to any legitimate goal of the state and is incompatible with the dignity of a man and the judicial process.

In the Massachusetts decision in *District Attorney for the Suffolk District v. Watson*, where the Constitution of the State of Massachusetts prohibited cruel or unusual punishment, the death sentence was also held, by six of the seven judges, to be impermissibly cruel.

In both cases the disjunctive effect of "or" was referred to as enabling the Courts to declare capital punishment unconstitutional even if it was not "unusual." Under our Constitution it will not meet the requirements of section 11(2) if it is cruel, or inhuman, or degrading.

Proportionality is an ingredient to be taken into account in deciding whether a penalty is cruel, inhuman or degrading. No Court would today uphold the constitutionality of a statute that makes the death sentence a competent sentence for the cutting down of trees or the killing of a deer, which were capital offenses in England in the 18th Century. But murder is not to be equated with such "offenses." The willful taking of an innocent life calls for a severe penalty, and there are many countries which still retain the death penalty as a sentencing option for such cases. Disparity between the crime and the penalty is not the only ingredient of proportionality; factors such as the enormity and irredeemable character of the death sentence in circumstances where neither error nor arbitrariness can be excluded, the expense and difficulty of addressing the disparities which exist in practice between accused persons facing similar charges, and which are due to factors such as race, poverty, and ignorance, and the other subjective factors which have been mentioned, are also factors that can and should be taken into account in dealing with this issue. It may possibly be that none alone would be sufficient under our *Constitution* to justify a finding that the death sentence is cruel, inhuman or degrading. But these factors are not to be evaluated in isolation. They must be taken together, and in order to decide whether the threshold set by section 11(2) has been crossed they must be evaluated with other relevant factors, including the two fundamental rights on which the accused rely, the right to dignity and the right to life.

The carrying out of the death sentence destroys life, which is protected without reservation under section 9 of our *Constitution*, it annihilates human dignity which is protected under section 10, elements of arbitrariness are present in its enforcement and it is irremediable. Taking these factors into account, as well as the assumption that I have made in regard to public opinion in South Africa, and giving the words of section 11(2) the broader meaning to which they are entitled at this stage of the enquiry, rather than a narrow meaning, I am satisfied that in the context of our *Constitution* the death penalty is indeed a cruel, inhuman and degrading punishment. . . .

The European Union Explains Its Views to a Friend

The continued use of the death penalty by the United States seriously troubles many of its closest friends in Europe. In the following memorandum, the European Union explains its own abolitionist views and appeals to the United States, on the basis of shared values, to join in abandoning what the EU regards as an inhumane and outmoded punishment.

EUROPEAN UNION MEMORANDUM ON THE DEATH PENALTY

"If I can prove that this punishment is neither useful nor necessary, I will have furthered the cause of humanity." Cesare Beccaria, *Dei delitti e delle pene* (1764)

The European Union (EU) is opposed to the death penalty in all cases and has consistently espoused its universal abolition, working towards this goal. In countries which maintain the death penalty, the EU aims at the progressive restriction of its scope and respect for the strict conditions, set forth in several international human rights instruments, under which capital punishment may be used, as well as at the establishment of a moratorium on executions so as to completely eliminate the death penalty.

The EU is deeply concerned about the increasing number of executions in the United States of America (USA), all the more since the great majority of executions since reinstatement of the death penalty in 1976 have been carried out in the 1990s. Furthermore, it is permitted to sentence to death and execute young offenders aged under 18 at the time of the commission of the crime, in clear infringement of internationally-recognised human rights norms.

At the dawn of a new millennium the EU wishes to share with the USA the principles, experiences, policies and alternative solutions guiding the European abolitionist movement, all the EU Member States having abolished the death penalty. By doing so, the EU hopes that the USA, which has risen upon the principles of freedom, democracy, the rule of law and respect for human rights, considers joining the abolitionist vanguard, including as a first step towards abolition establishing a moratorium in the use of the death penalty, and by this way becoming itself a paradigm for retentionist countries.

1. Europe: On the Road to Abolition

In Western Europe the death penalty issue aroused the attention of some circles within society at an early stage. Included among the instruments of both criminal law and criminal policy through ages, capital punishment soon raised a debate on humanitarian values. This evolution in attitudes to the death penalty began particularly in the context of the establishment of the democratic State in the 18th century and since then, step by step, it has gained the support of the peoples of the States nowadays assembled in the European Union.

In fact, the questioning of the legitimacy of the death penalty dawned in the context of the Enlightenment, at the end of the 18th century. At that time deprivation of liberty was the preferred means of criminal punishment, in parallel with the rise of classic criminal law. Although early attempts to repeal the death penalty were not a total success, several European countries had by then accepted the limitation of the death penalty to capital crimes and reformed their law accordingly. This trend towards restriction of the scope of capital punishment would continue throughout the next two centuries, although not without various backward steps due to particular political circumstances.

Nevertheless some of those countries went even further and definitively abolished the death penalty in their laws for ordinary crimes. Portugal led the way in 1867, immediately followed by the Netherlands. Sweden and Denmark joined this abolitionist movement after the First World War. After the Second World War, Italy, Finland and Austria did likewise. The mid-century was also the time for Germany to outlaw capital punishment, encompassing abolition for all crimes. In the 1960s and 1970s, the United Kingdom and Spain also became legally abolitionist for civil crimes.

In the meantime the trend towards abolition for all crimes, thus including crimes under military law or committed in exceptional circumstances such as during wartime, was also affirmed. Since the end of the 1960s, all EU Member States have absolutely abandoned the death penalty in law.

From this, it is clear that for the majority of Member States the total abolition of capital punishment was achieved in two stages of which the second was, in general, a lengthy process. Furthermore, it has to be stressed that, although countries such as the United Kingdom, Spain, Luxembourg, France, Ireland, Greece and Belgium maintained the death penalty in their laws into the second half of this century, executions took place quite rarely or else this form of punishment simply remained unused. In fact, a long period of time generally passed between the carrying out of the last execution and abolition of the death penalty, which leads to the conclusion that when European countries formally abandoned capital punishment they were already abolitionist de facto or even by tradition, capital punishment having clearly fallen into disuse in judicial practice.

On the other hand, while in some EU Member States abolitionist measures have met the deep sentiment of the population and thus corresponded to the accomplishment of a national tradition, in others the political decision towards abolition was not taken with the support of the majority of public opinion. Nevertheless in countries where this was the case, the decision did not result in any form of negative reaction, usually leading to minimal debate on the issue. Therefore, mention should be made of the fact that abolition itself contributed favourably to better-informed public opinion, which helped to shape different feelings among community members.

2. The Common Basis for Abolition: Values, Principles and Criminal Policy

The death penalty poses a set of distinct questions of a philosophical, religious, political and criminological nature. Although Member States' experiences in abolition varied in time, they shared common ground—that of the inhumane, unnecessary and irreversible character of capital punishment, no matter how cruel the crime committed by the offender. Besides, this justification now seems to be shared by the international community as a whole, insofar as both the Rome Statute of the International Criminal Court and the United Nations Security Council Resolutions establishing the International Criminal Tribunals for the former Yugoslavia and for Rwanda do not provide the death penalty among the range of sanctions, even when the most serious crimes, including genocide, crimes against humanity and war crimes are to be tried.

Humanistic values, ethical points of view and human rights reasons weighed in favour of the abolition of the death penalty. Effectively, for the European Governments the death penalty as a means of State punishment rapidly revealed itself as a denial of human dignity, which is a fundamental basis of the common heritage of the European Union as a union of shared values and principles.

At the same time, there is insufficient justification on either criminal or criminological grounds for maintaining such a punishment. First of all, it is scientifically undemonstrated that the death penalty and its application deter criminality any more effectively than other forms of punishment. Indeed, crime rate and the death penalty are independent realities, capital punishment and its execution failing to have a deterrent effect and thus to produce less violent societies. Besides, maintaining capital punishment would not fit the philosophy of rehabilitation pursued in the criminal justice systems of all EU Member States and according to which one of the penological aims of penalties is that of rehabilitating or resocialising the offender. Furthermore, emphasis is also placed upon the penological goal of prevention, understood as a process ante delictum (before crime) and post delictum (post-crime), implying the rejection of any form of brutality, either physical or psychological, with a view to promoting respect for human rights and preventing the development of an even more crime-ridden society. Last but not the least, capital punishment should not be seen as an appropriate way of compensating the suffering of crime victims' families, as this view turns the justice system into a mere tool of illegitimate private vengeance. This does not mean that European criminal systems are insensitive to victims' rights and interests. Quite the contrary. Legislation safeguarding those rights, as well as victims' assistance agencies and programmes are provided. Besides, there are appropriate alternatives to the death penalty which respond to their needs and ensure adequate assistance to them. Both offenders and victims' families stand in need of rehabilitation. As far as the latter are concerned, it is essential that the emotion caused by the loss they suffered is surmounted and this requires the availability of financial and psychological support.

In the realm of judicial practice, the irreversible nature of capital punishment has also to be taken into account. Even highly advanced legal systems, which rest upon the principle of the rule of law, including the principle of due process, are not immune to miscarriages of justice. That irreversibility removes any possibility of correcting such miscarriages of justice, allowing for the execution of innocent people. Judicial error, different interpretations of the law, conviction based on unclear and non-convincing evidence, as well as lack of adequate legal assistance at all stages of the proceedings, in particular where the offender is indigent, are just some of the circumstances which may result in the innocent being executed.

As a result, criminal policy programmes were intentionally humanised in order to pursue the view under which the State's actions should not have human beings as victims, but also that of the promotion of the human person as one of the major purposes of criminology. Maintaining the death penalty would, instead, bring to light undesirable expiatory features of criminal law. Accordingly, major reform initiatives were carried out, restructuring the criminal sanctions so as to make them more conducive mainly to the rationale of social rehabilitation and reintegration of the offender in the community, simultaneously taking into account the need to ensure the protection of society and to prevent crime, rather than punish it.

3. Envisaging Alternative Sanctions

Opting for a more humane, but also more effective, criminal justice system paved the way for considering appropriate alternative criminal sanctions to the death penalty. In fact, European lawmakers assumed that crime could be punishable by means of non-lethal penalties, such as long-term or life imprisonment. In practice, even when the death penalty was still contemplated in law, and even mandatory, either the judge would decide upon an alternative penalty by reason of mitigating circumstances or the sentence would be systematically the object of a pardon and thus commuted.

Imprisonment for life remains the usual alternative for very serious crimes. In any case, although nearly all Member States provide for this type of punishment in their respective penal codes either as a possibility or mandatorily, it is understood rather as a principle than as a common practice.

In some countries life imprisonment can indeed be replaced by temporary incarceration once there are mitigating circumstances. Furthermore, in practically all Member States parole can be granted to those sentenced to life after having served a certain term in prison and depending on other factors, such as good behaviour, signs of readaptation or illness. Commutation of the penalty by way of pardon is also provided for in almost all the sanctions systems concerned. Moreover, in some of these countries imprisonment for life simply can not be applied to juveniles or to the mentally ill.

As to long-term imprisonment, the present criminal policy in the EU Member States clearly shows a decreasing trust in the resocialising effect of long prison sentences and is moving towards keeping imprisonment to an absolute minimum.

It is well established that long-term imprisonment, and above all imprisonment for life, fails to achieve its criminal policy's goals, unless relevant measures are adopted in order to enable the return of the prisoner to social life at the appropriate moment. In this context, the possibility of parole is of paramount importance. In fact, a crime prevention policy which admits maintaining imprisoned for life a convicted person who has served in prison a term corresponding to the gravity of the committed crime and is no longer a danger to society, would fail to meet either recognised minimum standards for the treatment of prisoners or the goal of social rehabilitation which is achieved in view of the willingness and ability of the offender to a lead a law-abiding and self-supporting life. Moreover, it must be underlined that the United Nations (UN) Convention on the Rights of the Child expressly deals with the issue of imprisonment for life imposed on minors, stating that life imprisonment without the possibility of release shall not be imposed for offences committed by persons below 18 years of age.

4. The International Context

The de jure abolitionist trend endorsed by European legislators, clearly evident in the second half of this century, was also favoured by the international environment. In fact, abolition of the death penalty soon became an issue of international concern, contributing to the enhancement of human dignity and the gradual development of human rights.

In 1971, the United Nations General Assembly in Resolution 2857 (XXVI) affirmed the desirability of abolishing the death penalty in all countries. As for international abolitionist treaties, the Council of Europe took the first steps in 1983 by adopting Protocol No. 6 to the European Convention for the Protection of Human Rights and Fundamental Freedoms (ECHR) concerning the Abolition of the Death Penalty. In the framework of the UN a Second Optional Protocol to the International Covenant on Civil and Political Rights (ICCPR) aiming at the abolition of the death penalty was adopted in 1989. More recently, the Inter-American system for the protection of human rights followed the abolitionist vanguard and the Organisation of American States—of which the United States is a member—adopted the Protocol to the American Convention on Human Rights to Abolish the Death Penalty in 1990.

Furthermore, strict conditions under which the death penalty may be used are laid down in international human rights instruments, such as the ICCPR or the UN Economic and Social Council (ECOSOC) Safeguards Guaranteeing Protection of those Facing the Death Penalty. The EU seeks to ensure that in countries where the death penalty has not been abolished executions are carried out in accordance with those generally accepted safeguard standards. It particularly pays attention to: imposition of capital punishment beyond the most serious crimes; retroactive enforcement of the death penalty; imposition of capital punishment on pregnant women or new mothers and on persons suffering from any form of mental dis-

order; disrespect for procedural safeguards, including the right to a
fair trial and the right to petition for clemency; or inhumane enforcement of the death penalty. Executions under these circumstances are
contrary to internationally recognised human rights norms and ne-
glect the dignity and worth of the human person.

5. Juvenile Justice

The EU is equally concerned about the imposition of the death
penalty on persons below 18 years of age.

All the EU Member States reject the idea of incorrigibility of
juveniles. These States hold the view that the problem of juvenile
delinquency should be addressed bearing in mind that young offenders are in the process of full development, facing several difficulties of adaptation. In addition, poor backgrounds, lack of success
at school and dependence on drugs are just some of the social problems affecting them and fostering their criminal behaviour. As a result, they are less mature, and thus less culpable, and should not be
treated as adults, deserving a more lenient criminal sanctions system. This implies, among other things, rejection of the death penalty
for juveniles.

The European approach to juvenile justice is therefore deeply
consistent with internationally-recognised juvenile justice standards,
as enshrined in the following international human rights instruments: the UN International Covenant on Civil and Political Rights,
the ECOSOC Safeguards Guaranteeing Protection of those Facing
the Death Penalty, the UN Convention on the Rights of the Child
and the American Convention on Human Rights. In fact, the international norms in question expressly prohibit sentencing to death
persons below 18 years of age at the time of the commission of the
crime. A similar prohibition is set out in the fourth Geneva Convention of 1949 relative to the Protection of Civilian Persons in Time of
War and Additional Protocols of 1977 to the Geneva Conventions.

The EU and its Member States base their action on the inherent
dignity of all human beings and on the inviolability of the human
person.

Offenders are human beings who committed a crime but who
also enjoy an inherent and inalienable dignity, the very same dignity
claimed by rationalist philosophy, all relevant religions and by law,
the death penalty being a denial of human dignity.

The criminal justice system of a country, and in particular its
sanctions system, may reflect traditions and specific historical aspects of a society. However, the death penalty issue is, above political, legal or criminal considerations, a question of humanity. Hu-

manisation of the problem of capital punishment should be a decisive aspect of a people's life.

Long ago European countries, either in practice or in law, made a choice for humanity, abolishing the death penalty and thus fostering respect for human dignity. And this is an ultimate principle that the EU wishes to share with all countries, as it shares other common values and principles such as freedom, democracy, and the rule of law and safeguard of human rights. If it succeeds in reaching this goal, both the EU and those countries will have furthered the cause of humanity, as Beccaria foretold. The EU thus invites the USA to equally embrace this cause.

8

Organizations

The overwhelming majority of the organizations devoted to or active on the capital punishment issue are abolitionist.

Selected Organizations Based in the United States

American Civil Liberties Union—Death Penalty Project
Executive Director
122 Maryland Avenue NE
Washington, DC 20002
http://www.aclu.org/death-penalty/
(212) 549–2500

This division of the ACLU concentrates on efforts to end the death penalty through public education and legislative action. It has been particularly active in attempting to influence federal legislation on the subject. ACLU publications, and information about the organization's activities in general, are available from the national headquarters.

For those wishing to become active in local efforts of the ACLU, there are affiliate offices in every state and the District of Columbia. Some states have more than one. Addresses and telephone numbers can be found in the appropriate local telephone directories, at http://www.aclu.org/—or by calling or writing to the national office in Washington, DC. Other cities with offices include the following, listed by state:

Alabama (Montgomery)
Alaska (Anchorage)
Arizona (Phoenix)
Arkansas (Little Rock)
California (Los Angeles, San Diego, San Francisco)
Colorado (Denver)
Connecticut (Hartford)
Delaware (Wilmington)
District of Columbia (Washington)
Florida (Miami)
Georgia (Atlanta)
Hawaii (Honolulu)
Idaho (Boise)
Illinois (Chicago)
Indiana (Indianapolis)
Iowa (Des Moines)
Kansas (Kansas City)
Kentucky (Louisville)
Louisiana (New Orleans)
Maine (Portland)
Maryland (Baltimore)
Massachusetts (Boston)
Michigan (Detroit)
Minnesota (Minneapolis)
Mississippi (Jackson)

Missouri (St. Louis, Kansas City)
Montana (Billings)
Nebraska (Lincoln)
Nevada (Las Vegas)
New Hampshire (Concord)
New Jersey (Newark)
New Mexico (Albuquerque)
New York (New York)
North Carolina (Raleigh)
Ohio (Cleveland)
Oklahoma (Oklahoma City)
Oregon (Portland)
Pennsylvania (Philadelphia, Pittsburgh)
Rhode Island (Providence)
South Carolina (Columbia)
South Dakota (Sioux Falls)
Tennessee (Nashville)
Texas (Austin, Dallas, Houston)
Utah (Salt Lake City)
Vermont (Montpelier)
Virginia (Richmond)
Washington (Seattle)
West Virginia (Charleston)
Wisconsin (Milwaukee)
Wyoming (Laramie)

American Friends Service Committee
1501 Cherry Street
Philadelphia, PA 19102
(215) 241–7000
http://www.afsc.org/

One of the most active of religious organizations in the United States opposing the death penalty and all other forms of violence, whether committed by individuals or governments.

Amnesty International USA Program to Abolish the Death Penalty
322 Eighth Avenue
New York, NY 10001

(212) 807–8400
http://amnesty-usa.org/abolish/

Amnesty International USA (Regional Headquarters)

AIUSA Mid-Atlantic Regional Office
608 Pennsylvania Avenue NE
Fifth Floor
Washington, DC 20003
(202) 544–0200

AIUSA Midwest Regional Office
53 W. Jackson, Suite #731
Chicago, IL 60604
(312) 427–2060

AIUSA Northeast Regional Office
58 Day Street, Davis Square
Sommerville, MA 02144
(617) 623–0202

AIUSA South Regional Office
131 Ponce De Leon NE, #200
Atlanta, GA 30308
(404) 876–5661

AIUSA Western Regional Office
9000 W. Washington Bl., 2nd Floor
Culver City, CA 90232
(310) 815–0450

Winner of the Nobel Peace Prize, Amnesty International collects
and disseminates information about human rights abuses around
the world, including the United States. "Amnesty International
opposes the death penalty in all cases, believing it to be the ultimate cruel, inhuman and degrading treatment and a violation of
the right to life as proclaimed in the Universal Declaration of
Human Rights and other international human rights instruments." For general information, you may get in touch with any
of the regional offices listed above. For information about publications, write or phone the national office in New York.

Campaign to End the Death Penalty
National Office
P.O. Box 25730

Chicago, IL 60625
(773) 955–4841
http://www.nodeathpenalty.org/

Founded in 1995, the Campaign to End the Death Penalty now has many chapters across the country. Stresses "grassroots organizing" to win support for prisoners currently on death row. Publishes the on-line newsletter *The New Abolitionist*.

Catholics against Capital Punishment (CAPC)
P.O. Box 5706
Bethesda, MD 20824
(301) 652–1125
http://www.igc.org/cacp/

A Roman Catholic abolitionist group, which communicates Catholic teaching concerning the death penalty to federal and state legislators; encourages the clergy to speak out against the death penalty; and mobilizes Catholic laity opposition to it.

Citizens United for Alternatives to the Death Penalty (CUAAD)
PMB 297
177 U.S. Hwy #1
Tequesta, FL 33469
(800) 973–6548
E-mail: cuadp@cuadp.org
http://www.cuadp.org/

CUAAD works to end the death penalty in the United States through, "invigorated education about viable alternatives" and "strategic and tactical grassroots activism."

Clergy Coalition to End Executions
Suite 450 Gables One Tower
1320 So. Dixie Highway
Miami, FL 33146
(305) 794–3088
http://www.ClergyCoalition.org/

An "international interfaith coalition which supports alternatives to the death penalty."

Death Penalty Information Center
Executive Director
1320 18th Street NW
5th Floor
Washington, DC 20036
(202) 293–2531
http://www.deathpenaltyinfo.org/

Established to "serve the media and the larger community as a clearinghouse for data and resources on the myriad issues surrounding capital punishment," including "polls, academic studies, and newspaper coverage." Although it clearly opposes the death penalty, the Death Penalty Information Center attempts to provide objective information on the subject. It has several publications available, as well as a speakers' bureau of "informed sources on capital punishment, including unexpected voices [opposing the death penalty] from the law enforcement community and families of victims."

Defense for Children International USA
21 South 13th Street
Philadelphia, PA 19107
(215) 569–3996

This advocacy group for the protection of children has information on juveniles and the death penalty.

Hands Off Cain
P.O. Box 6966
New York, NY 10128
http://www.handsoffcain.org.

A "citizen's and parliamentarians' league for the abolition of the death penalty worldwide."

Innocence Project Northwest
University of Washington School of Law
1100 NE Campus Parkway
Seattle, WA 98105–6617
http://www.law.washington.edu/ipnw/

Dedicated to proving the innocence of the wrongfully convicted. Also provides links to other universities with similar projects

International Centre for Criminal Law & Human Rights (US)
110 East D Street, Suite A
Benicia, CA 94530
(707) 745–1362

An international organization that specializes in human rights laws.

Justice for All
P.O. Box 55159
Houston, TX 77255
(713) 935–9300
http://www.jfa.net/

A pro–death penalty criminal justice reform organization.

Loyola Death Penalty Resource Center
636 Baronne Street
New Orleans, LA 70113
(504) 522–0578

Collects information related to death penalty issues.

Mennonite Central Committee, U.S. Office
P.O. Box 500
215 12th Street
Akron, PA 17501
(888) 563–4646

Provides abolitionist literature and other educational materials.

Murder Victims' Families for Reconciliation
Director
2161 Massachusetts Avenue
Cambridge, MA 02140
(617) 868–0007
http://www.mvfr.org/

The director is William Pelke, the grandson of an elderly woman murdered by four teenage girls in Gary, Indiana. One of the girls was sentenced to death at the age of sixteen.

NAACP Legal Defense & Educational Fund
99 Hudson Street, 16th Floor

New York, NY 10013
(800) 221–7822

Once headed by Thurgood Marshall, the NAACP Legal Defense & Educational Fund (LDF) was founded by the National Association for that Advancement of Colored People in the 1940s. It is still allied with the NAACP, but it is no longer a part of it. Among its other activities, LDF helps to defend black defendants charged with, or convicted of, capital crimes. It opposes the imposition of the death penalty on others as well, including juveniles and mentally retarded people.

National Bar Association
Executive Director
1225 11th Street NW
Washington, DC 20001–4217
(202) 842–3900
http://nationalbar.org/

The national professional association for attorneys can provide information on legal questions surrounding the death penalty.

National Coalition to Abolish the Death Penalty (NCADP)
1436 U Street NW
Suite 104
Washington, DC 20009
(888) 286–2237
http://www.ncadp.org/

The most inclusive of the national groups working to end capital punishment, the NCADP helps consolidate the efforts of a broad range of national and local organizations and institutions active in the abolitionist cause.

National Criminal Justice Reference Service
P.O. Box 6000
Rockville, MD 20849–6000
(800) 851–3420
http://www.ncjrs.org/

A subdivision of the U.S. Department of Justice that provides information on all aspects of the U.S. criminal justice system, including the death penalty.

National Legal Aid and Defender Association
Death Penalty Litigation Section
1625 K Street NW
Eighth Floor
Washington, DC 20006
(202) 452–0620
http://www.nlada.org/

Devoted to the needs and interests of those actively engaged in defending people liable to receive the death penalty. Publishes a newlsetter, the *Indigent Defense*.

Northern California Coalition to Abolish the Death Penalty
1611 Telegraph Avenue
Suite 1501
Oakland, CA 94612
(510) 836–3013

An active branch of the National Coalition, which works to educate the public on death penalty issues by various means, including pamphlets and forums in high schools. Along with its other activities, the group participates in demonstrations against the death penalty; it was especially active in organizing the demonstrations outside San Quentin Prison in the weeks leading up to the execution of Robert Alton Harris.

Religious Action Center of Reform Judaism
2027 Massachusetts Avenue
Washington, DC 20036
(202) 387–2800

Affiliated with the Union American Hebrew Congregations, which represents the nation's Reform congregations, the Religious Action Center actively opposes capital punishment.

Washington Legal Foundation
2009 Massachusetts Avenue
Washington, DC 20036
http://www.wlf.org/

A "nonpartisan public interest law institution organized to engage in litigation and the administrative process in matters affecting the broad public interest," the foundation supports the retention of the death penalty. In addition to its efforts on behalf of capital punishment, it is active in promoting the "defense on individual rights," aiding crime victims, supporting a strong defense, and "challenging regulations which impede a free market economy." Publishes studies on matters of public policy, including the death penalty.

Selected Oranizations Based Abroad

Amnesty International
International Secretariat
1 Easton Street
London WC1X 0DJ
United Kingdom
44 020 7413 5507
http://www.amnesty.org/

The largest and best-known international nongovernmental organization dedicated to human rights.

Australian Coalition Against the Death Penalty
P.O. Box 577
Endeavour Hills VIC 3802
Australia
(61) 0411–538950
http://acadp.com/

A nonprofit activist organization for human rights, opposed to the death penalty.

**ECADP International (European Coalition
to Abolish the Death Penalty)**
Head Office
Postfach 1326
46363 Bocholt
Germany
Tel: + 49 2871 260515
http://www.ecadp.org/

ECADP Belgium (Country Representative)
E-mail: board@bel.ecadp.org (English, Dutch, and French)

ECADP Denmark (Country Representative)
Tel.: +45–97–40 76 28 (Danish, English, and German)
E-mail: board@den.ecadp.org

ECADP France (Country Representative)
Tel.: +33–4–90 75 94 75 (French, English, Italian, and German)
E-mail: board@fra.ecadp.org

ECADP Germany (Country Representative)
Tel.: +49–2871–26 05 15 (German and English)
E-mail: board@ger.ecadp.org
Press office: Tel.: +49–221–76 69 18 (German and English)
E-mail: press@ger.ecadp.org

ECADP Norway (Country Representative)
Tel.: +47–63–90 87 36 (English and Norwegian)
E-mail: board@nor.ecadp.org

ECADP Switzerland (Country Representative)
E-mail: board@sui.ecadp.org (German, English, Italian, and French)

ECADP The Netherlands (Country Representative)
Tel.: +31–75–621 96 15 (Dutch, English, and German)
E-mail: board@ned.ecadp.org

An international nonprofit organization, open to all who oppose the death penalty worldwide. Although international in scope, its primary focus is on the United States, presumably because, of the world's chief practitioners of capital punishment, it is the one most likely to be affected by international opinion.

Hands Off Cain—Brussels
Rue Belliard 97 (European Parliament)
113 Mon 229 B 1047
Brussels, Belgium
See **Hands Off Cain—New York**

Hands Off Cain—Rome
Via di Torre Argentina 76-00186
Rome, Italy
See **Hands Off Cain—New York**

Human Writes
27 Old Gloucester Street
London WC1N 3XX

United Kingdom
http://www.humanwrites.org/

Organizes letter writing to condemned inmates.

Inside-Outside
Postbus 1599
9701 BN Groningen
Netherlands
http://home.planet.nl/~inside-outside/

A Dutch group that organizes letter writing to condemned inmates.

International Centre for Criminal Law & Human Rights
Helmstraat 16C
Suite D2NL–6211
TA Maastricht, Netherlands
+ 31–43–350–0074
See **International Centre for Criminal
Law & Human Rights (US)**

LifeLines—Ireland
4 Chapel Manor
Chapelizod
Dublin 20
Ireland
http://homepage.eircom.net/~lifelines/Lifelines.htm

Organizes letter writing to condemned inmates.

LifeLines—United Kingdom
The Well House
Furneux Pelham
HERTS
SG9 0LN
012 79 777083
http://www.lifelines.org/

Organizes letter writing campaigns to condemned inmates.

Office of the High Commissioner for Human Rights
OHCHR-UNOG
8–14 Avenue de la Paix

1211 Geneva 10, Switzerland
Telephone Number (41–22) 917–9000
http://www.un.org/rights/index.html

The UN Commission on Human Rights, to which fifty-three states belong, examines, monitors, and publicly reports on "major phenomena of human rights violations worldwide," as well as human rights situations in specific countries or territories.

9

Print and Nonprint Resources

Books

Several of the books listed here are out of print, but they can be found in large libraries or through book search sites on the Internet.

Abbott, G. (Geoffrey). *The Book of Execution: An Encyclopedia of Methods of Judicial Execution.* London: Headline, 1995. 436 pp. $15.95. ISBN: 0747245819.

Extensive encyclopedia on the act of execution in all its historical forms. Includes the modern and familiar methods to the lesser known and unbelievably gruesome. Black and white illustrations.

Abbott, Jack Henry. *In the Belly of the Beast.* New York: Random House, reprint of 1981 edition. 166 pp. $12.00. ISBN: 0679732373.

Abbott had spent almost his entire teenage and adult life in prison by the time he wrote this book. Growing out of several passionate angry letters he had written to author Norman Mailer, it vividly describes a killing in which Abbott took part, as well as the dehumanizing and embittering effects of a long prison term. Introduction by Norman Mailer.

Acker, J. R., R. M. Bohm, and C. S. Lanier, eds. *America's Experiment with Capital Punishment: Reflections on the Past, Present, and Future of the Ultimate Penal Sanction.* Durham, NC: Carolina Academic Press, 1998. 595 pp. $35.00. ISBN: 0890896518.

An exploration of the use of the death penalty to deter crime. Includes law, psychology, sociology, philosophy, and criminal justice perspectives. Bibliographic references, tables, and figures.

Arriens, Jan, ed. *Welcome to Hell: Letters & Writings from Death Row.* Boston: Northeastern University Press, 1997. 255 pp. $45.00. ISBN: 1555532896.

Letters from condemned inmates to the pen-pal group Lifelines. Foreword by Sister Helen Prejean; preface by Clive Stafford Smith.

Bailey, Lloyd R. *Capital Punishment: What the Bible Says.* Nashville, TN: Abingdon Press, 1987. 112 pp. ISBN: 0687046262 (out of print).

Attempts to place Bible texts relating to the death penalty in the context of the time in which they were written, rather than to use particular texts to make a case either for or against capital punishment.

Baldus, David C., George Woodworth, and Charles A. Pulaski, Jr. *Equal Justice and the Death Penalty: A Legal and Empirical Analysis.* Boston: Northeastern University Press, 1990. 752 pp. $55.00. ISBN: 1555530567.

An extensive study of death penalty sentencing between the landmark *Furman* and *McCleskey v. Kemp* decisions of the Supreme Court. It concludes that, while procedures and results improved during the period, death sentencing remained unfair in its impact on disadvantaged minorities. Furthermore, "given the Supreme Court's decision in *McCleskey v. Kemp*, little improvement in this regard appears likely."

Ballinger, Anette. *Dead Woman Walking: Executed Women in England and Wales, 1900–1955.* Aldershot, England; Burlington, VT: Dartmouth, 2000. 374 pp. $89.95. ISBN: 184014789X.

A major study of women receiving the death sentence in England and Wales. Reviews in detail the lives and punishments of fifteen women executed in the twentieth century. Includes bibliographical references and index.

Beccaria, Cesare. *On Crimes and Punishments.* Edited and translated by David Young. Indianapolis, IN: Hackett Publications, 1986. 129 pp. $27.95. ISBN: 0915144999.

Originally published in Italian as *Dei delitti e delle pene* in 1764, this is the landmark essay that launched the great drive for abolition in the nineteenth and twentieth centuries. Beccaria attacked such widespread penal practices of the time as secret accusations and punishments, torture, and, of course, the death penalty. In his central argument, Beccaria declares "[t]hat a punishment may not be an act of violence." Furthermore, "it should be public, immediate, and necessary, the least possible in the case given, proportioned to the crime, and determined by the laws."

Bedau, Hugo Adam, ed. *The Death Penalty in America: Current Controversies.* New York: Oxford University Press, 1997. 524 pp. $40.00. ISBN: 0195104382.

A completely new edition of Bedau's classic. Bedau, one of the preeminent scholars on capital punishment, presents forty new essays by a variety of scholars, as well as updated statistics, and the texts of several recent Supreme Court decisions dealing with the subject. Covers legal, moral, race, and class issues from a wide variety of perspectives. Includes bibliographical references and index.

Berger, Raoul. *Death Penalties: The Supreme Court's Obstacle Course.* Cambridge, MA: Harvard University Press, 1982. 256 pp. $25.00. ISBN: 0674194268.

A distinguished defender of capital punishment looks at the Supreme Court's attitude toward the death penalty. In essence, the book is an argument against what Berger sees as a too broad reading of the "cruel and unusual" clause, which he believes is "depriving" the people of the right to decide whether or not they want criminals executed.

Berns, Walter. *For Capital Punishment.* Reprint edition. 226 pp. University Press of America, 2000.

The case for capital punishment, argued by one of its leading contemporary advocates.

Black, Charles L., Jr. *Capital Punishment: The Inevitability of Caprice and Mistake.* Rev. ed. New York: W. W. Norton, 1982. ISBN: 0393952894 (out of print).

A classic presentation of the abolitionist argument that the death penalty cannot realistically be applied fairly, and that any effort to apply it "inevitably" leads to tragic and uncorrectable mistakes.

Block, Brian P., and John Hostettler. *Hanging in the Balance: A History of the Abolition of Capital Punishment in Britain.* Winchester, UK: Waterside Press, 1997. 288 pp. ISBN: 1872870473 (out of print).

A history of the abolition of capital punishment in Britain. Includes bibliographical references and index.

Boissery, Beverly, and F. Murray Greenwood. *Uncertain Justice.* Toronto, Canada: Dundum Press, 2000. 285 pp. $22.99. ISBN: 1550023446.

Canadian women and capital punishment, 1754–1953. Includes index and bibliographical references.

Bovee, Marvin H. *Christ and the Gallows; or, Reasons for the Abolition of Capital Punishment.* New York: AMS Press, 1983 reprint of 1869 edition. ISBN: 0404624030 (out of print).

The classic collection of letters and essays by prominent opponents of the death penalty, including Henry Longfellow, Elizabeth Cady Stanton, and Bovee himself.

Bowers, William J., Glenn L. Pierce, and John F. McDevitt. *Legal Homicide: Death as Punishment in America, 1864–1982.* Boston: Northeastern University Press, 1984. 614 pp. $65.00. ISBN: 0930350251.

A historical review.

Brettschneider, Corey Lang. *Punishment, Property and Justice.* Aldershot, UK: Ashgate Publishing Company, 2001. 164 pp. $69.95. ISBN: 0754620646.

Examines the philosophical foundations of the death penalty and welfare. It explores the capital punishment argument in respect to traditional philosophical theories of punishment. Includes bibliographical references.

Carrington, Frank. *Neither Cruel nor Unusual: The Case for Capital Punishment.* New York: Crown, 1978. (out of print).

A forceful presentation of the pro–death penalty position.

Cheever, George B. *Punishment by Death: Its Authority & Expediency.* New York: AMS Press, reprint of 1842 edition. $37.50. ISBN: 040462409X.

The case for capital punishment, laid out by the clergyman who was, perhaps, its strongest nineteenth-century defender.

Chessman, Caryl. *Cell 2455 Death Row.* Englewood Cliffs, NJ: Prentice-Hall, 1954. Reissued, Westport, CT: Greenwood Press, 1969. 361 pp. ISBN: 837116317 (out of print).

The autobiography of Caryl Chessman, who was executed in 1960 for kidnapping. In "Author's Note," Chessman describes the book as a plea "for the criminally damned and doomed." The title is taken from the number of the author's cell on San Quentin's death row. Beginning with a description of the gas chamber death of a fellow prisoner, Chessman goes on to describe the life that brought him to the brink of a similar fate. It is a vividly written account of the author's criminal career, in which he maintains his innocence of the crimes for which he was condemned, and declares his determination "to cheat the executioner out of his day off and his hundred dollar fee." The book became a best-seller and helped to focus public attention on the issue of capital punishment in the mid-1950s.

————. *Trial by Ordeal.* Englewood Cliffs, NJ: Prentice-Hall, 1955. 309pp. Library of Congress Catalog No. 55-10671 (out of print).

An account by Caryl Chessman of his efforts to save himself from execution for robbery and kidnapping. It includes descriptions of his life in prison and his reflections on his own death sentence. (By 1955 he had been on death row for over six years.)

The Churches Speak On—Capital Punishment. Vol. 3. Detroit, MI: Gale Research, 1989. 165 pp. ISBN: 0810372207 (out of print).

Official statements from a variety of religious and ecumenical groups, including the Roman Catholic and Eastern Orthodox Churches, as well as various Protestant and Jewish organizations.

Cliff, C., ed. *Capital Punishment: A Bibliography.* Huntington, NY: Nova Science Publishers, 2000. 298 pp. $49.00. ISBN: 1560728620.

Examines current death penalty statutes in the United States. Includes detailed bibliographical references, subject and author indexes.

Costanzo, Mark, Ph.D. *Just Revenge: Costs and Consequences of the Death Penalty.* New York: St. Martin's Press, 1997. 206 pp. $22.95. ISBN: 031215559X.

Mark Costanzo, Ph.D., chair of the Department of Social Psychology at Claremont-McKenna College, disputes the usefulness of the death penalty through legal and logical arguments as well as emotional stories of life on death row, botched executions, and inmates' families. Includes bibliographical references and index.

Darrow, Clarence. *Attorney for the Damned: Clarence Darrow in the Courtroom.* Edited and with notes by Arthur Weinberg; foreword by William O. Douglas. Chicago: University of Chicago Press, 1989. 552 pp. ISBN: 0226136493.

A collection of courtroom speeches by the great criminal defense attorney.

———. *Clarence Darrow on Capital Punishment.* Evanston, IL: Chicago Historical Bookworks, 1991. (Paperback) 121 pp. ISBN: 9990800251.

The greatest courtroom opponent of the death speaks out on the issue.

———. *The Story of My Life.* Introduction by Alan M. Dershowitz. New York: Da Capo Press, 1996. 496 pp. ISBN: 306807386.

An autobiography of the renowned defense attorney, with accounts of several of his most famous cases.

Dicks, Shirley. *Young Blood: Juvenile Justice and the Death Penalty.* Amherst, NY: Prometheus Books, 1995. 295 pp. $30.00. ISBN: 0879759534.

Abolitionist Shirley Dicks address the problems with today's juvenile legal system, and urges reform. Topics covered include the waiving of juveniles into adult court, drugs, the mentally retarded, and case profiles.

Dicks, Shirley, ed. *Death Row: Interviews with Inmates, Their Families and Opponents of Capital Punishment.* New York: iUniverse.com, Inc., 2001. 160pp. $9.95. ISBN: 0595149103.

The first section of this three-part book deals with opponents of capital punishment, the second with people sentenced to death, and the third with the families of the condemned.

Ellis, Georgie. *Ruth Ellis, My Mother.* London: Smith Gryphon, 1995. 246 pp. ISBN: 1856850943 (out of print).

A memoir written by the daughter of the last woman executed by hanging in England. Sixteen pages of plates.

Evans, Richard J. *Rituals of Retribution: Capital Punishment in Germany, 1600–1987.* New York: Oxford University Press, 1996. 1014 pp. $85.00. ISBN: 0198219687.

Historian Richard Evans studies the death penalty in Germany from the seventeenth century through its abolition in Germany in 1945, and finally to its complete abolition in the East in the 1980s. Covers a wealth of new information due to the release of German Democratic Republic documents. Includes bibliographical references and index.

Farb, Robert L. *North Carolina Capital Case Law Handbook.* Chapel Hill: Institute of Government, University of North Carolina at Chapel Hill, 1996. 248 pp. ISBN: 1560112891 (out of print).

Gatrell, V.A.C. *The Hanging Tree: Execution and the English People 1770–1868.* New York: Oxford University Press, 1996. 654 pp. $19.95. ISBN: 0192853325

A study of the attitudes and emotions of the citizens toward "the Bloody Penal Code" that sent some 7,000 people to the gallows for crimes minor as well as severe. Challenges many conventional views of popular attitudes toward public executions at the time.

Gillespie, L. Kay. *The Unforgiven: Utah's Executed Men.* 2d ed. Salt Lake City, UT: Signature Books, 1997. 209 pp. $18.95. ISBN: 1560850981

Gillespie served on the Utah Board of Pardons and personally interviewed many inmates under sentence of death. Relates a rare insider's view of an American death row. Includes bibliographical references.

Gray, Ian, and Moira Stanley. *A Punishment in Search of a Crime.* New York: Avon, 1989. 400 pp. ISBN: 0380759233 (out of print).

Subtitled *Americans Speak Out Against the Death Penalty,* the book consists primarily of more than forty selections by opponents of capital punishment. Contributors include such prominent figures as author William Styron, Congressman John Conyers, and Hugo Adam Bedau, along with many lesser-known scholars, lawyers, death row inmates, and prison officials. Includes bibliography. Foreword by M. Kerry Kennedy.

Haines, Herbert H. *Against Capital Punishment: The Anti-Death Penalty Movement in America, 1972–1994.* New York: Oxford University Press, 1999. 253 pp. $19.95. ISBN: 0195132491.

Traces the abolitionist movement in the United States since 1972 with anti–death penalty organizations' records and interviews with the fight's leaders.

Henderson, Harry. *Capital Punishment.* 2d ed. New York: Facts on File, 2000. 208 pp. $45.00. ISBN: 0816041938.

Part of the Library in a Book series. Covers many death penalty issues from a variety of viewpoints, and includes an extensive chronology. Includes bibliographical references and Internet sources.

Hood, R., et al. *The Death Penalty-Abolition in Europe (1999).* Strasbourg: Council of Europe, 1999. 186 pp. ISBN: 9287138745.

From the abstract provided by the Council of Europe: "Europe is the first continent in which the death penalty has been completely abolished. The Council of Europe has been Europe's major defender of abolition and presently requires all countries seeking membership in its ranks to place a moratorium on the death penalty. This collection of texts by major European abolitionists includes voices from countries which have enjoyed abolition for many years, as well as from those where abolition has been a struggle against popular opinion."

Hood, Roger G. *The Death Penalty: A World-Wide Perspective.* 2d ed. New York: Oxford University Press, 1996. 307 pp. ISBN: 0198262825 (out of print).

Discusses the present abolitionist movement, capital punishment in practice, safeguards and standards, deterrence and public opinion. Includes bibliographical references and index.

Hook, Donald D., and Lothor Kahn. *Death in the Balance: The Debate over Capital Punishment.* New York: Free Press, 1990. 131 pp. ISBN: 06692090646.

The authors argue that society should overcome its ambivalence toward the death penalty and either enforce it consistently and wholeheartedly or abolish it altogether. Includes bibliography.

International Commission of Jurists. *Administration of the Death Penalty in the United States: Report of a Mission.* Geneva: The Commission, 1996. 265 pp. ISBN: 9290370947 (out of print).

A 1996 mission reports that public pressure and views of victims' families influence application of the death penalty, increasing "the likelihood of a miscarriage of justice."

Jackson, Jesse. *Legal Lynching: Racism, Injustice, and the Death Penalty.* New York: Marlowe & Co., 1996. 224 pp. ISBN: 1569247617 (out of print).

Passionately examines the questions the U.S. death penalty raises, including its impact after all other Western democracies have abandoned it. Includes bibliographical references and index.

Jasper, Margaret C. *The Law of Capital Punishment.* Dobbs Ferry, NY: Oceana Publications, 1998. 110 pp. $25.50. ISBN: 0379113317

Attorney Jasper presents arguments for and against the death penalty, death row demographics, and information about the death sentence internationally. Includes bibliographical references.

Johnson, Robert. *Death Work: A Study of the Modern Execution Process.* 2d ed. Edited by Roy R. Roberg. Pacific Grove, CA: Brooks/Cole, 1997. 250 pp. $38.95. ISBN: 053452155X.

Following a description of execution procedures from ancient times to the present, this book describes the process as it is carried out in the United States today. It details the experiences and impressions of condemned prisoners and executioners alike as they prepare for, and finally face, the grim ordeal.

Joyce, James Avery. *Capital Punishment: A World View.* New York: AMS Press, reprint of 1961 edition. ISBN: 0404624227 (out of print).

Using as a starting point an account of convicted kidnapper Caryl Chessman's efforts to save himself from the gas chamber, Joyce discusses the history of the movement to abolish the death penalty in Europe, Great Britain, and the United States, and ultimately in the United Nations. In later chapters, the debate over the death penalty is related to broader questions of war, peace, and nuclear deterrence. Includes bibliography and two appendices.

Koestler, Arthur. *Reflections on Hanging.* New York: AMS Press, reprint of 1957 edition. ISBN: 0404624235 (out of print).

Meditations on the death penalty by the renowned Hungarian-born author who was himself imprisoned under sentence of death in Spain for some time during the Spanish Civil War. Contains the famous abolitionist distinction: "The division is not between rich and poor, highbrow and lowbrow, Christians and atheists: it is between those who have charity and those who have not."

Koosed, Margery B., ed. *Capital Punishment.* New York: Garland, 1996. 1,200 pp. $295.00. ISBN: 0815322194.

The philosophical, moral, and penological debate over capital punishment. Includes bibliographical references.

Lawes, Lewis E. *Life and Death in Sing Sing.* Garden City, NY: Garden City Publications, 1928. (out of print).

An account of Lawes's thoughts and experiences as warden of the famous prison. It contains what Philip English Mackey has described as "the reformer's best attack on capital punishment."

Leopold, Nathan. *Life Plus 99 Years.* New York: Greenwood Press, reprint of 1958 edition. 381 pp. $55.00. ISBN: 0837172071.

An account of his experiences, and reflections on them, by the convicted killer who was spared a death sentence in 1924 and served the next 34 years in prison.

Lester, David. *The Death Penalty: Issues and Answers.* 2d ed. Springfield, IL: C. C. Thomas, 1998. 164 pp. $43.95. ISBN: 0398068224.

Dr. Lester examines topics including international attitudes toward the death penalty, executions in the United States, juries, public opinion, race, economic classes, and deterrence. Includes bibliographical references and indexes.

Mackey, Philip English. *Voices against Death: American Opposition to Capital Punishment, 1787–1975.* New York: Burt Franklin & Co., 1976. ISBN: 0891020624 (out of print).

An invaluable collection of essays, speeches, etc., by a wide variety of death penalty opponents from Benjamin Rush to Hugo Adam Bedau. Included, among many others, are Edward Livingston, Robert Rantoul, Jr., John Greenleaf Whittier, Walt Whitman, Horace Greeley, William Dean Howells, Clarence Darrow, Kathleen Norris, Caryl Chessman, and Thorsten Sellin. Includes a bibliography and an introduction by Bedau.

Manderson, Desmond, ed. *Courting Death: The Law of Mortality.* Sterling, VA: Pluto Press, 1999. 238 pp. $59.95. ISBN: 0745313663.

A collection exploring the relationship of law and mortality. Views from a wide variety of philosophers, theorists, and practitioners from the United States, Britain, and Australia. Includes bibliographical references and index.

Marquart, James W. (Walter). *The Rope, the Chair, and the Needle: Capital Punishment in Texas, 1923–1990.* Austin: University of Texas Press, 1994. 275 pp. ISBN: 0292751583 (out of print).

A detailed study of executions in Texas. Explores the opinion that slavery and lynchings led to the public approval of race-, class-, and gender-biased sentencing in capital cases. Includes bibliographical references and index.

Masur, Louis P. *Rites of Execution: Capital Punishment and the Transformation of American Culture, 1776–1865.* New York: Oxford University Press, reprint of 1989 edition. 224 pp. $19.96. ISBN: 0195066634.

A study of capital punishment during the first near century of United States history, with special attention to changing public attitudes toward hanging, particularly in the northeastern and mid-Atlantic states.

Mello, Michael. *Against the Death Penalty: The Relentless Dissents of Justices Brennan and Marshall.* Evanston, IL: Northwestern University Press, 1996. ISBN: 1555532616.

William J. Brennan and Thurgood Marshall were the two strongest opponents of capital punishment ever to sit on the U.S. Supreme Court. In this book, Mello analyzes the two justices' death penalty decisions and dissents and provides an analysis of the philosophical foundations for their views.

Mikhlin, Alexander S. *The Death Penalty in Russia.* Boston: Kluwer Law International, 1999. 183 pp. $65.00. ISBN: 904119312X.

Examines a century of the death penalty in Russia, its use both judicially and extrajudicially. Explores issues not often covered and looks at a society that has swayed between extremes on the issue, arguably more than any other.

Morriss, William E. *Watch the Rope.* Winnipeg: Watson & Dwyer, 1996. 196 pp. ISBN: 0920486258 (out of print).

Discusses the death penalty in Manitoba. Includes bibliographical references.

NAACP Legal Defense & Educational Fund Staff. *Death Row U.S.A. Reporter, 1975–1988 and 1989–1997 Supplements.* Buffalo, NY: W. S. Hein, various dates. (out of print).

A massive resource provided by what has long been one of the most active organizations opposing the death penalty.

Nelson, Lane, and Burk Foster. *Death Watch: A Death Penalty Anthology.* Upper Saddle River, NJ: Prentice Hall, 2000. 310 pp. $26.95. ISBN: 013085201525.

Short, nontechnical articles on important issues concerning the use of the death penalty today. Topics covered include how capital cases are determined, the selective application in cases involving women and juveniles, organ donation and physician participation, last words, and the innocent on death row.

O'Shea, Kathleen A. *Women and the Death Penalty in the United States, 1900–1998.* Westport, CT: Praeger, 1999. 404 pp. $69.50. ISBN: 027595952X.

Provides the stories of women who have been executed and of those on death row, as well as the legal history of capital punishment in states that have sentenced women to death. Includes bibliographical references and index.

Otterbein, Keith F. *The Ultimate Coercive Sanction: A Cross-Cultural Study of Capital Punishment.* New Haven, CT: HRAF Press, 1986. 164 pp. $16.00. ISBN: 0875363466.

Argues that the death penalty is, or has been, used by every culture at one time or another.

Paul, John II. *The Gospel of Life-Evangelium Vitae.* Boston: Pauline Books & Media, 1995. 176 pp. $4.95. ISBN: 081983078X.

The pope's encyclical letter on the sanctity of life in modern society.

Potter, Harry. *Hanging in Judgment: Religion and the Death Penalty in England.* New York: Continuum, 1993. 292 pp. ISBN: 0826406262 (out of print).

An analysis of the role of religious attitudes toward the death penalty in England; and the long-time active role of the Church of England in defending capital punishment. Includes much previously unpublished material from 1700 through to the last execution in 1969.

Prejean, Helen. *Dead Man Walking: An Eyewitness Account of the Death Penalty in the United States.* New York: Vintage Books, 1994. 276 pp. $13.00. ISBN: 0679751319.

A Roman Catholic nun's first-hand account of the path to the electric chair. She tells the story of her time as counselor and advisor to executed criminal Patrick Sonnier. Sister Prejean has worked with victim's families as well as inmates on death row and steadfastly opposes capital punishment.

Pucci, Idanna. Translated by Stefania Fumo. *The Trials of Maria Barbella: The True Story of a 19th Century Crime of Passion.* New York: Vintage Books, 1997. 296 pp. $14.00. ISBN: 0679776044.

The account of an New York immigrant who became the first woman to be sentenced to die in the electric chair. Written by the great-granddaughter of Cora Slocomb, the Italian aristocrat who organized the appeal that saved her life. A look into the Victorian-era plight of immigrants in American society, women's activism, and the legal system and due process at the turn of the century.

Radelet, Michael L. *Facing the Death Penalty: Essays on a Cruel and Unusual Punishment.* Philadelphia: Temple University Press, 1989. 264 pp. $34.95. ISBN: 0877226113.

Deals with the experiences of condemned inmates, and those working on their behalf. "Little support for capital punishment will be found in these pages." Includes a foreword by Henry Schwartzschild.

Randa, Laura E., ed. *Society's Final Solution: A History and Discussion of the Death Penalty.* Lanham, MD: University Press of America, 1997. ISBN: 0761807136.

A fair, if critical, exploration of the death penalty as it is practiced. Includes an excellent international history of the death penalty.

Russell, Gregory D. *The Death Penalty and Racial Bias: Overturning Supreme Court Assumptions.* Westport, CT: Greenwood Press, 1994. 170 pp. $55.00. ISBN: 0313288895.

An evaluation of the U.S. Supreme Court's assumption that "death qualified" juries do not add racial bias to the process. The first study to suggest that this procedure concentrates racial bias in juries.

Sarat, Austin. *When the State Kills: Capital Punishment and the American Condition.* Princeton, NJ: Princeton University Press, 2001. 324 pp. $29.95. ISBN: 0691007268.

Sophisticated analysis of recent American cases involving the death penalty and the impact it has had on American culture, as evidenced, for example, by popular films. Sarat explores the ethics of capital punishment and asks whether it can be compatible with democracy. Includes bibliographical references and index.

Sarat, Austin, ed. *The Killing State: Capital Punishment in Law, Politics, and Culture.* New York: Oxford University Press, 1999. 263 pp. $39.95. ISBN: 0195120868.

A collection of essays from ten scholars exploring the reasons the United States has continued to use the death penalty after other industrialized democracies have abandoned it. Includes bibliographical references and index.

Sarat, Austin, and Robert V. Wolf. *Capital Punishment: Crime, Justice and Punishment.* Philadelphia, PA: Chelsea House Publishers, 1997. $19.95. ISBN: 0791043118.

Surveys the history of the death penalty, describes different methods of execution, and uses case histories to discusses the legal and ethical ramifications. Written for young adults.

Schabas, William A. *The Death Penalty as Cruel Treatment and Torture: Capital Punishment Challenged in the World's Courts.* Boston: Northeastern University Press, 1996. 288 pp. $50.00. ISBN: 1555532683.

A comparative analysis of the national and international laws and court rulings on the subject.

———. *The Abolition of the Death Penalty in International Law.* 2d ed. New York: Cambridge University Press, 1997. 403 pp. $42.95. ISBN: 0521588871.

A study of the trend away from capital punishment in international law. Extensively revised to include developments since the first edition, published in 1933. Includes bibliographical references and index.

———. *The International Sourcebook on Capital Punishment.* Boston: Northeastern University Press, 1997. 264 pp. $65.00. ISBN: 1555532993.

The first of a projected series of yearbooks generated by the Center for Capital Punishment Studies of the University of Westminster, London. Contains articles, book reviews, and documents.

Scott, George R. *The History of Capital Punishment: Including an Examination of the Case for & against Capital Punishment.*

New York: AMS Press, reprint of 1950 edition. $38.50. ISBN: 0404624286.

A valuable standard work.

Seleoane, Mandla. *Death Penalty: Let the People Decide.* Lee Glen, FL: Vivlia Publishers, 1996. 98 pp. ISBN: 1868670473 (out of print).

Public opinion on capital punishment in South Africa. Includes bibliographical references.

Solotaroff, Ivan. *The Last Face You'll Ever See: The Private Life of the American Death Penalty.* New York: HarperCollins, 2001. $25.00. ISBN: 006017448X.

The story of executioners and the death sentence. Includes bibliographical references.

Sorell, Tom. *Moral Theory and Capital Punishment.* New York: R. Blackwell, in association with the Open University, 1988. 172 pp. ISBN: 0631153217 (out of print).

A philosophical examination of the possible justifications for the death penalty, concluding that it is a fit punishment for a limited category of murderers.

Stassen, Glen H., ed. *Capital Punishment: A Reader.* Cleveland, OH: Pilgrim Press, 1998. 229 pp. $20.95. ISBN: 0829811788.

Offers a wide variety of perspectives on the death penalty from theologians, writers, and ethicists. Offers a balance of pro– and anti–death penalty views. Includes bibliographical references.

Steffen, Lloyd H. *Executing Justice: The Moral Meaning of the Death Penalty.* Cleveland, OH: Pilgrim Press, 1998. 185 pp. $17.95. ISBN: 0829812199.

Includes discussions of Willie Darden, the theory of "just execution," and the right to life, liberty, and security.

Stevens, Leonard A. *Death Penalty: The Case of Life and Death in the United States.* Great Constitutional Issues: The Eighth Amendment. New York: Coward, McCann & Geoghegan, 1978. 160 pp. ISBN: 0698307011 (out of print).

A study of capital punishment as an issue in the United States, in the form of a detailed account of the historic *Furman* case. With a foreword by Michael Meltsner.

Szumski, Bonnie and others, eds. *The Death Penalty.* The Opposing Viewpoints series. St. Paul, MN: Greenhaven, 1986. 175 pp. ISBN: 00899083811 (out of print).

An anthology of writings both for and against the death penalty, from 1701 up to the 1980s. Selections are grouped under four chapter headings: "Three Centuries of Debate on the Death Penalty, " "Is the Death Penalty Immoral?" "Does the Death Penalty Deter Murder?" and "Should the Death Penalty Be Used for Political Crimes?" Notable authors include John Stuart Mill, Clarence Darrow, Horace Greeley, Walter Berns, and Ernest van den Haag. With bibliography.

Taylor, Mark Lewis. *The Executed God: The Way of the Cross in Lockdown America.* Minneapolis, MN: Fortress Press, 2001. ISBN: 0800632834.

The author, a professor of theology and culture at Princeton Theological Seminary with twenty-five years of involvement with prison reform, explores similarities between the imperial Roman régime in early Christian times to the American justice system. Includes bibliographical references and index.

van den Haag, Ernest, and John P. Conrad. *The Death Penalty: A Debate.* New York: Plenum, 1983. 305 pp. ISBN: 0306414163 (out of print).

An unusually extended debate on the issue, van den Haag supporting the death penalty and Conrad opposing it. Their intent "is to reach the thoughtful citizen who is concerned about the condition of criminal justice—its effectiveness, its humaneness, and its fairness." Foreword by Arthur J. Goldberg.

Vila, Bryan, and Cynthia Morris, eds. *Capital Punishment in the United States: A Documentary History.* Westport, CT: Greenwood Press, 1997. 337 pp. $55.00. ISBN: 0313299420.

Contains 112 documents with introductions; includes biographical accounts, Supreme Court decisions, position papers, congressional hearings, and more. Explores both pro– and anti–death penalty opinions. Includes bibliographical references and index.

Wawrose, Susan C. *The Death Penalty: Seeking Justice in a Civilized Society.* Brookfield, CT: Millbrook Press, 1997. 128 pp. ISBN: 0761300023 (out of print).

Examines the issue of capital punishment and highlights the Supreme Court cases that have shaped our approach to it and the arguments in favor of and against its use in a civilized society. Includes bibliographical references and index.

Williams, Mary E., ed. *Capital Punishment.* San Diego, CA: Greenhaven Press, 2000. 160 pp. $18.70. ISBN: 0737701412.

Contains thirty essays, from 1995 to 1999, addressing many aspects of the capital punishment debate by a variety of authors. Advanced reading level, although key points are highlighted. Includes bibliographical references and index.

Winters, Paul A., ed. *The Death Penalty: Opposing Viewpoints.* 3d ed. San Diego, CA: Greenhaven Press, 1997. 192 pp. $22.95. ISBN: 1565105109.

Written for young adults. Includes bibliographical references and index.

Woodward, Bob, and Scott Armstrong. *The Brethren: Inside the Supreme Court.* New York: Avon, 1981. 467 pp. ISBN: 0380521830 (out of print).

An inside look at the working of the U.S. Supreme Court from the 1969 through 1975 terms. It includes valuable information on the justices' deliberations concerning the death penalty and the Eighth Amendment's ban on cruel and unusual punishment that resulted in the historic *Furman* and *Gregg* decisions of the 1970s.

Pamphlets and Monographs

Costanzo, M., and L. T. White, eds. **"Death Penalty in the United States."** *Journal of Social Issues* 50, 2 (special issue, summer 1994).

A special issue examining the death penalty in context, the capital sentencing trial and focusing on public views of the death penalty, the deterrence effect of capital punishment, the U.S. Supreme Court's response to capital punishment, and sources of bias in the capital sentencing trial. References, tables, and figures.

Study shows that California homicide rates were, at best, unaffected by capital punishment. An increase in homicides during both abolition and retention of capital punishment was found.

Steib, V. L. **"Capital Punishment of Female Offenders: Present Female Death Row Inmates and Death Sentences and Executions of Female Offenders, January 1, 1973, to December 31, 1997."** Ada, OH: Ohio Northern University Law School, 1998. 19 pp.

Information on the numbers of females sentenced to death from 1973 through 1997, the executions of female offenders in the twentieth century, and the current numbers of female death row inmates. Tables and case summaries.

Texas Office of the Attorney General. *Capital Punishment Appellate Guide Book.* Austin, TX: Texas Office of the Attorney General, 2000. 18 pp.

A brochure to explain to families of homicide victims the appeals process for Texas capital cases starting with the trial and the direct appeal and continuing through post-execution.

Print Articles and Reports

Acker, James, David C. Brody, Talia R. Harmon, and J. Scott Richeson. **"Empire State Strikes Back: Examining Death- and Life-Qualification of Jurors and Sentencing Alternatives Under New York's Capital-Punishment Law."** *Criminal Justice Policy Review* 10, 1 (March 1999): 49–83.

Analysis of New York's death penalty legislation and discussion of survey data showing that New York's law provides a powerful inducement for jurors to produce unanimous sentencing verdicts in capital cases. References, notes, and tables.

Amnesty International USA. **"Death Penalty: No Solution to Illicit Drugs."** *International Review of Penal Law* (3d and 4th Trimesters 1996): 655–700.

Analysis of drug trafficking and drug laws in various countries concludes that the absence of capital punishment will not harm and may even strengthen efforts to address drug abuse and drug law offenses.

Bailey, W. C. **"Deterrence, Brutalization, and the Death Penalty: Another Examination of Oklahoma's Return to Capital Punishment."** *Criminology* 36, 4 (November 1998): 711–733.

A study of Oklahoma homicides examining the brutalization effects of the death penalty for various types of murder. Confirms that Oklahoma's return to capital punishment was followed by an increase in killings that involved strangers. Tables and references.

Center on Wrongful Convictions, Northwestern University School of Law. *Mistake and Perjured Eyewitness Identification Testimony in U.S. Capital Cases: An Analysis of Wrongful Convictions since Restoration of the Death Penalty Following Furman v. Georgia.* May 2, 2001.

Report of a study of eighty-six cases of legally exonerated death row inmates, which examines the prosecutors' reliance on faulty eyewitness testimony in obtaining their original convictions.

Culver, John H. **"Twenty Years after Gilmore: Who Is Being Executed?"** *American Journal of Criminal Justice* 24, 1 (fall 1999): 1–14.

Profiles 432 felons executed 1977–1997 since the U.S. Supreme Court decision in *Gregg v. Georgia* in 1976 established certain procedural safeguards. Raises questions about economic discrimination. List of cases and references.

Deak, A. **"About the Death Penalty."** *Belugyi Szemle* 33, 1 (January 1995): 55–57.

A discussion of capital punishment's historical background and arguments for its reintroduction in Hungary.

Garner, M. E. **"Capital Punishment for Minors."** *Journal of Juvenile Law* 15 (1994): 150–167.

The U.S. Supreme Court ruled in two cases involving juvenile murderers that the imposition of capital punishment on an offender who murders at age sixteen or seventeen does not constitute cruel or unusual punishment. A discussion of the degree to which the justices agreed. Notes.

Grant, Stefanie, **"A Dialogue of the Deaf? New International Attitudes and the Death Penalty in America."** *Criminal Justice Ethics* 17 (June 22, 1998).

A valuable discussion of the disagreement between the United States and much of the rest of the international community over U.S. attitudes toward capital punishment.

Haddock G., and M. P. Zanna. **"Assessing the Impact of Affective and Cognitive Information in Predicting Attitudes toward Capital Punishment."** *Law and Human Behavior* 22, 3 (June 1998): 325–339.

Examines the relative importance of affective information (feelings) and cognitive information (beliefs) in predicting attitudes toward capital punishment. References and tables.

Hauck, Brian, Cara Hendrickson, and Zena Yoslov. **"Symposium: The Death Penalty Debate: Capital Punishment Legislation in Massachusetts and Panel Discussion."** *Harvard Journal on Legislation* 36, 2 (summer 1999): 479–529.

Reviews the historical context of the debate about capital punishment in Massachusetts, explores constitutional restrictions on capital punishment legislation, examines proposed legislation to restore capital punishment. Includes the transcript of a symposium held on 12 April 1999. Footnotes.

Hennessy, James J., Vincent P. Rao, Jennice S. Vilhauer, and Joyce N. Fensterstock. **"Crime and Punishment: Infrequently Imposed Sanctions May Reinforce Criminal Behavior."** *Journal of Offender Rehabilitation* 29, 1/2 (1999): 65–75.

Investigates the probability of being incarcerated for committing a number of crimes including homicide, rape, robbery, and assault; and finds there was a negative correlation between murder rates and capital punishment. Tables, references.

Lanier, Charles S. **"Death Penalty in the Northeast."** *Criminal Justice Policy Review* 10, 1 (March 1999): 7–28.

A study of the status of capital punishment in the Northeastern United States and includes a list of states that authorize the death penalty; the number, race, and ethnicity of prisoners convicted and sentenced to die; and the number of prisoners executed. References, notes, and tables.

Liebman, James S., Jeffrey Fagan, and Valerie West. **"Death Matters: A Reply to Professors Latzer and Cauthen."** *Judicature* 84, 2 (September-October 2000): 72–99.

Takes issue with several claims made about capital punishment.

Plywaczewski, Emil W. **"Capital Punishment in Poland: The Debate Continues."** *International Journal of Comparative and Applied Criminal Justice* 24, 1 (spring 2000): 159–174.

Examines, in a time of rising violent crime rates, the possibility of reinstitution of capital punishment in Poland; a view that 75 percent of the population supports.

Sandys, M. **"Attitudinal Change among Students in a Capital Punishment Class."** *American Journal of Criminal Justice* 20, 1 (fall 1995): 37–55.

Twenty-three students who took part in a college class on capital punishment recorded their attitudes toward the topic on a weekly basis and also completed a one-year follow-up. Tables, notes, and references.

Sandys, M., and E. F. McGarrell. **"Attitudes toward Capital Punishment: Preference for the Penalty or Mere Acceptance?"** *Journal of Research in Crime and Delinquency* 32, 2 (May 1995): 191–213.

Information drawn from a study in which 514 adults in Indiana were interviewed by telephone about their attitudes toward capital punishment as well as their preferences for alternative sentences. Tables, notes, and references.

———. **"Beyond the Bible Belt: The Influence (or Lack Thereof) of Religion on Attitudes toward the Death Penalty."** *Journal of Crime and Justice* 20, 1 (1997): 179–190.

The rise in influence of religious leaders in the Republican party has led to interest in the role of religion in public policy issues, including capital punishment. Findings suggest that the role of religion in attitudes toward capital punishment may not generalize beyond the Bible Belt. Notes, references.

Sorensen, Jon, and Donald H. Wallace. **"Prosecutorial Discretion in Seeking Death: An Analysis of Racial Disparity in the Pretrial Stages of Case Processing in a Midwestern County."** *Justice Quarterly* 16, 3 (September 1999): 559–578.

Examines pretrial decisions to determine whether they had been influenced by race. Notes, tables, references, cases cited, appendix.

Wallace, D. H., and J. R. Sorensen. **"State Supreme Court's Review of Comparative Proportionality: Explanations for Three Disproportionate and Executed Death Sentences."** *Thomas Jefferson Law Review* 20, 2 (summer 1998): 207–276.

Analyzes the capital punishment review procedures used by the Missouri Supreme Court to determine that the death sentence in a case is not excessive when compared with cases that are similar in both the crime and the defendant. Tables, footnotes, and appended list of Missouri laws on aggravating and mitigating sentencing factors.

White, Linda. **"Reasoned Opposition to the Death Penalty."** *Crime Victims Report* 4, 1 (March/April 2000): 1–13.

The mother of a rape and murder victim explains her reasons for opposing the death penalty.

Whitehead, J. T. **"'Good Ol' Boys' and the Chair: Death Penalty Attitudes of Policy Makers in Tennessee."** *Crime & Delinquency* 44, 2 (April 1998): 245–256.

Summary of a survey of the attitudes toward capital punishment of Tennessee district attorneys general, chief public defenders, and state legislators. Tables, notes, references.

Wolfgang, M. E. **"We Do Not Deserve to Kill."** *Crime & Delinquency* 44, 1 (January 1998): 19–31.

Discusses the historical context of capital punishment and how it fits with classic and modern theories of punishment. Notes, references.

Wright, H. O., Jr., R. M. Bohm, and K. M. Jamieson. **"Comparison of Uninformed and Informed Death Penalty Opinions: A Replication and Expansion."** *American Journal of Criminal Justice* 20, 1 (fall 1995): 57–87.

A study of the impact of a college class on capital punishment on students' attitudes toward the death penalty. Tables, case citation, and references.

Videos

Born Killers: Leopold and Loeb (In Search of History)
Type: VHS
Length: 50 min.
Cost: $19.95
Source: A&E Store
http://www.aetv.com/
(888) 423–1212

Examines the evidence and provides contemporary news coverage and interviews with experts to present the story of the crime and trial that captivated America and that Clarence Darrow turned into a national referendum on the death penalty. From planning the "perfect crime" to the end of the story some half a century later.

The California Killing Field (American Justice)
Type: VHS
Length: 50 min.
Date: 1996
Cost: $29.95
Source: A&E Store
http://www.aetv.com/
(888) 423–1212

Includes interviews with law enforcement officials in two nations, relatives, and the attorneys who argued the case to tell the story of Charles Ng and his fight to avoid the death penalty by fleeing to an abolitionist country. A story that raises many questions on capital punishment and international law that remain to this day.

Capital Punishment (Bill of Rights in Action Series)
Type: VHS

Length: 23 min.
Date: 1982 (revised)
Cost: $79.00
Source: Encyclopedia Britannica Educational Corporation
6th Floor
310 S. Michigan Avenue
Chicago, IL 60604
(800) 554–9862

The key questions of deterrence, retribution, and Eighth Amendment rights are framed as arguments presented by prosecuting and defense attorneys in a trial.

Dead Man Walking
Type: VHS, DVD
Length: 122 min.
Cost: $11.99, $16.99

Based on the book by Sister Helen Prejean about the time she spent as a spiritual advisor and counselor to a death row inmate.

Death Penalty (American Justice)
Type: VHS
Length: 50 min.
Cost: $29.95
Source: A&E Store
http://www.aetv.com/
(888) 423–1212

Explores the arguments for and against capital punishment, including legal, political, and religious issues. Extensive interviews with experts on both sides of the debate. Includes a look at the case of Caryl Chessman, who appealed his sentence for twelve years. He was the last person put to death before capital punishment was declared unconstitutional in the 1960s.

The Death Penalty: Right or Wrong
Type: VHS
Length: 17 min.
Date: 1997
Cost: $59.95
Source: Library Video Company
P.O. Box 580

Wynnewood, PA 19096
(800) 843–3620
http://www.libraryvideo.com/

Offers commentary from students on both sides of this complex issue and encourages viewers to do further research on the topic.

Death Row Radical: Mumia Abu-Jamal (American Justice)
Type: VHS
Length: 50 min.
Cost: $19.95
Source: A&E Store
http://www.aetv.com/
(888) 423–1212

The case in recent history that has most become a lightning rod for the debate about capital punishment in the United States. On the night of 9 December 1981, Abu-Jamal intervened when he saw a police officer struggling with his brother. Exactly what happened is unclear, but Officer Daniel Faulkner was fatally wounded. The state won a conviction and Jamal was sentenced to death; he then took the fight to the public at large through many interviews and a book.

Death Row Women (American Justice)
Type: VHS
Length: 50 min.
Cost: $29.95
Source: A&E Store
http://www.aetv.com/
(888) 423–1212

Jailhouse interviews with the often-forgotten death row inmates, they talk about their crimes, their lives in prison, and their being unable to see their children and grandchildren grow up.

Earl Washington
Type: On-line video clip
Cost: No charge
Source: Death Penalty Information Center
http://www.deathpenaltyinfo.org/dpicmr.html

Earl Washington, a mentally retarded man with an IQ of 69 was convinced by police to confess to a crime in 1983. Sixteen years later, when DNA tests confirmed that Washington was innocent, he received a pardon.

Ethics and the Death Penalty
Type: On-line video, Powerpoint presentation
Cost: No charge
Source: Ethics Updates
http://ethics.acusd.edu/death_penalty.html

Presentation from 13 March 2001 by Lawrence M. Hinman of the University of San Diego.

Execution (Frontline)
Type: VHS
Length: 90 min.
Cost: $19.98
Source: The PBS Store
http://www.shop.pbs.org/
(877) PBS-SHOP

The story of Clifford Boggess and the almost ten-year wait for his execution.

Execution at Midnight: Death Row/Last Hours (Investigative Reports)
Type: VHS
Length: 50 min.
Cost: $29.95
Source: A&E Store
http://www.aetv.com/
(888) 423–1212

Follows several inmates in a Missouri prison through their last day; they reflect on their crimes, lives, and impending executions. Also includes interviews with those outside the gates protesting and applauding, and with the officials who carry out the sentences.

Gary Gilmore: A Fight to Die (Biography)
Type: VHS
Length: 50 min.
Date: 1996
Cost: $29.95

Source: A&E Store
http://www.aetv.com/
(888) 423–1212

Gilmore's death marked the return of capital punishment to the justice system in the United States. Includes interviews with friends, family, and law enforcement officials for a comprehensive view of Gilmore's life. Also features archival footage and news coverage about the debate over capital punishment that Gilmore's case brought on as he campaigned to die.

The History of Executioners (Investigative Reports)
Type: VHS
Length: 100 min.
Cost: $29.95
Source: A&E Store
http://www.aetv.com/
(888) 423–1212

Explores capital punishment from its first mention in the oldest legal document ever discovered to modern methods. Examines the debate over execution since almost the beginning of time. Includes interviews with judges, executed inmates' families, victims, and executioners.

Lawbreakers: Death Row Diaries
Type: VHS
Length: 50 min.
Cost: $19.95
Source: A&E Store
http://www.aetv.com/
(888) 423–1212

A look inside America's most notorious death house, Sing Sing, told from official records newly available. Includes the stories of Julius and Ethel Rosenberg and Louis Lepke Buchalter (the head of Murder, Inc.); provides new details and even more tales of the many executed who are long-forgotten.

Life or Death: A Battle Over Capital Punishment (20th Century with Mike Wallace)
Type: VHS
Length: 50 min.

Date: 1996
Cost: $19.95
Source: A&E Store
http://www.aetv.com/
(888) 423–1212

What is behind the resurgence of capital punishment in the United States when other Western nations are abandoning it? Traces the past thirty years of capital punishment and the current state of capital punishment in the United States. Includes interviews with advocates on both sides of the issue and looks at the famous cases of Gary Gilmore, John Spenkelink, and Ted Bundy.

Mario Marquez
Type: On-line video clip
Cost: No charge
Source: Death Penalty Information Center
http://www.deathpenaltyinfo.org/dpicmr.html

Mario Marquez, a mentally retarded man with an IQ of 65, was executed in Texas in 1995.

Nightline (15 April 1992)
Type: VHS
Length: 30 min.
Date: 1992
Cost: $14.98
Source: MPI Home Video
http://www.mpihomevideo.com/
(708) 460–0555

Host Ted Koppel leads a discussion of the (then) upcoming execution of Robert Alton Harris; the video features Harris's attorney, who was trying to block the execution; California's attorney general, whose office had prosecuted Harris and was asking for the execution to proceed; and a former California Supreme Court justice who had voted to uphold Harris's death sentence, but who believed that clemency should be granted in his case.

Presumed Guilty (American Justice)
Type: VHS
Length: 50 min.
Cost: $29.95

Source: A&E Store
http://www.aetv.com/
(888) 423–1212

The story of Rolando Cruz and Alex Hernandez, who were charged with a brutal crime. Despite a suspicious and circumstantial case against them, they were found guilty and sentenced to die. In 1995, they walked free and their case brought serious questions about the conviction of the innocent back to the death penalty debate.

"Retributive Punishment and Reconciliatory Punishment"
Type: On-line video clip
Cost: No charge
Source: Ethics Update
http://ethics.acusd.edu/death_penalty.html

The presentation of a paper by Edward G. Lawry of Oklahoma State University. Argues that "the revenge attitude inherent in retributive notions of punishment is incoherent based on the recognition that the agent of the avenging punishment is not of the same ontological type as the criminal, the original injuring party."

Sentenced to Die: Capital Punishment and the Eighth Amendment, 2d ed.
Type: VHS
Length: 33 min.
Date: 2001
Cost: $62.95
ISBN: 0–932765–71–8
Source: The PBS Store
http://www.shop.pbs.org/
(877) PBS-SHOP

The recent revelation of DNA evidence proving that certain death row inmates are innocent brings a renewed question of the possibility of executing the innocent. *Sentenced to Die* takes a look at capital punishment through the eyes of the individuals directly affected by it.

The Thin Blue Line
Type: VHS
Length: 101 min.

Date: 1988, reissued 2000
Cost: $8.99

This excellent documentary chronicles the case of Randall Adams, an innocent man convicted and sentenced to death for the murder of a Dallas policeman in 1977. At the time *The Thin Blue Line* was made, Adams was still in prison in Texas. The film was so persuasive that the case was reopened, and Adams was ultimately released.

Selected General Information Web Sites

A Capital Defender's Toolbox—Legal Resources, Jurisprudence, and More
http://www.karlkeys.com/cdw/index.htm

Capital Punishment, Death Row in Missouri
http://www.missourinet.com/CapitalPunishment/

Cornell's Death Penalty Project
http://www.lawschool.cornell.edu/library/death/

Death Penalty Curricula for High School Students
http://deathpenaltyinfo.msu.edu/

Death Penalty Institute of Oklahoma
http://www.dpio.org/

The Death Penalty, Pro & Con
http://crime.miningco.com/newsissues/crime/msub2.htm

Ethics Update—Punishment & the Death Penalty
http://ethics.acusd.edu/death_penalty.html

Looking at the Death Penalty—by David J. W. Vanderhoof
http://www.uncp.edu/home/vanderhoof/death.html

Second Optional Protocol to the International Covenant on Civil and Political Rights, Aiming at the Abolition of the Death Penalty. United Nations High Commissioner for Human Rights.
http://www.unhchr.ch/html/menu3/b/a_opt2.htm

UN Safeguards Guaranteeing Protection of the Rights of Those Facing the Death Penalty
http://www.unhchr.ch/html/menu3/b/h_comp41.htm

University of Alaska-Anchorage Justice Center Web Site—Focus on the Death Penalty
http://www.uaa.alaska.edu/just/death/

Yahoo! Death Penalty Directory
http://dir.yahoo.com/Society_and_Culture/crime/correction_and_rehabilitation/death_penalty/

Abolitionist Web Sites

Abolish Mailing List
http://dialup.oar.net/~Pcarelli/abolish/

Against the Death Penalty
http://www.geocities.com/icacpstudent/index.html

Association Rupture
http://www.associationrupture.org/

Canadian Coalition against the Death Penalty
http://www.ccadp.org/

The Case against the Death Penalty
http://ethics.acusd.edu/Bedeau.html x

Catholic Bishop's DP Web site
http://www.nccbuscc.org/sdwp/national/criminal/death/dpvat.htm

Citizens For a Moratorium on Federal Executions
http://www.federalmoratorium.org/

Citizens United for Alternatives to the Death Penalty
http://www.cuadp.org/

D.E.A.T.H.
http://donlemaire.homestead.com/deathpen.html

Death Penalty Information from the American Society of Criminology
http://sun.soci.niu.edu/~critcrim/dp/dp.html

Death Penalty Net
http://www.deathpenalty.net/

Death Penalty Perspective
http://home.flash.net/~rwcarlso/

Death Penalty USA Pages
http://www.agitator.com/dp/

Derechos
http://derechos.org/dp/

European Coalition to Abolish the Death Penalty
http://www.ecadp.org/

Fight the Death Penalty in the US
http://www.fdp.dk/

Italian Coalition to Abolish the Death Penalty
http://www.coalit.org/

Juvenile Death Penalty
http://www.abanet.org/crimjust/juvjus/juvdp.html

Lifespeak—Swiss Organization against the Death Penalty
http://www.geocities.com/EnchantedForest/Glade/3216/

The Other Side of the Wall
http://www.prisonwall.org/

Religious Organizing against the Death Penalty Project
http://www.deathpenaltyreligious.org./

Southern Center for Human Rights Death Penalty Information
http://schr.org/death-penalty-info/index.html

Stop the Death Penalty in Iran
http://www.ihrwg.org/CP/

Stop the Death Penalty Petition
http://slowdown.stanford.edu/dp/

You Can't Pardon a Corpse
http://www.compusmart.ab.ca/deadmantalking/

Selected Abolitionist Web Sites (State Specific)

California Coalition for Alternatives to the Death Penalty
http://www.igc.apc.org/sjpc/ccadp.htm

Coalition of Arizonans to Abolish the Death Penalty
http://www.caadp.org/

Coloradans against the Death Penalty
http://www.coadp.org/

Death Penalty Focus of California
http://www.deathpenalty.org/

Indiana Citizens to Abolish Capital Punishment
http://www.icacp.org/

Nebraskans against the Death Penalty
http://nadp.inetnebr.com/

New Jerseyans for a Death Penalty Moratorium
http://njmoratorium.org/

New Mexico Coalition to Repeal the Death Penalty
http://www.nmrepeal.com/

New Yorkers against the Death Penalty
http://www.nyadp.org/

Ohioans to Stop Executions
http://www.otse.org/

Oklahoma Coalition to Abolish the Death Penalty
http://www.ocadp.org/

Oregon Coalition to Abolish the Death Penalty
http://members.tripod.com/ocadp/

People of Faith against the Death Penalty—North Carolina
http://www.netpath.net/~ucch/pfadp/

Virginians for an Alternative to the Death Penalty
http://www.vadp.org/

Washington Coalition to Abolish the Death Penalty
http://www.scn.org/activism/wcadp/

Western Missouri Coalition to Abolish the Death Penalty
http://home.kc.rr.com/wmcadp/

Retentionist Web Sites

Canada Protest Page
http://www.tpg1.com//protest/federal/cp/cpmain.html

**Death Penalty in Indiana (maintained by the Clark County
Prosecuting Attorney)**
http://www.clarkprosecutor.org/html/death/death.htm

**The Death Penalty in North Carolina (maintained
by the North Carolina Dept of Correction)**
http://www.doc.state.nc.us/DOP/deathpenalty/index.htm

DPINFO—Death Penalty Information
http://www.dpinfo.com

**Pennsylvania Department of Corrections—
The Death Penalty in Pennsylvania**
http://www.cor.state.pa.us/deathp.htm

Pro-Death Penalty.Com
http://www.prodeathpenalty.com/

Texas Dept. of Criminal Justice—Death Row Information
http://www.tdcj.state.tx.us/statistics/stats-home.htm

The Ultimate Punishment: A Defense—Ernest van den Haag
http://www.pbs.org/wgbh/pages/frontline/angel/
procon/haagarticle.html

Wesley Lowe's Pro Death Penalty Web Page
http://www.geocities.com/~lurch7/cp.html

Selected Web Sites Devoted to Specific Cases or to Material by Inmates

Aaron Patterson
http://members.tripod.com/ccadp/aaronpatterson.htm

The Fratta Legal Defense Fund—on behalf of Robert Alan Fratta, "innocent man sentenced to death in Texas"
http://hometown.aol.com/jfriedbaue/index.html

The Case of Paul William Scott
http://www.derechos.net/doc/fyi/scott.html

Dead Man Talkin' by Dean Carter
http://utopia.ision.nl/users/annegr/deadman/talking.htm

Eddie Mitchell's Home Page
http://www.portland.quik.com/pssr/

Jamie Bruce McCoskey
http://savejamie.cjb.net/

Jeffrey Dicks' Homepage
http://members.nbci.com/jdicks/

Justice for Officer Faulkner
http://www.danielfaulkner.com/

Michael Moore (page written by his mother)
http://lonestar.texas.net/~acohen/michael_moore/

Miguel Angel Martinez
http://go.to/miguel.com

Mumia Abu-Jamal
http://www.mumia.org

Nicholas Yarris Home Page
http://www.just-rain.com/yarris/

Roger Keith Coleman
http://www.geocities.com/rkcolemaninfo/

Thomas J. Miller El
http://people.txucom.net/five/

Throw Away the Keys
http://members.aol.com/DKeasl5227/index.html

Virginia Larzelere
http://www.helpvirginia.com/

Selected Web-Site Articles and Essays

Bedau, Hugo Adam. **The Case against the Death Penalty**
http://www.aclu.org/library/case_against_death.html

Brown, David L. **The Bible's Teaching on Capital Punishment**
http://logosresourcepages.org/capital.html

Cassell, Paul G. **An Examination of Alleged Cases of Wrongful Conviction**
http://www.prodeathpenalty.com/guilt.htm

Cauthen, Kenneth. **Capital Punishment**
http://www.frontiernet.net/~kenc/cappun.htm

Coulter, Ann. **O. J. was "Proved Innocent"**
http://www.townhall.com/columnists/anncoulter/
ac000630.shtml

Criminal Justice Legal Foundation. **Death Penalty "Error" Study Has Errors of Its Own**
http://www.cjlf.org/releases/00–11.htm

Dunehew, Glenn. **What about Capital Punishment?**
http://www.forerunner.com/forerunner/
X0131_Capital_Punishment.html

Harrell, William Clark. **The Death Penalty and Due Process in Guatemala**
http://www.wcl.american.edu/pub/humright/brief/v4i2/
guatem42.htm

Harris, Bob. **Dissecting the Death Penalty**
http://www.motherjones.com/scoop/scoop5.html

Hart, John. **Death Penalty Serves Justice to Victims**
http://www.spub.ksu.edu/ISSUES/v099B/SP/n091/opn-
Hart–2–1.html

Henry, Gary. **Is Capital Punishment Sanctioned by Divine Authority?**
http://brasstacks.org/capital-punishment/capital-punishment-
outline.htm

Irvine, Reed. **AIM Report—The Death Penalty Saves Lives**
http://www.aim.org/publications/aim_report/2000/08a.html

Johansen, Jay. **Does Capital Punishment Deter Crime?**
http://my.voyager.net/jayjo/capdeter.htm

Kroll, Michael. **Executioner's Swan Song?**
http://www.salon.com/news/feature/2000/02/08/
death_penalty/index.html?CP=SAL&DN=110

Kroll, Michael. **Public Support Weakening, but the Death Penalty Will Be Slow to Die**
http://www.csindy.com/csindy/2000–02–16/yourturn.html

Mears, Michael. **The Death Penalty in the United States**
http://www.gidc.com/racial%20bias%20act%20article.htm

Mill, John Stuart. **Speech in Favor of Capital Punishment**
http://ethics.acusd.edu/Mill.html

Morrow, Lance. **Why I Changed My Mind on the Death Penalty**
http://www.time.com/time/nation/article/
0,8599,44196,00.html

National Science Foundation. **Capital Punishment Decisions Hinge on Jurors Who May Not Understand Their Task**
http://www.nsf.gov/od/lpa/news/press/pr972.htm

The New American. **Murders That Could Have Been Averted by Capital Punishment**
http://thenewamerican.com/focus/cap_punishment/
vo06no17_murders.htm

Pambianco, Robert V. **Evidence That the Innocent Are Executed Doesn't Exist**
http://www.courierpress.com/cgi-bin/view.cgi?200007/
05+viewpoint070500_news.html+20000705

Patel, Aanand N. **Enforce Death Sentences for Cold-Blooded Killers.** http://www-paradigm.asucla.ucla.edu/db/
issues/96/1.24/view.death.html

Pitts, Leonard, Jr. **Executioners Song Carries Faulty Lyrics**
http://www.mydrum.com/Pages/Lpitts/lp000630.htm

Rice, Charles E. **Retribution Is an Obligation**
http://thenewamerican.com/focus/cap_punishment/
vo03no13_retribution.htm

Smith, Michael. **Why I Was Right about Capital Punishment**
http://home.echo-on.net/~smithda/whyiwasright.html

Streib, Victor L. **Juvenile Death Penalty Today**
http://www.law.onu.edu/faculty/streib/juvdeath.htm

Tucker, Benjamin R. **Anarchism and Capital Punishment**
http://flag.blackened.net/daver/anarchism/tucker/tucker12.html

Webster, John. **Beyond the Game Justice Gets Done**
http://www.spokane.net/news-story-
body.asp?Date=061600&ID=s815224&cat=

Woolley, Wayne. **More Blacks Are Backing Capital Punishment**
http://detnews.com/1996/menu/stories/69081.htm

Young, Cathy. **Sexism and the Death Penalty**
http://www.salon.com/mwt/feature/2000/05/04/death/
index.html?CP=SAL&DN=110

Glossary

M any of the following terms have several meanings. Only those most relevant to the way in which the term is used in this book, or, more broadly, to the general subject of capital punishment, are included here.

abolitionist   One who opposes capital punishment and wants to see it abolished.

actual innocence   A claim that a defendant, or convicted person, did not commit the crime. Actual innocence can be distinguished from the merely legal innocence of someone found not guilty because of lack of proof, or whose conviction may be overturned on technical grounds.

appeal   A request to a higher court for it to review a decision made by a lower court, in the hope that the decision will be amended or overturned; the act of making such a request.

appeals court   *See* **Court of Appeals**

beheading   A method of execution in which the head is severed from the body by use of a sword, axe, guillotine, or other device. Once common in many countries, it is now in use only in Saudi Arabia and a handful of smaller Middle Eastern countries, the Congo, Mauritania, and Belgium.

Bill of Rights   The first ten amendments to the Constitution of the United States, which limit the power of the federal government and spell out the rights of individuals.

capital case   A criminal case in which the life of the defendant is at risk.

capital crime   An offense legally punishable by death.

capital punishment   The use of death as a legally sanctioned punishment for a crime.

capricious   Tending to change or vary abruptly, or without good reason; freakish, unpredictable. Critics complain that the death penalty is often applied capriciously.

charge An allegation of wrongdoing, especially a formal legal accusation that a particular person has committed a particular crime.

Chief Justice The presiding justice of the Supreme Court of the United States.

code The written law; the entire law on any subject.

commutation An alteration of the length or severity of a sentence that has the effect of lessening the punishment. State governors may sometimes commute a death sentence into a life sentence or some other, lesser penalty.

concurring opinion In the U.S. Supreme Court, a written opinion from a justice that agrees with the essential conclusion of the Court as a whole but that goes beyond it to make certain points with which the entire majority may not agree.

Constitution of the United States The fundamental and supreme law of the United States, as drafted by the Constitutional Convention in Philadelphia in 1787 and amended since.

constitutional That which accords with the Constitution of the United States; the U.S. Supreme Court is the final arbiter of whether a law (or practice) is constitutional.

convict One who has been convicted of a crime; one who is imprisoned as a result of being convicted.

court-appointed attorney A lawyer assigned by a judge to represent a defendant, usually because the defendant cannot afford to hire one him- or herself. Court-appointed attorneys are paid by the states, often at a lower rate than a privately hired attorney would charge, and defendants often complain that such attorneys do not represent them with the same care and skill they would devote to a private client.

Court of Appeals A higher-level court that hears appeals from decisions of lower courts and has the power to overturn those decisions. Each state has its own appeals court (or courts). The federal system has ten district courts of appeals.

crime An act forbidden by the criminal law; an offense against the public order.

criminal A person who has broken the law, or who has been convicted of a crime

criminal justice system The network of procedures and institutions— including the police and courts—by which society responds to crime.

death qualified jury A jury in a capital case, each member of which has sworn that he or she would be willing to sentence a guilty defendant to death should the proven circumstances of the case warrant it.

death row That section of a prison in which condemned prisoners are held awaiting execution.

decapitation *See* **beheading**

deter (deterrence, deterrent) To prevent or discourage someone from doing something. Retentionists argue that capital punishment deters potential criminals from committing capital crimes.

dissent, dissenting opinion In the U.S. Supreme Court, a written opinion disagreeing with a specific decision of the Court.

District Court *See* **U.S. District Court**

drawing and quartering A process, no longer in use, in which the body of a condemned criminal was torn apart—usually, although by no means always, after death.

drop The fall of the body in a hanging, the distance and force of which determines whether death comes by asphyxiation or by a broken neck.

Eighth Amendment The Eighth Amendment to the Constitution of the United States states: "Excessive bail shall not be required, nor excessive fines imposed, nor cruel and unusual punishments inflicted." Abolitionists argue that both specific means of execution and capital punishment by its nature are cruel and unusual, and therefore forbidden by this amendment.

electric chair The device used for carrying out electrocutions.

electrocution The form of execution that causes death by running a charge of electricity through the body of the condemned. The United States is the only country in which it is used.

execution The carrying out of a sentence, in particular the putting to death of someone convicted of a crime.

extraordinary crimes Crimes such as treason, or desertion from the military in time of war, which are sometimes treated tried and/or punished differently from ordinary crimes; for instance, some countries that have abolished the death penalty from ordinary crimes have retained it for these.

federal Pertaining to the United States as a whole or to the national government.

federal court One of the two major classifications of court systems in the United States, the other being the state courts. The federal court system deals with cases involving federal laws, as well as cases involving interpretations of the U.S. (federal) Constitution.

federal crime An offense forbidden by the laws of the United States, as opposed to the law of a particular state or states. Some acts can be both state and federal crimes.

federal law A law of the federal government, which applies across the entire United States; as opposed to a state law.

first degree murder The most serious degree of murder, and the one for which death is usually reserved. The laws of the states may define it differently.

garrote Any of several devices for killing a human being by strangulation. "Garroting" is execution by means of strangulation.

gas A method of execution in which death is produced by the release of toxic gas. It is used only in the United States, where it is employed by seven states.

gas chamber A small room used to execute prisoners by the release of deadly gas.

gibbet   A gallows; also, a structure from which hanged criminals are left to dangle as an example to others.

grant cert (to)   When the U.S. Supreme Court accepts a case for review.

"Great Writ"   The writ of habeas corpus.

habeas corpus   (Latin for "you have the body.") A writ, or order of a court, ordering the authorities holding someone in custody to produce the detainee and to justify his or her detention. Also, an appeal to the courts on behalf of a prisoner who claims that his or her detention is unjust.

hanging   A method of execution in which the condemned is dropped at the end of a rope. Death is produced by either a broken neck or asphyxiation.

headsman   An executioner who decapitates his victim with an axe.

homicide   The killing of one human being by another. Homicides are divided into three main categories: accidental homicides, justifiable homicides (such as killing in self defense, in the defense of others, or in a war), and murders.

impalement   A form of execution, no longer in use, in which the victim is killed by being pierced with a spear, stake, or other sharp device.

International Criminal Court   A court, established by international treaty in 1998, which has jurisdiction over such crimes as genocide, crimes against humanity, and war crimes. It does not have authority to impose the death penalty.

judge   A public official, either elected or appointed, who officiates at trials and renders legal decisions. In the United States, judges serve either in the federal or state court systems.

jurisprudence   The study or philosophy of the law.

juror   A member of a jury.

jury   A body of citizens legally impaneled to examine the facts of a case and make a decision as to the guilt or innocence of the defendant.

jury nullification   The refusal by a jury to convict a defendant whom they believe to be guilty of having committed the act with which he or she is charged, because they consider that the act was justified, or that the punishment the defendant would receive is too harsh.

justice   The quality of righteousness. In criminal matters, the notion that legal procedures need to be fair, court decisions accurate, and punishment both deserved and appropriate. Also, a member of the U.S. Supreme Court.

justice system   *See* **criminal justice system**

lethal injection   A form of execution that produces death by the effects of a toxic chemical injected into the veins of the condemned man or woman. It is the most popular method of execution in the United States.

lex talionis   Latin term for the principle of retribution expressed in the saying, "An eye for an eye and a tooth for a tooth."

"life means life"   *See* **life without parole**

life without parole   A lifetime criminal sentence requiring that the person so sentenced must never be released.

lynching   A murder committed by a vigilante group or other mob, often considered a form of unofficial execution by those who carry it out. Historically, lynching has been used to terrorize minorities, as well as to punish suspected criminals. It was used through the United States as a means of summary "justice" and was once particularly widespread in the southern United States, where it was used by whites to frighten and control the black population.

majority opinion   In the U. S. Supreme Court, an opinion that has received the votes of the majority of the justices.

mandatory   Required. In some jurisdictions, at some times in history, the death penalty has been mandatory for people convicted of certain crimes.

murder   The unlawful and deliberate killing of a human being, with legal malice. There are various degrees of murder, with different degrees of punishment for each. In most cases, only first degree murder is punishable by death.

ordinary crime   An offense against civilian law.

pardon   A release from punishment. The president has the power to pardon anyone accused or convicted of a federal crime. Many state governors have a similar power to cancel the punishment of anyone convicted of a state crime. Pardons may be granted because the pardoner believes the person to be innocent or believes that he or she has already received sufficient punishment.

penal   Having to do with punishments, particularly legal punishments.

penal system   The prison system.

penalty   A specific punishment, especially the punishment for a crime that is expressly prescribed by law.

penalty phase   That part of a trial which takes place after the defendant's guilt has already been determined, for the purpose of deciding what the punishment shall be.

penology   The study of prisons and of methods of controlling and/or rehabilitating criminals.

plurality opinion   In the U.S. Supreme Court (and elsewhere), a plurality opinion is one which receives more votes than any other but less than an absolute majority.

prosecutor   A legal officer of the state or federal government whose job is to present the government's case against a criminal defendant in court.

recidivist   A criminal who repeats his or her crime.

retentionist   One who favors the death penalty and wants it retained in the United States.

retribution   A punishment deserved because of some previous action of the subject.

review The reconsideration by a higher court of a decision of a lower court, with the possibility that the higher court may overturn it.

sanction Official approval of a punishment or reward; that which gives standing to a particular penalty and makes it binding. Also, a specific penalty designed to force people or institutions to behave in a particular way.

sentencing phase That part of a bifurcated trial which is held after the defendant's guilt has been established and which determines what the punishment shall be.

shooting A form of execution in which the death penalty is carried out by firing squad. It is currently used by only two states.

state court A court that is part of the judicial system of a particular state and that deals with violations of that state's laws and interpretations of that state's constitution.

state crime An offense forbidden by the laws of a particular state and committed within the borders of that state. A state crime is distinguished from a federal crime, although the same act may be both a state and a federal crime.

state law A statute of a particular state.

statute A law or formal regulation.

stoning A form of execution in which stones are showered on the victim until death is produced by brain damage or asphyxiation. It is a traditional form of execution in some Middle Eastern and Islamic countries and is currently in use in Iran and Pakistan, as well in some predominantly Arab countries.

Supreme Court of the United States The highest federal court in the country, charged, among other duties, with making the final determination in disputes over the meaning and application of the U.S. Constitution. It is also the court of final appeal for condemned criminals who claim that their constitutional rights have been violated.

United States Constitution *See* **Constitution of the United States**

U.S. District Court A constitutional court; the federal equivalent of a state court.

U.S. Supreme Court *See* **Supreme Court of the United States**

vigilante A person who takes the law into his or her own hands. Vigilante groups—or vigilance committees—appear where there is a general feeling that the legal system is not working to protect the public and keep order. They take it upon themselves to violently abuse those they consider enemies of society and sometimes to lynch them. Vigilante action of this kind is illegal, although at some times, and in some places, it has been tolerated by the legal authorities.

vigilantism Private citizens taking the law into their own hands. One reason put forward in support of capital punishment is as a means of preventing vigilantism.

warrant A written order from a court.

writ A warrant in a criminal case.

writ of certiorari A writ from a higher court, ordering the record of a legal proceeding to be brought to it. When a writ of certiorari is granted, it means that the higher court is accepting the case for review.

Index

Abbott, Burton, 63, 122, 123
Abbott, Jack Henry, 18
Abolition movement, 87
Abolition of the Death Penalty
    Act, 125
ACLU. *See* American Civil
    Liberties Union
Adams, Randall Dale, 59
Afghanistan, 92, 93
Africa, 20, 89
African Americans, 49, 50
Aggravating circumstances, 18
Alabama, 70
Alaska, 123
Albania, 89, 98
Alfred P. Murrah Building, 42, 45,
    57, 147, 153
All-American Council of the
    Orthodox Church in
    America, 74
Allen, Jerome, 141, 142
American Bar Association House
    of Delegates, 70
American Civil Liberties Union
    (ACLU), 190–191
  Capital Punishment Project, 49,
    59, 181
  Death Penalty Project, 295–296
  Foundation of Northern
    California, 38
  Project on Amnesty for
    Vietnam War Resisters, 181

American colonies, capital
    punishment in, 15, 16, 55,
    108, 109, 110
American Convention on Civil
    Rights, 72
American Convention on Civil
    Rights to Abolish the Death
    Penalty, 98
American Convention on Human
    Rights, 99, 139
American Federation of Labor, 116
American Friends Service
    Committee, 296
American League to Abolish
    Capital Punishment, 119,
    161, 170, 173
American Revolution, 16, 17, 179
American Society for Adolescent
    Psychology, 70
American Society for the
    Abolition of Capital
    Punishment, 114, 169
Amnesty International, 20, 21, 48,
    68, 69, 303
Amnesty International USA, 73
  Mid-Atlantic Regional Office,
    297
  Northeast Regional Office, 297
  Program to Abolish the Death
    Penalty, 296–297
  South Regional Office, 297
  Western Regional Office, 297

355

Amsterdam, Anthony Guy, 158, 159
Andover Seminary, 165
Angola State Prison, 43
Angremont, Louis Collot d', 111
Anti-Defamation League of B'nai B'rith, 181
Anti–Drug Abuse Act (1988), 140
Anti-Terrorism and Effective Death Penalty Act, 145
Argentina, 88, 133
Arizona, 102, 118, 120, 149
Arkansas, 16, 64, 125
Arkansas Court of Appeals, 134
Armed Forces Amendment Act 2000 (Malta), 151
Article 6 (International Covenant on Civil and Political Rights). *See* International Covenant on Civil and Political Rights
Ashcroft, John, 45, 153
Asia, 20, 89
Asian Americans, 52
Assyrian Laws, 107
Atlanta Constitution, 72
Attorney for the Damned (Darrow), 170
Auburn Prison, 116, 173
Austin Fletcher Chair (Tufts University), 161
Australia, 20, 89, 127, 128, 133
Australian Coalition against the Death Penalty, 303
Austria, 110, 160
Autry, James, 64
Azerbaijan, 145, 146, 148

Babylonian Code, 11
Bahamas, 148
Bahrain, 147
Baker, Nicole, 190, 191
Baldus, David C., 49, 50
Baldus study, 50
Baltimore, 174
Bangladesh, 70

Barfield, Velma, 133
Barnes, Harry Elmer, 187
Barzun, Jacques, 4, 24, 30, 32
Batson v. Kentucky, 134, 193
Beard, Angel Francisco, 148
Beccaria, Cesare, 17, 110, 157, 159, 161, 162, 178
Beck v. Alabama, 131, 193
Bedau, Hugo Adam, 53, 59, 119, 161
Beheading. *See* Decapitation
Belgium, 146
Bentham, Jeremy, 66, 67, 110, 157, 161, 162, 179
Benz, Tadea, 46
Bermuda, 150
Berns, Walter, 157, 162, 163
Biennial Convention of the Lutheran Church in America, 74
Bill of Rights (England), 109
Bill of Rights (U.S.), 111
Bishop's Conference of the Philippines, 91
Black, Charles L., Jr., 54
Blackmun, Harry, 50, 60, 61, 136, 140, 144
Blacks. *See* African Americans
Blasphemy, 11, 12, 152
"Blood money, " 93
Booth v. Maryland, 138
Bordeaux, 101
Bosche, Mariette, 152
Boston University, 161
Boswell, James, 56
Botswana, 102, 152
Bovee, Martin H., 163
Bowden, James, 72
Bowdoin College, 165
Bradford, William, 112
Braintree (MA), 120, 188
Brazil, 88, 98, 121, 131
Breaking on the wheel (method of execution), 203
Brennan, William Joseph, Jr., xi, 50, 51, 66, 136, 163, 165, 175

Britain, 108, 162
Brooklyn, 176
Brooks, Charles, Jr., 53, 131, 132
Brown v. Board of Education,
     174–175
Bryan, William Jennings, 170
Bryant, Charles, 43
Buchanan, James, 169
Buddhism, 94
Bulgaria, 139, 146
Bullington v. Missouri, 131
Bundy, Ted, 35
Burning (method of execution), 11,
     203
Bush, George Herbert Walker,
     142
Bush, George W., 103, 148
Butler v. McKellar, 193
Bye, Raymond T., 28

Cain and Abel, story of, 73, 91, 92,
     166, 233, 237
California, 121, 122, 127, 141, 142,
     186, 187, 302
California Trial Lawyers
     Association, 159
CAPC (Catholics against Capital
     Punishment), 298
Cambodia, 20
Cambridge University, 181
Campaign against the Death
     Penalty (India), 151
Campaign to End the Death
     Penalty, 297–298
Canada, 20, 66, 101, 129, 140, 141
     Supreme Court of, 101
Canute the Great, 14
Capital Punishment (UN study),
     124
Capitall Lawes of New England,
     72, 109
Catechism of the Roman Catholic
     Church, 91
Catherine the Great, 160
Catholic Bishops Conference of
     the Philippines, 151

Catholic Church. *See* Roman
     Catholic Church
Catholics against Capital
     Punishment (CAPC), 298
Caverly, Judge John R., 119, 183, 185
Cell 2455 Death Row (Chessman),
     18, 187
     decision in case of *State v.*
          Makwanyane and Mchunu
          excerpted, 267–286
Champion, Jane, 109
Chandler, David, 140
Chaskalson, Arthur, 267, 293
Cheever, Rev. George B., 165, 167
Chessman, Caryl, 18, 121, 124, 142,
     186, 188
Chicago, 116, 163, 182–183
Chicago and Northwestern
     Railroad, 169
Child Welfare League of America,
     70
Chile, 153
China, 21, 88, 89, 90, 93, 150, 153
Christ. *See* Jesus Christ
Christ and the Gallows: Or, Reasons
     for the Abolition of Capital
     Punishment (Bovee), 163
Christian Reformed Church in
     North America, 74
Cincinnati, 181, 182
Citizens United for Alternatives to
     the Death Penalty
     (CUAAD), 298
Civil disobedience, 161
Class distinctions, 13
Clemency, 62, 64
Clergy Coalition to End
     Executions, 298–299
Clermont (NY), 174
Clinton, William Jefferson, 145,
     176
Code of King Hammurabi, 107
Code of Theodosius, 108
Coker v. Georgia, 129, 130, 193
Coleman, Roger Keith, 60, 61, 140,
     142, 143, 189

Coleman v. Thompson, 140, 193, 194

College of New Jersey, 168

College of Philadelphia, 179

Colombia, 114, 118

Colorado, 10, 117

Columbia University, 181

Comoros, 147

Comprehensive Violent Crime Control Act of 1991, 142

Conference on the Human Dimension (Conference on Security and Cooperation in Europe), 139

Congo, Democratic Republic of, 21

Congregation for the Doctrine of the Faith, 91

Congressional Medal of Honor, 168

Considerations on the Injustice and Impolicy of Punishing Murder by Death (Rush), 180

Constantine, 108

Constitution of the United States. *See* U.S. Constitution

Continental Congress, 179

Convention on the Rights of the Child (United Nations), 99

Cooper, Paula, 138

Copeland, Ray, 139

Cornell University, 162

Coronado, Manuel Martinez, 147

Costa Rica, 98, 115

Cote d'Ivoire, 151

Council of Bishops of the Russian Orthodox Church, 92

Council of Europe, 145, 146, 148

The Courts, the Constitution and Capital Punishment (Bedau), 161

Crime, Its Cause and Treatment (Darrow), 170

Crimes, ordinary, 88

Crimes punishable by death, 18, 19

Crowe, Robert E., 5

Crucifixion, 151, 202, 203

"Cruel and unusual punishment," (U.S.) 18, 64, 66, 115, 116, 150

"Cruel, inhuman or degrading punishment, " (South Africa), 267

Cuba, 89

Curtis, Newton M., 167–168

Daeubler-Gmelin, Herta, 102

Dahmer, Jeffrey, 35

Dalai Lama, 94

Dale, Thomas, 108, 109

Dallas, 66, 78

Dallas, Alexander James, 168–169

Dallas, George Mifflin, 114, 168–169

Darden, Willie, 60

Darrow, Clarence, 4, 119, 169–170
    plea in the case of Leopold and Loeb, 119, 182–185

Davis, Allen Lee, 150

Davis, David Brion, 17

Death Is Different: Studies in the Morality, Law and Politics of Capital Punishment (Bedau), 161

Death penalty
    alternatives to, 13, 14
    biblical references to, 73, 91, 92, 166
    as deterrent, 5, 6, 26, 30
    inconsistencies in the administration of, 52, 55
    indigent defendants and, 47, 48, 69, 133
    keeping order, as a means of, 9, 10
    minorities and, 13, 14
    origins of, xi, 3, 11, 13
    race and, 48, 51, 135, 136, 141
    sense of justice and, 6, 7
    special costs of, 37, 40
    suicide, as a form of, 32, 33
    underrepresented groups and, 47, 52
    uniqueness of, 6, 8

Death Penalty Focus, 57

Death Penalty Information Center, 20, 39, 299
Death qualifying juries, practice of, 134
Debs, Eugene V., 169
Decapitation, 12, 13, 14, 15, 17, 151, 201
Defense for Children International USA, 299
Defense of Capital Punishment, 166
Delaware, 123, 124
Democratic Republic of Congo, 150, 151
Denmark, 131
Denning, Lord Justice, 7
Department of Defense Authorization Act of 1986, 134
Department of State, U.S., 181
Dickens, Charles, 57, 229
Pictures from Italy excerpted, 229–233
Disciples of Christ, 74
District of Columbia, 128, 143
Divine, Moral and Martial Laws, 108, 109
Diya. See "Blood money"
DNA, 60, 61
Dobbert, John, Jr., 130
Dobbert v. Florida, 130
Dodd, Westley Allen, 4, 5, 34, 37, 43, 45, 67, 68, 143, 144
Domingues, Michael, 99
Douglas, William O., 40, 47, 58
Draconian Code, 11, 107
Drawing and quartering, 203, 204
Drug "kingpins," 136
Duffy, Clinton T., 47, 67
Dugan, Eva, 120
Dugger v. Adams, 137
Dukakis, Michael, 33
Duke's Laws, 109

Eberhart, A. O., 37
ECADP. See European Coalition to Abolish the Death Penalty.

Echegaray, Leon, 149
ECHR. See European Convention for the Protection of Human Rights and Fundamental Freedoms
Ecuador, 98, 114, 117
Egypt, 107
Eighth Amendment, 45, 61, 65, 111, 115, 116, 123, 130, 136, 138, 163, 165, 175
Einstein, Albert, 4
Eisenhower, Dwight D., 164, 182
El Salvador, 132, 147
Electrocution, 116, 150, 200
Ellis, James, 39
Endmund v. Florida, 132, 133, 194
England, 108, 109, 112, 113, 115, 121, 179
Engle, Joe, 65
An Enquiry into How Far the Death Penalty Is Necessary in Pennsylvania (Bradford), 112
An Enquiry into the Consistency of the Punishment of Murder by Death, with Reason and Revelation (Rush), 180
An Enquiry into the Effects of Public Punishments upon Criminals and upon Society (Rush), 180
Episcopal Church, 74
Equal Protection Clause, 50
Erlich, Isaac, 29
Essay on Crimes and Punishments (Beccaria), 110, 159–160
EU. See European Union
Europe, 94
European Coalition to Abolish the Death Penalty (ECADP), 303
Belgium, 303
Denmark, 303
France, 304
Germany, 304
International, 303
The Netherlands, 304

Norway, 304
Switzerland, 304
European Convention for the
    Protection of Human Rights
    and Fundamental Freedoms
    (ECHR), 97, 98, 132, 146, 278
European Convention of Human
    Rights. *See* European
    Convention for the
    Protection of Human Rights
    and Fundamental Freedoms
European Parliament, 103
    "Resolution on the Death
    Penalty," 264–267
European Union (EU), 100, 103,
    104
    "Memorandum on the Death
    Penalty," 286–293
Evangelum Vitae (Gospel of Life),
    91, 92
    excerpted, 233–237
Execution
    of the incompetent, 69, 137,
    138
    of juveniles, 60, 70, 96, 99, 100,
    136, 138, 150, 151, 292
    public, 12, 17, 55, 58, 93, 94, 113
    televising of, 56, 57, 147, 153
    U.S., number of, 19
    *See also specific methods; names of
    executed individuals*
*Executioner: Pierrepoint: The
    Amazing Autobiography of the
    World's Most Famous
    Executioner,* 176

The Face of Justice (Chessman), 187
Fall Creek (IN), 112
*Federal Republic of Germany v.
    United States,* 194
Fellowship of Reconciliation, 74
Fifth Amendment, 111, 115
Fiji, 131
Fisher, Trevor, 148
Five Year Meeting of Friends, 74

Florida, 19, 20, 39, 53, 70, 75, 128,
    130, 132, 133, 135, 137, 141,
    150
*For Capital Punishment: Crime and
    the Morality of the Death
    Penalty* (Berns), 163
Ford, Alvin, 135
Ford v. Wainwright, 135, 194
Fort Worth, 66
Fourteenth Amendment, 61, 115,
    165, 175
France, 66, 101, 111, 114, 120, 121,
    170–171, 229
Francis, Willie, 18, 121
Franciscan Sisters of Mary
    Immaculate, 46
Frankfurter, Felix, 158
Franklin, Benjamin, 110, 179
Franks, Bobby, 119, 123
French Revolution, 14, 57, 111,
    171
Fugate, Carol Ann, 123
Furman v. Georgia, 10, 18, 51, 53,
    127, 128, 129, 138, 159, 165,
    175, 182, 194, 238, 259
Furman, William, 127

Gacy, John Wayne, 35
Gallatin, Albert, 168
GAO (General Accounting Office),
    51
Garrett, Johnny Frank, 46, 47
Garroting (method of execution),
    204
Gas (method of execution), 200
Gaskins, Donald, 141
Gein, Ed, 35
General Accounting Office (GAO),
    51
General Assembly of the Christian
    Church (Disciples of Christ),
    74
General Assembly of the
    Presbyterian Church (USA),
    74

General Assembly of the
Unitarian Universalist
Association, 74
General Assembly of the United
Nations, 95, 98, 139
General Association of General
Baptists, 74
General Board of American
Baptist Churches, 74
General Conference of the United
Methodist Church, 74
General Convention of the
Episcopal Church, 74
General Synod of the Reformed
Church in America, 74
General Synod of the United
Church of Christ, 74
Genesis, 91, 92, 166
Geneva Convention Relative to
the Protection of Civilian
Persons in Time of War, 99
Georgetown University, 162
Georgia (nation), 147
Georgia (U.S. state) 18, 29, 30, 49,
59, 128, 129, 130, 135, 136,
141
Georgia Board of Pardons and
Paroles, 72
German Democratic Republic, 135
Germany, 66, 101, 102, 149, 180
Gerould, Daniel, 15
Gilmore, Bessie, 129, 191
Gilmore, Gary Mark, 32, 43, 129,
157, 190, 191
Gilmore v. Utah, 194
Gladiatorial games, 12
Goldberg, Arthur J., 124
Gomez, Jose Antonio, 153
Governing Board of the National
Council of Churches of
Christ in America, 74
Graham, Barbara, 18
The Great Writ. *See* Habeas corpus
Greece, 88, 114
Greeley, Horace, 55

Gregg v. Georgia, xi, xiii, 18, 30, 32,
53, 60, 63, 64, 128, 165, 175,
177, 181, 182, 194
decision excerpted, 238–264
Guatemala, 145, 147
Guillotin, Joseph-Ignace, 15, 111,
170–171
Guillotine, 14, 15, 111, 121, 170,
171

Habeas corpus, 40, 60, 61, 132, 139,
140, 142, 178
Haiti, 20, 135
Halifax gibbet, 15
Hallowell (ME), 165
Hammer, David Paul, 152, 153
Hampton, Lloyd Wayne, 32, 33, 43
Hand, Samuel, 7
Hands Off Cain, 299
Brussels, 304
New York, 304
Rome, 304
Hanging, 13, 65, 120, 143, 200
Harris, Robert Alton, 57, 142, 143,
178
Harvard University, 161
Hawaii, 123
Haymarket anarchists, 116
Hayward, Susan, 123
Haywood, Big Bill, 170
Healey, John, 48, 54
Hearst, William Randolph, 26
Henley, William Ernest, 153
Henry VIII, 108
Herrera, Leonel, 61, 62, 144, 178
Herrera v. Collins, 61, 144, 194, 195
Hill, Joe, 118
Hittite Code, 107
Hong Kong, 20
Horton, Willie, 33
House of Commons, 124
Houston, 66
Howard University, 166, 174
Human Writes, 304–305
Huntsville Penitentiary, 131

I Want to Live! (movie) 18, 123
Iceland, 120
Illinois, 169
"In Favor of Capital Punishment"
    (Barzun), 30
In re Kemmler, 116, 150, 195
India, 151, 279, 281
Indiana, 63, 112
Indiana Supreme Court, 138
Industrial Workers of the World
    (IWW), 118
Ingle, Joseph B., 171–172
Innocence Project Northwest, 299
Inside-Outside, 305
Inter-American Commission on
    Human Rights, 148
Inter-American Court of Human
    Rights, 99
International Centre for Criminal
    Law & Human Rights, 305
International Court of Justice, 103,
    149
International Covenant on Civil
    and Political Rights, 70, 95,
    98, 99, 133, 139, 277, 278
International Criminal Court, 148,
    149
*International Encyclopedia of the
    Social Sciences*, 28
International law, 269, 270
International Rescue Committee,
    181
*Introduction to the Principals of
    Morals and Legislation*
    (Bentham), 162
"Introductory Report to the
    System of Penal Law
    Prepared for the State of
    Louisiana, " 174
"Invictus" (Henley), 153, 154
Iowa, 115
Iran, 29, 70, 87, 100, 112, 150
Iraq, 70, 89
Islam, 92, 94
Islamic Law. *See* Sharia
Israel, 122

Italy, 121, 229
IWW (Industrial Workers of the
    World), 118

Jackson, Andrew, 168, 174
Jackson, Robert H., 177
Jamaica, 152
Japan, 94
Jefferson, Thomas, 17, 110, 168
Jesus Christ, 34, 74, 108
John Paul II, Pope, 91–91, 149
Johnson, Lyndon, 175
Johnson, Samuel, 56
Jon, Gee, 119
Jones, Leo, 60
Joyce, William (Lord Haw Haw),
    176
Judaism, attitudes toward the
    death penalty, 90, 91
Judeo-Christian beliefs, 72, 74, 90
Judicial Committee of the Privy
    Council (Commonwealth),
    153
Jurek, Jerry Lane, 128
Jurek v. Texas, 128, 195
Justice and Equality (Bedau), 161
Justice for All, 300

Kamenar, Paul, 41, 47, 65
Kansas, 117, 120, 128
Kansas Legislative Research
    Department, 39
Kazis, Israel, J., 74
Kemmler, William, 116
Kendall, George, 108
Kenosha (WI), 163
Kentucky, 120
Ketch, Jack, 172
Kindler, Joseph, 141
Kindler v. Canada, 276, 278
Kinne, Norman, 78
Kinsman (OH)
Kirchwey, George W., 28
Knight, Goodwin J., 63, 122
The Koran. *See* Qur'an
Koresh, David, 147

KQED-TV, 57
Kvale, O. J., 40

LaGrand, Karl, 102, 194, 217
LaGrand, Walter, 102, 103, 149,
    194, 217
Laos, 153
Latvia, 146, 147
Law enforcement, improved, 77,
    78
Law of the Twelve Tablets, 11, 107,
    108
Lawes, Lewis E., 66, 67, 119, 170,
    173
Lawyers Constitutional Defense
    Committee, 181
Lecter, Hannibal, 92
Leopold, Nathan, Jr., 5, 34, 119,
    123, 170, 182, 185
Lethal injection, 58, 64, 65, 201
*Letters Containing an Account of the
    Late Revolution in France*
    (Romilly), 178
Libya, 146
Liechtenstein, 135
Life and Death in Sing Sing (Lawes),
    173
Life imprisonment, 75, 76
"Life means life" laws, 35, 36, 75,
    76
Life Plus 99 Years (Leopold), 185
LifeLines (UK), 305
Lincoln, Abraham, 169
Lincoln University, 174
Livingston, Edward, 112, 113, 174
Lockett v. Ohio, 130, 195
Lockhart v. McCree, 134, 135, 195
Loeb, Richard, 5, 119, 123, 170,
    182, 185
London School of Economics and
    Political Science, 162.
Los Angeles Police Department,
    28
Louis, Antoine, 111, 171
Louisiana, 16, 18, 43, 48, 112, 113,
    174

Lovat, Lord, 110
Luxembourg, 131
Lynching, 10, 11

Mackey, Philip English, 54, 180
Mailer, Norman, 191
Maine, 113, 115, 116, 165
Maine Law, 113
Malawi, 148
Malta, 151
Mandela, Nelson, 147
Man's Judgment of Death (Lawes),
    173
Marshall, Thurgood, 45, 134, 135,
    136, 140, 165, 174, 174–176,
    182
    dissent in case of *Gregg v.
        Georgia*, 260, 264
Marwood, William, 115
Maryland, 174
Mason, Morris, 69
Massachusetts, 33, 90, 120, 126,
    133, 163, 165
Massachusetts Bay Colony, 72, 109
Maxwell v. Bishop, 125, 195
McCarthy, Joseph, 164
McCleskey v. Kemp, 50, 135, 136,
    139, 140, 141, 195, 196
McCleskey v. Zant, 139, 141, 142,
    196
McCleskey, Warren, 50, 135, 136,
    139, 140, 141
McCree, Ardia, 134
McGautha v. California, 127, 196
McMillen, Walter, 144, 146
McNamara, James, 170
McNamara, John, 170
McVeigh, Timothy, 42, 45, 57, 58,
    147, 153, 154
Meet the Murderer! (Lawes), 173
"Memorandum on the Death
    Penalty" (EU), 286–293
Mennonite Central Committee
    U.S., 74, 300
Mennonite Church, 74
Mentally ill, executing, 68, 69

Mentally retarded, 64, 65, 137, 152, 154
Mexico, 89, 118, 132
Michigan, 114
Mill, John Stuart, 41, 42
Millay, Edna St. Vincent, 189
Milwaukee, 177
Minnesota, 29, 37, 118
Missouri, 118, 119, 149, 163
Mitigating circumstances, 130
Mogae, Festus, 102
Montana, 70
Mother Teresa, 74
Murder Victims' Families for Reconciliation, 300
Murrah Building. *See* Alfred P. Murrah Building
Murray v. Giarrantano, 137, 196

NAACP. *See* National Association for the Advancement of Colored People
Nashville (TN), 171
National Academy of Sciences, 29
National Assembly (France), 111, 170
National Association for the Advancement of Colored People (NAACP), 174, 175
  Legal Defense and Education Fund, 174, 300
  Legal Defense and Educational Fund Capital Punishment Project, 49
  Legal Defense Fund, 125, 159
National Bar Association, 301
National Coalition to Abolish the Death Penalty (NCADP), 159, 181, 301
National Commission on the Reform of Federal Criminal Laws, 125
National Conference of the Campaign against the Death Penalty (India), 151

National Council of Churches of Christ in America, 74
National Criminal Justice Reference Service, 301
National Legal Aid and Defender Association Death Penalty Litigation Section, 302
Native Americans, 16, 112, 114
NCADP (National Coalition to Abolish the Death Penalty), 159, 181, 301
Nebraska, 151, 163
Nepal, 150
Netherlands, 115, 132
Nevada, 119
New Delhi, 151
New Hampshire, 113
New Jersey, 163, 164
New South Wales, 128, 133
New York (colony), 109
New York (state), 113, 116, 125, 163, 167, 168, 173
New York City, 67, 122
New York Herald, 28
New York League to Abolish Capital Punishment, 119
New Zealand, 91
Newsweek, 64
Ng, Charles, 141, 276, 278
Nicaragua, 99
Nigeria, 100, 131, 150
Nixon, Richard, 176
Nobel Peace Prize, 172
Norris, Kathleen, 119
North America, 89
North Dakota, 118
Northern California Coalition to Abolish the Death Penality, 302
Norway, 117, 131

Oceania, 20
O'Connor, Sandra Day, 70, 136, 177
O'Dell, Joseph, 60

Office of the High Commissioner
     for Human Rights, 305–306
Ohio, 63, 169
Oklahoma, 70, 100, 129, 136
Oklahoma City, 45, 57, 147, 153
Oman, 150
On Crimes and Punishment
     (Beccaria), 17
*On the Value and Inviolability of
     Human Life* (John Paul II),
     233–237
Ordinary crimes, 88
Oregon, 39, 118, 119, 124
Organization of American States,
     98, 99
Orleans (U.S. territory), 174
Osborne, Thomas Mott, 67, 73, 76,
     77
Ossining (NY), 173
Ottoman Empire, 13
Oxford University, 162

Pakistan, 70, 100, 150, 152
Panama, 98, 117
Parent Teacher Association, 70
Paraguay, 98, 148
Paris, 171
Payne v. Tennessee, 140, 196
Peine fort et dure (method of
     execution), 204
Pelletier, Nicolas, 111, 131
Penn, William, 16, 109
Pennsylvania, 16, 109, 110, 112,
     113, 114, 141, 170
Pennsylvania Law Review, 158
Penry, John Paul, 137, 152
Penry v. Lynaugh, 137, 196
Perry, Rick, 154
Peru, 131
Philadelphia, 114, 168, 170
Philippines, 95, 135, 145, 149, 151
Phoenix (AZ), 176
Pictures from Italy (Dickens),
     excerpted, 229–233
Pierce, Franklin, 169
Pierrepoint, Albert, 65, 67, 176

Polk, James, 169
Popot, Canon, 67
Pornography, 182
Portland (OR), 161, 190
Portugal, 115, 129
Powell, Lewis Franklin, Jr., 135, 136
Presbyterian Church (USA), 74
Priestly, J. B., 187
Princeton University, 169, 179
Prisons (as alternative to death
     penalty), 13, 14
Proffitt v. Florida, 128, 196, 197
Progressive Conservative Party
     (Canada), 141
Protocol No. 6 (European
     Convention for the
     Protection of Human Rights
     and Fundamental
     Freedoms), 97, 98, 132, 146
Provost (UT), 190
Public opinion polls, 21, 75
Puerto Rico, 118, 119, 120, 185

Quakers, 16, 73, 109
Qur'an, 93

Radelet, Michael L., 58
Rand School of Social Science, 181
Ratzinger, Cardinal Joseph, 91
Reagan, Ronald, 134, 176
Recidivism rates, 33, 35
Rector, Rickey Ray, 64, 65
Reed, Stanley, 64
Reed College, 162
Rehabilitation, 76, 77
Rehnquist, William Hubbs, 40, 60,
     134, 177–178
Rehnquist Court, 164, 178
Religious Action Center of Reform
     Judaism, 302
Reiner, Ira, 8
Resolution 39/118 (UN General
     Assembly), 95, 96
"Resolution on the Death Penalty"
     (European Parliament)
     excerpted, 264–267

Retribution, 7, 44, 47, 75
Revolutionary War. *See* American
    Revolution
Rhode Island, 17, 114
Richards, Ann, 63
Robertson, Pat, 37
Rohatyn, Felix, 101
Roman Catholic Church, 74, 90,
    91, 92, 94, 95, 229, 233
Roman Coliseum, 150
Roman Empire, 108
Roman Law of the Twelve Tablets.
    See Law of the Twelve Tablets
Roman Republic, 11, 12
Rome Diplomatic Conference, 148,
    149
Romilly, Sir Samuel, 162, 178–179
Roosevelt, Eleanor, 97
Roosevelt, Theodore, 41
Rosenberg, Ethel, 122
Rosenberg, Julius, 122
Royal Commission on Capital
    Punishment, 30, 34
Rudolph v. Alabama, 124
Rumbaugh, Charles, 133, 134
Rush, Dr. Benjamin, 17, 36, 110,
    111, 157, 160, 179–180
Russia, 110, 146, 150
Russian Orthodox Church, 92
Russian Revolution, 188
Rust-Tierney, Diann, 59, 62, 181
Rwanda, 150

Sacco, Dante, 189
Sacco, Nicola, 120, 157, 188, 190
Sacramento Bee, 39
St. Joseph (MO), 186
St. Louis (MO), 149
Salem witchcraft executions, 109,
    110
Samp, Richard, 11, 54, 60
San Marino, 114, 115
San Quentin Prison, 63, 67, 74,
    122, 123, 142, 187
Saudi Arabia, 21, 92, 93, 94, 100,
    150, 151

Sawyer v. Whitley, 143, 197
Scalia, Antonin, 138, 176
Schwarzchild, Henry, 49, 180–181
Schweitzer, Albert, 187
Scopes, John, 170
Scott, James (Duke of Monmouth),
    172
Scottish maiden, 15
Second Optional Protocol
    (International Covenant on
    Civil and Political Rights),
    98, 139
Sellers, Sean, 100
Sellin, Thorsten, 29
"Separate but equal" doctrine, 175
Serial killers, 34, 35
Sermon on the Mount, 73
700 Club, 37
Shakespeare, William, 8
Sharia, 92, 94
Shaw, George Bernard, 66
Shevardnadze, Eduard, 147
Shooting (method of execution),
    199
Simmons v. South Carolina, 197
Sing Sing Prison, 173
Sixth Amendment, 125
Slack v. McDaniel, 197
Smith, Adam, 160
Smith, George C., 51, 65
Socrates, 108
Somalia, 100
Somers, Jerome, 90
Souter, David, 144
South Africa, 102, 147
    Constitutional Court of, 145, 267
    *State v. Makwanyane and
        Mchunu* excerpted (abolition
        of capital punishment)
        267–286
South America, 94
South Braintree (MA), 120, 188
South Carolina, 138, 141
South Carolina v. Gathers, 138, 197
South Dakota, 118
South Korea, 150

Southern Coalition on Jails and
   Prisons, 171–172
Southern Poverty Law Center, 159
Spain, 131
Spence, David, 60
Spenkelink, John A., 131
Stanford Law School, 177
Stanford University, 159
Stanford v. Kentucky, 138, 197
Stark (prison), 60, 131
Starkweather, Charles, 123
State ex rel. Francis v. Resweber, 121
   197, 198
State v. Makwanyane and Mchunu,
   excerpted, 267–286
Stephen, James, 6, 26, 42
Steuenberg, Governor, 170
Stevens, John Paul, 136, 140, 144
Stewart, Potter, 10, 11, 30, 181–182
Stoning, 93, 201, 202
The Story of My Life (Darrow), 170
Styron, William, 56, 57
Suicide, execution as form of, 32,
   33, 180
Supreme Court of the United
   States. *See* U.S. Supreme
   Court
Switzerland, 121
Synod of the Christian Reformed
   Church in North America, 74

Tajikistan, 149
A Tale of Two Cities (Dickens), 229
Talley, Alfred J., 4, 7, 119
Teepen, Tom, 67, 68
Tennessee, 113, 118
Texas, 29, 39, 48, 53, 59, 61, 62, 63,
   64, 66, 67, 78, 103, 128, 131,
   133, 144, 147, 148, 154
Texas State Board of Pardons, 47
Thackeray, William Makepeace, 56
The Thin Blue Line (movie), 59, 337
Thompson v. Oklahoma, 136, 198
Thompson, William Wayne, 135
Thoughts on Executive Justice
   (Romilly), 178

Toulouse, 101
Trial by Ordeal (Chessman), 187
Tribe, Lawrence, 175
Trop v. Dallas, 123, 198
Tucker, Karla Faye, 148
Tufts University, 161
Turkmenistan, 150
Tuscany, 110, 160
Twenty-Thousand Years in Sing Sing
   (Lawes), 173
Tyburn Prison, 172

Ukraine, 149
Ulmanis, Guntis, 146
"Uncontrollable brutes," 3, 5, 33,
   34
Union of American Hebrew
   Congregations, 90
Union of Soviet Socialist
   Republics, 20, 122
Unitarian Universalist
   Association, 74
United Church of Christ, 74, 171
United Methodist Church, 74
United Nations, 21, 95, 97
United Nations Commission on
   Human Rights 96, 133, 149,
   150, 151
United Nations Economic and
   Security Council, 137
United Nations General Assembly,
   95, 98, 139
United Nations Subcommission
   on the Promotion and
   Protection of Human Rights,
   150
United States v. Jackson, 124, 125,
   198
U.S. Code of Military Justice, 134
U.S. Constitution, 16, 45, 61, 111
   See also specific amendments
U.S. Criminal Code, 117
U.S. Supreme Court, 38, 49, 60,
   115, 121, 142
   on "death-qualifying" juries,
   134, 135

on execution of African
Americans, 50
on execution of juvenile
offenders, 70, 71, 99, 136, 138
on execution of the insane, 135
on execution of the mentally
retarded, 137, 152
on habeas corpus, 40, 60, 61,
139, 140
Office of Legal Counsel, 177
on right of appeal, 138, 140,
143, 152, 153
on right of legal counsel for
appeals, 137
on right to psychiatric
assistance, 69
on timing of constitutional
claims, 136
*See also specific cases and
decisions*
Universal Declaration of Human
Rights, 121
University of Chicago, 162
University of Edinburgh, 179
University of Iowa, 162
University of Pennsylvania Law
School, 158
University of Redlands, 161
Uruguay, 98, 117
Utah, 118, 129
Utilitarianism, 162

van Buren, Martin, 169
van den Haag, Ernest, 6, 7, 41, 73, 77
van Venison, Harold B., 120
Vanzetti, Bartolomeo, 120, 157,
188, 190
Vatican, 91
Venezuela, 98
Vengeance, 7, 44, 47
Vermont, 125
Versailles, 120
Victim impact evidence, 46
Vienna Convention on Consular
Relations, 148

Vigilantism, 9, 11
Violent Crime Control and Law
Enforcement Act, 145
Virginia, 29, 108, 109, 110, 140, 143,
148, 168
*Voices against Death: American
Opposition to Capital
Punishment, 1781–1975,*
(Mackey), 180
Voltaire, 160

Warren, Earl, 164
Warren Court, 164
Washington (state) 37, 101, 118,
119, 143
Washington Legal Foundation, 11,
41, 47, 51, 65, 302–303
Washington Post, 42
Washington State Prison, 143
Weems v. United States, 117, 198,
199
Weinberg, Arthur, 170
West, Louis Joylon, 30, 32
West Jersey (American colony), 16
West Virginia, 125
Western Australia, 133
Wharton School, 164
White, Byron, 176
Wilkerson v. Utah, 115, 199
Wilkins v. Missouri, 138, 199
William the Conqueror, 14, 108
Williams, Clayton, 63
Wisconsin (state), 8, 9, 17, 29, 114
Wisconsin (territory), 163
Woods, John C., 32
Woods, Richard, 148
Woodson v. North Carolina, 199

Yale University, 162, 181
Yeltsin, Boris, 150
Yemen, 100, 150
Yugoslavia, Federal Republic of,
20

Zachariah, 91

About the Author

Michael Kronenwetter is a freelance writer and newspaper columnist. Born in West Palm Beach, Florida, Kronenwetter grew up in Wausau, Wisconsin. Leaving there as a young man, he lived in a variety of places, including New York City, Carlsbad, New Mexico, and Longueuil, Quebec. He met and married his wife, Pat, in Kingston, Ontario. Eventually, they moved back to Wausau, where they have raised their two children, Catherine and Jay, in the house in which Kronenwetter himself was raised. Among his more than thirty books for adults and young adults are *Prejudice in America, How to Write a News Article, Journalism Ethics, Protest!,* and the *Encyclopedia of Modern American Social Issues* (ABC-CLIO). Several of his books have appeared on the New York Public Library's prestigious annual list of Notable Books for the Teen Age. He has written in a variety of other forms and media, including fiction, poetry, and CDs. His script for the filmstrip *America's Power and Prestige since Vietnam* was honored by the National Educational Film Festival in 1983.